HIGH
IN
AMERICA

HIGH IN AMERICA

The True Story behind NORML and
the Politics of Marijuana

PATRICK ANDERSON

THE VIKING PRESS   NEW YORK

First published in 1981 by The Viking Press
625 Madison Avenue, New York, N.Y. 10022
Published simultaneously in Canada by
Penguin Books Canada Limited

LIBRARY OF CONGRESS CATALOGING IN PUBLICATION DATA
Anderson, Patrick, 1936–
High in America.
Includes index.
1. Marijuana. 2. Stroup, Keith, 1943–
3. National Organization for the Reform of Marijua-
na Laws. 4. Marijuana—Law and legislation—
United States. I. Title.
HV5822.M3A53   363.4'5   80–51772
ISBN 0–670–11990–3

Printed in the United States of America
Set in Linotron Century Expanded

For Gene and Mike

HIGH
IN
AMERICA

Introduction

One Saturday evening in November of 1972, my wife and I drove into Washington for dinner at a Georgetown restaurant. It was a celebration, of sorts. Since the early spring we had worked as volunteers for George McGovern in the rural Virginia county in which we live. We'd been delegates to the state Democratic convention; we'd knocked on doors and registered voters and worked the polls on election day. We'd done all the things Americans do when they believe passionately in a political cause.

On election night, of course, Richard Nixon wiped us out. Our anti-war candidate for president lost about as decisively as you can lose an election in America. That was why Ann and I were dining in an excellent French restaurant that Saturday night: We were celebrating the end of the campaign, the fact that at least the disaster was behind us, and for better or worse we could get on with our lives.

After dinner we dropped by the nearby home of Larry and Louise Dubois. Larry, a writer I had met that summer, was tall, dark, and excitable; Louise was petite, blond, and serene. On this Saturday night there were eight or ten people sitting around their living room talking and drinking wine and listening to a Grateful Dead album. One of the guests was an attractive, dark-haired woman in her twenties named Kelly Stroup (rhymes with "cop"), who was talking about her and her husband's adventures at the Democratic convention in Miami Beach that summer. I asked her what they'd been doing there.

"We lobby for marijuana-law reform," Kelly said.

"You what?"

"My husband is the head of NORML," she said, and went on to tell me about her husband, Keith Stroup, and about the National Organization for the Reform of Marijuana Laws, which he had founded two years before.

I was thirty-six years old, and didn't know much about marijuana —I'd tried it only twice—and I'd never heard of NORML. I did, however, know a little something about writing for magazines. In the previous six years, in addition to writing my first three books, I'd written articles for *The New York Times Magazine* on such political figures as Larry O'Brien, Henry Kissinger, Clark Clifford, Ralph Nader, and Bill Moyers, and if there was anything I was sure of, it was that the adventures of a pro-marijuana lobbyist in Washington would make good copy.

On Monday morning I called an editor at *The New York Times Magazine* and told him I had a natural for them. Shortly thereafter I joined Stroup on a trip to Texas, where, among other things, we visited the state prison and met young men who had been sentenced to as much as twenty-five years' confinement for smoking and/or selling marijuana.

My article on NORML appeared in the *Times Magazine* the next month, and though properly "objective," it was certainly favorable to the cause of marijuana-law reform. I was not part of the drug culture, but it seemed blindingly clear to me that people should not go to jail for smoking marijuana—not for a day, much less for the ten- and twenty-year sentences I'd encountered in Texas. A few months earlier, in March of 1972, Richard Nixon's own National Commission on Marijuana and Drug Abuse, after conducting the most exhaustive study of marijuana ever made in America, had concluded that it was virtually harmless and that people should not go to jail for smoking it. Nixon didn't agree with his commission, but I did, and still do.

I started dropping by NORML's office from time to time, to see how Stroup's work was coming and, more generally, to enjoy the wonderful panorama of people who wandered in and out: reporters, political activists, drug dealers, groupies, law students, scientists, Yippies, rock musicians, and assorted other notables and crazies. A busy little world revolved around Stroup as he dashed about his ground-floor office, with the marijuana posters on its walls and the bust of George Washington on the mantel. Whether playing host, making introductions, fielding phone calls, yelling orders to his staff, rolling joints, dropping names, or denouncing his political adversaries, he was always onstage, starring in his self-created role of outlaw lobbyist.

Stroup was thirty then, and certainly one of Washington's most colorful political figures. He was a turned-on Nader, a funny, fast-talking, charming, very bright lawyer-activist. Angry and hot-tempered at times, he was always competitive, always the politician, quick to turn every situation to his own advantage. But he was also candid and introspective with his friends, dedicated to his cause, and quick to laugh at himself and at the madness of it all. It was a dispiriting time in Washington, and one of Stroup's most attractive qualities was his enthusiasm. He was always up, always ready to fight the next battle, and if he was sometimes frustrated by NORML's political setbacks, he was never discouraged and never dull. He saw himself as a professional manipulator, employed by the marijuana smokers of America to manipulate national drug policy to their advantage, and he believed it an honorable pursuit.

By then NORML, in its second year, was becoming the catalyst of a national movement to reform the nation's marijuana laws. Stroup's endless wheeling and dealing had brought together an unlikely alliance that ranged from out-and-out drug freaks to young lawyers who smoked and resented the laws that defined them as criminals to nonsmoking scientists and clergymen and civic leaders who simply thought the laws were wrong. As NORML's support grew, Stroup searched for new ways to bring pressure on the political system. There was nothing he could do to change the Nixon administration's zealous anti-drug policy, but NORML was starting to challenge the marijuana laws and to work with state legislators who wanted to enact the Marijuana Commission's recommended policy of "decriminalization," which simply meant that people could be fined, but not jailed, for marijuana use.

Stroup loved the constant intrigue and manipulation. He was a power groupie, one who lived for the deals, the leaks to the press, the political gossip, the daily crises, the delicious high that is obtained only at the center of the action. Like any lobbyist, he was first of all selling himself, and he took pains to develop his public persona of Mr. NORML, the cool and collected pot politician, party-giver and ladies' man. In fact, he had to an extent modeled himself after NORML's first financial patron, Hugh Hefner. But there was another, darker side to Stroup's personality, an angry side. He was angry in part at the drug laws and at a political establishment that, as he saw it, loved to guzzle its whiskey but denied his generation the right to enjoy its drug of choice. At another level Stroup was angry at his past, angry at a small-town Baptist boyhood in Dix, Illinois, that for years he had only wanted to escape. There was a certain Jekyll-and-Hyde quality to Stroup. If he could be charming and considerate, he could also be abruptly cold, self-righteous, and intensely critical of others, including his close friends and allies, if they did not match him in their dedication to the cause. This duality seemed to flow from the influence of two quite dissimilar parents: a father with a small-town politician's live-and-let-live attitude and a mother who was a devout Southern Baptist and not at all tolerant of the sins of the world.

In the fall of 1975 I was asked to conduct a *Playboy* interview with Stroup. By then the reform movement had scored some major victories. In 1973 Oregon had ended criminal penalties for smoking, and in the summer of 1975 five more states had done the same: Alaska, California, Maine, Colorado, and Ohio. NORML had provided national leadership to this burst of reform, by gaining publicity for the issue, by advising state legislators on what strategies and expert witnesses might be most effective, and often by paying the expenses for those outside witnesses to go to testify. Moreover, NORML had begun a far-ranging legal program, which involved both aid to individual defendants and court challenges to the constitutionality of state and federal marijuana laws, and to the federal government's ban on the medical use of marijuana. For many years the government had treated marijuana smokers pretty much as it pleased, but now NORML was rallying some of the brightest young lawyers in America to the smokers' defense.

As I studied the marijuana debate in preparation for my interview with Stroup, I began to think of it in terms of a war, a terrible civil war. I was struck by the parallels between this issue and the other great nation-dividing issue of the time, the war in Vietnam. In both cases the political establishment had been hell-bent to convince young Americans of something they refused to believe: that they should go die in Vietnam, in one case; that they should not smoke marijuana, in the other. In the minds of many Americans the two wars seemed to have blended: The slippery little Vietcong in Southeast Asia had become the dope-smoking hippie at home, and it was somehow imperative that the government's armed forces search out and destroy him. The same mentality that could say we had to destroy a village to save it in Vietnam could argue that we had to send a college student to prison to save him from marijuana.

The marijuana war was being waged on one front as a military conflict, in which tens of thousands of police and narcotics agents busied themselves arresting millions of young people for smoking and/or selling the weed. But as NORML, the Marijuana Commission, President Nixon, Sen. James Eastland, and others began a national debate on the issue, it became increasingly a propaganda war, fought through the media, as the pro-marijuana and anti-marijuana forces battled for the hearts and minds of millions of nonsmoking Americans who would ultimately determine the outcome of the conflict in the political arena.

In 1976 I spent six months as Jimmy Carter's speechwriter and had an opportunity to view the marijuana issue from the perspective of a presidential campaign. If there is anything to be learned in a national campaign, as it moves endlessly from city to city, rally to rally, enclave to enclave, it is that America is an incredibly large, diversified, and potentially explosive nation, less melting pot than tinderbox. The divisions are all there—black and white, Protestant and Catholic, North and South, immigrant and blueblood—waiting for politicians to exploit them. Now to that list has been added the division between those who enjoy drugs and those who fear them. The issue had been exploited in 1972, when McGovern supported decriminalization and Nixon opposed it. Nixon's followers denounced McGovern as the candidate of the three A's—acid, amnesty, and abortion, marijuana having been transformed by political hyperbole into "acid," or LSD.

Fortunately, the drug issue was not exploited in the 1976 campaign. Carter had endorsed decriminalization early in his campaign. I had assumed he was motivated by a combination of intellectual honesty and political necessity: the former because he knew his sons had smoked, the latter because the issue was important to a lot of young activists and to rock stars, like the Allman Brothers, whose support he sought. Having endorsed the no-jail concept, he rarely mentioned it unless asked, for he was aware of the basic political fact that the great majority of voters were anti-marijuana. His opponent, Gerald Ford, waffled on the issue. He said he didn't want smokers to go to jail, but he never quite endorsed decriminalization. Still, he never tried to exploit the issue, perhaps in part because he, too, had sons who had smoked and a wife who said she might have if it had been around in her younger days.

If marijuana had become an issue in the 1976 campaign, it would probably have been because some of us on the Carter staff occasionally smoked, not only among ourselves but with friends in the media. It was a crazy thing to do, but people do a lot of crazy things in a political campaign. (Consider the candidates, the one proclaiming lust in his heart, the other forever bumping his head and forgetting where he was. What were *they* smoking?) Alcohol was by far the drug of choice on the campaign, but sometimes, late at night in somebody's hotel room, we'd share a joint or two, and in the small, gossipy world of the campaign that fact could have leaked and been transformed into a great drug scandal. Looking back on it, I think our smoking was symbolic, a gesture of defiance, of individuality, against the insane and dehumanizing pressures of a national political campaign. The reporters were my friends, but our respective roles in the campaign made us antagonists. By smoking we were making a separate peace.

During the campaign I would sometimes receive calls and memos from Stroup, who was busy pinpointing his potential allies in a Carter administration. I was one, although less crucial to Stroup's hopes than Dr. Peter Bourne, Carter's friend and advisor on health issues, whom Stroup had known for several years. When NORML held its annual conference in December of 1976, a month after Carter won the election, Stroup had persuaded Bourne to be its keynote speaker and me to be cohost (with Christie Hefner and Garry Trudeau) at a fund-raising party afterward. Unfortunately for Stroup's ambitions, I had by then decided I was not cut out to be a politician, or even a politician's speechwriter, and I parted company with Carter just before his inauguration.

Stroup also had his problems with Jimmy Carter, who had been president less than a month when Stroup decided he was backing away from his campaign commitment to decriminalization. Stroup angrily

—and rashly—leaked an embarrassing story about Chip Carter, the president's son, to reporters, and thereby outraged Peter Bourne and members of the Carter family. Stroup continued to mix socially with some of the younger, more adventuresome members of the Carter administration, including Chip Carter, but he was increasingly at odds with it on policy. This culminated in a lawsuit NORML brought to stop the government from supporting a program in which the Mexican government sprayed marijuana fields with the herbicide paraquat.

I knew about NORML's fight with the government over paraquat, but I was still shocked by a phone call that reached me in France one evening in July of 1978. My wife and I were having dinner at L'Hôtellerie du Val-Suzon, a wonderful country inn outside Dijon, when the call came from a friend of mine, a reporter with the Washington *Post*.

"What do you know about Peter Bourne and Ellen Metsky and the drug scandal?" my friend asked.

"About *what?*"

"Oh, God, haven't you *heard?* Bourne wrote Metsky a Quāālude prescription and used a phony name, and then Keith blew the whistle on him about using coke at the NORML party and he had to resign, and the whole town's gone crazy, and don't you know *anything?*"

I really didn't know anything, except that from my perspective, sitting there in a French country inn, the whole thing sounded insane. When I got back to Washington a few weeks later, I found that to be the case. Bourne, whom I knew and liked, had been caught using a false name in writing out a Quāālude prescription for a patient. Then, with Bourne already in serious trouble, Stroup helped Jack Anderson break a story about Bourne's having used cocaine at a NORML party eight months earlier. Bourne denied the charge, but several witnesses supported Stroup's account.

Once again Stroup had acted rashly, out of anger toward the administration over the paraquat issue, and this time his anger was self-destructive. His attack on Bourne was considered irresponsible by many of NORML's supporters. By the end of the year, realizing he had lost much of his effectiveness, Stroup left NORML to start a law firm. By then, the seventies were coming to a close, NORML was struggling to stay afloat, a new anti-marijuana political movement was gathering momentum, and one era in the long national debate over drugs was coming to an end.

This book is about Stroup's adventures, NORML's work, and the political war over the marijuana issue in America, an increasingly bitter confrontation between two groups of angry Americans. On one side are millions of smokers, many of them well educated, successful people who resent being defined as criminals for using what they regard as a mild but enjoyable drug. Opposing them are angry parents who see increasing marijuana use by adolescents as a threat to their children's health and well-being. Both sides have their scientists to cite—those who say marijuana is virtually harmless and those who believe it presents real or potential health hazards—and both sides have their political champions, although as the 1980s began, the momentum was clearly with the parents' anti-marijuana movement.

The marijuana debate is an increasingly complex one, and there are many perspectives from which to view it: historical, scientific, economic, legal, cultural, sociological, political. My focus in this book is mainly on the politics of the issue and, beyond that, on its human dimension. As a writer, I have been fascinated by the mixture of comedy and tragedy that has surrounded the issue, and by the wonderful variety of people who became caught up in it in the 1970s. The cast of characters includes Stroup, an admirably flawed protagonist; Peter Bourne, a well-intentioned man who ventured beyond his political depth, Hugh Hefner, who scorned drugs for years, then suddenly found marijuana giving him unexpected pleasure, and a cocaine investigation causing him unexpected pain; Gordon Brownell, a Ronald Reagan adviser who was transformed by psychedelic drugs into a pro-marijuana politician; Sue Rusche, a liberal Atlantan who became an anti-drug crusader; Tom Forcade, a smuggler turned Yippie who made a fortune with a pro-drug magazine; Frank Demolli, a college freshman whose love of marijuana won him a twenty-five-year prison term; and Bob Randall, a teacher who challenged the government because he needed marijuana to save his eyesight. I knew most of these people, and I thought them all caught up in political currents they could barely understand, much less control, currents that tossed their lives about, challenged them, changed them, defined them, and sometimes destroyed them. Few controversies in recent years have touched more Americans' lives than has the drug issue, and to examine that issue is, I think, a way of looking at America in the 1970s, perhaps as good a way as any.

Where to begin? One place would be the celebrated NORML party in December of 1977, a party at which many worlds intersected, a party that seemed to be NORML at its zenith but proved to be the beginning of the end.

1

It was destined to be Washington's party of the year, even before the great cocaine scandal. One participant recalled it enthusiastically as the moment when "the drug culture met the Establishment —everybody came out of the closet at last." Each year a big Saturday-night party climaxed NORML's annual conference, and each year the NORML party had become more fashionable, more talked about—"outlaw chic," some called it. This one, on a bitter-cold December night in 1977, promised to be the biggest and best of all.

Because three or four hundred guests were expected, the party was for the first time being held away from NORML's offices on M Street NW. Keith Stroup, NORML's national director, had asked two of his friends, Fred Moore and Billy Paley, co-owners of the Gandy Dancer, a fashionable Capitol Hill restaurant, to suggest a suitable location for the party, and they in turn had consulted another of Stroup's friends, a young man who worked in the Carter administration. This young man had arranged to borrow the big town house on S Street, not far from DuPont Circle, in Northwest Washington.

The young man from the Carter administration arrived early, to make sure the food and the band and the security men were all in place, and as the first wave of guests poured in, he was increasingly pleased with his selection. The town house was perfect for a big, noisy, get-it-on party. An architect had bought and restored the house a few years earlier, opening up its inside so that the stairs were exposed and you could see all the way from the basement level to the fourth floor. The house was like a huge stage on which everyone could see everyone else performing. The only real privacy to be found was in a small bedroom on the top floor, and the young man from the Carter administration had promised the owner that it would be kept closed off, except perhaps for a few special guests. Otherwise, as people streamed in downstairs, they were thrown together in a way that demanded intimacy. It was cold outside but hot and loud inside; introductions were unnecessary, and flirtations were inevitable. The rock band began to beat out a tune, the psychedelic juggler began to toss balls up into flashing strobe lights, the music and shouts and laughter became deafening, and soon many guests were very open about their drug use.

Silver trays were being passed among the guests. Some held caviar; others, hand-rolled joints made of the finest domestic marijuana, seedless, which on the open market sold for as much as $400 an ounce. This very expensive, hand-cultivated marijuana had been grown by a young Southern farmer who had first tried the drug as a helicopter pilot with the U.S. Army in Vietnam. When he returned home, he brought with him some choice Laotian marijuana seeds, and he proceeded to convert his family farm to a new cash crop. Illegal marijauna soon made him rich, and, what's more, he believed in the weed, believed it liberated men's minds, believed it should be legal. He became an early supporter of NORML, and it had become a tradition that each year he would donate a few pounds of his finest product to the NORML party. That afternoon two young NORML employees had watched a football game on television, tripped on a hallucinogenic drug called MDA, and patiently rolled the several hundred superjoints that now were being circulated on the silver trays.

Many people had brought their own drugs, of course; to serious drug users a party like this was an opportunity to show off their "special stash." Soon joints glowed like fireflies in the dark, crowded rooms. Soon, too, some guests produced small vials and spoons and began to snort cocaine. To the uninitiated it might have seemed an unpleasant, even an offensive sight—men and women sucking white powder up their noses—but to others "snorting" cocaine was no stranger than smoking cigarettes or sipping wine. Indeed, in an America still deeply divided over drugs, this party could be seen in vastly different lights. To its guests it was simply a great party, and perhaps also a symbol of their defiance of repressive drug laws. But to millions of other Americans this party would seem a different symbol: It was degeneracy, decline and fall, Babylon on the Potomac.

Not everyone at the party was using drugs, of course, although most of the guests were professionally concerned with drugs in one way or another. There were lawyers, Congressional aides, state legislators, and other young politicians from around America who had worked with NORML on marijuana-law reform. There were scientists from government agencies and great universities, men and women who were concerned both with the possible harm and the possible benefits of drugs. There were lawyers and writers and administrators from Washington's ever-expanding drug-abuse bureaucracy (for one man's problem is another man's bureaucracy), which included the Drug Abuse Council, the National Institute on Drug Abuse, and the Food and Drug Administration. These experts had participated that weekend in NORML conference workshops on such topics as "Marijuana and Science" and "Research and Regulation."

Some guests at the NORML party had achieved a degree of celebrity. A few were born to it: Christie Hefner, the slender, pretty daughter of *Playboy*'s publisher; Billy Paley, the son and namesake of the CBS founder; David Kennedy, one of Robert Kennedy's sons. There were eight or ten guests whose celebrity flowed from their association with Jimmy Carter, the nation's new president. They were young men and women, still in their twenties, who had climbed onto Carter's improbable bandwagon, served as advance men and staff assistants in his campaign, and been rewarded with jobs in the White House and in executive agencies, jobs that paid enough to support the expensive tastes in drugs that many of them had acquired.

There were a good many news-media people present, too, young writers and reporters from the Washington newspapers and television stations and from the out-of-town newspaper bureaus. These journalists were not working, although this party might have made quite a good story. They were young reporters who, although in theory objective, were in fact sympathetic to NORML and its cause, for they used marijuana and other drugs and they were, therefore, technically criminals, although they tended to consider themselves very responsible citizens. In a sense the young media people and the young political people, however much they might disagree on other matters, were united as drug users and as victims of the double standard that surrounded drug use in America. At the Washington *Post*, no less than in the Carter White House, young people who were part of the drug culture rarely admitted that fact to their superiors, who were usually part of the alcohol culture and tended to think that marijuana or cocaine use was a sign of irresponsibility. It was said that sex was the "dirty little secret" of the Victorian era; in the America of the late 1970s drug use seemed to have become the secret vice, the one that almost everyone enjoyed and almost no one admitted to.

There were some guests at the NORML party that evening who were emissaries from the very heart of the drug culture: Yippie political activists; marijuana growers and smugglers; pilots in what was called the MAF, or Marijuana Air Force. One of the Yippies, Aaron Kaye, had achieved a certain celebrity by throwing pies in the faces of Mayor Abe Beame, singer Anita Bryant, and others whose political views he found distasteful. Aaron Kaye was not a wealthy man—the next day he would have to borrow six dollars to buy a pie—but there were several young men at the NORML party who had become marijuana millionaires, either through smuggling or through the sale of rolling papers and other paraphernalia. The most celebrated of these tycoons was a small, intense man named Tom Forcade, who had first been a Yippie, then became a smuggler, then started a phenomenally successful magazine called *High Times*, which was to drugs what *Playboy* was to sex.

The thirty-year-old Forcade had contributed tens of thousands of dollars to NORML, and he had flown down from New York for the party like a royal prince on tour. He wore a white suit, a white hat, and sharkskin cowboy boots, and he was accompanied by an entourage of *High Times* writers and executives. He had rented the biggest suite at the Hyatt Regency, the conference headquarters, and the *High Times* hospitality suite soon became immensely popular, perhaps because Forcade's "bar" served cocaine instead of whiskey.

Another young man at the party that evening might, with any luck, have been a marijuana millionaire. He was bright and ambitious, he had been a business major in college, and he had been in the rolling-paper business at a time when fortunes were being made. But Mark Heutlinger had worked for Amorphia, a group in California that used the profits from its Acapulco Gold papers to finance pro-marijuana politics, and when Amorphia went broke, he had ended up as NORML's business manager. This evening he had volunteered to guard the front door.

It was an important job but not an entirely pleasant one. There was a long line of people waiting outside in the near-zero cold, and many of them did not have invitations. Moreover, the doorknob had somehow fallen off, and Heutlinger had to use a screwdriver to twist the lock open every time he let someone in. The job had one important fringe benefit, however: The people he admitted were often so grateful that they would press drugs on him—a hit of this, a snort of that—so that as the evening progressed, Mark Heutlinger was complaining less and less and smiling more and more. Still he was glad when Keith Stroup arrived, around nine-thirty, because he wanted to propose an open-door policy: They should let everyone in, rather than making people wait out in the cold while he checked invitations. Heutlinger thought it was the obvious thing to do, but he didn't want to do it without Stroup's approval. It was, after all, Stroup's party.

Stroup arrived fashionably late, with his nine-year-old daughter at his side, and in answer to Heutlinger's question he cried, "Hell, yes, let 'em all in," a decision that drew cheers from the twenty-odd people waiting in line. Stroup beamed—it was the sort of dramatic gesture he loved—and then he plunged headlong into the party, for this was his element, his world. He had founded NORML in 1971, viewing it as a public-interest lobby that would use Ralph Nader–style techniques to change the marijuana laws. Improbably, he had made a success of it; many people on Capitol Hill thought that, dollar for dollar, NORML was the most effective lobby in Washington.

But Stroup was more than an effective lobbyist; he had made himself a star. In a city of dull, careful men he was an outlaw, an adventurer, and finally a celebrity who hung out with the likes of Hunter Thompson, Hugh Hefner, and Willie Nelson. He caused a stir as he pushed through the crowded party, pumping the hands of the men, kissing and hugging the women, taking a hit of grass here, a snort of cocaine there, getting high rather quickly and not much caring. Keith Stroup was on top of the world this evening. He had survived the Nixon years, and now Jimmy Carter was president; he had friends in high places, and the prospects for the movement he headed seemed bright indeed. He was a few weeks short of his thirty-fourth birthday, a slender, good-looking, rather intense man who was just under six feet tall, wore rimless glasses, and kept his dark-blond hair trimmed at shoulder length. For the party he had dressed in jeans, a Pierre Cardin shirt, and a blue velvet dinner jacket, topped off by the burgundy bow tie that was his trademark.

Stroup was inevitably a controversial figure, even within this world he had created. Some saw him as a latter-day Jay Gatsby. Like Fitzgerald's bootlegger-hero of the 1920s, Stroup had rejected his drab Midwestern origins and created a glamorous new persona for himself. Others seeking a literary analogy might have compared Stroup to Budd Schulberg's opportunistic Sammy Glick. There was some truth in both views, for Stroup was a politician and as such many-sided. He was idealistic enough to have started a marijuana-law-reform program and tough enough to have made it succeed. He was a fast-talking, fast-moving, high-energy performer, a magnetic figure, an actor who this evening, at this gaudy party, was glorying in his favorite role: Mr. Marijuana, the Man from NORML, the Prime Minister of Pot.

He left his daughter watching the juggler with a friend and fought his way upstairs. He was pleased to see so many young professionals present, people who even a year earlier might not have ventured into a NORML party. He wondered if some of these very respectable people might think it dangerous here, might fear the police would break down the door at any moment. In theory, they could all have been arrested, but in reality, Stroup knew, this party was one of the safest places in Washington that evening. Stroup's friend in the Carter administration had been an advance man during the campaign, and he understood how police officials relate to political power. He had called the precinct station that afternoon and told the police about the party, and he had pointedly mentioned that numerous people from the White House, the District government, and Capitol Hill would be among the guests. That was why police cars kept cruising past the town house all evening: not to stop the drug use in progress inside but to make sure that no politically important people were murdered, mugged, or otherwise molested as they walked to and from their cars.

Upstairs, Stroup joined two of his favorite people, Christie Hefner and Hunter Thompson. Christie was twenty-four, slender, and very pretty, with long brown hair and a bright, disarming smile, She was also an ambitious, sophisticated feminist who fully intended to take control of her father's publishing empire someday. She and Stroup had met some five years earlier, when she was still in college and he was hanging out at the Playboy mansion, trying to win her father's favor. They had become close friends and though they had their separate careers and their various romantic entanglements, once or twice a year they would slip away to spend some time together, getting high and giggling at the madness of it all.

If Christie Hefner was a princess of the drug culture, forty-year-old Hunter Thompson was its poet laureate. He had written brilliantly, violently, of presidential politics in the pages of *Rolling Stone*, excoriating Hubert Humphrey as a senile old whore; Ed Muskie as a demented, drug-numbed geek; Richard Nixon as a blood-sucking vampire. His book *Fear and Loathing in Las Vegas* ranked with Tom Wolfe's *Electric Kool-Aid Acid Test* as a classic of the drug culture. Absurdly, he had achieved his greatest celebrity not for his writing but as the model for the Doonesbury comic strip's drug-crazed character Ambassador Duke. He was a Hemingway of his generation, a writer-adventurer whose talent was in constant danger of being overshadowed by his much-publicized nonliterary exploits. In fact, Thompson lived a quiet life outside Aspen, Colorado, most of the time, but in his public appearances, such as this one at the NORML party (he was on the organization's advisory board), he was very much "on" as a celebrity, always puffing on a joint or swigging a beer, talking loudly, arguing politics. He made some people uncomfortable, for he was a big, rugged-looking man, and there was an aura of violence about him, as if at any moment he might explode.

When Stroup joined Thompson and Hefner, the writer began immediately to fire insults at him: "Stroup, it's clear to me that you're a neurotic paranoid and you're destined to fuck up badly and bring us all down. I'm not sure I want to remain associated with this organization with you at the helm."

Stroup replied in kind. It was the sort of celebrity banter both men were skilled at, a show they put on for the people pressed around them. Stroup recognized, without resentment, that Thompson was the only person at the party who ranked higher on the national-celebrity scale than he did. But after a while something unexpected interrupted their banter. Christie Hefner grabbed Stroup's arm, said she felt dizzy, said perhaps she should sit down.

"Oh, my God," Stroup said with a groan. He knew at once what the problem was: those joints they had been smoking as they talked, the young Southern farmer's very expensive, very powerful marijuana. As Stroup moved quickly to find Christie a place to sit and to send for a glass of water, he was unaware of another event that was causing a good deal of excitement downstairs.

Peter Bourne had arrived.

He came by himself, entering the town house at a little after ten. In truth, he had not wanted to come. He had addressed the previous year's NORML conference, and he had been embarrassed when television cameras recorded people smoking marijuana in the audience as he spoke. More recently, he and Stroup had clashed over Bourne's support of the paraquat program. Still, Bourne did not want to seem to be snubbing NORML, whose members were part of his political constituency, and so he had dropped by the party, thinking his mission there to be business much more than pleasure.

He could hardly have received a warmer welcome. He had no sooner stepped in from the cold when people began crowding aound him, shaking his hand, hugging him, giving him the VIP treatment that reflected both his political importance and the genuine affection that many people felt for him.

Dr. Peter Bourne, who was in his late thirties then, had been a popular, respected figure in the drug-abuse field in Washington since 1973. That year he had come up from Atlanta, where he had directed Gov. Jimmy Carter's drug-treatment program, and had become assistant director of Richard Nixon's Special Action Office for Drug Abuse Prevention. He left the Nixon administration the next year, however, because he had a more urgent political priority: helping to make Jimmy Carter president. He took a part-time job with the privately financed Drug Abuse Council, but he devoted his best energies to the Carter cause. Now Carter was president, and Bourne was his closest adviser on drug policy. Already, in his first year in office, Carter had called for the decriminalization of marijuana and for a ban on barbiturates. People in the drug field assumed that Bourne had prompted these and other presidential decisions, and they hoped to lobby Bourne a bit that night for their own pet projects. In Washington, as everyone knew, a few words in an informal setting might do more good than a hundred official memoranda.

Still, most of the people who would lobby Peter Bourne that night also genuinely liked him. After the Nixon years it seemed a minor miracle to have as the president's senior adviser on drug policy someone as intelligent, humane, and open-minded as Bourne. By White House standards, Peter Bourne was a most unusual man. There was something gentle, even vulnerable, about him. He was a soft-spoken, self-effacing man, almost shy, a man who seemed determined never to give offense. Some of his friends feared he was not as canny a politician as he fancied himself, feared he might be too decent to survive in the jungle of Washington politics. But he had his office in the White House, with easy access to his friend the president, and he was obviously surviving very well.

As Bourne entered the town house, he encountered a friend, a woman named Ann Zill, who worked for Stewart Mott, the General Motors heir, and a financial supporter of NORML. Bourne and Zill tried to stay together, but it wasn't easy with the people crowding around and the rock band playing, so they began to push their way upstairs. At one landing a door burst open and Hunter Thompson staggered out. He was snorting loudly, jerking his head violently, flailing his arms about. It wasn't clear whether he was snorting cocaine or just giving his imitation of some crazed cocaine snorter. The party was full of surprises like that. A woman downstairs passed out, and an ambulance was called. By the time the ambulance arrived, the woman was fine, and the problem was then to get the ambulance crew to leave.

Bourne stopped for a moment to talk with a tall, bearded man named Craig Copetas, a writer for *High Times* who for the past year had been singing Bourne's praises in his magazine. A Yippie leader named Dana Beal approached them and offered Bourne a hit from his joint. Copetas, feeling very protective toward his White House friend, waved the Yippie away.

Other people pressed around Bourne, and he and Ann Zill became separated. Soon he was joined by another woman, also a friend of several years, who worked in what was called the "drug-abuse-prevention field" but who was, in her private life, a not-infrequent user of illicit drugs. She and Bourne talked, other people joined them, joints began to circulate, and soon Bourne was enjoying himself, glad he'd come to the party after all.

Upstairs, Christie Hefner had recovered from her dizzy spell, and Keith Stroup was enjoying the party. He was a bit high, and when the woman friend of Bourne's rushed up to him, he did not at first understand what she was saying.

"Peter's here," she whispered urgently. "He wants to get high."

"Peter who?" Stroup asked, confused.

"Peter *Bourne*," said the woman who was also a close friend of Stroup's. "He's on his way up here, and he wants to do some coke. Do you have any?"

Stroup happened not to have any cocaine on him, but he moved quickly to take command of the situation. Soon he had people scurrying in all directions. Craig Copetas set off in search of the *High Times* stash, the woman went downstairs to check with a NORML aide, and another friend of Stroup's called a nearby dealer and told him to bring over eight grams of his best cocaine at once.

Having drugs, or having easy access to drugs, was part of Stroup's outlaw mystique. He did not pass out drugs in school yards or otherwise seduce the innocent (there being, some would say, precious few innocents left to seduce in America). Still, he understood the uses of temptation; if some reporter or politician wanted an ounce of good marijuana, Stroup could often help out. His job, after all, was to make marijuana use respectable, and one way to do that was to encourage respectable people to smoke. Some months later, with the wisdom of hindsight, it would be clear that the last thing Keith Stroup should have done was to provide cocaine for Peter Bourne. Indeed, he should have done everything in his power to stop Bourne from using cocaine. But that was not Stroup's instinct.

Bourne finally made his way to where Stroup was standing with Thompson and Hefner, and more celebrity chitchat ensued. Stroup could not have been happier. To have the president's drug adviser present added a final touch of legitimacy to the party and, by implication, to everything Stroup had been fighting for these seven years. Moreover, to have Peter Bourne side by side with Hunter Thompson was a perfect symbol of Stroup's achievement. He had built a coalition that included drug-using crazies, eminent scientists, and influential politicians. Stroup was laughing, joking, smoking a joint, talking a mile a minute, when Bourne's friend appeared at his side and said she'd found some coke.

Soon Stroup suggested that a few of them go upstairs to a private room and have a little "toot"—drug users' slang for cocaine use. Bourne smiled and said that sounded fine.

It took a few minutes to get everyone upstairs. The process was a bit awkward, since some people were invited and others were not. The stairs up to the little room on the fourth floor had been roped off, and an ex–Secret Service man was guarding the way. But because the stairway was open, scores of people could see Stroup, Bourne, Thompson, and the others going upstairs, and most of them suspected what was happening. Most NORML parties had a room like that, where the elite could partake of their favorite drugs in private.

The room upstairs was T-shaped, with one small area that held a desk and chair and another area, down a few steps, that contained a bed and a television set. There was also a balcony, where people went from time to time for fresh air. Almost everyone who went upstairs felt a sense of relief. The party downstairs was so noisy and crowded that this little room seemed an island of sanity.

Hunter Thompson made his way to the television set, accompanied by his young friend David Kennedy and by John Walsh, an editor with the Washington *Post*. They were soon engrossed in the UCLA–Notre Dame basketball game, and Thompson, a sports nut, was engaged in what he called "creative betting" with Walsh: betting a dollar on which way the ball would bounce, on whether a shot would go in or out, on almost anything. They thought they might stay and watch television awhile, because *Saturday Night Live* came next, with Willie Nelson as the guest star.

About ten people had assembled in the room with the desk. Stroup, Bourne, and Copetas were the core of the group, and the others clustered around them included a young woman from *High Times*, the young Carter aide who had helped organize the party, and two young women from the Carter administration who were friends of Bourne's. When Bourne's woman friend joined the group, she looked uncertainly at Copetas, then at Stroup.

"Is this all right?" she asked.

Stroup knew what she meant. He turned to Copetas. "This is all off the record, right?"

Copetas quickly agreed. The last thing he wanted to do was to hurt Peter Bourne. So the woman gave Stroup the "bullet" she had borrowed downstairs—a small, bullet-shaped container that holds cocaine and that, when twisted a certain way, measures out a hit of cocaine, much as cap spouts on whiskey bottles measure out one drink.

There was some talk about the bullet, and how it worked, and about drug paraphernalia in general and how elaborate and expensive it had become. There was some banter, too, about the young woman from *High Times*, who was olive-skinned and was wearing a loose black dress, and thus was somehow christened the "Lady from Peru." People were high enough for the joke to seem quite hilarious. Still, there was some awkwardness about the cocaine, and finally Stroup took the bullet and gave himself a "one-and-one"—a hit in each nostril—and then passed it on to the next person. The process took a minute or two for each person. There was a certain protocol to drug use; one did not rush things or otherwise appear uncool. As the bullet slowly made its way around the circle toward Peter Bourne, one young woman, a friend of his from the campaign, whispered to him that he should not be doing this, but he only laughed self-confidently. Bourne had a fatal desire to be one of the boys. When the bullet reached him, he too took a one-and-one. All around the room people were stunned. And well they might have been, for they were witnessing one of the turning points in the war over drug policy that had been so bitterly contested in America in the 1970s.

More people crowded into the room, and there was more joking and laughter. Some lines of coke were laid out on a little hand mirror on the desk top, and people took hits from that, using a rolled-up bill to inhale the powder. There were jokes about whether it was a one-dollar bill or a hundred-dollar bill. Peter Bourne and the woman from *High Times* were deep in conversation. After a while Bourne's other friend decided to take the bullet and go back downstairs. She said she didn't think they should use up all the coke that had been lent to her, but she was really leaving because she felt uncomfortable about using cocaine in this company.

When she was gone, and the bullet with her, the woman from *High Times* produced a vial, one with a spoon attached to it by a tiny chain, that held a small amount of cocaine. She gave it to Copetas, who measured out a spoonful and passed it on to Bourne.

Copetas did not feel comfortable about what was happening. As a journalist he saw this scene with double vision. Part of him knew what an explosive story this was, and he feared that even if he didn't write it, someone else would. He felt, too, the sudden silence in the room. As soon as he could, Copetas left Bourne and joined Hunter Thompson at the television set. Thompson threw his arm around Copetas, sighed loudly, and declared, "My God, man, we'll all be indicted now."

Copetas's *High Times* colleague was uncomfortable, too. She had been having a fine time downstairs. She loved this big, loud, sprawling party. There were different pockets of energy everywhere, she thought, and so many terrific people. She'd never expected Washington to be such fun. Then Craig had asked if she was holding any coke, and had whisked her up here, and suddenly she was doing coke with the president's drug adviser. And she had liked Bourne, liked him a lot. He was such a gentle person—so unlike the crazies she dealt with at her magazine. Still, she had to smile when he did the coke; he hardly knew how. When he finished, she reached up and wiped a speck of cocaine off the end of his nose. He was such a nice man, gave off such good vibes, and yet there was something about this scene that gave her bad vibes, too. It was very confusing. After a while she and Copetas went out on the balcony, and they agreed that the whole thing was crazy.

Soon Peter Bourne decided to leave. Again, as he and Stroup descended the open stairway, hundreds of people looked up at them with curiosity. When Bourne finally made his way to the front door, where Mark Heutlinger was still on duty, the NORML aide shook his hand enthusiastically. "We really appreciate your coming, Dr. Bourne," he said. "You don't know what this means to us."

Bourne was barely out the door when people began rushing up to Heutlinger, asking if it were true that Bourne had done cocaine. Upstairs, Stroup was starting to get the same question. In a way he was as surprised at what had happened as everyone else: "Can you *believe* Peter did that?" he asked a friend. But he quickly realized where his interests lay, and so he sought out the writers who had been upstairs and reminded them that it was all off the record, and as people continued to ask him whether Bourne had used cocaine, he dismissed the reports as rumors, crazy bullshit.

It was not late, only midnight or so, but Stroup was tired—he'd been up until dawn the night before—and he was increasingly concerned about all the questions he was getting about Bourne. He sensed it was time for a strategic withdrawal, and so he found his daughter, who had fallen asleep downstairs, and got a friend to drive them back to the Hyatt Regency.

The party raged on without him. At four o'clock two policemen came to the door and suggested, very politely, that it was time to call it a night. Mark Heutlinger, still on his feet, told the band to stop playing and persuaded most of the remaining guests to leave. There were, however, ten or fifteen people passed out. Heutlinger checked to make sure each of them was breathing—they were, he recalled later, "sleeping and smiling"—and then he got permission for them to spend the rest of the night where they were. On that hospitable note, the 1977 NORML conference party ended.

More precisely, the party ended and the gossip began. Gossip is what most people in Washington have instead of money or power —glittery scraps of information they can exchange to show their importance—and talk of Bourne's cocaine use became a staple of Washington gossip for weeks. To some, of course, it was more than mere gossip; one man's gossip is another man's scoop. Not long after the party, a writer for Jack Anderson's column confronted Stroup about Bourne's rumored cocaine use; Stroup refused to comment. Another reporter, who had attended the party but had not been upstairs, typed up a detailed account of drug use at the party, for future reference. For good reporters, nothing is ever wasted.

The Bourne incident simmered for months, seemed to have died out, then suddenly exploded into public view the next summer. It was a tragedy for Peter Bourne, but he was not the only person harmed by the affair. Keith Stroup, who contributed to Bourne's downfall, was soon under pressure to resign from NORML. Jimmy Carter was hurt politically by the scandal, once more embarrassed by a member of his inner circle. Finally, the Bourne affair hurt the movement for drug-law reform to which Bourne, Stroup, and Carter were all, in different ways, committed. There were larger political forces at work, of course, but the Bourne incident put the Carter administration on the defensive about drug policy. It destroyed NORML's political effectiveness and it emboldened the hard-liners who opposed any reform of the drug laws. The political pendulum, which had been moving toward reform throughout the 1970s, and which seemed to have reached a peak with Peter Bourne's arrival in the White House, was swinging back the other way. "The drug-law reform movement vanished up Peter Bourne's nose," one participant later said bitterly.

It was one of those rare moments in Washington when the link between personality and policy was crystal clear. At the highest levels, politics becomes a test of character, and the pressures are such that few men pass the test with flying colors. Peter Bourne and Keith Stroup were friends (although Stroup understood better than Bourne old Joe Kennedy's dictum that in politics you have no friends, only allies), and they shared common goals, yet they were on a collision course, one that in the end would highlight each man's limitations. Peter Bourne's weakness was that he was not tough enough to play the political game at those levels. He did not see the dangers that surrounded him until he was overwhelmed by them.

Stroup's was a different flaw, almost the opposite. He was an angry man, angry at his past, angry at the drug laws and the people who made them, and that very anger had made him an effective agent of political change. He had known how to respond to the Nixons and Agnews and Mitchells who had symbolized U.S. drug policy when he started NORML—he fought them with all he had—but he found it difficult to play the more subtle, more restrained political game that is called for when the people in power are your friends. When he became convinced that Peter Bourne had turned against him, he reacted angrily, and his anger contributed to his own downfall. It was a complex, contradictory situation, but one point was clear. The cocaine scandal that rocked Washington in the summer of 1978 was not a fluke, not an accident. Bourne and Stroup, like all of us, were prisoners of their pasts, acting out roles for which a lifetime had prepared them. All that happened was part of all that had gone before.

2

Keith Stroup, who would in time become Mr. Marijuana, had a boyhood as American as apple pie. Born two days after Christmas 1943, he grew up on his parents' 160-acre farm on the outskirts of the hamlet of Dix, in Southern Illinois. His parents, Vera and Russell Stroup, were hard-working, God-fearing people, pillars of their community. Russell Stroup's people had farmed in the area, but by the 1950s he was a successful building contractor who drove a Lincoln Continental and was the area's unofficial Republican political leader. Vera Stroup's parents, Irvin and Effie Hawley, lived nearby. Irvin had been a miner—in time he died of black lung—and Effie worked in a dress factory and spent her weekends quilting. As a boy Stroup loved to go squirrel hunting with Grandfather Hawley, who always made a point of saving the squirrel heads, which were considered a great delicacy when cooked, for his grandsons.

Keith had a brother, Larry, who was exactly one year older, and the two boys were expected to work hard at home and in their father's construction company. If they didn't, or if they missed Sunday school or talked back to their parents, Russell Stroup was quick to whip off his belt and administer fast, firm discipline. He believed in the age-old admonition about sparing the rod and spoiling the child. The elder Stroups were Southern Baptists, fundamentalists who in theory opposed drinking, smoking, dancing, and related worldliness, although in practice Russell Stroup liked a drink now and then, a fact that grieved his wife. Vera Stroup was the more zealous of the two. She was a cheerful, rather shy woman who believed that truth and salvation were to be found in the Good Book, strictly interpreted, and who used her considerable strength of character to see that her husband and sons lived by its admonitions.

Both Stroup boys grew up in the church, often winning gold stars for their perfect attendance at Sunday school, but their behavior was often far from perfect. Like other boys of that time and place, they sometimes shot cats, blew up mailboxes with cherry bombs, got in fights, and avoided their chores, and once, when they were in their early teens, a solemn delegation appeared at the Stroup home: the local Baptist minister, a touring evangelist, and several stalwarts of the Pleasant Hill Baptist Church. Russell Stroup ordered his sons onto their knees. The visitors had come to pray for the two boys, whose behavior of late had put the future of their souls in doubt. The brothers were horrified to find themselves surrounded by weeping, chanting, praying adults. The Baptist religion was increasingly a social embarrassment to Keith, although he could not reveal that awful fact to his parents. Church continued to be central to his life, particularly the tent revivals that came to town twice a year and were a much-awaited highlight of community life. Years later, when Stroup had become Mr. Marijuana and was preaching his own version of hellfire-and-damnation on the college lecture circuit, he would laugh at how much he had learned from those backwoods evangelists who had saved his soul twice yearly in his youth.

From boyhood, the Stroup brothers exhibited very different personalities. Larry was an excellent student who married his high-school sweetheart, became a successful businessman, and was always comfortable with the Baptist Church, the Midwest, his parents, and his father's political conservatism—with everything, in short, against which his younger brother would rebel. In later years Larry thought *he* was what Keith had rebelled against, that since he, the older brother, had been a conformist, Keith had been forced to become a rebel to gain attention and to carve out a separate identity for himself.

Keith always thought he had been rebelling against what he saw as his father's strict discipline, and, beyond that, against the hypocrisy and oppression of his hometown and his church. Russell Stroup, when his younger son shocked the family by becoming a marijuana lobbyist, thought that the boy had taken after his mother, that he had inherited her moral zeal but had applied it to a quite different social standard. Vera Stroup, for her part, didn't think Keith resembled her to any great degree. She really didn't know how to explain his behavior (nor did she ever stop praying that he would return to the teachings of the Church), but she suspected that the turning point had come when he was thirteen and left his hometown of Dix to confront the temptations of Mount Vernon, Illinois, the nearby city where he attended high school.

The move from the little elementary school in Dix to the high school in Mount Vernon was in fact traumatic for Keith. He had grown up as a leader in Dix, but when he started riding the bus to his new school, he discovered that his status had abruptly changed. The Mount Vernon kids who were the social elite of the high school looked down their noses at the country kids who rode the yellow buses in from places like Dix. They viewed the bus riders as farm kids, hillbillies, people of no social consequence. Stroup was indeed a farm boy, but an ambitious one, and he moved quickly to solve the crisis in his young life. Rather than be stigmatized by emerging from the school bus each morning, he simply quit riding the bus and began hitchhiking the ten miles to school each day.

It was Stroup's first effort at image-making, at setting himself apart from the crowd, and it was a success. He was bright and articulate as well as ambitious, and he soon won the social acceptance he so badly wanted. He was voted into Mount Vernon's exclusive "teen club"; in time he was elected a class officer, dating prom queens, and hanging out in the Mount Vernon pool hall with the high school's "in" crowd. Sometimes he even visited the local country club, to which some of his new friends belonged.

As he spent more and more time with his new friends in Mount Vernon, Stroup was increasingly embarrassed by his home, by his father's poor grammar and his mother's religious fervor. He was embarrassed, too, when he visited his new friends' homes and realized how much he didn't know about art and music, or when he went to dinner at the country club and confronted the classic uncertainties over which fork to use. He had by then offended his parents by leaving the Pleasant Hill Baptist Church, near Dix, to attend a Methodist church in Mount Vernon—the move was social, not theological—and it would have hurt them more if they'd known he and his friends soon quit going to church at all.

His parents of course resented the amount of time he spent with his new friends in Mount Vernon. His mother was upset when he and some friends were stopped by the police for driving a car in someone's yard and were required to wash police cars for several Saturday mornings. To the boys, of course, that "punishment" was a badge of honor. His parents understood that their younger son was rejecting their values, their culture, and it pained and angered them. "What's wrong with you?" his father once demanded. "We're country people and we're proud of it. Why isn't Dix good enough for you?" There was, of course, no answer to the question, except the universal, unutterable truth: It just isn't.

Keith Stroup grew up resenting his father's strict discipline and his lack of social polish, but the fact remained that he learned his politics from him. Russell Stroup had for years been Dix's most active Republican. He was a stocky, white-haired, long-winded man, a classic courthouse politician, a horse trader, a teller of tales, the country bumpkin who invariably outfoxes the city slicker. For years he kept on good terms with the district's Republican congressman, and he was at least on speaking terms with Sen. Everett Dirksen. In 1968 Russell Stroup would reach the pinnacle of a lifetime of party loyalty as one of a group of downstate Republican leaders called to Chicago for a personal meeting with candidate Richard Nixon.

In the little town of Dix, Russell Stroup talked up Republican candidates, handed out their campaign literature, gave them advice on local matters, and in return had a measure of influence with them and their staffs. When a farmer wanted his road blacktopped, or when two aspirants sought one postmastership, it was to Russell Stroup that they appealed for a political boost. When the family visited Washington during Keith's teenage years, they rated VIP treatment on Capitol Hill and a tour of the White House—routine constituent treatment by Capitol Hill standards but dazzling to a family from Dix, Illinois. And as Russell Stroup's construction business flourished in the late 1950s, his custom of holding fish fries had grown into an annual summer event to which hundreds of friends and political associates were invited.

Years later Stroup would joke that those fish fries had inspired the annual NORML conference parties, to which everyone who was anyone in his world was invited.

His father's political involvement affected him in another important way. Russell Stroup had a friend named Frank Walker, a Mount Vernon lawyer and a state representative. When Walker ran unsuccessfully for Congress, the elder Stroup was his campaign manager. Frank Walker was the most impressive man Keith knew in those days, and it was his example that made him decide, while still in high school, that he wanted to be a lawyer; or, more precisely, that being a lawyer was the best route to the money and social status he saw as his goals in life.

Stroup's final break with his parents came just a few nights after he graduated from high school—third in his class of three hundred. He and some friends had started meeting weekly to play poker and drink a few beers. They'd held their poker parties in the other boys' houses, and Stroup thought he'd received his parents' permission to hold one at their house. Perhaps he had, but around midnight, when the laughter became too loud, his parents came down from their bedroom and ordered his friends to leave at once—his mother in tears, his father shouting, both outraged that he had brought drinking and gambling into their home. Stroup, equally outraged, left with his friends. He hitchhiked to Yellowstone National Park, found a job, and didn't return home—or bother to tell his parents where he was—until Labor Day. After a brief, tense reunion with his parents, he was off to the University of Illinois at Urbana-Champaign. It was the fall of 1961.

Stroup's first step in college, like that of any ambitious young man of that era, was to join a fraternity. He lacked the connections or social graces to be invited into one of the Big Three fraternities—he arrived at college sporting an elaborate flattop haircut—but he joined Theta Chi, which prided itself on being one of the top ten of the forty-odd fraternities on campus. He let his hair grow out and was chosen social chairman of his pledge class, and soon he was busy with the two great preoccupations of frat boys in those days: dating sorority girls and drinking beer. At the end of his sophomore year Stroup was elected vice-president of Theta Chi for the next year. It was a great honor. It meant he had a shot at being president of his fraternity, and perhaps an officer of the interfraternity council. He was on his way to being a certified Big Man on Campus.

Still, there were problems. One was money. His father's construction company had failed a few years earlier. The family farm had to be
sold to pay debts, and Vera Stroup took a job as a nurse's aide. Russell
Stroup went to work as a federal housing official—a reward from the
Republican party for years of faithful service. What all this meant to
Keith was that he was on his own as far as his college expenses were
concerned. He could earn about half of what he needed from summer
and part-time jobs and borrow the other half from government
student-loan programs, but he was usually a few months behind in his
fraternity-house bill. Once, when it seemed he'd never get caught up,
he went to his rich uncle—his father's older brother, who'd had the
good fortune to have oil discovered on his farm—and asked for help.
The uncle declared that he'd gladly lend the young man $500, provided
he'd sign a pledge promising not to smoke or drink until graduation.
As it happened, smoking cigarettes and drinking beer were basic to
Stroup's collegiate life-style, so he declined the offer.

Drinking would soon lead to Keith's downfall. First, in his sophomore year, there was a drunken frat-house prank in which he and some
accomplices ordered pizzas sent to the sorority house across the
street, then sneaked across to steal pizzas off the truck when it
arrived. They were caught, and Stroup was put on probation. That
summer, not wanting to go home to Dix, Stroup attended summer
school. He rented an apartment and soon gave an informal rush party
that was thrice illegal: It was off campus, beer was served, and women
were present. Worse, a campus cop's son had attended and told his
father, and the next thing Stroup knew he had been expelled from
college for "conduct unbecoming a student."

Stroup's world had collapsed. Overnight he had gone from BMOC to
an embarrassment to his fraternity, an outcast, a reject. He was too
stunned to do anything but flee. He headed west, lit out for the
territory, like Huck Finn. In later years he would see his expulsion
from the university as the first step in his radicalization. Broke,
disgraced, jobless, hitchhiking west, he wanted to think something
was wrong, that the university had been hypocritical, that he was
being punished unfairly for doing what everyone did, for drinking beer
and chasing girls. But he had no support for his resentment. His
friends, his family, his fraternity brothers—all accepted that he had
broken the rules and had been justly punished. And the social

conformism of the time was such that he was half convinced they were right.

He caught a ride to Portland and found a job repossessing furniture for a loan company. But there was no future in that, and when the university refused to readmit him the next semester, he hit upon a fallback position: He joined the Peace Corps.

Stroup had not been much impressed by the Kennedys or caught up in the liberal idealism of the New Frontier. His interest was campus politics, not national politics. He and a fraternity brother had attended the first big civil-rights march on the University of Illinois campus, but as observers rather than participants. It was a candlelight procession in honor of some murdered civil-rights workers, and Stroup thought it moving but not particularly relevant to his life. In 1964 he would be vaguely pro-Goldwater.

Stroup's joining the Peace Corps was less a political statement than a shrewd social move. If he couldn't get back into college, the Peace Corps would give him a certain status, certainly more than he would gain repossessing furniture in Portland.

The Peace Corps sent him to New Mexico to train for "rural community action" in Colombia. It was not a prize assignment; from what he could determine, his community action would consist of building public toilets. He soon noticed that everyone in his training class was a loser of some sort—college dropouts, like himself; people of dubious intellectual achievement—and that there were other classes in which the bright, young Ivy Leaguers trained for the showcase projects. The truth dawned: "They've put me in a class full of fuck-ups," Stroup raged, unable to accept the possibility that he was himself something of a fuck-up. Furious, he quit the Peace Corps. Told he had to write a letter of explanation to get severance pay, Stroup gladly responded with a five-page denunciation of the testing and classification program that had, as he saw it, failed to recognize his talents. It was the first of many disagreements he would have with the government.

He attended a small college in Kentucky for a semester, sometimes bootlegging beer and whiskey for spending money, and in time the University of Illinois readmitted him. Stroup's fraternity brothers, far from welcoming him back, still considered him an embarrassment, his illegal party having got the fraternity in trouble. Stroup lived in the frat house for a while, but having seen the real world, he was no longer impressed by the Joe College world. He was running a Texaco station part-time, and it amused him to show up for meals in his grimy overalls while his fraternity brothers were trying to impress their dates.

He was as resentful toward the university as he was toward his fraternity. He was on probation, obliged to report to the dean once a month, like an ex-convict reporting to his parole officer. By then, Stroup cared only about getting his degree. He did, in August of 1965, and he left the next day for Washington, D.C. "I got the fuck out of the Midwest without a wasted minute," he would later recall.

In Washington he quickly enrolled in law school at Georgetown University, found an apartment, got another government loan to help with expenses, and dropped by Senator Dirksen's office. There, playing on his father's political contacts, he talked his way into a $50-a-week job as an office boy. It was menial work, but it provided him a useful view of Capitol Hill, and a sense of how Congress operates, and left him in no great awe of the people there. Senator Dirksen himself—the Republican leader, the silver-tongued orator, his father's great hero—struck Stroup as a comic character at best and an incoherent old drunk at worst. "*This* man is helping run the country?" he would ask himself. It amused him greatly one day, while operating the machine that signed the senator's name to his letters, to spot a letter to his father and to scribble at the bottom "Hey, Dad, you didn't think *he* signed them, did you?"

The next summer, when Stroup was seeking a better-paying job, someone in Dirksen's office suggested that he contact the senator's friend Bobby Baker about a job at Baker's Carousel Hotel, in Ocean City, Maryland.

Bobby Baker was under indictment then, awaiting trial on the tax-evasion and other charges that would eventually send him to prison, but he remained a popular, legendary figure in Washington. He was a child of the Senate. He had gone there as a teenager, from his home in Pickens, South Carolina, to be a page, and while still in his twenties he had become the protégé of the powerful Senate majority leader, Lyndon Johnson. Baker was famous for his detailed knowledge of the senators—their pet projects, their likes and dislikes, which way they might lean on a given issue. And he knew, too, which senator liked a drink, which had a roving eye, which might be interested in a profitable business deal. He was a smart, charming, ingratiating young man, a reflection of the Senate's darker side, perhaps, but a man who in his prime understood the realities of Washington as well as anyone of his generation.

Stroup and Baker hit it off, and Stroup was hired to wait tables at Baker's hotel. Soon he advanced to manager of the hotel's nightclub, and at the end of the summer Baker offered him a job in his Washington office, the one that handled his various business interests. Baker saw in Stroup the same instinctive political skill that he himself had brought to Washington some years before, and Stroup, for his part, liked Baker and was tempted by his offer. They were, indeed, a great deal alike, enough alike for Stroup to realize that Baker, however charming, was in a lot of trouble, and definitely not someone to hitch his wagon to. So he thanked the older man and returned to law school.

Something else happened to Stroup in Ocean City that summer: He fell in love.

Her name was Kelly Flook. She was dark-haired, vivacious, and very pretty, and in some ways she was much like Stroup. She, too, had grown up on a farm—near Jefferson, Maryland—had gone off to college at the state university, and was something of a rebel, or at least she wanted to be. She had been a tomboy, an independent, outgoing girl who grew up driving a tractor, and by her high-school years she was dreaming of a career as an interior decorator. But when she went off to college, her parents convinced her that this wasn't realistic, that she was destined to be a wife and mother. In those prefeminist days the advice seemed indisputable, so Kelly chose to be a home-economics major, vowing that if she was to be a housewife, she would learn to be the best. Then she took a summer job as a waitress in Ocean City and fell in love with Keith Stroup.

He seemed to be just the husband she'd dreamed of. He was bright and funny and attractive, clearly destined to be a great success as a lawyer, and he shared her goals of a family, a comfortable home, a good life. At the summer's end she returned to Washington to live with Stroup while she finished college at the nearby University of Maryland and he completed his second year of law school.

The next summer Stroup worked for a lawyer he knew in Mount Vernon, back in Illinois. The lawyer made a great deal of money, more than $100,000 a year, and at the end of the summer he offered Stroup a job and said he would make him a partner in two years. It was a tempting offer financially, and it fit perfectly with what for several years had been Stroup's general plan: to return home, practice law, and then go into politics, perhaps by running for Congress. But now, facing a decision, he realized he couldn't go home again. He saw Southern Illinois as a cultural wasteland. He couldn't live there, not for a million dollars a year. He was hooked on Washington, on its glitter and intrigue, and the only question was what niche he might find for himself there.

While he worked for the Mount Vernon lawyer that summer, Kelly came out to spend a month with him. They were to be married at the end of the summer, and this was a chance for her to be with Keith and to get to know his parents. The encounter did not turn out ideally, at least as far as Keith's mother was concerned. Mrs. Stroup was not sure her son should be marrying so early, she didn't approve of Kelly's long hair, and she definitely disapproved of the young couple's living together under her roof before their marriage. By the time the summer was over, Kelly had come to see her future in-laws quite differently from the way Keith did. He saw his father as crude and oppressive, and his mother as a kind, long-suffering Christian, but Kelly saw Mr. Stroup as a warm, good-natured man, a man who liked a drink and a laugh, and Mrs. Stroup as cold and narrow-minded, always trying to force her strict religious views on others. Kelly could never understand why Keith resented his father so, because, as she saw it, if you allowed for the generational difference, Keith *was* his father, in the way he liked to drink, to joke, to talk about politics.

There was a problem as the newlyweds settled into their first apartment and Stroup completed law school: The nation was at war, and as Stroup's graduation neared, his most urgent priority was to avoid the military draft. Two of his college fraternity brothers had already died in Vietnam, and he wanted no part of the war. He hoped to win some kind of deferment, but they kept changing the rules; deferments for both marriage and fatherhood had been discontinued. If he couldn't get a deferment, he knew an anti-war psychiatrist who would testify he was homosexual. If that failed, he planned to go to Canada. He was annoyed when Kelly said she'd rather go to Canada than have him say he was gay; after all, she knew better than anyone that he was not.

The fact that a rather straight, rather conservative, and devoutly heterosexual young law student would consider fleeing the country or declaring himself homosexual suggests the desperation that millions of young men felt in those days. There are few things like the prospect of an early death in a distant land to cause young people to rethink their political assumptions. Stroup had always been preoccupied with looking out for himself, but the war forced him to think for the first time in generational terms. In law school Stroup had been exposed to liberal ideas and had begun to find new heroes. One was Phil Hirschkop, a recent Georgetown Law graduate who was making a name for himself representing leaders of the anti-war movement. Stroup and other law students who were threatened by the draft began to attend anti-war rallies and to look for leadership to the Hirschkops and Naders and others who were challenging the government on every possible front.

Stroup and many of the lawyers of his generation were, in fact, professional mutants. They had been trained to serve the American establishment, but the war had forced them to be anti-establishment. They remained intensely competitive, but prestige had become not a high-paying job with a major law firm but rather a low-paying job with Ralph Nader or some other public-interest cause. The war produced a generation of reformers; Stroup, when he eventually seized upon the marijuana issue to make his name, was only one of the more colorful of them.

When Stroup saw a note on the law-school bulletin board that the newly formed National Commission on Product Safety was interviewing, he was quick to respond. The most urgent reason was his hope that it might qualify him for a "critical skills" deferment from the draft. A secondary reason was a sense that the commission's pro-consumer role appealed to his budding liberalism. After he was hired as one of four young lawyers on the commission, he found out that two of the other three had applied, as he had, in hopes of a deferment. He and another lawyer from the commission, Stuart Statler, consulted a draft lawyer who, after hearing their stories, laughed and said, "Fellows, there's no way they can draft you." They would apply for a critical-skills deferment; if that failed, they would seek conscientious-objector status; and by the time all appeals had been exhausted, they would be beyond draft age. As it turned out, Stroup's draft board back in Mount Vernon granted his critical-skills deferment without debate. Too many hometown boys had died in Vietnam, and the draft board was exempting anyone it could.

Safe from the draft, Stroup could concentrate on his new job. The

Product Safety Commission was called for by President Johnson and created by Congress, but its spiritual father was Ralph Nader, that unique political genius who in a few years had forged the American consumer movement into a major political force. The commission, which had only a two-year mandate, was feared and bitterly resisted by industry, and it soon began to investigate and publicize such problems as soft-drink bottles that exploded, toys that harmed children, and lawn mowers that maimed people.

Stroup soon joined the pro-consumer faction on the commission's staff. Consumerism seemed to him to follow logically from his anti-war position: People had a right to buy soft drinks in bottles that did not explode in their faces, just as they had a right not to be sent to die in a senseless war. It was David versus Goliath in either case: the average guy versus big government and big industry. For Stroup, two years with the Product Safety Commission was like a graduate course in practical politics. He and the other pro-consumer staff members planned their strategy *sub rosa* with Nader and with Michael Pertschuk, an influential Senate aide who later became a controversial chairman of the Federal Trade Commission. Stroup learned how the commission's public hearings could be stacked, one way or the other, by the choice of witnesses. He learned how important it was to make your case with dramatic photogenic examples that would attract the media, like that of the little black girl who'd been blinded by an exploding bottle. He learned how a low-level staff member could outflank his boss by a timely leak to Jack Anderson or to some other columnist. That was the most lasting lesson he learned—the power of the media, the art of the leak—and he would make ample use of it soon, when he started his lobby for the consumers of marijuana.

Something else was contributing to Stroup's thinking by the end of the decade: He was becoming a regular marijuana smoker.

In college he'd been vaguely aware that a few students smoked marijuana, but they'd been considered the artsy-craftsy crowd, oddballs. Stroup's only drug use in college—except for beer and whiskey, which of course weren't thought of as drugs—had been the amphetamine pills that he and some of his fraternity brothers had used to stay awake and study for exams. They had got them from another fraternity brother, a football player who had an unlimited supply and who therefore made a little spending money by selling them. Stroup and a few friends soon realized that the pills—"black beauties," they were called—not only kept you awake but gave you a fine sense of euphoria, and once in a while they took them just to get high. But booze remained by far his and his friends' drug of choice in college.

He smoked marijuana a few times in law school without ever getting high. At the commission, however, he became friends with another young man who introduced him to serious smoking and who, in time, would become his partner in NORML: Larry Schott, who had made his way to the Product Safety Commission for the good and simple reason that he had married a senator's daughter. Schott, who was a few years older than Stroup, was a black-haired, dark-complexioned man of Alsatian ancestry who had grown up in a small town near Indianapolis, where his father was a tool-and-die maker in a GM plant. After high school Schott went to work for the telephone company, and he might have continued there except that in 1961, so as not to be drafted, he joined the National Guard. During his six months of training he met a lot of college boys, and he decided to enter college himself. At age twenty-one he entered Indiana University, where he soon met and married a young woman named Sandy Hartke, whose father was the state's maverick Democratic senator, Vance Hartke.

In 1964, Larry and Sandy moved to Washington, where he enrolled in the University of Maryland, from which he later graduated. Then, with a boost from his father-in-law, he became the Product Safety Commission's chief investigator. Schott and Stroup soon became close friends. Many of their colleagues at the commission were Easterners, Ivy Leaguers, often Jews, and they felt a special kinship as two young Midwesterners from working-class backgrounds. Keith and Kelly had moved to a town-house development in suburban Fairfax County, and Schott often visited them there, sometimes bringing his friend Joe Sharp, a short, muscular, good-natured man with long red hair. Joe had sold cars and real estate in the Washington area and was starting to sell marijuana. The first time Stroup got really high—so high he couldn't sleep that night—it was from eating marijuana brownies made with Joe Sharp's dope. Another time he and Kelly smoked while playing bridge with some friends. They hadn't even mastered the art of rolling joints, but someone had an old cigarette-rolling machine. Soon they were stoned, and the bridge game was forgotten. Keith rocked so obsessively in a rocking chair that the chair broke. Then he became convinced that someone was about to murder his and Kelly's new daughter, and he raced home to save her. At another party they got so high that the walls seemed to be closing in, and they all ran out into the street for safety. Another time, Larry Schott, Joe Sharp, and a friend of Joe's, a long-haired, tough-looking biker named Ronnie, came to dinner. Kelly prepared her specialty, roast duck, but they all got stoned before dinner, and someone dropped the duck, and then Stroup became paranoid, convinced that Ronnie was going to kill them all. After a few parties like that the neighbors began to grumble, and one evening someone yelled in their door "Fucking hippies"—which upset Keith and Kelly, who were, after all, hardworking, respectable, middle-class Americans.

In fact, Stroup was getting into the marijuana culture. He and his friends were spending less time playing bridge in their suburban apartment and more time getting high and going into Washington to see *Fantasia* or *Yellow Submarine*. He had never owned any sound system more elaborate than a clock radio, but after the first time he got high and listened to rock music on Schott's expensive stereo, he hurried out to buy one of his own. Guided by Larry Schott and Joe Sharp, he began to attend rock concerts by the Rolling Stones, Neil Young, Elton John, and Leon Russell, and to find out that rock music often reflected his own views on politics and drugs.

Marijuana was an all-purpose drug. It made you laugh, it made sex seem better, and it had political significance as well. Stroup not only quit drinking whiskey but came to scorn it. The first time Joe Sharp brought an ounce of dope by the commission's office to share with them, they knew it was a symbolic moment: They might be working for the government, but they would defy it, too, scorn its rules and regulations. Stroup and Schott began to let their hair grow longer; their sideburns were down to their earlobes and sinking fast. They were caught up in a political rebellion along with millions of other young Americans. They were turning on, and if not quite dropping out, they were at least covertly rejecting a society that supported the war and chose Richard Nixon as its leader.

Keith and Kelly moved in the summer of 1970 from their rented suburban town house to a house at 2105 N Street NW, in Washington. Stroup had decided that the suburbs were sterile, the habitat of Nixon's "silent majority"; Kelly felt isolated there, alone all day with her infant daughter. Kelly's uncle had left her $10,000, and they used half of it for a down payment on the new house, which was located in a racially mixed neighborhood, a mile or so from the White House. Soon, as the great Washington anti-war rallies were held, Stroup would invite demonstrators to camp out on their floor. At the appointed hour they would all smoke some grass and then go march and chant and shake their fists at Richard Nixon.

One day Joe Sharp was arrested while driving his Volkswagen van in Washington. He was stopped for a traffic violation, and the police found a small amount of marijuana in the van. He called Stroup, who went and bailed him out. Stroup was outraged at the way his friend has been treated. As he saw it, Joe had been stopped arbitrarily, because he had long hair and was driving a van with a peace sticker on it. The incident caused Stroup to focus for the first time on the marijuana issue. He knew, as everyone did, that tens of thousands of young people were being arrested each year on marijuana charges; Joe's arrest had simply made that fact personal for him. It infuriated him to think that he was classified as a criminal by the marijuana laws, and that he could be arrested, jailed, perhaps fired from his job, all for using what he viewed as a mild intoxicant.

Law students were taught that for every wrong there is a remedy, and it seemed to Stroup that marijuana smokers were the victims of a great social wrong. Joe Sharp had won his case, on the grounds of an illegal search, but you obviously couldn't fight the government on a case-by-case basis. There should be some way to help marijuana smokers as a group, as Nader had helped consumers as a group, but for the moment Stroup could not see what it was.

As 1970 began, Stroup and Schott, who had by then separated from Sandy, faced a more urgent problem than the marijuana laws. The Product Safety Commission was going out of business that summer, and they would be out of a job. As he pondered his future, Stroup realized that he was pulled in opposite directions, caught between cultures. Part of him still cherished conventional goals, but another part was drawn toward public-interest law, something like what Nader had done, something anti-establishment, but he didn't know what.

Stroup and Schott often discussed some kind of marijuana project. Perhaps a Nader-style program to change the laws. But how would you finance it? Perhaps some kind of "bust insurance," to pay for bond and legal fees for persons arrested. They even discussed the idea of producing a marijuana-related board game, a smoker's Monopoly. Stroup had other, non-marijuana-related ideas as well, for the idea of making a lot of money was very attractive to him. One was for a pizza-franchise business. Another was a scheme to fly women to London for legal abortions. Another involved pork bellies. Then, on the Fourth of July 1970, one of his get-rich-quick schemes blew up in his face.

He persuaded Kelly to let him invest $5000 of her money with Joe Sharp, who would go to California and bring back several hundred pounds of marijuana. Stroup hoped to double his investment. But once Joe headed for California, the jitters began. He was supposed to be back in five days, but he wasn't heard from for ten. Stroup was in panic when Joe finally called. Everything was fine, he said. He'd just been doing a little partying on the Coast. He was home, and the trip had been a great success. Stroup breathed a sigh of relief.

Joe, reflecting his business success, had rented a comfortable house in a respectable neighborhood in Arlington, Virginia. Unfortunately, he, his flashy new car, and the company he kept were all quite conspicuous in the neighborhood. The postman had warned Joe that police were watching his house, but he ignored the warnings, and on the Fourth of July, soon after his return from California, the police, armed with shotguns, raided Joe's house, arrested everyone there, and seized several pounds of marijuana.

Keith and Kelly had been invited to spend the Fourth at Joe's house, but they had gone to Ocean City instead, to spend a few days at the Carousel Hotel. When Stroup got a phone call that evening, telling him of Joe's arrest, he was close to hysteria. If Joe named him as one of his partners, he would be arrested, jailed, ruined. He imagined the police breaking down his door at any moment. He and Kelly were staying in a room with a balcony overlooking the ocean. It was a stormy night, and Stroup spent hours on the balcony, watching lightning flash above the churning sea, almost ready to jump. Should he flee? Or give himself up? What would happen to his family? There were tears, embraces, promises: If he got out of this mess, he would never smoke again, never even *look* at marijuana again.

Around midnight there was a knock at the door. Stroup grimly opened the door, expecting the police, but instead it was Joe, grinning his mad doper's grin. Everything was cool. He had made bond. He would never rat on his friends. The police hadn't even got all the dope; most of it was safely hidden in a "stash house." Stroup would even get his money back. Stroup felt as if he'd been raised from the dead. There

were tears, handshakes, laughter. Finally, Joe produced some of his
California grass and they all got stoned.

When Stroup's job at the Product Safety Commission came to an end
that summer, he moved to a $16,000-a-year position with the American
Pharmaceutical Association, a lobby for the nation's pharmacists. He
never took the job very seriously, for by then he was obsessed with
starting some sort of marijuana-law project, and he and Schott were
starting to spend all their spare time seeking out ideas and support for
the new venture.

One thing Stroup and Schott did not know, as they talked endlessly
about the marijuana laws and how to change them, was that across
America other people were thinking the same thing. In San Francisco
a talented young man named Blair Newman was starting a nonprofit
corporation called Amorphia, which was going to sell rolling papers
and use the proceeds to work for marijuana-law reform.

At about the same time, on the Upper West Side of Manhattan, two
young lawyers named Guy Archer and Frank Fioramonti were talking
about introducing a marijuana-legalization bill in the state legislature.
Also in New York at that time, officials of the rich and prestigious Ford
Foundation were concerned about the explosion of drug use in America
and about the probability that the Nixon administration would respond
to it only with negative, law-and-order programs. Their concern would
soon lead to the creation of the Washington-based Drug Abuse
Council, which would press for drug-law reform.

By 1970 these groups and others were responding in different ways
to the fact of widespread drug use and widespread imprisonment of
drug users. Soon the various groups would discover one another.
Sometimes they would form alliances; sometimes they would do battle
for control of the emerging reform movement. But Stroup and Schott,
as they planned their marijuana project, were unaware of the other
reformers, and their plans drew upon their own experience as young
men in Washington: Nader's example, their work at the Product Safety
Commission, their fairly sophisticated understanding of the political
process. They kept coming back to the idea of a Nader-style operation,
a public-interest lobby, one that would represent straight, middle-
class smokers like themselves, one that would use legal means to
change what they saw as unjust laws.

By the fall, Stroup even had a name for his proposed project: the
National Organization to Repeal Marijuana Laws. Acronyms were

fashionable, and NORML seemed a good one. Schott, more cautious, insisted the R should be "reform," not "repeal." No, Stroup declared, you had to be out front about it: They wanted repeal.

One of the people Stroup turned to that fall, as he sought advice and encouragement, was a former attorney general, Ramsey Clark. He had read Clark's book, *Crime in America*, and had been deeply impressed, not simply by Clark's call for legalization of marijuana but by Clark's compassion and social vision. In his darker moments Stroup feared this whole idea for a marijuana-law-reform program was crazy, but if Ramsey Clark thought it made sense, then perhaps it would be worth pursuing.

Ramsey Clark was then one of the most controversial men in America. He was a tall, jug-eared Texan who as Lyndon Johnson's attorney general had championed the legal rights of the poor and called for an end to wiretapping, for tighter gun controls, and for the abolition of the death penalty. Richard Nixon, running for president on a law-and-order platform in 1968, largely ran against Clark, who became Nixon's symbol of the "jellyfish" liberal who was not tough on crime and criminals.

Clark had a law office in Washington. He also had a secretary who was very skeptical about callers who wanted to talk about marijuana. Eventually Stroup talked his way past her, however, for the first of what became several conversations with Clark. To Stroup's immense relief, Clark took his plan seriously. In essence what Clark said was this: Do it. What do you have to lose? You're a lawyer, and if it doesn't work, you can always do something else. But if you believe in your idea and you don't give it a try, you'll regret it the rest of your life.

Once, speaking of the opposition Stroup might expect, Clark reflected on the criticism he had received when, after leaving office, he visited Hanoi with a group of anti-war leaders. He viewed this as a mission of peace, but when he returned, he was confronted by reporters asking if he wasn't a traitor, if he hadn't given aid and comfort to America's enemy. Clark recalled the outrage, the helpless fury, he had felt, the same kind of anger and frustration he had felt when Martin Luther King was killed. But you can take the criticism if you know you're right, Clark said. It can be tough, but you can take it.

Clark had one specific suggestion: Make it the National Organization for the *Reform* of Marijuana Laws, not *Repeal*. "Repeal" was a scare word, Clark cautioned, but there was a long and honorable tradition of political reform in the United States. Stroup had been unconvinced when Larry Schott made the same suggestion, but he followed Clark's advice at once.

Clark gave Stroup the names of six or eight small foundations that might support his project. Stroup quickly approached them all, and one by one they turned him down. It was a discouraging time. Marijuana-law reform was too hot an issue for these traditional supporters of liberal causes. Then, one Sunday afternoon, Keith and Kelly went for a walk and dropped by Ralph Nader's office, and a lawyer named John Esposito asked if they'd tried the Playboy Foundation.

Stroup had never heard of the Playboy Foundation, but he was soon on the phone with its staff director, Margaret Standish. By early February, Playboy had dispatched one of its senior executives, Bob Gutwillig, to Washington for a talk with Stroup, Schott, and a third young man who had joined forces with them, Larry Dubois.

Dubois was a writer, a tall, thin, bearded, energetic man of about Stroup's age who had attended Princeton, worked in *Time*'s Washington bureau, and then set out on a free-lance career. The way he and Stroup met was typical of the way Stroup was operating that winter. Keith had read a book called *Marijuana: The New Prohibition*, by John Kaplan, a law professor at Stanford. Kaplan, a political conservative, had been hired by Gov. Ronald Reagan to recommend a new state marijuana policy. He studied the issue in depth and recommended that marijuana be made legal. Reagan quickly fired Kaplan, who published his report in book form. When Stroup called Kaplan, seeking ideas and support for NORML, Kaplan suggested that he seek out a "young conservative" named Dubois who had reviewed his book favorably for William Buckley's *National Review*. It turned out that Dubois lived not far from Stroup in Washington, and he was not a conservative at all but a liberal and a marijuana smoker who happened to have become friendly with Buckley. Dubois shared Stroup's enthusiasm for NORML, and he became Stroup's close friend and a member of NORML's board of directors.

After the meeting with Gutwillig, Stroup submitted his proposed program, which included a pamphlet explaining the marijuana laws, a direct-mail fund-raising program, model legislation, a newsletter, and public-service television spots. Stroup asked for about $20,000 for the first six months of the program. Also, he counted on a free advertisement in *Playboy* to bring in tens of thousands of dollars more.

Stroup was invited to come to Chicago and meet Hugh Hefner and members of the Playboy Foundation's board. Upon arrival he went to dinner with Burton Joseph, the Chicago lawyer who headed the foundation. Stroup proceeded to get drunk; as a committed smoker he had lost his capacity for alcohol. At noon the next day, as he waited, nervous and hung over, to see Hefner and the foundation's board of directors, Stroup met a slender, funny, fast-talking woman who would soon become important in his life: Bobbie Arnstein, Hefner's executive assistant, who reassured him that Hefner was extremely interested in his proposal. Why else would he have got up for a noon meeting, which for Hefner was like getting up at dawn?

As the meeting began and members of the foundation's board began to question him, it was clear that many of them were extremely skeptical about venturing into the marijuana controversy. All of which mattered not, because Hugh Hefner liked the idea of NORML, for reasons that were not immediately clear to some of the people who were close to him.

Hefner was not at that time a frequent marijuana smoker. He would take an occasional puff if a friend passed a joint his way, but he did not keep marijuana for his personal use or allow its use in his mansions. Nor had America's growing marijuana controversy touched his very sheltered life. None of his friends had been busted for marijuana; nor did he have any reason to think the authorities would ever concern themselves with whatever occasional drug use might go on in his mansions. Still, he was aware that thousands of people were being arrested for smoking marijuana, and that fact outraged him, for reasons that were basic to Hefner's very complex nature.

Hefner, looking back on his youth in a 1980 interview, recalled two great influences on his boyhood. One was a strict Midwestern Methodist upbringing that left him sexually repressed, with a deep, painful conflict between his emotional needs and his acquired sense of right and wrong. As Hefner saw it, he had spent his adult life freeing himself from puritanical sexual repression, and he had, through his magazine, helped millions of other Americans fight that same battle for sexual liberation.

The other great influence on the young Hefner was movies. As a teenager he had been an usher in a movie theater, and Hollywood's world of illusion often seemed more real to him than the world that awaited him outside the theater. Of the hundreds of movies he saw, none made a greater impression on him than those of Frank Capra. In Capra's films, such as *Mr. Smith Goes to Washington* and *Meet John Doe*, the hero was always a lone idealist who challenged the powers that be. That became Hugh Hefner's vision of the future: of himself, no longer young and lonely and uncertain and anonymous but a knight on a white charger who would slay the dragons of intolerance and, not incidentally, win the fair princess who awaited him in some shining tower.

Hefner had, as an adult, acted out his boyish fantasies to a remarkable degree—not only his sexual fantasies, although it was for those that he was most famous, but also his political fantasies of the lone crusader. In founding *Playboy*, he successfully challenged the obscenity laws. His Playboy Foundation challenged the sex laws that in many states were used to jail homosexuals or even heterosexuals who had engaged in "crimes against nature." Thus, to Hefner, a challenge to the marijuana laws was consistent with his commitment to the cause of individual freedom.

He therefore instructed his foundation to support NORML. But because he was a cautious man and his commitment was to the issue, not to Stroup or NORML, he advised going slowly. Thus, a few days later, Stroup got a call from Burton Joseph that shocked him. The foundation would give him $5000 to get started.

"Five thousand dollars?" Stroup raged. "Do you think I'm going to quit my job and go out into the cold, cruel world for *five thousand dollars*?"

Joseph assured him that the five thousand was just a start, that if he did a good job, there would be more money. Stroup was uncertain. He had envisioned an $18,000 salary for himself and enough money to guarantee at least a year's program. If NORML folded, he might lose his house, and he wondered if any respectable law firm would hire a failed marijuana lobbyist. He was burning a lot of bridges for $5000. He talked to Schott and Dubois, and they encouraged him. But they were not the ones taking the chance. Finally he made his decision: He would do it. The money arrived, he quit his job, and NORML was in business.

3

What Stroup did not fully understand, as he started NORML, was that ne was injecting himself not so much into a social issue—in the sense that the League of Women Voters might concern itself with clean air—as into a war, a very one-sided war against marijuana and its users that had been raging for a long time. It was a war that had been aggravated both by the war in Vietnam and the election of Richard Nixon, but its origins went back at least to the turn of the century.

The origin of the word "marijuana" is unclear. One scholar suggests it derives from *mariguango*, Portugese for "intoxicant." Another scholar thinks it came from "Maria y Juana," Mexican slang for soldiers and whores in the era of Pancho Villa. Whatever its orgin, "marijuana" is the word by which Americans have come to know *Cannabis sativa*, which most of the world calls "Indian hemp." It is a weedlike plant that requires little or no cultivation, will grow almost anywhere there are hot summers, and can reach a height of ten or fifteen feet. Its fibers can be used to make rope, baskets, bags, cloth, even sheets and napkins. Moreover, its leaves, if smoked or eaten, produce a state of intoxication. There are references to its use as an intoxicant in Chinese literature dating back to 2000 B.C. and in Greek medical journals dating to 500 B.C. From earliest times, one scholar notes, there has been dispute as to whether the hemp plant lined the road to Utopia or to Hades.

The first American crop of Indian hemp was planted in 1611 near Jamestown, Virginia, and soon there was a thriving hemp-farming business in the Colonies, providing bagging, marine rope, and clothing. George Washington was a hemp farmer, and modern marijuana cultists have used enigmatic notes in his diaries to claim the father of our country as a smoker. In truth, if anyone in those days knew marijuana was an intoxicant, it was a well-kept secret. Hemp remained a crop, like corn or cotton, but one that was doomed by the abolition of slavery and the decline of the ship-building industry. (Then, as now, whiskey was the American passion; Washington called alcohol "the ruin of half the workingmen in this Country," and Jefferson warned with his usual prescience that we would soon become "a nation of sots.")

Across the Atlantic the use of hashish, a more powerful, compressed form of marijuana, became fashionable among French intellectuals in the 1840s. Baudelaire, Balzac, and others formed the Club des Haschischins and held weekly meetings in an elegant apartment on the Ile Saint-Louis. Their hashish supply came from a friendly physician, who obtained his supply from Algeria. Hashish can be smoked, like marijuana, but the Frenchmen chose to eat it, which produces a far more intense state of intoxication than smoking.

There is no evidence that this experimentation among French artists influenced Americans, but in 1854 an American writer named Bayard Taylor published a magazine article about his experience with hashish while visiting Damascus, and one of the readers of his article was an impressionable eighteen-year-old college student named Fitz Hugh Ludlow, who soon became the first American to proclaim to his countrymen both the joys and the horrors of hashish.

Ludlow was born in 1836, in New York City, the son of a prominent abolitionist minister. He grew up in upstate New York, a well-educated, widely-read, religious young man, and he found that Taylor's article on hashish moved him "powerfully to curiosity and admiration." He therefore managed to obtain some hashish from a doctor, who kept it on hand as a sedative, and soon he was eating large quantities of the drug. As a result, he had hallucinogenic experiences much like the LSD trips college students would embark on more than a century later.

After two years of hashish use, the twenty-year-old Ludlow wrote a remarkable memoir called *The Hasheesh Eater,* which was published anonymously in 1857 and was devoted almost entirely to depicting, in the ornate prose of the era, the heavens and hells of drug use. In his mind Ludlow had voyaged through the universe; he had spoken to God, visited magical kingdoms; he had been attacked by devils with red-hot pitchforks. By the time he wrote the book, drugs had caused in him periods of suicidal depression, and the book was intended to discourage drug use, although it may have had the opposite effect. One avid reader of *The Hasheesh Eater* was an eighteen-year-old student at Brown University named John Hay, who was moved to obtain and eat some hashish. He told a friend it was "a marvelous stimulant to the imagination," and after graduation he looked back on the days when he "used to eat Hasheesh and dream dreams" in a "mystical Eden." Drug use did not impede Hay's later career. At age twenty-two he became an aide to President Lincoln, and he was later a distinguished novelist, poet, and secretary of state.

America was developing a serious drug problem in the late nineteenth century, but it had nothing to do with hashish. The hollow-needle hypodermic syringe was invented in 1854, and during the Civil War, injecting wounded soldiers with morphine was common. Morphine addiction was widespread after the war, so much so that it was called "Soldier's illness." Moreover, the postwar era saw a proliferation of patent medicines, most of them opium-based. By the turn of the century there were an estimated twenty to thirty thousand drug addicts in America, mostly as a result of the patent medicines. The typical addict was white, male, and rural, and public opinion toward him was sympathetic: He was seen as a sick person but not as a criminal.

Attitudes were changing, however. The severity of the addiction problem was one reason, and another was the rise of immigration. Native Americans—mostly Protestant, with Puritan heritage —tended to look down on the newcomers, and one reason was the supposed immorality of the latter, which was thought to manifest itself both in drunkenness and in drug addiction. When Congress passed the Harrison Narcotic Act of 1914, to regulate patent-medicine sales, it in effect declared that drug addicts were criminals. The Harrison Act, according to Dr. Norman Zinberg, assistant professor of psychology at Harvard, "ushered in the modern era of repression of drug use." In time the new law did reduce the number of opium addicts in America, and by then the forces of morality had moved on to a new target: the prohibition of alcoholic beverages in America.

It was against this cultural and political background that marijuana use was introduced to America early in the century by Mexican field-workers who came across the border into Texas and other Southwestern states. By the early 1920s New Orleans had become a marijuana-importing center, with boatloads of the weed arriving from Mexico, Cuba, and Texas and moving upriver to St. Louis and cross-country to other large cities. Black dockworkers in New Orleans were soon smokers, as they and other laborers learned that a marijuana high made their routine chores more bearable. New Orleans jazz musicians were also discovering the weed. Louis Armstrong once recalled, of his early days in New Orleans, "One reason we appreciated pot was the warmth it always brought forth. . . . Mary Warner, honey, you sure was good and I enjoyed you 'heep much.' But the price got a little too high to pay, law wise. At first you was a misdemeanor. But as the years rolled by you lost your misdo and got meanor and meanor." Armstrong was arrested for marijuana possession in Los Angeles in 1931 and spent ten days in jail before he was released with a six-month suspended sentence.

As Armstrong's comment suggests, the spread of marijuana was soon followed by the imposition of harsh sanctions against it. Marijuana use was made a felony in Louisiana in 1925, and many other states followed. The first states to act were Southern and Southwestern, and their motivation was primarily racial. Marijuana was seen, correctly, as a drug primarily used by blacks and Mexicans. This was a time when lynchings were frequent and racial fears were growing. There were rumors that marijuana gave black men superhuman strength, violent sexual desires, and otherwise caused them to challenge their ordained place in society. Newspapers attributed horrible crimes by blacks and Mexicans to marijuana use. By 1930, the year the federal Bureau of Narcotics was created, sixteen states had passed laws against marijuana, and Harry Anslinger, the head of the new bureau, soon made a federal marijuana prohibition his top priority.

Harry Jacob Anslinger, America's first great anti-marijuana crusader, was born in 1892 in Altoona, Pennsylvania, attended Penn State, embarked on a diplomatic career, made a name for himself pursuing rumrunners in the Bahamas, and by 1929 had switched to the Treasury Department and become assistant commissioner of prohibition. By then, of course, the prohibition of alcohol was recognized as a colossal failure, but despite that fact, or perhaps because of it, America was soon to attempt a new prohibition, this time of marijuana.

Anslinger was known for his hard-line views on the enforcement of Prohibition, an attitude that would not change when he turned his attention from liquor to marijuana. The Prohibition laws made it a crime to sell, manufacture, or transport liquor, but not to buy it. Anslinger proposed in 1928 that the purchase of liquor be made a crime, with six months' imprisonment for a first conviction and two to five years for a second conviction. Cooler heads prevailed—the Hoover administration had enough troubles without locking up all the nation's whiskey drinkers—but when Anslinger became commissioner of narcotics, there was no opposition to his hard-line policy toward drugs other than alcohol.

Anslinger was a contemporary and a rival of the most formidable bureaucrat in American history, J. Edgar Hoover. Both men headed law-enforcement agencies despite having had little or no law-enforcement experience; both men's success came from their brilliance as bureaucrats and their ability to use the press to serve their purposes. Hoover, over the years, had far more to work with: He had the Red Menace, Bonnie and Clyde, the Nazi Menace, atom spies, and an endless succession of Public Enemies, and he used them to make himself a national hero, feared and deferred to by the presidents he served. Anslinger, by contrast, had little to capture the public imagination except a weed that was smoked by a relatively small number of poor blacks and Mexicans, plus a few jazz musicians and intellectuals. It was therefore a tribute to his imagination and energy that he was able to turn this little-known and relatively innocuous plant into the Killer Weed, a menace to life and health that would soon strike fear into the hearts of millions of God-fearing, law-abiding Americans who had never smoked marijuana, had never seen any, and had never known anybody who had.

By 1936, as legislation to outlaw marijuana was nearing Congress, he and his agents were busy giving out blood-curdling tales of marijuana-inspired crime and violence, tales that enlivened hundreds of newspaper and magazine articles. One favorite anecdote, which turned up in article after article, concerned the polite young man in Florida who smoked one reefer, then picked up an ax and killed his father, mother, sister, and two brothers. Never in history have so many mothers been ax-murdered, so many virgins lured into white slavery, so many siblings decapitated, as in the heyday of Anslinger's anti-marijuana campaign. The spirit of the era was most perfectly captured in the 1936 movie classic *Reefer Madness*, in which casual marijuana use was shown to lead swiftly to murder, rape, prostitution, addiction, madness, and death.

In the spring of 1937, testifying before the House of Representatives on the anti-marijuana bill, Anslinger granted himself a good deal of historical and literary license when he declared, "This drug is as old as civilization itself. Homer wrote about it, as a drug which made men forget their homes, and that turned them into swine. In Persia, a thousand years before Christ, there was a religious and military order founded which was called the Assassins, and they derived their name from the drug called hashish which is now known in this country as marijuana."

Almost no one had anything good to say about marijuana at the congressional hearings. The only serious dissenting voice was that of Dr. W. C. Woodward, legislative counsel for the American Medical Association, who protested, first, that future medical uses might be found for marijuana, and, second, that no serious evidence had been presented to support the charges that marijuana caused crime and violence. For his trouble, Dr. Woodward was insulted, ridiculed, and sent on his way.

The bill—officially, the Marijuana Tax Act—was passed, and became law on October 1, 1937. Soon, many more states passed laws making the use or sale of marijuana a felony. In the next few years there would be various scientific studies that said that marijuana was not addictive and did not cause crime or personality change or sexual frenzy, but these were invariably ignored or denounced.

In 1938 New York mayor Fiorello La Guardia appointed a team of scientists from the New York Academy of Medicine to study the medical, sociological, and psychological aspects of marijuana use. The study included tests on seventy-seven inmates in the city jails. A report was issued in 1944 that directly challenged everything Anslinger and the Bureau of Narcotics had been saying. It said smoking marijuana did not lead to mental or physical deterioration, to addiction, or to crime or violence. It was the most complete study of marijuana ever conducted in America, but Anslinger quickly denounced its "superficiality and hollowness" and charged that its authors "favored the spread of narcotic addiction." Perhaps more significant was the response of the American Medical Association. Several years earlier, the AMA spokesman was ridiculed at the congressional hearing when he questioned Anslinger's anti-marijuana orthodoxy. The AMA saw the error of its ways, and in 1945 an editorial in the *Journal of the American Medical Association* said of the La Guardia report, "Public officials will do well to disregard this unscientific, uncritical study, and continue to regard marihuana as a menace wherever it is purveyed." Thereafter the AMA was solidly in the anti-marijuana camp.

As the 1940s began, the Second World War stole the spotlight from Anslinger and his "devil's weed," but he had done a remarkable job. He had created a mythology that made it impossible to debate a marijuana issue in America: There was no issue, because marijuana was universally accepted as so insidious a drug that society had no choice but to use the harshest measures against it.

It was possible to grow up in the America of the 1950s in blissful ignorance of marijuana. It was something, like flying saucers, that happened to other people. Robert Mitchum, the actor, was jailed for smoking marijuana in Los Angeles, and Candy Barr, one of the great Texas ladies of her time, was sent to prison for possession; Norman Mailer and Jack Kerouac wrote about smoking the weed. But this was not the mainstream. If the average young American wanted to get high, he or she did so in the same way that dear old dad had in decades past: with beer busts and gin dins, with purple passions and hurricanes, with mint juleps and Singapore slings, with Scotch, bourbon, vodka, wine, and all the other forms of alcoholic delight that were easily available and socially acceptable. The first question, then, is why, in the mid-1960s, did large numbers of young Americans choose to risk imprisonment to get high with a new intoxicant, marijuana?

There are various theories. Dr. Norman Zinberg, one of the nation's leading experts on drug issues, thinks television has been a major factor in conditioning young people to use drugs. Television presents a restricted world, he says, a world confined to a twenty-four-inch box, and young people turned to marijuana and other drugs as a means of "boundary diffusion," of freeing their minds from an imprisoned view of reality.

Sen. James Eastland, after holding hearings in 1974 on the "marijuana-hashish epidemic," concluded that "the epidemic began at Berkeley University at the time of the famous 1965 Berkeley Uprising" and warned that "clearly subversive groups played a significant role in the spread of the epidemic."

Dr. Robert DuPont, a senior government drug-policy figure in the mid-1970s, suggests that a multiplicity of factors contributed to the spread of marijuana: the "baby boom" and the pressures it put on the schools; the breakdown of the family; the prevalence of television, which he says makes young people look for "quick, passive gratification"; and, finally, a kind of "me first" attitude throughout society.

Another factor, perhaps the crucial one, in turning young people toward marijuana was the war in Vietnam.

Once the war was over, almost everyone wanted to forget it, the people who opposed it no less than the people who made it. But the trauma was real; the scars ran deep, perhaps deeper than anyone yet understands. The war cut a generation adrift. Millions of young Americans who had grown up reciting the Pledge of Allegiance were suddenly chanting "One, two, three, four, we don't want your fucking war." And they were the lucky ones; the unlucky ones were being maimed and killed in a country that few Americans had heard of a few years before. It was a time of madness, an Orwellian time in which "peace with honor" meant more bombing, and in which villages had to be destroyed in order to be saved. Confronted with this madness, millions of young people rejected the culture that had produced the war—rejected their parents, their past—and set out to build their own counterculture, their own world, and it was imperative that the new world be as different as possible from the one they had left behind.

It was a time of symbols. Long hair was a symbol. Casual clothing was another. Rock music became a symbol, too—bad times often create good art—and Frank Sinatra gave way to Bob Dylan, Patti Page to Janis Joplin. Dylan, more than any artist of his time, looked into the eye of the madness and fused it with his personal vision. Songs like "Tombstone Blues" and "Desolation Row" are nothing less than distillations of the madness, art at the edge of the abyss. On one great

1965 album he sang two songs that seemed to state definitively both the madness and the possibility of escape from it. One song, "Subterranean Homesick Blues," told it all in three minutes: the police, the paranoia, the drugs, the alienation. It even gave a name to the terrorists who were still to come: the Weathermen. The other song, "Mr. Tambourine Man," was at once an invocation of the muse and an exquisite hymn to drugs. (Several years later Hunter Thompson dedicated *Fear and Loathing in Las Vegas* to Dylan, specifically "for 'Mr. Tambourine Man.'")

Marijuana, like rock music and long hair, was another symbol of rebellion for the young. It was illegal, it produced a nice high, and it drove parents up the wall: Who could ask for more? Young blacks had smoked during the civil-rights movement of the early 1960s, and they passed the habit along to young white activists, and as the civil-rights movement gave way to the anti-war movement, marijuana-smoking began to spread rapidly. Pot was not easy to come by at first, unless you grew your own, but the law of supply and demand operates in a counterculture as elsewhere, and soon informal distribution networks spread across the country and into other countries.

If smoking spread in the mid-1960s for essentially negative reasons —defiance of authority—its proponents would nonetheless argue that the custom endured, and reached millions of otherwise undefiant people, for a positive reason: It was fun, and it provided a better high than alcohol.

Marijuana became the Achilles' heel of the counterculture. The dominant culture might hate the dirty clothes and the long hair and the rock music, but it was difficult (not impossible, but difficult) to punish people for those offenses. It was simplicity itself, however, to arrest young people for the weed in their pocket. J. Edgar Hoover, in a 1968 memo to all FBI field offices, said, "Since the use of marijuana and other narcotics is widespread among members of the New Left, you should be alert to opportunities to have them arrested by local authorities on drug charges." Others might equivocate, but Hoover saw the marijuana issue with perfect clarity: It was a way to put his enemies in jail. Throughout the drug debate, up to the present day, there has been that ugly undercurrent. Many sincere people may worry about health hazards or teenage drug abuse, but there are always those in authority who simply want power over other people's lives.

Because of the war and the angry passions of the time, marijuana became politicized, evolving into a central symbol in the most bitter generational dispute in American history. To the young, smoking marijuana (or pot, dope, grass, weed) became a kind of communion, a rite that affirmed generational unity, that demonstrated their willingness to run risks with their peers. But that very willingness made smokers all but defenseless against police.

Smoking spread, too, in another, quite different way. If millions of young Americans, particularly college students, began smoking while protesting the war in Vietnam, hundreds of thousands of others began smoking while they were in Vietnam fighting that war. When they returned home, many GIs brought their smoking habit back to the small towns and working-class lives that awaited them. They, too, were often arrested.

Originally the drug laws had been aimed at immigrants and at the poor blacks and Mexicans who were virtually the only marijuana users in America. Now it was young, white Americans, with their long hair and their dirty talk, who had become the foreigners, the alien culture, the threat to respectable America. And so the marijuana arrests rose: from 18,000 in 1965 to more than 220,000 in 1970, the year Stroup first conceived of NORML.

Inevitably, the mounting arrests led to the first stirrings of protest and political action. As best as anyone can say, the American legalization movement began on August 16, 1964, when a young man walked into a San Francisco police station, lit a joint, and asked to be arrested. His lawyer was an ultraconservative civil libertarian named James R. White III, who proceeded to form LeMar (for Legalize Marijuana), which sponsored the first marijuana-law-reform demonstrations in America in San Francisco's Union Square in December of that year.

LeMar soon began to spread. Poets Ed Sanders and Allen Ginsberg started a chapter in New York early in 1965 and organized demonstrations outside several prisons. By 1966 there were chapters in Cleveland, Berkeley, and Detroit, where the poet John Sinclair was among the founders. In the fall of 1966 a graduate student named Mike Aldrich began organizing a chapter on the Buffalo campus of the State University of New York. The chapter would fold in time, but Aldrich would be a key figure in the legalization movement for years to come.

Michael R. Aldrich was a slight, bespectacled, bookish young man

who grew up in South Dakota, discovered marijuana as an undergraduate at Princeton, smoked hashish while a Fulbright scholar in India,
and then returned to SUNY's Buffalo campus to seek his doctorate. He
soon became friendly with Leslie Fiedler, the literary critic. When
Aldrich started the LeMar chapter, he persuaded Fiedler to be its
faculty adviser. He also persuaded Fiedler to let him write his thesis
on "Cannabis Myths and Folklore." Mike Aldrich, soon to be Dr.
Michael R. Aldrich—"Dr. Dope" to his friends—thus began a career
that would combine his passion for drugs, history, and scholarship.

   LeMar's chapters began to fold after the violence at the Democratic
convention in Chicago in August of 1968. Most activists by then
thought their very survival was at stake and that focusing on the
marijuana issue was a luxury they couldn't afford. Just after Chicago,
however, Aldrich and Sanders started the *Marijuana Review.* By
1970 LeMar consisted mainly of Aldrich and of occasional issues of the
Review, a journal of interest only to hard-core smokers. Aldrich had
also worked as Allen Ginsberg's secretary and written a book entitled
Free Marijuana, which he couldn't get published; his publisher said it
was "too emotional." Just then, with LeMar fading and Dr. Dope's
future uncertain, Aldrich got a call from Blair Newman, who said he
had a plan to work for legal marijuana. They founded Amorphia, the
California group that soon would contest NORML for leadership of the
reform movement.

   By 1970 marijuana was becoming an issue in presidential politics. In
1968 Richard Nixon had campaigned for law and order, but drugs had
not been at the core of the issue. When Nixon needed to make good on
his law-and-order promises, he turned to drug control as his surest
bet, and, aided by John Mitchell and G. Gordon Liddy, he declared a
much-publicized war on marijuana, heroin, and other drugs.

   Such was the national mood when Stroup began NORML. It could be
said that to start a marijuana-law-reform program at the peak of the
Nixon era was an act of madness. Victory was too distant a goal even
to define. To stay solvent and out of jail would be a considerable
achievement. Still, as an ambitious young lawyer-activist looking for
an issue to call his own, Stroup had chosen well. He would later say
that discovering the marijuana issue in 1970, with no one working on
it, was like finding out in 1965 that no one was opposing the war in
Vietnam. He had a potential constituency of millions of smokers. He
had potential allies, too, in people like Ramsey Clark and John Kaplan,

who were calling for a more rational policy toward marijuana. The immediate challenge was to unite all these people, from hippies to Harvard professors, in a political alliance. The larger challenge was to confront the mythology, to persuade millions of nonsmoking Americans that the problem was not "reefer madness," as they had been told for so long. It is unwise, certainly, to abuse any drug, but the challenge to NORML was to convince America that the time had come to refocus its concerns; that when a nation began putting thousands of its young people in prison for using a mild intoxicant, the problem had become something larger, something deeper, than reefer madness, something that might more properly be called American madness.

4

Stroup's dream, as NORML opened its doors early in 1971, was to build a national political organization, representing smokers and financed by them, that would focus political pressure on the federal and state governments to reform the marijuana laws. His reality was $5000 from the Playboy Foundation, an office in the basement of his home, and one paid employee besides himself: his $100-a-week secretary, Dinah Trachtman, who had been Schott's secretary at the Product Safety Commission. The question was how to make the dream come true, how to advance from his basement into the national political mainstream.

There was no precise model for what he hoped to do. Nader came closest, but even Nader had not championed the consumers of an illegal drug. Still, if NORML had no exact precedents to follow, it had several obvious needs. Money was the most obvious. Another was the kind of big-name endorsements that could give NORML respectability. Another was mass support from smokers who would send in their dues, write their congressmen, and otherwise create a political presence. There was a need for a larger Washington staff, too, and for publicity to generate money and mass support. And there had to be substance, a program, specific actions and victories that would justify public support. NORML faced the same Catch-22 as any new reform group: You need money to build a program, and you need a program to attract money.

Underlying the obvious need for money, publicity, and a program was the basic question of how NORML defined itself. On this, Stroup had been lucky. The first important people he had talked to, Ramsey Clark and John Kaplan, were lawyers who had studied the issue dispassionately and concluded that marijuana should be legal. That was Stroup's view, too, and it was reflected in the first letters he wrote to Playboy. But that winter, as he talked to people at Playboy and to lawyers and scientists whose support he wanted, they told him again and again they could not be associated with any organization that advocated the use of marijuana. Thus, by the time NORML began operations, Stroup had changed his emphasis: NORML was not pro-pot, only anti-jail. If asked, Stroup would say that he personally thought marijuana should be legal and regulated, as alcohol was, but NORML's official goal was simply to end criminal penalties for its use. He was thus on solid political ground from the outset.

In the first months of NORML's existence, Stroup did not seek publicity, because he knew he had little to publicize. Instead he concentrated on trying to persuade prominent people to join what he called NORML's "advisory board of directors." This was not the real board of directors, which had power over money and consisted of Stroup, Schott, Dubois, and a few other close friends. The advisory board had certain vaguely defined duties—in theory it met once a year, and in reality some of its members *did* advise Stroup—but its most immediate role was to give Stroup some impressive names to print on NORML's stationery. Seeking recruits, Stroup wrote liberal politicians; he wrote celebrities whose children had been busted; he wrote scientists who had made moderate statements on marijuana; and he wrote people recommended to him by friends in Washington's left-wing community. In March, at the suggestion of Marcus Raskin, the cofounder of the Institute for Policy Studies, Stroup wrote to Max Palevsky, the California liberal who had made a fortune in Xerox stock and who, the next year, would be one of George McGovern's biggest financial backers. A meeting was arranged in Palevsky's suite at the Madison Hotel the next time he was in Washington.

The talk was rather formal, until Palevsky asked, "What about your own drug use?"

Stroup hesitated. He had no idea how Palevsky felt about drugs, and for the most part he was minimizing his own drug use in those days. He would sometimes tell interviewers, "I *have* smoked, but I'd be crazy to now," which, if true, was not the whole truth. But he decided to be candid with Palevsky.

"I smoke a lot of dope," he said, "and I've been experimenting with hallucinogens."

Later he thought Palevsky had been testing him, and he must have passed the test, for the California millionaire soon joined NORML's advisory board and became an important financial backer, contributing more than twenty-five thousand dollars over the decade.

Another important lead came from Burton Joseph, who urged Stroup to contact Aryeh Neier, the national director of the American Civil Liberties Union. Neier not only agreed to serve on the advisory board but provided NORML with free office space in New York and put Stroup in touch with the ACLU's state coordinators, who sometimes became NORML's state coordinators.

Stroup did not always get his man, or his woman. There was no one he more admired and wanted on his advisory board—nor anyone whose name he more often dropped—than Ramsey Clark, but Clark was not yet willing to link himself officially with the marijuana lobby. One problem was that Clark was defending the Berrigan brothers, two anti-war clergymen who were accused, incredibly enough, of plotting to kidnap Henry Kissinger. One of the government informants was a drug dealer, a fact Clark hoped to use to discredit the witness, and he feared that effort might backfire if he was himself linked to a pro-marijuana lobby. After the Berrigan trial was over, Clark did join NORML's board and helped in many other ways as well.

Another big name Stroup went after in that first spring was Margaret Mead, the celebrated anthropologist, who had been critical of the marijuana laws. He wrote to Mead in May, asking if she would serve on his advisory board. He followed up his letter with a call, during which she said she was leaving for a trip abroad and would prefer not to make a decision until she returned. Stroup brooded over this rejection overnight, then called her back, full of zeal and indignation: This was important. People were in jail. How could she say no? He succeeded only in offending Mead and ending any hope of her support.

He had an urgent need for pro-marijuana scientists to combat the reefer-madness mythology. Early in 1971 he read *Marijuana Reconsidered*, a scholarly work by Dr. Lester Grinspoon of the Harvard Medical School, who concluded that marijuana was essentially harmless. He quickly called Grinspoon, who soon agreed to serve on NORML's advisory board and to testify on its behalf before legislative panels. He also recommended that Stroup contact his Harvard colleague Dr. Norman Zinberg, who had written extensively on drugs and who also became an advisory board member and, in reality, an important personal adviser to Stroup. There was a certain chain-letter quality to Stroup's search for support: One scientist would recommend another, until by May of that first year Stroup had a pool of nationally respected scientists he could call upon to rebut the more outrageous scientific claims against marijuana.

In mid-April Dinah Trachtman and Kelly Stroup represented NORML on a television show called *Women Take a Stand*, and they came back with enthusiastic reports about two other panelists: an elderly woman doctor who believed marijuana should be legal, and a senior official of the federal Bureau of Narcotics and Dangerous Drugs (BNDD), who seemed to think that people should not be jailed for smoking. Stroup was quick to follow up on the lead, and thus recruited two of the most unusual and politically useful of NORML's early supporters: Dr. Dorothy Whipple, a seventy-year-old professor of pediatrics at Georgetown University, and John Finlator, deputy director of the BNDD. "We ripped off the number-two narc," Stroup liked to boast of Finlator's recruitment to the cause, although in fact the law-enforcement official came voluntarily. When Stroup called him that spring and said he'd like to meet him, Finlator laughed and told him to call back after he retired at the end of the year. Stroup did, and Finlator joined NORML's board and also issued a statement that putting people in jail for marijuana use was not stopping them from smoking, was ruining lives, and was wasting the time of law-enforcement officers. Because of who he was, Finlator's statement made front-page news.

That Dorothy Whipple would take up the cause of legal marijuana in her seventies was a surprise only to those who did not know this remarkable woman. She was born in 1900 into an old New York family—a Whipple signed the Declaration of Independence—and as a young girl she decided she wanted to be a doctor, no easy feat for a woman in those days. When she was married in the early 1920s, to an economist named Ewan Clague, she kept her own name ("Dorothy Whipple is *me*," she says), although that, too, was quite rare then. She, her husband, and their children settled in Washington, where she practiced and taught medicine. (She also found time, at age sixty-six, to take a two-week raft trip down the Amazon.) During the 1970s she found that more and more of her teenage patients were using drugs. She was shocked, and moreover she realized she was quite ignorant about drugs. "I decided that if I was responsible for these young people, I should know something about drugs," she says. "I read all the books I could and I interviewed scientists who'd studied drugs. In the course of my investigation, my attitudes changed." She concluded that although drug use among the young should be discouraged, marijuana should be made legal and regulated. In 1971 she published a book, *Is the Grass Really Greener?*, which spelled out the facts on drugs in her usual no-nonsense manner.

Dr. Whipple became, along with John Finlator, one of NORML's star witnesses at state legislative hearings across the nation. Once, in the interest of research, she invited Keith and Kelly to her home to introduce her and her husband to marijuana. Their visit came during Easter week, so the Stroups brought a toy Easter egg filled with good grass. They all smoked, got a little high, got hungry ("got the munchies," Kelly recalls), and raided the refrigerator. The experiment was pronounced a success, although Dr. Whipple decided she preferred to stick with a cocktail before dinner. Some months later, when she was testifying before the Minnesota legislature, a state senator asked if she had ever smoked pot. "Why, yes, sir," she replied innocently. "Haven't you?"

For Stroup, struggling to overcome the image of the marijuana proponent as a sinister, drug-crazed hippie, such allies as the grandmotherly Dr. Whipple and the square-jawed, white-haired ex-narc, Finlator, were gifts from the gods. By the end of the year, NORML's advisory board included not only Aryeh Neier, John Finlator, and Drs. Grinspoon, Zinberg, and Whipple but Margery Tabankin, president of the National Student Association; Dr. Edwin Schur, a criminologist at Tufts University; Burton Joseph, of the Playboy

Foundation; Canon Walter Dennis, of the Cathedral Church of St. John the Divine, in New York; former senator Charles Goodell, of New York; and Dr. Benjamin Spock, the child-health expert and anti-war spokesman.

In those first few months Stroup reached out in many directions, seeking whatever help he could get. He wrote to Jann Wenner, the publisher of *Rolling Stone*, asking for a free ad, which Wenner provided. He wrote to Peter Fonda, who had played the dope-smoking Captain America in the movie hit *Easy Rider*, asking for his help. He wrote to a judge in Kentucky who'd outraged his community by saying smokers shouldn't be jailed. He advised the head of the Society of Ultimate Logic, in Corpus Christi, Texas, that he didn't think the Nixon Supreme Court would accept religious freedom as a justification for marijuana use. All this was fine, sometimes fun, sometimes useful, but it wasn't going to change the marijuana laws. Then, in April, Stroup began to focus his and NORML's attention on a political target that was of immense importance to America's smokers: the National Commission on Marijuana and Drug Abuse, which was about to hold public hearings on the marijuana issue and would then recommend what national policy on the drug should be.

The Marijuana Commission, as it came to be called, was created by the Drug Reform Act of 1970, largely because of the efforts of Rep. Ed Koch, a Democrat who lived in Greenwich Village and later became mayor of New York. The 1970 drug act was a distinctly mixed bag. On the one hand, the Nixon administration wanted a tough drug law to highlight its law-and-order campaign. On the other hand, in Congress, as elsewhere, there existed by 1970 a growing awareness of the need for drug-law reform. Both sides won a partial victory. The Nixon administration won the reclassification of marijuana as a dangerous drug, which all but eliminated its medical use, a decision that NORML would fight throughout the decade. The reformers won the reduction of the federal penalty for possession of marijuana from a felony to a misdemeanor. Actually, few people are prosecuted under the federal law, but it is traditionally a model for state laws, and the 1970 act set off a wave of reform at the state level. Within two years, first-offense marijuana possession had been reduced to a misdemeanor in almost every state. This simply meant that in most states you could be sentenced to up to a year in jail for possession, but not more than a year.

The federal law did not go far enough to satisfy Ed Koch, who believed that if a serious commission looked at the facts, it would recommend the end of all criminal penalties for marijuana use. He therefore added to the 1970 act a provision for the creation of the Marijuana Commission, which was to hold hearings in 1971 and issue a report on national marijuana policy in 1972. The goal of NORML and all reform groups was to persuade this top-level commission that people should not be jailed for smoking marijuana. For NORML, especially, as it struggled for credibility, the hearings would be an opportunity to prove its effectiveness, to gain publicity, and to meet virtually everyone in America who was professionally concerned with the issue, pro or con. NORML's dealings with this government commission would, in effect, be the first real test of its political potency.

At the outset, the Marijuana Commission gave every appearance of being hostile to reform. President Nixon appointed nine of the commission's thirteen members, including its chairman, Raymond P. Shafer, a former Republican governor of Pennsylvania. The ones Nixon did not appoint were members of Congress: two liberal senators, Harold Hughes and Jacob Javits; and two conservative congressmen, Paul Rogers and Tim Lee Carter. The commissioners were mostly white, middle-aged, and, with three or four exceptions, conservative. The reformers feared that, whatever Ed Koch had intended, this Nixon-appointed commission existed only to rubber-stamp the government's well-known anti-marijuana, anti-drug ortho-doxy. Still, the commission existed, it would be a battleground for publicity, and if NORML was indeed to be a credible, respectable spokesman for reform, it would have to show that it could deal with the commission.

Stroup therefore wrote Chairman Shafer in mid-April and as a result was invited to meet with the commission's executive director, a young lawyer named Michael Sonnenreich. Stroup knew enough about Sonnenreich's background to view him with misgivings. Sonnenreich had previously been assistant chief counsel of BNDD, and he was known as a Nixon loyalist, one of a group of conservative young lawyers who had ridden to power on Nixon's coattails. Still, knowing all this, Stroup was stunned at the curt rejection he received when he told Sonnenreich he hoped to testify at the first commission hearing, in Washington on May 17. In essence Sonnenreich told him, We'll decide who testifies, we have enough pro-marijuana witnesses, and we don't need you.

Stroup's shock soon turned to despair. If NORML could not even testify before the Marijuana Commission, it might as well disband; all its pretensions to respectability, to working within the system, would be a joke. The Nixon administration would have destroyed NORML by ignoring it. Groping for a next stop, Stroup asked Ramsey Clark if he would testify before the commission on behalf of NORML, and when Clark said yes, Stroup thought he had solved the problem. Certainly the commission could not refuse to hear a former attorney general.

So Stroup went back to see Sonnenreich, only to be told bluntly that the commission didn't need Ramsey Clark, either. Desperate, Stroup fought back with a technique he had learned at the Product Safety Commission: a leak to the press.

He called columnist Jack Anderson's office and told a young reporter named Brett Hume about Sonnenreich's rejection of both himself and Clark. The column that followed, implying that the commission was anti-marijuana, was an embarrassment to the commissioners, who, whatever their views, wanted to appear to be open-minded. Chairman Shafer quickly called Clark to say he would be welcome to testify before the commission. A while later Sonnenreich called Stroup and invited him to testify at the commission's second set of hearings, in San Francisco in June.

Stroup's leak to Jack Anderson, suggesting that the commission was a stacked deck, had embarrassed the commission, but it was far more embarrassed on May 1 when President Nixon declared, at a news conference, "Even if the commission does recommend that it [marijuana] be legalized, I will not follow that recommendation."

Stroup's response to Nixon's anti-marijuana outburst was to demand equal time from the television networks under the "fairness doctrine." He didn't get it, because the networks claimed they had given the other side of the marijuana issue in their news shows, so he had to settle for sending a written response to Nixon's statement to several hundred newspapers.

As the first day of the hearings drew near, Stroup's concern focused on two anti-marijuana psychiatrists who were to be the leadoff witnesses. The two witnesses had previously published an article that linked marijuana use with mental illness, based on a study of thirty-eight young people with histories of mental disorders. Stroup had nationally known psychiatrists who would dispute the study, but that was not the point.

All the way back to Harry Anslinger's heyday, marijuana hearings had always led off with scientific horror stories that grabbed the headlines while dull scientific rebuttal went unnoticed. The fact that the commission had scheduled the two anti-marijuana psychiatrists as its first witnesses convinced Stroup that the commission wanted only to set off another round of reefer-madness headlines. He had Dr. Zinberg and other scientists who had agreed to come to Washington and rebut the study, but the key was timing. A rebuttal the next day wouldn't matter. He somehow had to steal the commission's thunder.

On the morning of the first hearing, Stroup and Schott were stationed outside the hearing room in the massive Rayburn Office Building, passing out their press releases and alerting reporters to the NORML press conference at noon, right down the hall. Stroup even put up his own sign announcing the news conference, next to the sign that said the commission was meeting in the hearing room.

Stroup attended the hearing, and as the noon break neared, he was pleased to hear a reporter he knew, William Hines, of the Chicago *Sun-Times*, ask Chairman Shafer a question: What about charges by Keith Stroup, the head of NORML, that the commission was rigged? Shafer responded indignantly that perhaps Mr. Stroup should speak for himself.

On cue, Stroup stood up and invited everyone to NORML's news conference, which began a few minutes later in a nearby hearing room that had been provided by a friendly member of Congress, James Scheuer, a Democrat from the Bronx. NORML's news conference featured vigorous rebuttals of the anti-marijuana study by several nationally known scientists, and the upshot was that they blunted the anti-marijuana testimony and stole the first day's headlines. The Washington *Star*'s headline, for example, read "Marijuana Study Challenged." NORML's victory was complete when its scientists got equal time with the anti-marijuana scientists on the CBS Evening News that night.

Stroup assumed the commission would be outraged by his performance, but he didn't care. He assumed the commission was already outraged by his leak to Jack Anderson. No matter. He saw NORML locked in an adversary role with the commission, and if they could not be friends, he thought he could at least force them to respect him.

For Stroup, one of the important by-products of the three commission hearings was the opportunity it provided to meet potential allies in the reform movement. It was at the hearings, for example, that he first met Dr. Andrew Weil, a Harvard-trained expert on mind-altering drugs who would soon introduce Stroup and his friends to the hallucinogenic drug MDA, and also Dr. David Smith, of the Haight-Ashbury Medical Clinic, who joined NORML's advisory board.

At the hearings in San Francisco in June, Stroup had his first contact with Amorphia, the California legalization group. Stroup already regarded Amorphia as a potential rival, and was quick to tell people that it was a hippie, pro-pot group, whereas NORML was straight and only anti-jail. Mike Aldrich, the LeMar activist who had joined Amorphia, was testifying, and Stroup watched with cool professional curiosity. Aldrich appeared in a rumpled Brooks Brothers suit, sporting an Indian headband and wearing his pale-brown hair in a long ponytail. He was accompanied by a short-haired man who was wearing a suit, tie, and porkpie hat and whom he introduced as his "spiritual and financial adviser, Allen Ginsberg." It was true: Ginsberg's own guru had told him he was too concerned with his image, so he had shaved the long hair and full beard he had worn for years.

Aldrich read a statement to the commission, tracing the history of marijuana and calling for study of alternative forms of legal regulation, and then at its conclusion he leaped to his feet, raised one fist defiantly, and shouted, "We want free, legal backyard marijuana." Immediately, thirty or forty of his hippie followers jumped to their feet and began cheering. Stroup, watching, was grudgingly impressed. The fellow might be a freak, he thought, but he knew how to turn out his troops. Stroup and Aldrich chatted warily, and agreed to meet in September at the National Student Association convention in Denver to discuss ways they could work together.

At the third set of hearings, in Chicago, Stroup for the first time met the New York reformers, Guy Archer and Frank Fioramonti. They were a kind of Mutt and Jeff team: Archer was tall and easygoing, Fioramonti short and intense. They had become friends at Columbia Law School, and by 1970, when Fioramonti was a lawyer for the City of New York and Archer was in private practice, they spent a lot of evenings together, smoking marijuana and denouncing the marijuana laws. That fall they read a law-journal article about proposals to legalize marijuana, and they talked with Franz Leichter, a state assemblyman from Manhattan's Upper West Side, about introducing such a bill. Early in 1971, working with Leichter and several other young pro-marijuana lawyers, they drafted a bill to permit legal sale of marijuana in liquor stores, under the supervision of a state regulatory agency.

The bill got nowhere, but Archer and Fioramonti were by then committed to the reform cause. They organized the Lawyers Committee to Legalize Marijuana, and they found hundreds of New York lawyers willing to sign petitions and otherwise work for reform. In the summer of that year they got themselves invited to testify before the Marijuana Commission, at its final hearings in Chicago, and it was there that they met Stroup. The encounter boosted everyone's morale. All three of them sometimes thought they were crazy to be working for marijuana-law reform, and for Stroup to meet two talented lawyers working on the issue in New York, and for the New Yorkers to learn of Stroup's national ambitions, was cause for celebration. Archer and Fioramonti had not been thinking in national terms, but Stroup had been thinking in terms of New York, and Archer and Fioramonti would soon become NORML's men there.

At the first Marijuana Commission hearing, various of the commissioners had seemed hostile to pro-reform witnesses. When John Kaplan said that one reason to end criminal penalties for smoking was that millions of people were ignoring the law, a commissioner asked if Kaplan also favored legalizing auto theft. There were many barbs like that, but by the second and third hearings, the mood of the commission seemed to change. Some of the commissioners began to ask friendly questions, and one or two would chat with Stroup during breaks. This new mood, plus encouraging reports from his sources on the commission staff (who were, he had learned, often sympathetic to his cause), made Stroup optimistic. That fall, in the first issue of NORML's newsletter, he wrote, "I'm guessing the commission will recommend the repeal of all criminal penalties for simple possession of marijuana. They've heard it from so many people so often it's going to be hard to avoid."

He wouldn't know until the next spring if his optimism was justified, but in the meantime he could take pride in a textbook example of how a media-wise David can hold its own with an establishment Goliath. NORML may or may not have done anything to change the commission's thinking, but Stroup had clearly used the commission to reap maximum publicity and political contacts for himself.

NORML's news conference at the first Marijuana Commission hearing, when Stroup used his pro-marijuana scientists to rebut the anti-marijuana studies, had been the pot lobby's first publicity splash. Stroup's instinct had been to go slowly with the media, to wait until he had more to talk about. If reporters came to him, he would talk to them, but he wasn't going to them empty-handed. It was a good policy, in part because the reporters who sought him out tended to be the younger ones who were favorably disposed to his cause. One day that summer a young wire-service reporter appeared, chatted awhile, confessed that he was a smoker, and said he wanted to do a feature on NORML. When he asked what the pot lobby had accomplished, Stroup was overcome by candor and replied, "Not a hell of a lot." The feature that resulted, although friendly, was headed "Washington's Feeblest Lobby" and treated NORML as something of a joke. Moreover, Stroup had foolishly agreed to be photographed with the plastic marijuana plant he kept in his basement office. The story and picture received front-page play in hundreds of newspapers, and Stroup was mortified. Instead of the earnest young public-interest lawyer of his self-image, the feature made him seem an ineffectual hippie with a marijuana plant in his office.

Then, after a week or so, he began to notice that his mail had gone up sharply. In time he realized that the wire-service story, however embarrassing to him, had introduced NORML to millions of people. Like all politicians, he was learning that the only bad publicity is no publicity.

In those early days he would fly halfway across the country for a local television show or a campus lecture. He wanted the exposure, and in a sense he was trying out his act on the road, preparing for an eventual opening in Washington. He was trying to build local chapters, too, and by the end of the year, NORML had organizers on nearly a hundred campuses, including fourteen in New York State alone. In Nashville NORML's volunteer coordinator persuaded Kris Kristofferson to give a NORML benefit concert and to cut NORML's first public-service radio tape, which consisted of Kristofferson singing a few bars of "Me and Bobbie McGee" and saying that marijuana smokers shouldn't be tossed in jail. Kristofferson, the Rhodes scholar turned country songwriter, was a fitting spokesman for NORML, for many of his great early songs, like "Sunday Morning Coming Down," not only had specific references to marijuana but in their free-flowing lyricism reflected something very like a stoned consciousness.

One substantive issue that NORML tried to address that summer concerned a BNDD program to use a powerful herbicide called "2,4-D" to kill marijuana plants that grew wild in many Midwestern states. NORML's inquiries forced the Department of Agriculture to admit it knew nothing about the harm that might befall people who smoked the poisoned plants, but it was soon clear that the Bureau of Narcotics and Dangerous Drugs was not concerned with that issue. The spraying continued despite NORML's protest, and the incident foreshadowed the confrontation six years later when NORML sued the government to stop the spraying of Mexican marijuana fields with paraquat.

The first issue of *The Leaflet*, NORML's newsletter, went out to its members that fall. It was a well-written, handsomely designed, six-page publication that reflected the straight, nonhippie tone that Stroup wanted for NORML. It also reflected the fact that, in terms of its own progress, NORML did not have a great deal to report at that point. The lead article was an account of a Vietnam veteran in Ohio, with no previous arrest record, who had been sentenced to twenty to forty years in prison for being present when a friend sold marijuana to an undercover agent. There was also an account of the case of John Sinclair, the radical poet who was sentenced to ten years in prison in Michigan for allegedly giving two joints to an undercover agent. *The Leaflet* account noted, "Since his sentencing, freedom and humanity have been denied John Sinclair. He is in administrative segregation in Jackson prison. For 22 of 24 hours each day, he is in solitary confinement. He is allowed to exercise and eat only with the prisoners in the special administrative segregation. He is allowed to shave and shower once a week. His mail is censored and copied." The article noted that NORML had filed an *amicus curiae* brief with the Michigan supreme court on Sinclair's behalf, its first such action.

The Leaflet also had long reports on the Marijuana Commission's hearings and the herbicide-spraying program, a feature on Rep. James Scheuer, of New York, who favored drug-law reform, and reports on two American Bar Association committees that had called for legalization. For comic relief, *The Leaflet* told of the gift memberships that

NORML had sent to President Nixon and Attorney General John Mitchell. Both men had responded. Mitchell asked that his name be deleted from membership. A Nixon aide wrote, "At the President's direction, we are forwarding the materials about your work to officials of the Department of Justice. With the President's best wishes."

No one at NORML was sure if that was a joke or a threat, or maybe both. The paranoia level was always high at NORML, since there was usually an ounce or two of marijuana around. Once, in the early days, a crew-cut, middle-aged man appeared and said he wanted to volunteer. Stroup shrugged and put him to work, but at the end of the day, when the man asked if Stroup knew where he could score a pound of marijuana, he threw him out. Sometimes Stroup wished the BNDD would charge in and arrest them all. It would give them a million dollars' worth of publicity; Nader, after all, had got his real start when General Motors foolishly put a private detective on his trail. But the government had apparently learned from GM's mistakes, and NORML's staff and guests smoked with impunity.

It soon became obvious that NORML was a one-man show. Larry Schott, Larry Dubois, and Kelly Stroup helped out as they could, but Keith was NORML, and NORML was for him an all-consuming passion. That fact was painfully clear, above all, to Kelly, who felt herself losing her husband to his political crusade, and the fact that she agreed with the issue did not make it any easier. She had come to regret that NORML's office was in their basement, for a number of reasons, not the least of which was that the house was constantly filled with people who were smoking, sometimes dealers, and she lived in fear of a police raid. She didn't know what would happen to her baby daughter if she and Keith were both arrested. Sometimes as she put Lindsey to bed at night, she wondered if she would be able to convince the police that she hadn't known anything about all that grass they'd found in the house.

And there were other problems. Lindsey wasn't even two, but she answered the phone not with "Hello" but with "Marijuana reform!" And there was the question of money. Keith was paid at a rate of $18,000 a year, but when Kelly worked for NORML, she was paid $2 an hour. When she protested, Keith snapped, "We can't have a mom-and-pop operation." There were also her fears that he was having affairs with other women. She had dreams about his affairs sometimes, very specific dreams, but when she pleaded with him to be honest with her, he only denied there were other women at all.

One night when Keith was away, two young men with a gun forced their way into the house and demanded money and drugs, and Kelly was sure she and her daughter would be killed. When the robbers finally left, Kelly realized that she couldn't even call the police, because they'd find marijuana when they came to investigate. By the fall of that first year, Kelly was urging Keith to move NORML's office out of their home, to give them some kind of a private life. But of course that was impossible, because NORML didn't have money for another office.

Everything always came back to money. By September 15 NORML had taken in almost $24,000: $14,125 from Playboy, $7550 in memberships, and about $2100 in donations. It was enough for survival but not for a real national program, with paid organizers and legal challenges and mass mailings and everything Stroup dreamed of. For a while that fall he and Schott thought their money problem was solved. *Playboy* had given NORML a free full-page ad. Headed "Pot Shots," it showed mug shots of a young man arrested for marijuana, and it told a little about NORML and urged readers to send their $7 ($5 for students) to join. As the ad's mid-August publication drew near, Stroup and Schott would sit in the basement office each night getting high and dreaming of all the money that would soon be pouring in. A similar *Playboy* ad for the Vietnam Veterans Against the War had drawn about $100,000 and in their fantasy the NORML ad might draw twice that amount, maybe more. After all, the war was an old issue, but theirs was new, and there were millions of smokers out there waiting to send their money to someone who would lead them out of the wilderness.

The flood of money never began; there was hardly a trickle. Six thousand dollars came in, but nothing like they'd dreamed of. When Stroup returned to reality, he thought he knew what the trouble had been. People had heard of the VVAW, but they knew nothing about NORML. At best, it was just a name; at worst, the more paranoid smokers would think the ad a trick by the government to get their names for John Mitchell's files.

It was, for Stroup, the last straw. The first year of NORML had not been all fun and games. There was the constant concern about money and the threat of arrest. There had been plenty of rejections, plenty of reporters and politicians who'd laughed in his face, plenty of nights when there was nothing to do but go home and get stoned with Schott and Dubois and curse a nation that didn't care about the smokers who were rotting in jail. That was the worst part, the prison mail that had started to pour in, hundreds of letters from guys who were serving six months or six years for a couple of joints or a couple of ounces. NORML answered every letter, and sometimes it asked a volunteer lawyer to look into an unusual case, but it was maddening to keep sending those letters that really said nothing but "I'm sorry you're in jail; enclosed is our brochure." The truth was that NORML had nothing to offer them yet, no real legal program, no legislative plans, nothing but brochures and an impressive advisory board and a lot of good intentions.

"This is a fucking sham," Stroup raged to Schott one night after the *Playboy* ad had flopped. "We're nothing but a pen-pal operation. I won't go on like this."

The more he thought about it, the angrier he became. He'd given NORML all he had, and Playboy was playing games with him, giving him $5000 here, $5000 there, but never the kind of money he needed. He wouldn't take it any longer. He would go to them and say "Put up or shut up; get in or get out."

Stroup did indeed make a formal request to the Playboy Foundation that fall for more money. He put it in writing, neatly typed, well reasoned, each penny justified, and it was presented to the staff and the board of the Playboy Foundation and considered, in the somber way that foundations make decisions. But all that probably mattered a great deal less than the fact that for several months Hugh Hefner had been hearing good things about NORML. For that, Stroup could thank two women, Michelle Urry and Bobbie Arnstein.

He met Michelle first, and soon was half in love with her, as were a great many men. She was in her late twenties then, a very beautiful, very intelligent, very gentle woman who had already risen to be *Playboy*'s cartoon editor, an important post at the magazine, since Hefner himself started as a cartoonist and took intense interest in what cartoons appeared in his magazine. Michelle had grown up in Canada, the daughter of a prosperous businessman, and had gone to UCLA. After college she visited a friend in Chicago and decided to stay there, mainly because she loved the architecture, the classic buildings, and she took a job as a clerk-typist at *Playboy*. That was in 1965. She kept pestering the editors for an editorial job, but they said they had no openings. It was Hefner himself who noticed her filing papers in his office one day, liked her, and said she could be an apprentice cartoon editor, his assistant, his protégée. One day he told her there was a vacant apartment on the ground floor of the mansion, and she could rent it for $125 a month if she wished. It was a wonderful bargain, but she hesitated. What strings were attached? None, Hefner assured her. She asked if she could have men in. (The Bunnies, who lived on the top floor, were not allowed to.) Of course, Hefner said. But why me? she said, persistent. Because we think you'll make a contribution, he said. You like people and you'll be fun to have around. And so she moved in, and it *was* fun, but after a year or so she moved out again, because she wanted her privacy, and because she was a very sane woman who soon realized that life in Hefner's mansion was essentially insane, unless you were Hefner.

Michelle was one of the first people Stroup met in the *Playboy* world, and she was fascinated by him from the first. To begin with, he was the fastest-talking man she'd ever met, and she herself was someone who thought and spoke very quickly. For another, he had that strange way of saying tough, angry things in a soft, gentle manner, it was almost like a speech impediment. She was struck, too, by the contrast between the way he looked and what he said. He always wore three-button suits when he came to *Playboy*, and his granny glasses, and he had that wonderful silky blond hair that kept falling down in his eyes, and he looked like a Yalie, a young stockbroker, or an IBM executive, but he kept talking about *dope*! And he was so impassioned when he spoke, so sure you agreed with him. He talked about the kids rotting in jail and the corrupt, cynical, whiskey-drinking politicians, and he assumed you shared his outrage, or that he could convince you purely through his logic.

It happened that Michelle did agree with him. She had several friends who'd been arrested for marijuana, and she was impressed to meet this very smart, dynamic young lawyer who thought the laws could be changed. They kept seeing each other, whenever he was in Chicago, and she continued to be impressed with him, although she thought she really didn't understand him. He was so detached from everything; she didn't think he really gave himself emotionally to anyone except his child, and she couldn't imagine what his marriage could be like. He didn't have time to enjoy people; he was always on the run. There was something else about him that bothered Michelle, who had grown up with piano and ballet lessons, who had studied architecture and design in college, who loved music and the theater, who in time would marry a sculptor: Keith was a hick, a hayseed. It took her a while to understand that, because he was so sophisticated about everything relating to politics and marijuana. But he was so unsophisticated about everything else. He didn't know which fork to use. He invariably said "Just between you and I." He'd never been to Europe, and he seemed to have no interest in books or music or art; his limits, the vast gaps in his education, constantly surprised her. And yet she found them endearing, too.

Most important, she thought his work was important, that he could make a difference, and so she wanted him to know Hef better. That was when she began to tell her friend Bobbie Arnstein about him, because Bobbie was Hef's executive assistant, the person who if she chose could see that Keith had a chance to sell Hefner on himself and NORML.

All Stroup knew was that one day Michelle picked up her office phone and called Bobbie and said she wanted to send her friend Keith over to the mansion to meet her. What he didn't know was that there were other calls in which she'd discussed him with Bobbie in great detail. She had to, because Bobbie was fragile, paranoid about people using her to get to Hefner. So Michelle had made a very careful decision before she passed Keith on to Bobbie, just as Bobbie would make her own decision before she passed him on to Hef. Then, the decision made, she called Bobbie and told her, Bobbie, you'll love him; he's so sweet; he's adorable; so innocent in a way, but he's very smart and his work is important and he needs to know Hef.

Thus, one afternoon that fall, Stroup made his way to Bobbie's office on the third floor of the mansion, near Hefner's own office. She was busy when he arrived, and she sent him down to her three-room suite on the second floor of the mansion, where she had lived for several years. He put on a record—The Band's first album, Bobbie's favorite that summer—and ordered a glass of wine. Bobbie, right off, introduced him to the wonders of the mansion; all you did was pick up the phone and dial 20, and you could get anything you wanted to eat or drink, twenty-four hours a day. (Not even the president, in the White House, commands that sort of service.) He looked around the apartment, which was very modern, a little spooky, and blatantly erotic. There were no windows, and the walls, ceilings, and floors of the main room were all black. Bobbie collected kinetic art; there was a three-dimensional figure of a man in a business suit tearing open his shirt to reveal a Superman crest—every corporate executive's fantasy, Stroup guessed. There was another puzzling, troubling piece that showed half a male body and half a female body—the upper half, in each case—joined at the point where their sex organs would have been.

Bobbie joined him after a while, and they smoked a joint and talked. Stroup saw from the first that Bobbie was much different from her friend Michelle. Michelle was serene; Bobbie was frenetic, defiantly burning her candle at both ends. Bobbie lived in the mansion; Michelle had a life apart from the *Playboy* world. For a long time Stroup had thought of Michelle as someone far above him, untouchable, unreachable, a fantasy figure, but he never felt that way about Bobbie. They were too much alike. He knew that if he and Bobbie had been strangers, at a party with a hundred people, they would have found each other.

As they talked the first day, Stroup noticed the book *Be Here Now*, by Baba Ram Dass, at her bedside; the author was formerly Richard Alpert, in the days when he and Timothy Leary were pioneers of the movement toward LSD and other hallucinogenic drugs. Stroup was starting to use hallucinogens, mostly MDA, and he had read the book, and his and Bobbie's talk soon turned to drugs. At the time, Stroup was simply trying to be as impressive as he could to this very important, very attractive woman as she alternately flirted with him and interrogated him. Later, when he understood her better, he realized she was sizing him up in a number of ways. For one thing, she was deciding whether or not Hefner would like him. If he was just an ambitious lawyer on the make, Hefner might support his program but not want to socialize with him. There was also the question of whether Stroup was someone Bobbie might enjoy. She soon decided he was.

"You need to get to know Hef better," Bobbie said, when it was time for her to get back to work.

"I want to, but I don't know how," he said.

"The best way is to make the flight from Chicago to L.A. with him sometime."

"I'm available."

"Anytime?"

"Anytime at all," he said.

She called a few days later and asked if he could fly to Los Angeles with Hefner the next week.

"Sure," he said.

"Do you have any business in L.A.?"

"Not really."

"Well, don't tell Hef that," she said.

Stroup flew to Chicago on the appointed day of the following week and went to the mansion for what Bobbie had said would be a two-o'clock departure. It turned out that Hefner was not ready to go until six that evening—still early in his day—and so Stroup spent several hours just hanging out. He played pinball for a while and, not wanting to be in the way, waited in Bobbie's suite for most of the time, listening to The Band play "Up on Cripple Creek" and "The Night They Drove Old Dixie Down," listening to Robbie Robertson discover America.

Bobbie came in once and said that she'd decided not to make the trip. When Hefner went to Los Angeles, she explained, it was finally possible for her to catch up on her work in Chicago.

"Bobbie, you're not going to put me on that plane alone, are you?" Stroup protested.

It was true that he was terrified of getting on the plane with Hefner without Bobbie, but there was another reason for his protests. There was a current of flirtation between them, and if he was going to Los Angeles, he didn't want her staying behind in Chicago. She dragged it out, protesting, teasing, enjoying the game, and finally she agreed to go. At six in the evening she took him out to the driveway beside the mansion where two Mercedes limousines were waiting to take Hefner's party to the airport.

Two other friends of Hefner's, actor Warren Beatty and writer-cartoonist Shel Silverstein, joined the flight to California in Hefner's $5.5 million converted DC-9, known as the *Big Bunny*. As they flew, looked after by four "jet Bunnies," Hefner encouraged Stroup to tell about NORML's work and particularly about its challenges to the laws in Texas, the one state where many young men were still getting long prison sentences for simple possession. The talk soon shifted, however, from drugs to sex, not an uncommon subject in the *Playboy* world, and then it shifted again, to the subject of women and their many new demands.

This was 1971, a year when the women's-liberation movement was gathering momentum, a time when many men were finding their women embracing dangerous new ideas. Hefner, who at that time kept one girl friend in his Chicago mansion, another girl friend in his Los Angeles mansion, and of course enjoyed the favors of countless other young women, confessed that he could not rid himself of male possessiveness, that he could not surrender the double standard, that he sought sexual freedom for himself but he could not grant it to his women. He said he knew it was intellectually dishonest, but it remained part of his emotional makeup. Beatty and Silverstein confessed to the same incapacity. All this, at least, Stroup could identify with, because the serious problems he was starting to have with his wife arose at least in part from his passionate belief that different rules should guide her sexual behavior and his own.

Bobbie had told Stroup they would have to play it loose when they arrived in Los Angeles, as to whether he went to the mansion with her and Hefner; it was, after all, Hefner's home, and if he and Stroup had not hit it off during the flight, he might not have wanted Stroup visiting there. But Bobbie thought the chemistry had been good and waved Stroup into one of the waiting limousines, and he was on his way to his second Playboy mansion of the day.

When they arrived, Hefner and Bobbie went to their respective rooms, and Bobbie sent Stroup out to the game room, where he could amuse himself with pool, pinball, or any of the dozens of penny-arcade games that lined the walls. After a while Bobbie and Hefner reappeared, along with Barbi Benton, Hefner's Los Angeles girl friend, and Hefner gave Stroup a tour of his thirty-room mansion and the five-and-a-half-acre grounds. Hefner had stocked his grounds with such an assortment of wildlife that he was required to register it as a zoo: There were doves, monkeys, flamingos, peacocks, parrots, rabbits, and even a pet llama.

Stroup, dazzled by Hefner's glittering pleasure dome, was still uncertain of his place in it. He didn't even know where he was to spend the night. Bobbie settled that by taking him to her room. She took some downers, to offset the uppers she'd been on all day, and they talked for a while and then made love. It was for Stroup all wonderfully exciting, and yet unsettling, too. There was an element of role reversal that troubled him, for Bobbie had been very much in control of the situation. Still, the next morning, when she told him that she and Hefner would be very busy that day and arranged for a limousine to take him back to the airport, he decided that his trip had been a considerable success.

All this was part of the background when Stroup went back to the Playboy Foundation in the fall of 1971 and said NORML had to have more money. The final decision was Hefner's, and that summer and fall, when from time to time some mention of NORML penetrated Hefner's very insulated world, it was usually Bobbie or Michelle saying what a good job Keith was doing, and they were among the handful of people Hefner paid attention to.

On November 24 the Playboy Foundation agreed to give NORML cash and free printing that amounted to $100,000 a year.

5

As 1972 began Stroup had big money from Playboy and big plans to go with it. One of his first decisions was to move NORML's office from the basement of his home to a rundown row house a block away, in the middle of a restaurant's parking lot on Twenty-second Street. He opened two new offices, too. One, in New York City, was headed by the tall, likable Guy Archer, who had left his Wall Street law firm to work with NORML. The other, in Phoenix, was run by a short, energetic drug dealer who vowed he had given up dealing in order to work for legalization.

There was movement on the political front. Two other reform groups—BLOSSOM, in Washington State, and Amorphia, in California —were determined to put pro-marijuana initiatives on the ballot in their states, and Stroup had to decide how NORML should relate to them. Moreover, the Marijuana Commission's report, due in March, was rumored to be favorable, and Stroup hoped it would set off a national election-year debate on marijuana. Then, if a Democrat could beat Nixon in November, the revolution might be at hand.

Such were the fantasies as 1972 began. The reality was that Stroup and his closest friends, Larry Schott and Larry Dubois, had entered a period of drug use that was both destructive to their personal lives and harmful to their work with NORML. They had begun using hallucinogenic drugs, particularly MDA, a substance developed by Dow Chemical Company and produced illegally in clandestine laboratories.

Stroup was introduced to MDA by Dr. Andrew Weil, a twenty-eight-year-old Harvard-trained expert on mind-altering drugs. Weil had studied drugs in Haight-Ashbury, at the National Institute of Mental Health, and in such places as the Amazon basin, where he investigated tribal drug use. When he met Stroup at a Marijuana Commission hearing in mid-1971, he was working on a book called, *The Natural Mind: A New Way of Looking at Drugs and the Higher Consciousness*, wherein he argued, among other things, that "stoned thinking" was superior to "straight thinking."

Weil, who was living in the Washington area, called Stroup and invited him and Kelly to dinner. Their talk soon focused on hallucinogens, or "psychedelics," such as MDA, LSD, and mescaline, and what Weil saw as their mind-expanding qualities. Stroup had heard all these "higher consciousness" arguments before from freaks he had met in his travels, but to hear them now, from this very sophisticated, articulate, Harvard-trained scientist, was far more impressive.

Weil stressed that the hallucinogenic experience would help Stroup in his work, and he added that he had a friend at Harvard who could supply some excellent MDA. Stroup, never shy about new drug experiences, was soon on a plane to Boston. He spent an evening with Weil's friend, a chemist who was making large quantities of MDA. The chemist was impressed to meet Stroup, having read about him in *Playboy*, and he showed him around his lab and told him about a problem he'd had recently. There is a point in the production of MDA when the mixture is highly explosive, and the chemist's lab had blown up. That was bad enough, but then the FBI, thinking that radicals were starting to bomb the Harvard campus, had swarmed over the damaged lab, causing widespread panic among Harvard's MDA-tripping community. As it turned out, the FBI never discerned the true nature of the blast, and the lab was soon back in production. When Stroup returned to Washington, he took with him several hundred tabs of MDA, enough to keep him and his friends in outer space for months.

Stroup was curious about the hallucinogens and saw them as a natural step up from marijuana. By then, marijuana was part of his daily life. It relaxed him, it was fun, but it was no big thing: It was the equivalent of a couple of beers at the end of the day. MDA was not a couple of beers. Once you swallowed the little pink pill, you were gone for eight hours; you were on the bus and there was no getting off. The first rush could be frightening, but after that the drug *was* mind-expanding, or so it seemed. Music, for example, became more intense, more meaningful, far more so than with marijuana. MDA brought a sense of intimacy, a sense of community. You became intensely interested in the people you were with. You wanted to know all about them, and so you talked a mile a minute, seeking communication, seeking understanding. Your ego seemed to fade away, you cared more about others than about yourself, you saw the unimportance of the individual in the universe.

MDA was an immediate sensation with Stroup and his friends, one of whom, after his first trip, proposed that they fly immediately to Cambridge and buy up the chemist's entire supply and put it in a bank vault, lest they run out of this priceless substance.

Stroup and Dubois and their wives, Schott, and two or three other couples, close friends of theirs, began to make MDA-tripping the center of their lives. On weekends they would gather at someone's house and get high and listen to records and sip endless soft drinks, because MDA made you so thirsty. Or they would go outdoors. There was an urge to be outdoors when you were tripping, to climb mountains, to get close to God, and since there were no mountains nearby, they would go wander through Rock Creek Park or sit by the Potomac for hours, watching the sea gulls.

Once they went to a ballet at the Kennedy Center while they were tripping. Stroup, very high, felt himself become a part of the dance, caught up in the syncopation, but when the intermission came and the audience got up, he freaked out, because it seemed that they were all part of the dance, everyone but himself. He ran out of the theater, racing across streets, oblivious of traffic, and he might have been killed if one of his friends hadn't caught up with him.

His work was affected. After a weekend of tripping he would be irritable, depressed, and later he felt that his judgment had been impaired by the drug. Once, starting off on a trip to another city, Stroup bought himself a pair of high-heeled, three-toned shoes. The purchase seemed perfectly logical at the time, but later he thought it was crazy. What was a middle-class reformer doing turning up at a meeting in pimp shoes? Worse, Stroup never got around to arranging to testify before the Democratic Platform Committee that spring, simply because he was too incapacitated by MDA to do his job.

But the worst, most destructive part of it was the sex. MDA was the aphrodisiac of drugs; it was often called the "love drug." The sense of intimacy it created led inevitably to sex. Moreover, it created a sense of community, of sharing, of new relationships, that could lead to great complications. There was talk among Stroup and his friends of living together communally. They never did that, but as 1972 progressed, there were far too many instances of one friend ending up in bed with another friend's mate. It all seemed fine when you were tripping, but when you came down, you faced the reality of guilt, anger, broken friendships, collapsing marriages. Stroup's period of heavy tripping lasted a year, and when it was over, he had come to view hallucinogenic drugs with sharply divided emotions. He thought, on the one hand, that they could be useful, broadening. In later years he always thought he could spot people who had tripped, as they tended to be introspective, relaxed, not hung up on rigid rules and concepts. On the other hand he saw hallucinogens as having great potential for abuse, and he thought he and his friends had tripped far more than was good for them.

He also tried LSD for the first time that winter. He'd gone to Lehigh University to make a speech, and after his speech he went back to a fraternity house where he was to spend the night. He was playing pinball when a boy offered him a tab of LSD. Stroup laughed, thinking that frat-house life had certainly changed since his day, and swallowed the tab. Soon he was caught up in the worst drug experience of his life.

An LSD trip, Stroup came to think, could be a good, useful experience, if you undertook it with a friend who could guide you through it, reassure you so that when the walls started to melt or a tree started to attack you, your friend could remind you that it was only the acid, that you hadn't really lost your mind. Unfortunately, Stroup had no such guide on his first acid trip. The fraternity boys were either tripping themselves or indifferent to his plight, so he spent the night in the basement, seeing the walls close in, not sure who he was or where he was, thinking he was dying, thinking he was dead, thinking he had lost his mind, suffering all the agonies of a very bad trip. By morning he had come down enough to catch his plane back to Washington, but he wanted no more of LSD, at least not for a while.

For better or worse, Stroup was still running NORML, and one of his prime concerns in those days was how he should relate to the various other reform groups that were scattered around the country. There were quite a few of them, often with wonderful acronyms: BLOSSOM (Basic Liberation of Smokers and Sympathizers of Marijuana), CAMP (Committee Against Marijuana Prohibition), CALM (Citizens Association to Legalize Marijuana), COME (Committee on Marijuana Education), POT (Proposition of Today), SLAM (Society for the Legalization and Acceptance of Marijuana), MELO (Marijuana Education and Legalization Organization), and STASH (Student Association for the Study of Hallucinogens).

From the first, Stroup sought out such groups. He wanted to know them, wanted to exchange ideas with them, and of course he wanted NORML to emerge as their national leader. For the most part Stroup found these groups to be composed of freaks, hard-core smokers, people who viewed smoking as a sacrament, people who might be kind and well-meaning but who, politically speaking, were still living in the Stone Age.

One such group, which Stroup worked with in early 1972, was BLOSSOM, in Washington State. A legalization bill had been introduced in the Washington legislature in 1970, but its sponsor was unable even to find a cosponsor for it. It was in the aftermath of this legislative disaster, in December of 1970, that BLOSSOM was formed. Its leader was a big, bearded mountain man named Steve Wilcox, who wrote to Stroup in April of 1971, as soon as he read about NORML in *Playboy*. Wilcox and six or eight followers were living a communal life in some cabins beside a lake outside Olympia. Convinced that marijuana could save a world gone mad, frustrated by the legislative defeat, Wilcox and his friends dreamed of a legislative initiative on the 1972 ballot. They filed official notice of their intent early that year and had to submit the signatures of 102,000 registered voters by July 7 in order to get the initiative on the November ballot.

Voter initiatives are provided for in the constitutions of more than twenty states. In theory they are a way for people to bypass a balky legislature and make law themselves. The voter initiative seemed ready-made for marijuana's true believers, who tended to talk only to themselves and thus to think there was vast (the pun is unavoidable) grass-roots support for legalization, waiting only to be proved by a direct vote.

In state after state Stroup argued against the initiative approach, and in state after state he thus made himself suspect to hard-core smokers. Stroup began with the assumption that there was no state where a majority of voters favored legal marijuana. It seemed to him that if you lost your initiative, you were at a political dead end. If you went back to the legislature, your opponents could say, with some logic, Forget it; the people have spoken.

As Stroup saw it, to win an initiative, even at best, would require a huge outlay of money on advertising and public education, and that sort of money was not available. Logic demanded a legislative strategy. In a legislature you only had to persuade, say, two hundred men, not millions of voters, and they were politicians who perhaps could be reached by some combination of reason and pressure. In any event, you could keep going back to a legislature, year after year, picking up a few more votes each time, until you had your majority.

The real difference between Stroup and the freaks was their timetables. Stroup was braced for the long haul. The freaks, living on the edge, in despair, in fear of arrest, wanted to gamble everything on one roll of the dice.

Stroup made his first of several trips to visit the BLOSSOM people in the spring of 1972. Wilcox and his friends met him at the airport, and soon they were pressing their best weed on him. That was a ritual he encountered almost everywhere he went, and he was never entirely comfortable with it. It was always possible that his new friends with their "special stash" might attract the police— or, for that matter, might *be* the police. But Stroup always smoked with them. He had to, to prove he was one of them, willing to run risks with them. He and the BLOSSOM people dropped by the water-bed store that was their headquarters, then drove out to their cabin beside a lake near Olympia to spend the night. The cabin had a gorgeous view, but it lacked electricity and running water. The BLOSSOM people, who were mostly vegetarians, lived a simple life there, staying high most of the time. It was a ritual always to have at least one joint in circulation, like an eternal flame.

They talked most of the night. Stroup explained his reservations about an initiative, but the others were unconvinced. Washington is *different*, they insisted; the people are *with* us. Stroup thought Wilcox and the others were decent, well-intentioned people but hopelessly naïve politically. In the long run he didn't think there was anything he could do for them, except possibly give them a little money.

The next morning, Saturday morning, Stroup got up, shaved with cold water, ate pancakes on a deck overlooking the lake, and then they all set off for the state capital, where BLOSSOM was holding a rally in support of its signature-gathering campaign. Two or three hundred students and street people were waiting there on the capitol steps, along with several watchful state troopers.

The two guest speakers at the rally were Stroup and the state legislator who'd introduced the unsuccessful legalization bill. As Wilcox introduced Mr. NORML, the Washington political celebrity who had come to back their efforts, he casually lit a joint, took a hit, and handed it to Stroup. Oh, shit, Stroup thought, I've come to a smoke-in.

Stroup assumed he would eventually be arrested on a marijuana charge. He rationalized that it would be a useful experience. A few days in jail might fire his resolve, and it might also increase his credibility with people like these. Still, he saw no reason to hasten his incarceration by smoking on the capitol steps in front of the state troopers.

But he did. He had no choice. He took a hit, grinned at the crowd, and passed the joint on. And nothing happened. The state troopers were observing that day, not making arrests. Stroup made his speech, tried to raise his audience's political consciousness, tried to make them see themselves as part of a political movement, but he didn't think he had much success.

BLOSSOM never got the 102,000 signatures. A few weeks later many of its people were arrested on marijuana charges, and thereafter their energies were directed at staying out of jail. Stroup was sorry but not surprised. He still thought initiatives were not the way—much less smoke-ins—and a lot of people were going to be busted until they figured that out.

A group like BLOSSOM was no threat to NORML. It was only in Amorphia that Stroup encountered a serious rival. Blair Newman, Amorphia's founder, was a brilliant and creative young man who had grown up in the Washington, D.C., area, the son of a successful real-estate woman. He dropped out of college, grew a beard, discovered hallucinogenic drugs, ran a record store, started an all-rock radio station, and by 1968 was talking about starting some sort of legalization lobby in Washington. When that didn't work out, he moved to San Francisco and began to give very serious thought to the rolling-paper business. As a businessman he saw there was a great deal of money to be made from the marijuana boom, from selling rolling papers and other paraphernalia.

Had Newman stopped there, he would have become a millionaire, as did several other young businessmen who arrived at the same conclusion at about the same time. But Newman was also interested in social change. He believed that marijuana should be legal, and it was his inspiration to create a nonprofit organization that would sell rolling papers and use the proceeds to work for legalization. He believed that smokers, given a choice, would buy his papers, knowing the profits would be used in their own interests, rather than those made by the "profiteering" paper companies.

Newman spent more than a year studying the international cigarette-paper industry, finding $16,000 in start-up money, and negotiating a contract to import papers from Spain. Once here, the papers would be put in his copyrighted Acapulco Gold packets and sold. But there was one remaining question: his credibility. Would the smokers trust him? Or would they think his "Amorphia: The Cannibis Cooperative" was just another rip-off?

Newman's very shrewd solution was to recruit Mike Aldrich to come to San Francisco and be the codirector of Amorphia. Once Aldrich agreed, Amorphia had instant credibility with LeMar's supporters, with people like Ginsberg and Leary and Sinclair, with the readers of *Marijuana Review*, indeed with all the radical left that concerned itself with the marijuana issue.

By late 1970, as Amorphia was starting business—and as, across the continent, Stroup was trying to figure out how to finance NORML—Newman had his long-range plan clearly in view. Amorphia's profits would go for a pro-legalization program that would include a media campaign, a news service, a speakers' bureau, court tests of marijuana laws, and expert witnesses to appear before state legislatures—a program, in short, very much like the one Stroup was proposing to Playboy. The money would be there. Newman estimated that for each 10 percent of the rolling-paper market Amorphia could seize, it would net $150,000 a year. Moreover, when marijuana became legal—by 1980, Newman estimated—Amorphia could produce high-quality marijuana on communal farms, import the best foreign marijuana, and once again use the profits for social change. He estimated that the legal marijuana market would be about $3 billion a year. If Amorphia could control one sixth of that, it would gross $500 million a year, and should have a profit of $30 million a year to put into social action.

It was a bold plan, to say the least, and for a time all went well. By 1972 Amorphia's gross was something like $300,000.

Yet Amorphia was pulled in too many directions at once. It is hard enough to start any new business, and it is almost impossible when the profits, desperately needed for expansion, are given away for political action. It is difficult to start a new business, too, when its key executives spend large amounts of time tripping on psychedelic drugs. Perhaps if Newman's business skill could have been combined with Stroup's political talent, a formidable program might have emerged, but that was not to be. The movement was too small, and their egos were too big, for the two of them to work together. They would soon become bitter enemies, and the only question was which of them would force the other out of the movement.

In September of 1971, when NORML and Amorphia met at the National Student Association convention in Colorado, there was some political back-and-forth: Stroup said he was thinking of starting a California NORML; Newman said he was considering a Washington office. To fight, or to merge? An uneasy compromise was reached by December: Blair Newman moved to Washington, worked out of Stroup's basement office, and called himself codirector of Amorphia and deputy director of NORML. Both Newman and Stroup were convinced they had co-opted the other.

At about that time there was great excitement in California. The idea of a pro-legalization initiative on the 1972 ballot was spreading like wildfire.

In October a forty-year-old Foster City lawyer and law professor named Leo Paoli began to think about an initiative. He called John Kaplan, the law professor who had written *The New Prohibition*. Kaplan agreed to help, and suggested that Paoli also call Mike Aldrich.

There were a series of meetings, and by early December the

reformers had reached their first serious disagreement. Kaplan wanted the initiative to propose full legalization, using the alcohol model, with marijuana sold in liquor stores and with quality control enforced by a new state agency. But there were two serious objections to that. One was legal: State legalization would be in conflict with federal law. The other was ideological: Mike Aldrich wanted no part of a commercial, state-controlled, alcohol-model marijuana system. Amorphia, he declared, would support no initiative that did not permit personal cultivation: free backyard grass.

Amorphia got its way. The reformers rallied behind a simple decriminalization proposal, which said no person in California over the age of eighteen could be punished criminally for growing, processing, transporting, possessing, or using marijuana.

By January of 1972 a new group, CMI, the California Marijuana Initiative, had been created to direct the campaign, and a state coordinator had been found for it. His name was Robert H. A. Ashford, and he was a twenty-seven-year-old, Harvard-trained San Francisco lawyer who had been active in the anti-war movement and was willing to devote himself full time to CMI. Ashford was an intense, charismatic figure, controversial from the first, and he and Stroup and Newman were soon engaged in a bitter three-way rivalry.

Stroup opposed the California initiative when he first heard about it, because he thought it would fail, but when it became clear that Californians were going ahead, he had no choice but to lend his support. Stroup's uncertainty about the initiative was intensified in late December when he returned one morning from a trip to Chicago to find Kelly and Blair Newman waiting at his home. They were nervous, uneasy, bleary-eyed, the way people were when they came down from an MDA trip. Stroup knew what was coming even before they got the words out.

His marriage was already in serious trouble. Kelly had found out about a number of his affairs, and she had told him, "Fine, I still love you, but it's an open marriage now. You can have your freedom, and I'll have mine, too." Stroup, preoccupied with his work, had not taken her seriously, but now, as she confessed that she and Newman had tripped on MDA and spent the night together, he was forced to. He might have used the occasion to reflect on his shortcomings as a husband, or her needs as a wife; instead he flew into a rage, threw

Newman out of his house, and soon moved out himself, into a small room in NORML's new row house on Twenty-second Street, a room he painted blood red, as if to reflect his violent state of mind.

The breakup of the marriage was long and painful. For more than a year they would separate, then try again, for the sake of their daughter, and because Stroup at some level still believed in marriage and was guilt-ridden at his failure. But he was emotionally incapable of either accepting sexual freedom in his wife or denying it to himself. Nor was there any possibility that he would cut back on his work or his travels. NORML was his life, and his family came second; there was nothing he could do about it. One irony of the situation was that drugs, particularly MDA, helped their marriage, at least as far as Kelly was concerned. She had found that when they were tripping, Keith would relax, would lose the hostility he seemed to feel for her, would be sensitive and loving. Once, when they were separated and she'd been seeing other men, he came and spent Christmas with her and they tripped, and they had a wonderful time. He told her, "Kelly, I can handle it intellectually, but I can't handle it emotionally." That summed up the problem. What she saw as equality he saw as a deliberate attempt to torture him in the one way that could cause him the most pain.

Stroup's unhappiness after his separation was made worse because he had almost no communication with his parents. Later that year, stoned, Stroup told a writer, "I love this job, but it hasn't been all fun. When I go home, my parents don't want to talk about my work. They think it's somehow illegal. I tell them, 'Don't be ashamed of me. I think I'm doing a moral thing. You don't have to agree with me, but I wish you'd just think I'm a nice person who's doing something he believes in.' "

After Stroup threw Newman out of his home, it was open warfare between NORML and Amorphia. Stroup started telling people that Amorphia was the "biggest setback to marijuana reform since Harry Anslinger." Newman fired back with an article, published in many underground newspapers, entitled "The Playboy Corporation vs. the People," which charged that Stroup was Playboy's front man in a scheme to take over the legal marijuana market.

That was the state of the reform movement as spring of 1972 arrived: CMI was struggling to collect half a million signatures for its initiative, and Stroup and Newman were trying to destroy one another. Then, on March 22, something of great importance to them all occurred back in Washington: The Marijuana Commission issued its report.

The thirteen-member commission, aided by a large staff, had spent a year preparing its report on marijuana. It had held three sets of public hearings, and countless private meetings with public officials and with private citizens, including one group of respectable Americans, doctors and lawyers, who were marijuana smokers. Members of the commission had traveled to many foreign nations to talk to scientists and political leaders. The commission had carried out major public-opinion surveys to determine the number of people who smoked and national attitudes toward smoking. It was the most exhaustive study of marijuana ever conducted in the United States, perhaps in the world, and the commissioners were citizens above suspicion. Appointed by Richard Nixon, they included two U.S. senators, two U.S. representatives, a Republican governor, and various public-health officials, scientists, and law-enforcement officials.

But on March 22, to the surprise of almost everyone, including themselves and the president who appointed them, this eminently respectable group reported to Nixon and to the nation that marijuana, smoked in moderation, is in effect harmless and that its private use should be legal and even its public use punished not by jail but only by a fine.

Here, to be precise, is what the commission said about the effects of marijuana.

There is no evidence that experimental or intermittent use of marihuana causes physical or psychological harm. The risk lies instead in the heavy, long-term use of the drug, particularly of the most potent preparations.

Marihuana does not lead to physical dependency. No torturous withdrawal symptoms follow the sudden cessation of chronic, heavy use. Some evidence indicates that heavy, long-term users may develop a psychological dependence on the drug.

The immediate effects of marihuana intoxication on the individual's organs or bodily functions are transient and have little or no

permanent effect. However, there is a definite loss of some
psychomotor control and a temporary impairment of time and
space perceptions.

No brain damage has been documented relating to marihuana
use, in contrast with the well-established damage of chronic
alcoholism.

A careful search of literature and testimony by health officials
has not revealed a single human fatality in the United States
proven to have resulted solely from the use of marihuana.

On the basis of these scientific findings, the commission made
specific recommendations for federal marijuana policy. Stripped of the
legal jargon, they were these:

—Possession or use of marijuana in private would "no longer be
an offense," which in effect meant it would be legal.
—The private distribution of small amounts of marijuana for no
profit or "insignificant remuneration" would be legal.
—Possession of up to an ounce of marijuana in public would be
legal, although the marijuana could be confiscated.
—The possession of more than an ounce of marijuana in public
would be punishable by a fine of up to $100, as would its public
use.
—Public distribution of small amounts for no profit would also be
punishable by a fine of up to $100.
—To grow or sell marijuana for profit would remain criminal,
felony offenses.

The commission thus advocated a policy toward marijuana that went
by the mind-numbing name of "decriminalization," and that they
presented as a policy of official "discouragement," but the fact
remained that as far as the use of marijuana was concerned, it came
very close to legalization. Just how this supposedly conservative panel
came up with such a radical proposal became a matter of speculation.
(Some years later, at the prison farm where he was confined, former
attorney general John Mitchell would grumble to other, pro-drug
inmates that he'd always known Raymond Shafer was too wishy-
washy to run that commission.) One of the more liberal members of the
commission would later say in an interview:

We operated under unusual circumstances. Law-enforcement
people were very cooperative with us, because we were per-

ceived as conservative. They were very candid about how they practiced selective enforcement. We talked to "hanging judges" who were quite proud of throwing the book at marijuana smokers. We talked to federal officials who admitted they'd lied about marijuana for years—it had been official policy to lie. Some of us were impressed by the secret meetings we had with successful people, doctors and lawyers, who were smokers—they obviously didn't belong in jail. After a while it became very hard to maintain the old myths. Of course, some of us had children who smoked.

Another factor was simply how damn much money we had. We could do anything we wanted, go anywhere we wanted. If someone said there was evidence of brain damage among smokers in Morocco, we'd go take a look. Some of us visited as many as thirty countries, and time after time the same thing would happen. We would talk to the government officials and they would give us the official line: marijuana use is very serious, we are concerned about it, we want to work with your government to stamp it out. Then, that night, we'd go out drinking with them, and they'd tell us the truth: they thought marijuana was harmless, but the Nixon administration wanted a hard line and they feared economic reprisals if they didn't go along. It all came down to money. We saw so much corruption. In one country, the king's brother had the hashish concession. We went to some countries where they would let the Americans out of prison before we arrived, and to others where they wouldn't let us see the dungeons where they kept them. By the time it was all over, and we'd seen all we had seen, there was really not much debate. No one could argue that people should go to jail for smoking marijuana.

As is often the case with high-level commissions, the staff had no small role in the Marijuana Commission's conclusion. The two key staff members were Michael Sonnenreich, the staff director, and Richard Bonnie, a University of Virginia law professor who worked closely with Sonnenreich in drafting the commission report. Bonnie had in fact published an article in the *University of Virginia Law Review* in 1970 in which he called for decriminalization of possession of four ounces or less of marijuana. One member of the staff said, "Bonnie was always for decriminalization, and Sonnenreich reached that conclusion—he was an honest man, despite his reputation as a Nixon loyalist—and they simply had to mold the concensus, being very careful how they presented the issues to the commissioners, until the commissioners did what they wanted them to do."

In the course of its report the Marijuana Commission dismissed many of the reefer-madness myths of the past: that marijuana was addictive, that it led to violence, and that it led to heroin and other hard drugs. Of the latter, the so-called "stepping stone" theory, the commission said, "The fact should be emphasized that the overwhelming majority of marihuana users do not progress to other drugs. They either remain with marihuana or forsake its use in favor of alcohol. . . . This so-called stepping-stone theory first received widespread acceptance in 1951 as a result of testimony at Congressional hearings. . . . When the voluminous testimony given at these hearings is seriously examined, no verification is found of a causal relationship between marihuana use and subsequent heroin use." What the commission found is that peer-group pressure is the greatest factor on what drugs people use.

The commission's proposed decriminalization policy, while familiar to people in the drug field, was a new idea to the nation at large. One of the first public figures to respond to it was President Nixon. He had appointed the commission and asked them for a national marijuana policy. They had responded with findings and recommendations that if ahead of their time politically were nonetheless bold and sophisticated. The decriminalization concept was an attempt to find a compromise between two powerful forces: widespread opposition to marijuana use on the one hand and, on the other, a growing sense that to jail people for smoking was a punishment that far exceeded the crime.

The issuance of the Marijuana Commission report was a crucial moment for American drug policy. Another president might have endorsed the report, supported it with the power and prestige of his office, reversed federal policy, and set off a wave of legal reform in states across the nation. Had that happened, there might have been decriminalization, if not outright legalization, in all of America by 1980. It was not inconceivable that even Nixon might have accepted the commission's report: If he could climax a lifetime of zealous anti-communism by going to China to embrace Chairman Mao, he might advocate not putting people in jail for smoking marijuana.

But it was not to be. Two days after the report was issued Nixon told a news conference, "I oppose the legalization of marijuana and that includes sale, possession, and use. I do not believe you can have effective criminal justice based on a philosophy that something is half-legal and half-illegal."

By saying he opposed the legalization of marijuana, Nixon simply ignored the decriminalization concept that the commission hoped could bring a truce in the nation's marijuana war. The commission, struggling with a hard social issue, and Nixon, content to play election-year politics with the issue, were not speaking the same language.

While Nixon was rejecting his commission's recommendations, NORML was embracing them. At first the report had set off a flurry of debate within the pot lobby. Some of Stroup's advisers, notably Harvard's Dr. Grinspoon, wanted to reject the decriminalization concept. It was not intellectually honest, they said: If marijuana was indeed harmless, it should be legal. These purists felt the commission should have called for legalization and put forth a plan for its implementation.

Stroup argued that NORML should embrace decriminalization as a necessary step toward legalization, and this became NORML's official position, although it criticized the commission on some secondary issues, particularly the idea that marijuana use might prove to be a fad. It was one of Stroup's most important decisions. The Marijuana Commission soon went out of business, and its recommendations would soon have been gathering dust had it not been for NORML. Instead, as Stroup and other reformers testified before state legislatures across America, they made the Marijuana Commission's report their Bible. They praised the parts of it that were useful to them (the scientific findings and the no-jail recommendation) and ignored the parts that were not useful (the idea of discouragement). Two years later when the anti-marijuana forces launched a major counteroffensive, they rather lamely complained that the Marijuana Commission's report had been "misinterpreted," which was another way of saying they had been outfoxed.

It was a busy summer for Stroup. In July he, his wife, his daughter, and Schott piled into Stroup's VW van and drove to Miami Beach for the 1972 Democratic Convention. In a sense there was not much for them to do there: McGovern was going to be the nominee, and he was on record as favoring decriminalization. (Indeed, the eventual

McGovern-Shriver ticket was what Stroup called a "double-bust"
ticket, in that both candidates had children who had been arrested on
marijuana charges.) What the NORML delegation was mainly doing was
"working the Left"—getting to know other reform groups, such as the
farm workers, the gays, the feminists, the Yippies, and so on. Stroup
spent a part of each day in the People's Park, often hanging out at the
Pot Tree, where the Yippies smoked and sold dope. It was there that
he met Tom Forcade, the Yippie leader who would later become his
close friend.

The next month, August, NORML held the first People's Pot
Conference at the St. Mark's Episcopal Church on Capitol Hill. About
three hundred delegates came from thirty-six states, and NORML had
put together an impressive program for them. An economics professor
led a discussion of legalization. Dr. Grinspoon gave a biting critique
of the Marijuana Commission report, calling it "half a loaf," but
Rep. James Scheuer replied that in light of the political realities,
the report was "a minor political miracle." An attorney reported
on a lawsuit NORML had brought to force the government to end
or reduce marijuana penalties. John Sinclair and Lee Otis Johnson,
two well-known political activists who had been imprisoned on
marijuana charges and had recently been released from prison,
led a discussion of the use of marijuana laws against political dis-
senters.

It was a good program, but Stroup wasn't sure all the delegates
were making the most of it. Many of them seemed mainly interested in
sitting out under the trees and getting high. On the last day of the
conference Stroup was standing outside the church talking to Ed
Miller, a bearded, balding disc jockey from Fort Worth. As they
talked, Miller started the engine on his car, produced a small bag of
marijuana, and calmly raised the hood of his car and put the bag on the
engine. The idea was that the heat of the engine would dry the grass.
He never got that far, however, because two plainclothes policemen
appeared and put him under arrest. A crowd gathered, and as the
cops led the disc jockey away, John Sinclair was calling for everyone to storm the police station to demand Miller's release. Stroup
insisted he would go alone to bail Miller out. Stroup got his way,
barely, and the People's Pot Conference broke up with that final

*   *   *

confrontation between the revolutionaries and the reformers.

Back in California a massive effort was under way on behalf of the marijuana initiative. It was hampered, however, by constant infighting between CMI, Amorphia, and NORML.

The situation improved somewhat after May 1, when a tall, neatly dressed, twenty-eight-year-old Republican named Gordon Brownell became CMI's statewide political coordinator. Brownell was to remain a central figure in the reform movement throughout the decade, and he was, with the possible exception of Stroup, its most politically sophisticated leader.

Gordon Brownell's father worked for thirty-five years as a sales representative for the American Can Company. Gordon lived most of his first fourteen years in Westfield, New Jersey, and later graduated from high school in Cape Elizabeth, Maine. He got his undergraduate degree from Colgate and his law degree from Fordham, where he was vice-president of his class. He was always the most conservative member of his family; his parents were Baptist and Republican, but they leaned toward the Eastern, liberal wing of their party. Gordon, by contrast, was a fervent Goldwater supporter in 1964. He worked on the Nixon campaign in New York in 1968 and was rewarded with a job at the White House as an assistant to Harry Dent, the South Carolinian who was a top Nixon political adviser.

In May of 1970, anxious for more political experience, Brownell became an assistant to the director of the Reagan reelection campaign, but before the Reagan campaign ended, Brownell had been turned on by drugs and turned off by the Reagan-Nixon brand of politics.

Brownell had smoked marijuana while in law school, as did most of his classmates. He didn't smoke during his year in the Nixon White House; but he did smoke with other young Reagan campaign workers. His turning point came when he began using mescaline, a drug that was, for him, truly mind-expanding. He was introduced to the drug by a young woman, also a worker in the Reagan campaign, with whom he had fallen in love. Their first mescaline trip together was at the Grand Canyon—the most stunning experience of his life.

Reagan's victory was not in doubt, and in mid-October, three weeks before the election, Brownell and the young woman drove for a weekend at the Grand Canyon—her first visit, his second. On Saturday morning they drove around the rim of the canyon, taking in its spectacular vistas, and in the afternoon they returned to their campsite, built a fire, and took mescaline. As the mescaline took effect, Brownell had a sense of flying, soaring above the canyon, becoming one with its vast beauty. He could not have said who he was. It was an ego-shattering experience; he was one with the universe. For a time it seemed that both he and the woman were outside their bodies and had achieved a spiritual and psychic union that was more powerful and more beautiful than any emotion he had ever known or imagined. He had a sense of being born anew, and in fact Gordon Brownell's life would never be the same again.

Soon, the use of marijuana and of psychedelic drugs helped him confront the great contradiction in his life: that the politicians he was working for regarded him and his closest friends, including the woman he loved, as criminals because they used drugs.

"I look upon the hallucinogenic drugs as an enlightening, illuminating experience," Brownell said later. "They made me see the contradiction between my work for Reagan and my belief in individual freedom. I was working for people who pretended to believe in individual freedom, but they didn't when it came to cultures they disapproved of. Up until then I'd been very much the upwardly mobile young man on the make. My drug experience totally redirected me, into the direction I've been going ever since. It was an eye-opening, mind-opening experience; if it wasn't for the drugs, I might have stayed on the same path forever. I came out of it with a clear sense of what I wanted for myself. I didn't want to spend the next twenty-five years working for a dying generation. Once I realized that, I felt a great sense of freedom. Of course, it was a painful and confusing time for me, because I had to break off personal and political relationships with people I'd been close to, and I couldn't explain it, because it would have only confirmed their view that drugs ruined people's lives. But I saw myself differently.

"The young woman crystallized for me that it was people like her who were most important to me, not the politicians who called us criminals. I thought the Republican party had blown the youth vote over the war, and I saw the marijuana issue as a way to win back that vote, and also to be true to a libertarian, small-government philosophy. I saw the older Republicans choosing to ignore reality. I was present once when Reagan and his advisers talked about marijuana. It was the first time I saw that the emperor had no clothes. I thought, These people don't know what the fuck they're talking about. That was when I started to question the whole thing. If they didn't understand the marijuana issue, what did they understand?"

After Reagan's reelection, Brownell moved to the village of Anchor Bay, some 120 miles north of San Francisco. He spent about nine months working on a novel called "Jessica's Story," about drugs and the young woman he had loved. In the fall of 1971, with his money running out and his novel unpublished, he accepted an offer from his friend Kevin Phillips, the conservative writer, to come to Washington for four months and help him start a newsletter. One day in September he saw an item about NORML in the Washington *Star*. He realized immediately what he wanted to do—to use his political skill on behalf of drug-law reform—and he quickly called Stroup.

Brownell soon became close to Stroup, Schott, and Dubois. He wanted a job with NORML, but Stroup didn't have a place for him. Brownell also met Blair Newman that winter, during Newman's brief stay at NORML, and the following spring, as CMI got under way, Newman invited Brownell to come to work for Amorphia, for $125 a week, and be assigned full time to CMI.

That suited Brownell, and one evening in the early spring of 1972 he went by Stroup's house to break the news. "He blew up," Brownell recalls. "He viewed it as me going over to the enemy. He literally threw me out of his house when I told him, but the next morning he called to apologize."

Brownell gave CMI an immediate boost. He was the only person in the operation with experience running a statewide political campaign. Moreover, the big, soft-spoken Brownell was able to mediate between the large egos of Stroup, Newman, and Aldrich. He organized a massive signature-gathering effort outside the polling places on June 6, primary day, with some 2000 CMI volunteers assigned to key precincts. The effort was successful: By the June 19 deadline CMI had gathered 522,000 signatures, and the marijuana initiative was on the November ballot.

In the fall CMI had two main activities: voter registration, since its natural supporters were people who didn't always vote; and winning whatever free publicity it could for the issue.

There were certain types of standard publicity available to them.

Gordon Brownell, as a Reaganite turned pot activist, could give interviews, and CMI staged several news conferences in which scientists spoke in favor of reform. But the greatest amount of publicity generated on behalf of CMI came from the antics of one Keith Lampe, who held the honorary title of entertainment director of Amorphia, and had previously been the Yippies' publicity director. A one-time correspondent for the Hearst newspapers before he turned on, dropped out, and became a founder of the Yippies, Lampe in 1972 was forty years old, a slender, bespectacled man with a ponytail and a long, scraggly black beard. Throughout the summer and fall, Lampe masterminded a series of media happenings that generated publicity for the cause, although the publicity was too exotic to please some of CMI's more staid supporters. There was, for example, the stoned Ping-Pong game, in which Lampe and an artist named Arthur Okamara played a match high on marijuana. Another of Lampe's creations was Jocks for Joynts. Dave Meggyesy, former NFL star linebacker, was chairman of the Jocks, whose goal was to demonstrate that marijuana enhanced, rather than impaired, their athletic abilities. At one point the Jocks challenged an anti-marijuana organization to a softball game, the Jocks to play stoned; the anti-pot forces declined, and the Jocks claimed a great moral victory.

Lampe was also the genius behind Mothers for Marijuana and Grannies for Grass. As he saw it, he was putting a friendly face on the issue, showing that smokers were not all sinister hippies but also mothers, grandmothers, people who liked Ping-Pong and softball. Not everyone agreed. Lampe's antics enabled Stroup to grumble that CMI was a bunch of freaks who wanted to settle a serious issue in a softball game.

But the real issue was never softball; it was money and control of the legalization movement. Stroup, as he contemplated CMI, had mostly negative feelings. In the first place, he didn't think the initiative could pass, and he was too wedded to a legislative strategy to grant any value in a defeat. Moreover, he had to consider what a CMI victory in California would mean to him. Almost certainly, if the initiative won, Bob Ashford, the CMI director, would (with some justice) proclaim himself the national leader of the reform movement and would set out to direct initiatives in other states. If that happened, NORML might be out of business.

The crunch came in July when Ashford sent the Playboy Foundation an impressive fifty-page request for $80,000 to help finance CMI's fall campaign. Stroup, learning of this, opposed it every way he could. His power came from having exclusive access to Playboy's money, and he wasn't about to share that money with anyone. CMI's request was turned down, and its members were furious at Stroup. In an effort to ease the situation Stroup sent the likable Guy Archer from New York to California with a copy of the movie *Reefer Madness*. Stroup had discovered that spring that the film was in the public domain, and he bought a copy from the Library of Congress for $297. It was the bargain of the year. NORML used it for fund-raising, because 1970s smokers found hilarious its portrait of young people driven to crime and madness by a single reefer. Archer raced up and down California, showing the film on college campuses, asking a dollar donation for admission, and he raised $16,000 for CMI, enough to protect Stroup from charges that he had done nothing for the California Initiative. Indeed, he had not done nothing, only as little as possible.

On election day the initiative won a third of the votes—33.47 percent, or 2,733,120 votes. It received 51.26 percent of the votes in San Francisco County, 71.25 percent in Berkeley, and ran ahead of McGovern in four counties. CMI immediately claimed a moral victory. Stroup, in Washington, grumbled that anytime you lose by two to one, you haven't done very damn well.

CMI was closer to the truth, as Stroup would in time concede. There is a certain relativity in politics. For the Democratic candidate for president to get 40 percent of the vote is a disaster, but for a poorly financed proposal for what amounted to legal marijuana to get a third of California's votes was certainly a victory. California politicians, considering the CMI vote, and the thousands of volunteers who worked for CMI had to ask themselves what would happen if all that energy was directed for—or against—them. They would realize, too, that time was on the marijuana movement's side—that 33 percent would inevitably become 51 percent, as more and more people smoked.

Still, as 1972 came mercifully to a close, the immediate reality was that CMI had lost, the Marijuana Commission report had caused no dramatic turnabout in national opinion, and Richard Nixon had been overwhelmingly reelected. The prospects for the reform movements, to put it mildly, were not bright.

6

January 20, 1973, was a cold, overcast, gloomy day in Washington, a dismal day for all those who opposed Richard Nixon. At noon Nixon took the oath of office for the second time and then led a heavily guarded motorcade back down Pennsylvania Avenue to the White House. A few blocks away, Keith Stroup and his NORML colleagues were among the tens of thousands chanting, dope-smoking, anti-war, anti-Nixon demonstrators who marched in a "counterinaugural" parade that culminated with defiant rhetoric at the Washington Monument.

One of Stroup's companions that morning was his friend Joe Sharp, the red-haired drug dealer who had turned him on to marijuana three years earlier and had since gone underground, a fugitive from a marijuana charge in Virginia. Joe Sharp's appearance was somehow symbolic of the uncertain future that NORML and all the political left faced that gloomy Saturday morning. Stroup and his friends were not fugitives, but their immediate prospects did not seem a great deal brighter than Joe Sharp's.

The election had proved that the political center was further to the right than most liberals had been willing to admit. The revolution wasn't coming. The reality was Nixon, and the only hope for reform was a straight, middle-class approach. For Stroup, Schott, and others at NORML it was a time to stop tripping, to cut their hair, to watch their rhetoric, to mind their manners. Bob Dylan had said it years before: You don't need a weatherman to know which way the wind blows.

Still, two winds were blowing as the new year began. Large forces were at work, poised for confrontation. On the one hand, the forces of reform were gathering momentum. The Marijuana Commission's report was a rallying point not only for smokers but for many lawyers, scientists, parents, politicians, and civil and religious leaders who were impressed by its conclusions. Yet, in opposition, there remained the seemingly immovable object of Richard Nixon, politically supreme and unyieldingly opposed to reform.

It was war. Marijuana arrests had risen year after year as the conflict escalated; in 1973 they would exceed 420,000. It was a war and as in the one in Vietnam, new weapons were constantly being introduced. The anti-skyjacking searches at the nation's airports were resulting in twice as many arrests for marijuana as for weapons, and narcotics agents were starting to use police dogs to sniff out marijuana in the nation's high schools. The newly-formed Drug Enforcement Administration was Washington's fastest-growing agency; it had an army, a navy, an air force (as, increasingly, did the nation's drug smugglers). As this zealous new bureaucracy was challenged by the reformers, it fought back, like any bureaucracy, with more arrests, more raids, higher body counts.

One night in April of 1973, Herbert Joseph Giglotto, a boilermaker, and his wife, Louise, were asleep in their suburban house in Collins-ville, Illinois, when armed men broke into their bedroom. Giglotto later recalled, "I got out of bed; I took about three steps, looked down the hall, and I saw men running up the hall dressed like hippies with pistols, yelling and screeching. I turned to my wife. 'God, honey, we're dead.'" The intruders threw Giglotto down on his bed, held a loaded gun to his head, tore the house apart, and warned, "You're going to die unless you tell us where the stuff is." Then the leader of the raiders said, "We've made a mistake," and the men departed.

The raiders were from ODALE, the Office of Drug Abuse Law Enforcement, a special White House–directed agency that Richard

Nixon created when he could not prod other federal agencies to enforce the drug laws as vigorously as he desired. In their zeal ODALE's warrantless raiders often raided the wrong houses. In the aftermath of the Giglotto raid the New York *Times* reported there had been hundreds of similar raids across America, during which at least three innocent citizens were killed. (A jury later acquitted the men who terrorized the Giglottos, apparently because they felt such errors were justified in the name of vigorous law enforcement.)

Nixon's concern about drug-law enforcement was largely political. Having run for president in 1968 on a law-and-order platform, Nixon believed he needed tangible proof of an anti-crime crusade to be reelected in 1972. Unfortunately, the federal government has very little crime-fighting responsibility. Nixon therefore looked to drug control as an area in which the federal government had some authority and one, also, that would be politically popular. One of the masterminds of Nixon's war on drugs was the ineffable G. Gordon Liddy, whose projects included Operation Intercept, in September of 1969, wherein tens of thousands of tourists were searched at the Mexican border in a crackdown on smuggling. Few drugs were found, and thousands of tourists were forced to sit in the hot sun for up to six hours, but Liddy was not discouraged. Another of his pet projects was ODALE, a two-fisted, gun-toting outfit, undeterred by formalities such as search warrants.

Eventually, after a congressional investigation into its abuses, ODALE as such was disbanded, but it set the tone for the Nixon administration's attitude toward drugs and drug users: all-out, unconditional war. The Supreme Court, venturing onto the field of battle, sided with Nixon's law-and-order forces. In a six-to-three decision it upheld the power of police to search people who had been stopped for minor traffic violations. One of the cases involved a man who was stopped for driving without a license and was found to possess several marijuana cigarettes. Justices Douglas, Marshall, and Brennan dissented, calling the decision a betrayal of the Constitution.

As in all wars, it became increasingly hard for the civilian populace to remain unaligned. As more and more people were arrested, an increasing number of individuals and groups felt obliged to take a stand. Indeed, such glimmers of hope as the reformers saw in the early months of 1973 had mainly to do with the growing number of voices calling for reform. The National Education Association, the National

Council for Churches, and the Central Conference for American Rabbis, for example, all called for decriminalization. The two most important endorsements, however, came from Consumers' Union and the American Bar Association.

Consumers' Union's 632-page report, "Licit and Illicit Drugs," called for the immediate decriminalization, and eventual legalization, of marijuana. As Stroup saw it, the CU report had bitten the political bullet that the Marijuana Commission had avoided. The commission clung to the idea that marijuana use might fade away, and therefore saw decriminalization as the end of reform, but CU declared that marijuana was here to stay and there should therefore be "an orderly system of legal distribution and licit use."

The ABA's call for decriminalization at its 1973 meeting in Washington was the result of several factors, one of which was an intensive lobbying effort by NORML. Frank Fioramonti, NORML's legislative counsel and a member of the ABA's committee on alcoholism and drug reform, managed to get a decriminalization resolution on the agenda for the annual meeting. He brought in a dozen young lawyers to lobby actively among the several hundred delegates to the convention. This effort, plus support for decriminalization by the ABA's president-elect, Chesterfield Smith, and its past president, Whitney North Seymour, was enough to pass the resolution by a vote of 122 to 70. The vote came despite the argument of one lawyer, who said he spoke for the U.S. Army's judge advocate's office, that marijuana had been responsible for untold violence by drug-crazed GIs in Vietnam.

The ABA endorsement was of particular importance because of its well-known conservatism and its prestige among lawyers and state legislators. Another endorsement from the right came when William F. Buckley, Jr., put himself and his *National Review* on record in favor of decriminalization. Buckley's conversion came about because of the efforts of a young Texan named Richard Cowan, who showed up at NORML's door one day in 1972 and told Stroup he was a Yale graduate, a conservative, an aspiring writer, and a smoker who wanted to do something for reform.

Cowan was short-haired and neatly dressed, not the typical NORML volunteer, and Stroup was suspicious: It was always possible he was a narc. But, as with other volunteers, he gave him a menial job, to see if he really wanted to work. Cowan's job was to read and respond to the prison letters that came in daily. Soon after he started, Cowan stumbled into Stroup's office in tears, overcome by the prisoners' stories. Well, Stroup thought, if he's a narc, he's a soft-hearted one.

Cowan in time reported that he was personally close to Bill Buckley and was working on a pro-marijuana piece for the *National Review*. Stroup remained skeptical, but one day that winter Cowan rushed into his office with the journal, which had a cover picture of a dozen young people being booked on marijuana charges and a headline announcing that the time for marijuana-law reform had come. Buckley had not only printed Cowan's article but had added his own editorial declaring that he agreed entirely with Cowan that there was no justification for jailing marijuana smokers. Buckley went on to confess that he had himself tried marijuana, but only, he explained, on his sailboat, outside the three-mile territorial limit, where U.S. laws did not apply. He added, "To tell the truth, marijuana didn't do a thing for me."

The Buckley-Cowan statement soon moved conservative columnist James J. Kilpatrick to join the call for decriminalization and to declare, "I don't give a hoot about marijuana, but I care about freedom!" To both Buckley and Kilpatrick the marijuana issue turned on the question of personal freedom, the right of the individual to be left alone by big government, and they had the intellectual honesty to take a position they knew would offend many of their conservative followers.

Buckley's conversion to decriminalization contributed indirectly to an extremely important alliance that Stroup formed in 1973. Soon after Buckley spoke out, he decided to devote one of his *Firing Line* television programs to the marijuana issue. Having taken a controversial stand, Buckley wanted to justify it to his fellow conservatives, and for his star witness he chose Dr. Thomas Bryant, the handsome and articulate president of a new, eminently respectable private institution called the Drug Abuse Council.

The Drug Abuse Council was created in 1971 by the Ford Foundation, which is both extremely rich and cautiously liberal. (It was, in effect, the liberal establishment's government in exile during the Nixon years.) This action reflected the Ford Foundation's concern about the nation's ever-widening drug-abuse problem—heroin in the slums, tranquilizers in the suburbs, marijuana and hallucinogens on the campuses—and its fear that the Nixon administration would react to the problem only with negative, law-and-order programs. The Drug Abuse Council was to be a specialized think tank, an independent voice evaluating drug programs and recommending public policy. Because of political pressures, law-enforcement officials had always dominated government drug policy, and moderates had been afraid to speak out. The Drug Abuse Council was intended to correct this imbalance.

As head of the council the Ford Foundation picked Tom Bryant, who was in his early forties and had degrees in both law and medicine and experience in the federal anti-poverty program. It also saddled him with an ultraconservative board of directors, one that one scientist said "didn't know marijuana from heroin, but knew that it didn't want to be embarrassed." At first Bryant moved carefully, sponsoring fellowships and academic studies, but he was under pressure from his young, liberal staff to do more on the marijuana issue, and that was his own instinct as well.

Then came the invitation for Tom Bryant to discuss marijuana on William Buckley's television show. Bryant was glad to accept, for it was the kind of exposure that was good for him and for the council. But on the afternoon of December 20, the day before he was to tape the Buckley show, Bryant became alarmed. He wasn't sure he knew enough about all the legal, medical, and political complexities of the marijuana issue to discuss it for a half hour on television. His staff had brought him scores of books, memos, and policy papers on marijuana —far too many to do him any good. He needed a briefing from an expert, and one of his project officers, a young woman named Jane Silver, had an idea: Why didn't they ask Keith Stroup to come in and brief Bryant?

At that point Stroup knew Bryant only casually. They were very different types: the freewheeling pot lobbyist and the cautious foundation executive. But Stroup had already become friendly with several members of Bryant's staff, including Jane Silver; Bob Carr, a forty-year-old former college professor who was the council's top writer; and Mathea Falco, a lawyer and Senate aide who would later have a top drug policy job in the Carter administration.

Silver called Stroup, who raced the six blocks from NORML's shabby row house on M Street to the Drug Abuse Council's elegant suite of offices in the high-rent district of L Street and gave Bryant an intensive three-hour briefing. The next day Bryant taped the Buckley program, and when it was shown, in early January, everyone agreed he had done very well. Thus was born the NORML–Drug Abuse Council alliance.

The incident underscored a basic fact about the drug-policy field in those days: If you wanted to deal with the marijuana issue, you had to deal with Stroup, because he simply knew more about it than anyone else. In Washington, as elsewhere, knowledge is power. Traditionally in Washington there is some obscure congressional aide or bureaucrat who has become the world's leading expert on any given issue, so his boss can appear wise on that issue when the need arises. But since no such government expert existed on the marijuana issue, that role fell to Stroup by default.

In mid-1973 Bryant joined NORML's advisory board and thus lent his and the Ford Foundation's prestige and credibility to the dope lobby. He also made Stroup a $200-a-month consultant to the council—not an insignificant amount of money to Stroup in those days. Most important, the council began giving grants of up to $30,000 a year to NORML's "nonpolitical" spinoff, the Center for the Study of Non-Medical Drug use. Money given to the center was used for such "nonpolitical" purposes as lawsuits, publishing costs, and the like, which of course freed other NORML money for its political activities. Indirectly, the council was subsidizing NORML's political and legislative program, helping NORML do things that the council thought needed doing but that it legally could not do.

The alliance benefited both parties. It gave NORML money, credibility, and increased access to the ultrarespectable scientists and policy makers who clustered around the council. For Bryant, alliance with NORML was a move to the left. As Stroup saw it, NORML had, in effect, become the political arm of the Drug Abuse Council. It was a delicate arrangement, given the tax laws and the Ford Foundation's sensitivity to criticism that it was subsidizing liberal political causes, but it was one that for several years was crucial to NORML's success.

NORML had a flurry of publicity in January of 1973, first a news story in the Washington papers, then a major article in *The New York Times Magazine*. The first came about when Stroup, Schott, and Dinah Trachtman invaded the New Senate Office Building one Monday afternoon carrying large cardboard boxes that contained several hundred small plastic bags of a chopped-up, greenish-brown substance that looked very much like marijuana.

Guards stopped Stroup and company at the door and insisted on inspecting the boxes. When the guards spied the mysterious weed, they said the visitors could not enter without first getting approval from higher authority.

Stroup put on a great show of indignation, insisting that he and his friends had a constitutional right to enter, that they were peacefully petitioning their elected representatives. The guards were unimpressed, and some pushing, shoving, and shouting ensued. The Stroup whispered to Dinah to find a phone and call the newspapers, and he and Schott took off down the corridor with the guards in hot pursuit. They eventually took refuge in Sen. Charles Percy's office, where Stuart Statler, their friend from the Product Safety Commission, was working.

When this Keystone Kops scene had run its course, reason prevailed, and the NORML forces were permitted to deliver a bag to each member of Congress. An attached letter explained what it was all about:

Dear Congressman:
THE ENCLOSED BAGGIE DOES NOT CONTAIN MARIJUANA! Actually, it contains tobacco, a legal but potentially more harmful drug. If the contents were marijuana, you would be subject to criminal arrest! . . .

The letter went on to give some facts from the Marijuana Commission's report and to urge support of the Hughes-Javits-Koch decriminalization bill. That bill never got anywhere, but Stroup's bag stunt did get NORML some free publicity. His knock at tobacco also inspired a North Carolina congressman to demand a chemical analysis of the substance in the bags, to make sure it really wasn't marijuana after all.

The *Times Magazine* article, which appeared on January 21, dealt in part with a trip Stroup had made to Texas the previous month.

Texas was then one of two states in the Union (Rhode Island was the other) where simple possession of marijuana was a felony, punishable by up to life imprisonment. Nor were the Texas laws an idle threat. There were some seven hundred young men in Texas prisons for simple possession of marijuana, serving average sentences of about ten years. Thirty had sentences of thirty years or more, and thirteen had been sentenced to life. Half of the seven hundred marijuana prisoners were first offenders, and a third were younger than twenty-two.

In other states reformers were trying to reduce marijuana penalties from a misdemeanor to a civil fine—decriminalization—but in Texas the effort was still to reduce the penalty for possession from a felony to a misdemeanor. A bill to do that had failed in 1972, and a new bill was to be introduced early in 1973. It was to support that bill that Stroup made his trip to Austin, the state capital.

Stroup's visit to Texas was fairly typical of his work in many states at that point. He had four target groups: the legislature, the media, NORML supporters, and prisoners in the state prison.

The first night, he met with Steve Simon, NORML's Texas coordinator, and eight or ten other supporters. They sat around someone's apartment smoking and talking about what was happening in Texas and elsewhere. Simon had written NORML a year earlier, angry about the use of lie detectors by the state government to determine if job applicants smoked marijuana; he had gone on to be one of NORML's most active coordinators.

The next day, Stroup met with two young men who were central to the reform effort in Texas: Griffin Smith, a lawyer and legislative aide, and Ron Waters, a modish, twenty-two-year-old legislator from Houston who had been elected on a pro-marijuana platform. (Asked if he smoked, Waters replied smoothly, "That's irrelevant.") To these two reformers Stroup was valuable as a source of information on strategies in other states, and as a source of expert witnesses. Anyone who was trying to reform the marijuana laws in Texas needed all the help he could get, and a major source of Stroup's power was his ability to produce witnesses like Dr. Whipple and Dr. Grinspoon.

Stroup gave numerous newspaper and television interviews while he was in Texas. He got a good press, partly because he was articulate and statistic-laden, partly because he said things that were still shocking in Texas (that he smoked marijuana and liked it), and partly, it appeared, because most of the young reporters who interviewed him had reason to support his cause.

Finally, on Saturday morning, Stroup, Waters, and a UPI reporter named Jurate Kazickas, who was a tall, stunning blonde, arrived at the Ferguson unit of the Texas prison system, a large, modern facility located near Huntsville, in central Texas. They were greeted by a polite young assistant warden who had arranged for them to meet with several young men serving sentences there on marijuana charges. Stroup's purpose in being there was to gain publicity, to encourage the prisoners, and to gather material that might be used for articles or radio tapes.

Eventually they settled down in the assistant warden's office for a talk with ten prisoners serving time for marijuana. Stroup, grand-standing, tried to bully the young assistant warden a bit: Did he think it was right that these men were locked up for smoking a harmless weed? But the young prison official only replied, very politely, that it was a shame, but he reckoned the law had to be enforced. The prisoners were anxious to know about the chances for a new law in Texas and—the crucial point for them—if reduced penalties might be made to apply retroactively to those already in jail. Stroup and Waters told them what they could, and then asked each prisoner to tell his story.

One was a husky, twenty-year-old Mexican American named Pete Trevino, who said he had grown up in an orphanage and was about to enter college on a football scholarship when he was convicted of selling several ounces of marijuana. By his account, the judge, noting that he was an orphan, said, "Son, we'll give you a home," and sentenced him to forty years.

Another was Frank York, a very straight young man from a small town, married and the father of two daughters, plump and balding at twenty-one, who had been a cemetery-lot salesman before being sentenced to five years for his second conviction for possession of a few ounces.

Another was Coy Whitten, a handsome man of twenty-nine, married and a college graduate, who was serving twelve years for possession.

It went on like that. The prisoners told depressingly similar stories: widespread marijuana use among their friends; an "it can't happen to me" attitude; arrest by undercover agents; headline-seeking prosecu-tors; and finally conviction, wives and children left behind, and the incredible reality of long, long sentences.

Almost to a man they declared, despite the presence of the assistant warden, that they believed they'd one nothing wrong, that it was the law that was wrong, and that they'd smoke again when they got out.

Another prisoner they talked to that day was Frank Demolli, who was twenty years old and had been eighteen and a freshman at the University of Texas when he was arrested. Demolli was not one of the All-American boys whom Stroup from time to time uncovered and publicized—the student-body president who got two years for one joint. No, Demolli had been a campus hippie who'd been dealing marijuana and other drugs and had been caught red-handed with twenty-one pounds of weed. His red hair was trimmed short in prison, but it had been long, shoulder length, when he went to trial; that had been one of the several mistakes that had led to his downfall. He was five feet seven and weighed about 120 pounds. He wore glasses and was rather homely, with a sad, owlish face that had become only sadder and more owlish in prison, where he lived in constant fear of being beaten, raped, or murdered by larger, more violent inmates.

Demolli's father was a noncommissioned officer in the air force, and Frank had lived all over the world and had read more books than most college freshmen. That was another part of his problem: Until he entered prison, most of his ideas about the world came from books. He was the kind of kid who would read *The Prophet* or *The Way of a Pilgrim* and confuse the way the world ought to be with the way it is. He had gone to high school in Germany for three years and then graduated from a high school in Rapid City, South Dakota, where he was on the school wrestling team. It was in South Dakota that he was first exposed to drugs. Having great faith in books, he read a book called *The Marijuana Papers,* concluded that marijuana would not hurt him, and began smoking marijuana and using LSD.

He decided to enroll in the University of Texas because he had been born in Texas, when his father was stationed there, and because he had a romantic notion of Texas as an exciting, wide-open place where he could make new friends and seek new truths. When he arrived in Austin, in September of 1970, he found that everyone he met was into marijuana and LSD. His first day there, someone sold him ten tabs of LSD for $20; he resold them at a profit, and his career as a dealer was begun. Soon he met another freshman called Laredo Slim, who was from the border town of Laredo and knew a dope-smoking border guard there, a Vietnam veteran, who would bring marijuana across from Mexico for half the profits. Soon Demolli and his friend Danny were buying twenty pounds from Laredo Slim every other weekend. They were middle men, buying a pound from Slim for $85, then selling it for $100: easy money, and free dope, too.

Of course, it wasn't just the money. Demolli believed in marijuana, believed it was a path to truth and awareness. Perhaps more important, being a dealer gave him an identity. The University of Texas was a very large, very rich university, with its social life dominated by sororities and fraternities; Demolli, a funny-looking little guy from South Dakota, was never going to make that scene, but by dealing and by letting his red hair grow long, he soon became a character in the freak scene, the hippie scene, and that was all he needed. Some years later he tried to capture what it had been like.

"We had fought against the war together, grown our hair long, balled our brains out, immobilized ourselves with Panamanian red, Mexican dirt weed, Colombian gold, Oaxacan, Michoacán, touched God with orange barrel, blotter, and clear light. We were all part of the Austin scene in January, 1971. We were outlaws with cars screaming down the drag, drivers yelling out to passersby, 'What is truth?' Some of us were sure we were on to something with LSD and marijuana. Even as we saw the scene deteriorate into guns, speed, smack, and rip-offs, we still believed love and peace could come out of dope. University life was wide open in those days. No one gave a screw about school. Just dope, women, the Armadillo, music, and going out to the country."

Frank Demolli's fantasy world began to crumble on the afternoon of January 7, 1971, when he and his partner Danny drove to the Greyhound station to pick up a shipment of dope from Laredo Slim. Other times, they had gone to Mexico themselves, made the big deal, felt the excitement of outfoxing the border guards, been big shots flashing their money and telling their ladies to take all the dope they wanted. But this time they were in a hurry, so they'd asked Slim to ship their twenty-one pounds up by bus. Demolli marched up to the package desk, flashed his fake ID, signed for the package, and carried it back out to Danny's green Camaro. They were congratulating each other on another successful mission when a black Chevy squealed to a halt beside them and the two men jumped out and pointed guns at their heads and yelled, "Up against the wall, you motherfuckers."

The next thing Frank Demolli knew his bail had been set at $20,000 and he was in the drunk tank of the county jail. The local media proclaimed the capture of two major drug dealers.

Soon he had a lawyer, one who was sent to him by his codefendant, Danny. The lawyer assured him that he could take care of his case, that the search was probably illegal, that at worst they could get him off with probation, but there was the question of money: five thousand dollars, in fact, if the case went to trial. The lawyer seemed to think Demolli, being a drug dealer, had plenty of money. He didn't, but he scraped up $500, and the lawyer got him out on bail. Soon he was driving a cab to try to earn money for his legal fees. When that didn't bring enough money, he returned to dealing. As the spring progressed and he awaited trial, Demolli was dealing more than ever before, this time with all the profits going to his lawyer. Once he hitchhiked to Tucson to buy some marijuana and cocaine. A friend wired him $300 to make the deal. When he went to Western Union to pick up his money, a seedy-looking guy came up and started talking to him and asked if he was looking for weed. Demolli was suspicious, but the fellow quoted a good price, so he finally went with him and his skinny girl friend to see a dealer. But the seedy-looking guy, who called himself Jess, said he would have to take the $300 and Frank would have to wait in the car. Frank protested, but Jess said the skinny girl, Donna, would wait with him, and from the way Donna was rubbing up against him, it looked as though it might be an exciting wait. So they waited five or ten minutes, and the girl was talking about meeting him later, and finally she said she'd go see what was keeping Jess. And she disappeared.

It was another ten or twenty minutes before Demolli could face the fact that he'd been ripped off. His new friends were gone, and his $300 was gone with them. He was so furious that he went to the police to report a swindle. The police laughed at him.

Demolli's lawyer had got his bond reduced to $5000, but for some reason it was raised back to $20,000 and he was forced to return to the county jail. He turned himself in, carrying copies of the Bhagavad-Gita, *The Joyous Cosmology*, and his German textbook. Most of his fellow inmates were also there on drug charges, and it was on that tour of the county jail that he first saw a rape, two tough speed freaks ganging up on a high-school kid who'd been busted when a traffic cop found an ounce of weed in his glove compartment. Demolli was in for a week before his lawyer got his bond reduced again, and he vowed then that he'd never go back. He'd run first, become a fugitive. Still, his lawyer kept telling him not to worry.

He dropped out of school, kept dealing, kept driving a cab, kept giving all his money to his lawyer, and finally in May his case came to trial. By then he had given a lot of thought to his trial. He had decided, for one thing, that he would not cut his shoulder-length red hair. By leaving his hair long, he would show the jury that he was being honest with them. Then, when he explained to the jury that all marijuana did was make you giggle, that the government's scare stories were false, the jury would believe him. He had decided, too, that after he had explained to the jury how harmless marijuana was, and after they had given him probation, he would thank them and promise them that he was going to quit smoking marijuana. He had decided it wasn't worth the hassle. His education was more important, he wanted to get his degree in social work. He'd had enough of Texas, however; as soon as the trial was over he was going to fly to Germany and see his parents and enter college there. Maybe he would come back to Texas later, but for now there was just too much hassle, too much madness.

The morning of his trial, Demolli realized he didn't even own a suit, so he borrowed one from a friend. The only trouble was that his friend was three inches taller and sixty pounds heavier, so Demolli, in his baggy suit and with his long red hair, looked rather like Bozo the Clown. He and his friends broke up with laughter. Oh, well, he thought, it'll give the jury something to laugh about.

When he got to his lawyer's office, he had his first surprise of the day. His lawyer said he'd decided not to let him testify. Demolli guessed that was all right. He'd never liked the idea of pleading innocent: Since he was obviously guilty, that seemed dishonest. He was sorry he wouldn't get a chance to explain to the jury about marijuana, how it was just a giggle, but he guessed it didn't matter. Probation was probation, no matter how you got it.

Demolli's next surprise came when prospective jurors were being questioned. The assistant prosecutor asked if any of them would object to sending a person to prison for life for possession of even a seed of marijuana, if that was the law. A few said they would object, and they were excused.

The next surprise came when the flamboyant local district attorney appeared to argue the case himself. In his opening statement he talked about the defendants as purveyors of corruption, men who tried to pervert children, men who made money off a vile substance that was spreading like a cancer through society, leading to heroin, to untold human tragedy. Demolli began to feel some concern. It did not sound like the statement of a prosecutor who would agree to probation. Still, the jury couldn't possibly believe all that junk about perverting children and about marijuana's leading to heroin. Marijuana was just a giggle.

There were only a few witnesses. The arresting officers said someone at Greyhound had smelled the marijuana and called them. They brought out the twenty-one one-pound bags and piled them on the prosecution table, a veritable mountain of marijuana.

Demolli's lawyer called no witnesses. Demolli took this as proof that they had the probation all locked up. Instead he made a brief summation. He said his client was sorry for what he had done, and he asked the jury to act with compassion.

Then the prosecutor got up. His cowboy boots clicked on the floor as he paced restlessly back and forth before the jury. He shouted that Demolli said he was sorry, but he had refused to say where he had got the twenty-one pounds of marijuana. That was true; when he was arrested, Demolli had said it was against his code of honor to cause trouble for anyone else.

The prosecutor said Demolli might look young and innocent, but he was in truth a pusher, the kind who hangs around the junior high schools luring Austin's young people into trying marijuana, into lives of corruption.

What should we do with someone who was arrested with twenty-one pounds of that filth? the prosecutor asked. We should put him in prison for forty-two years, he declared, two years for each pound.

Forty-two years, Frank Demolli thought. That's a lot of probation.

This is our chance to show the rest of the country that we Texans can stop the dope traffic, the prosecutor said, to show the dope pushers that we mean business.

The judge gave his instructions, and the jury retired to the jury room. Everyone else left the courtroom, too, and Demolli was alone there with the twenty-one pounds of marijuana. He started to laugh. It was as if the game were over and he could take his toys and go home. Giggling, he walked over and put his ear to the jury-room door. He heard a man say he wanted to give this kid thirty-five years.

But wasn't he a college student? a woman asked.

No, that was just a lie, a man said.

Demolli wondered if he should go into the jury room and set them straight about himself and his case. Just then an elderly bailiff came in and told him to get away from the door. Demolli went over to the bailiff and told him his ideas about marijuana, and asked if the bailiff couldn't see that there was nothing wrong with him.

"I think you're crazier than hell," the bailiff said with a snort, and walked away.

Demolli's lawyer and an assistant prosecutor came back in with cups of coffee. The assistant prosecutor was very friendly, and Demolli could tell from his tone that everything would be all right. They weren't mad at him. It was just a game. They wanted to scare him.

Then the jury came back in. Their foreman was the man who'd been yelling about thirty-five years. He gave the verdict to the judge. The judge read it and summoned Demolli and his lawyer to the bench. Demolli could feel his baggy pants flopping against his legs. The jury foreman gave Demolli an odd smile. Then the judge read the verdict.

"The jury hereby sentences you to no more than twenty-five years in the Texas Department of Corrections."

Demolli's head went light. He couldn't think or speak. His lawyer shook his hand and wished him luck. Someone put handcuffs on him and led him out of the courtroom. It was a fat jailer he'd met when he was arrested. Back then, when he left the jail, he'd told the fat jailer he'd never be back.

"They all come back," the jailer said, as he locked Demolli in the drunk tank.

Twenty-five years, he thought. Why, I'll be forty-three when I get out.

They're trying to scare me, he decided.

Then he began to cry and scream and pound on the steel door. Eventually he fell asleep.

What Frank Demolli and thousands of other young men like him had no way of understanding was that they had become pawns in the very-high-stakes game of presidential politics. Richard Nixon had, in effect, slammed the cell door on them when he rejected the Marijuana Commission's report and then proceeded to win forty-nine of the fifty states in the 1972 election. If that election seemed to prove anything to would-be presidents, it was that the American people wanted tough-ness, against rebellious communists in Asia and against rebellious dope smokers at home. Two of the men who hoped to succeed Richard Nixon as president in 1976, Ronald Reagan and Spiro Agnew, were already demonstrably tough on drugs. A third, Gov. Nelson Rockefeller, of New York, set out in January of 1973 to demonstrate that he was no less so.

Early in 1973 Rockefeller introduced anti-drug legislation that was by far the most punitive in the nation. His program was directed mainly at "hard" drugs. Possession or sale of heroin, cocaine, or LSD could lead to life in prison. However, the Rockefeller bill defined hallucinogenic drugs in such a way as to include hashish and some of the stronger varieties of marijuana, so that in theory you could go to prison for life for smoking high-quality marijuana. For garden-variety marijuana the Rockefeller bill let stand New York's existing penalties, which allowed one-year prison terms for more than an ounce.

Among the many voices raised against Rockefeller's proposed law were those of NORML's two men in New York, Guy Archer and Frank Fioramonti. The previous year, once he had got his $100,000 a year guarantee from Playboy, Stroup had proposed that their Lawyers Committee become New York NORML. Archer agreed to leave his law firm and become NORML's $1000-a-month state director, and Fioramonti continued to work with NORML on a volunteer basis and later became the New York coordinator when Archer moved to Hawaii to reenter private law practice.

NORML deliberately limited its opposition to the provisions of the New York bill relating to marijuana. This was a political decision. Stroup thought it was hard enough to challenge the marijuana laws without taking on the laws on hard drugs as well. He thought, for example, that heroin addiction should be treated as a medical problem, but if he started sounding "pro-heroin," he would alienate politicians who were barely willing to support marijuana reform. It was a joke at NORML that the next step would be NORCL, the National Organization for the Reform of Cocaine Laws, but Stroup thought the next generation of reformers would have to fight that battle.

In time, the provision of the Rockefeller law that made possession of certain forms of hashish and marijuana punishable by life in prison was dropped. Otherwise, Rockefeller got the tough laws he wanted. Eventually the courts would rule much of his law unconstitutional, and state officials would find other parts unworkable, notably the "mandatory minimum sentences" that ruled out plea-bargaining.

Still, the political reality in the spring of 1973 was that the nation's most powerful governor, riding roughshod over liberal objections, had passed the nation's toughest new drug law. There was every reason to think that the Rockefeller law would be the model for new laws in other states, laws that would reflect not the restraint of the Marijuana Commission but the rhetoric of Richard Nixon and the politicians who hoped to succeed him as president.

Then, late that spring, there were unexpected stirrings in the state of Oregon.

7

In the fall of 1972 Steve Kafoury, a thirty-one-year-old Portland teacher and social worker, was running for the Oregon state legislature. Several times, as he went door to door in search of votes, the same odd scene occurred. As soon as he knocked on the door, he would hear people rustling around inside. Someone would peek out a window. Finally a young person would open the door and Kafoury would smell the distinctive odor of marijuana within.

Kafoury had smoked and soon he was promising the young people, whenever this happened, "If I get elected, I'll do something about this. You won't have to be paranoid anymore!"

He was elected, and he did do something. In less than a year, in large part because of Kafoury's leadership, Oregon became the first state to end criminal penalties for possession of small amounts of marijuana—to enact, in other words, the decriminalization policy the Marijuana Commission had recommended a year before.

Stephen Kafoury was born in 1941 in Portland, where his father manufactured women's clothing. The family was Democratic, and politics was often the focus of dinner-table conversation; Kafoury can remember being heartbroken when Stevenson lost to Eisenhower in 1952, when he was eleven. He went to Whitman College, in Walla Walla, majored in history, graduated in 1963, and joined the Peace Corps, which sent him to Iran for two years. Returning home, he earned a master's degree in education from Reed College and then went to work in Portland's black community, where he founded an alternative school and worked to help low-income black youths get into college. After a few years of this he began to see the importance of political action, and he ran for the state legislature.

Elected, Kafoury was appointed to a special committee on alcohol and drugs, whose chairman said he was interested in lowering the drinking age to eighteen and doing something about marijuana-law reform. Kafoury, as he studied the political situation, found a good deal of support for reform. The influential Portland City Club had called for reform, as had the state's ACLU and Democratic party. Pat Horton, the thirty-year-old Lane County district attorney, had quit prosecuting possession cases, and Republican governor Tom McCall had testified for reform before the Marijuana Commission. Even more important, Kafoury found a widespread sentiment within the state legislature that it was time for reform. There was opposition, and there was confusion as to what the reform should be, but he began to think some kind of a bill could pass.

As he planned his legislative strategy, Kafoury made two crucial decisions. The first was to push for the most liberal bill possible. The second was to enlist the support of a sixty-one-year-old Republican hog farmer named Stafford Hansell, who he hoped could sway the votes of other conservative legislators.

Kafoury's bill proposed to remove all criminal penalties for the private use or possession of up to eight ounces of marijuana or for the cultivation of up to two plants. It was a liberal bill, and when it came to the floor of the state legislature in mid-June, it sparked heated debate. The day's emotional highlight was the speech by Stafford Hansell, the bill's floor manager. He was playing to a packed gallery, and he made the most of his opportunity.

"Mr. Speaker, members of the assembly," he began, "since it became known that I was to carry HB 2003, the marijuana-decriminalization bill, I've received letters, telephone calls, and looks of disbelief from my fellow legislators, all indicating that Hansell has finally flipped completely, with the old Devil winning out. In response to those who do not know me well, I want to prove to you that there are no telltale needle marks on my arms." He paused to pull up his sleeves. "I am not a dope addict. I haven't smoked a cigarette for twenty-five years, nor had a drink of intoxicating beverage, inclusive of whiskey, wine, or beer, for twenty-four years. In other words, there is no element of conflict of interest as I speak in support of HB 2003. Neither was I captivated by the eloquence of Representative Kafoury. I am speaking because I wish to, because I believe the issue should be faced by each and every legislative body in the United States."

Slowly, Hansell held up his exhibits for the legislators and the gallery to see: a cup of coffee, a bottle of aspirin, sleeping pills, amphetamines, a pack of cigarettes, a bottle of beer, a bottle of wine, a bottle of whiskey, and finally a marijuana cigarette. He spoke at length on the health hazards of each item and the penalties for their use. Then he concluded, "Having explored all the basic components of the marijuana situation, I am convinced we could and should take steps to decriminalize its use. Prohibition was not the answer to our alcohol problem in 1919, nor is it the answer to the marijuana problem in 1973."

He sat down amid an ovation that was richly deserved. The fact that Stafford Hansell was a hog farmer had tended to detract from the more basic fact about him: At a time when the great leaders of his political party, the Nixons and Rockefellers and Reagans, were content to play politics with the marijuana issue, Stafford Hansell was that rarest of creatures in the political jungle: an honest man.

His impassioned plea was not, however, persuasive to his colleagues in the Oregon legislature. When his bill came to a vote, after more oratory on both sides, it was soundly defeated.

The reformers were shattered. And yet, a day or two later, Steve Kafoury began to sense that all was not lost. Hansell's speech had received a vast amount of publicity, and there seemed to be a sense, both in the legislature and the state as a whole, that an opportunity had been lost. Quickly, Kafoury introduced a new, more moderate bill, one that did not allow cultivation and that classified possession of up to an ounce as a noncriminal violation, punishable by a fine of up to $100. This bill passed easily a few days later.

NORML had played no role in the passage of the Oregon bill. Stroup knew a bill had been introduced there, but NORML had been focusing its attentions on a number of other states where reform bills seemed more likely to pass, mainly by sending in Stroup, Dr. Whipple, John

Finlator, or other pro-reform witnesses. When Stroup heard that a bill was about to pass in Oregon, his first thought was, My God, the states are starting to move without us! He hurried to Oregon, met Kafoury, and was with him on the night the decriminalization bill passed. To Stroup's amazement, Kafoury was disconsolate. Marijuana was still illegal, he said, and there was a $100 fine.

"My God, man," Stroup said, "this is the first state to stop locking people up, this is the biggest thing that ever happened to marijuana reform."

Slowly, Kafoury began to think that he'd won a victory after all.

In the aftermath of the Oregon victory it seemed possible that several other states would pass decriminalization bills before the year was out. Stroup's instinct was to jump on the bandwagon and to try, if possible, to seize its reins. NORML redoubled its efforts in the various states that were considering bills, sending in witnesses, trying to convince legislators that the Marijuana Commission had provided the blueprint, Oregon had led the way, and the time had come for every state to act.

The breakthrough didn't come. In the Massachusetts senate, just a few weeks after the Oregon bill passed, a similar bill was defeated by a twenty-six-to-thirteen vote. Another bill was defeated in a floor vote in Maine, and bills in Maryland, Rhode Island, Montana, Hawaii, and Connecticut all died in committee. The Oregon success was not as easily transportable as Stroup had hoped, but he rationalized that 1974 would be the breakthrough year.

There was even a problem back in Texas. Stroup had gone there several times in the spring of 1973 as hearings were held on a reform bill. He arranged for testimony by John Finlator and also by Richard Cowan, the young Texas conservative who'd written the *National Review* article. He put together a group called Concerned Parents for Marijuana Reform, made up of people whose children were imprisoned, and its officers testified. The new law, which passed on May 29, reduced possession of marijuana from a felony to a low misdemeanor, which carried up to six months imprisonment for possession of up to two ounces, up to a year's imprisonment for possession of up to four ounces, and continued felony penalties for larger amounts. Sale of marijuana was reduced to a two-to-ten-year offense, and the law provided for persons imprisoned to apply for resentencing under the new, lower penalties. It was hoped that this retroactive provision would soon free most of the seven hundred marijuana prisoners in the Texas prison, but that proved not to be so simple. Gov. Dolph Briscoe declared that the resentencing provision infringed on his exclusive right of pardon and parole. Frank Demolli, whose twenty-five-year sentence could have been reduced to ten years under the new law, filed suit against the governor. NORML entered the case as *amicus curiae*, in a legal effort headed by Gerald Goldstein, a young San Antonio lawyer who had been working with NORML on Texas drug cases.

Frank Demolli was then in his third year of confinement. He was twenty-one and was no longer the innocent lad who thought marijuana was a giggle. He'd spent a year in the county jail in Austin, while his case was on appeal. A lot of other inmates were dopers and bikers. He watched some bikers kick one kid half to death for smearing their colors, which they'd painted on the cell wall. Another time, a kid came in with ten hits of LSD sewn in his pants. It was the purest acid Demolli had ever used; he had a great trip, a day's escape. Once, he watched as a big guy started to beat and rape an obnoxious inmate; when Demolli and the others realized what was happening, they pulled him off. Demolli was learning to live with violence, to accept fear as a way of life.

Eventually, when he was sent to the Ferguson unit of the state prison, he started taking college courses. He noticed a NORML ad in *Playboy* one day and wrote a letter. It was a few weeks later that Stroup and the others visited the prison. Demolli was shaken when he saw Stroup's long hair. It reminded him of his trial, when he'd refused to cut his own long hair, so that the jury would be impressed with his sincerity, and he wanted to warn Stroup to watch out, that it was dangerous to wear your hair long in Texas. Demolli and the other prisoners were upset, too, by the sight of Jurate Kazickas, the tall, blond reporter. Demolli had seen only one or two women in his eighteen months behind bars, and had touched none, and to be that close to such a beautiful woman made him want to cry.

But the biggest thing Demolli got out of Stroup's visit was an appreciation of the power of the media. The warden and his assistants were like gods in the prison world, and yet they were clearly worried about the possibility of bad publicity; they feared these reporters who, thanks to recent court rulings, could enter their prisons and ask questions and talk to inmates. Demolli began to see that perhaps he could help himself if he could learn to use the media and if he could win the help of friendly politicians like Ron Waters, who had seemed so shaken by what he saw in the prison. So Demolli, who was already editor of the prison newspaper, became a letter writer. He wrote hundreds of letters to newspapers and to legislators, urging support of the marijuana-law-reform bill.

The bill passed, but the governor refused to enact the resentencing provision, and eventually Demolli's lawsuit against the governor was rejected by the Texas court of criminal appeals. It was a cruel blow, but Demolli kept on writing letters. The issue was no longer legal; it was political. Liberal legislators, and some Texas newspapers, were putting pressure on Governor Briscoe to parole the marijuana prisoners. In time Briscoe did parole some, in a program called Project Star, but he refused to parole "pushers" like Demolli. By then several legislators had taken an interest in this case, including Ron Waters, Ronnie Earle, and a woman named Sarah Weddington. Eventually Ronnie Earle went to Briscoe and urged him to parole Demolli. He pointed out that Demolli was causing a stink, that he'd keep on stirring up publicity as long as he was behind bars. The governor said that if Demolli was causing him trouble in prison, he'd only cause him more if he got out. Earle said no, that Demolli had parents in Colorado, and he'd go there if released. Briscoe said he would parole the boy if he would get out of Texas. Demolli was more than happy to agree to that condition. He was freed, and he hastened to Colorado, where he took a job as a copy editor with a newspaper and enrolled in college. He had spent four years in prison.

There were some important additions to NORML's staff in 1973 and 1974.

First, Larry Schott joined the staff full time as Stroup's deputy. Schott ran the office when Stroup was traveling, edited *The Leaflet*, and in time headed up NORML's Center for the Study of Non-Medical Drug Use.

Another important addition came when a tall, intense, chain-smoking young legal scholar named Peter Meyers marched into NORML's office in the summer of 1973 and announced that he wanted to bring a right-of-privacy suit to test the constitutionality of the federal marijuana law. Stroup and Schott were skeptical. They'd seen other young lawyers rush in and say the same thing, then disappear after a week or two. Still, Meyers had impressive credentials. As a law student at George Washington University he'd studied under John Banzahf, who assigned his students to undertake Nader-type suits against federal agencies, and he'd been involved in several important cases. Stroup decided to give Meyers a try.

That summer the Supreme Court had made its historic ruling on abortion. It said, among other things, that in the first three months of pregnancy the mother's interests are paramount and that her right of privacy included a right to abortion. To Peter Meyers it seemed clear that if the right of privacy covered abortion, an act that millions of people viewed as murder, it must also cover the right to smoke marijuana in one's home.

By October, Meyers had filed NORML v. U.S., in which he, working in collaboration with Ramsey Clark, set out to establish that the federal marijuana law was in violation of the right of privacy, and thus unconstitutional.

It was a tricky question. The right of privacy—the idea that one's home is a sovereign domain—has never been absolute. The state can break down a man's door if he is, say, murdering his wife or manufacturing bombs in his basement. The question was whether marijuana was such a serious offense that it justified governmental intrusion into private conduct. It was the sort of question that courts traditionally prefer to leave to the legislatures, and in this particular case, the courts moved very slowly. Not until 1980 would NORML get a ruling on its test case.

In the meantime, Meyers had made himself invaluable as he headed up NORML's expanding program to challenge the marijuana laws in federal and state courts. Calls and letters poured into NORML every day from people who were in jail, or seemed headed there, on drug charges. NORML referred as many as possible to its growing national network of lawyers who defended drug cases for reduced fees, or even *pro bono*. Meyers himself could become involved in only a few of the cases that came to his attention, and Stroup urged him, in choosing those cases, to look for ones that were particularly unusual or outrageous and would thus attract media attention and public support.

One example was the case of Roger Davis, a black political activist who was convicted in Wytheville, Virginia, in 1974, of selling nine ounces of marijuana. He was sentenced to forty years in prison. Both NORML and the ACLU joined in his appeal, providing lawyers to assist and advise Davis's own lawyers, and after Davis had served three years in prison, a federal judge freed him on the grounds that the forty-year sentence amounted to cruel and unusual punishment and was thus unconstitutional. Such a case, in addition to helping an individual defendant, was useful to NORML politically. Very few marijuana defendants were sentenced to forty years, but Stroup's horror stories, as he called such cases, served to remind millions of people that such sentences were still very possible.

Another well-publicized case concerned the Piedras Negras jail break, in which a Texan whose son was imprisoned in a Mexican border town on a drug charge hired three other men to get him out. Armed with shotguns, the men crossed the border, raided the jail, freed the son and thirteen other Americans, and escaped back to Texas. There was no U.S. law against raiding a Mexican jail, but U.S. prosecutors, under pressure from angry Mexican officials, charged the raiders with conspiring to export weapons (their shotguns) without a license. NORML entered the case at the urging of Gerald Goldstein, the San Antonio lawyer who was becoming one of NORML's most active volunteers. For NORML, the jail break case was an opportunity to publicize both the inhumane conditions in Mexican jails and the way U.S. officials catered to the Mexican government. NORML often tried to publicize the stories of young Americans who were arrested on drug charges in Mexico and other foreign countries. Sometimes the people had in fact possessed drugs, sometimes they were framed, but in either case they were often tortured, deprived of all legal rights, and in effect kidnapped, since the surest way out of a Mexican jail is to bribe corrupt officials. U.S. officials, for their part, rarely showed concern for Americans who were in Mexican jails on drug charges. To NORML, and to others in the drug culture, the Piedras Negras raiders were not criminals but heroes, and their story ended happily when Goldstein won a reversal of their convictions.

Meyers directed NORML's major legal challenges to the government, including the 1978 suit to stop the paraquat spraying in Mexico and the suit to permit the medical use of marijuana, and he also brought a series of lesser-known suits against federal agencies. One caused the

U.S. Parole Commission to modify its parole regulations so that marijuana offenses were classified among the least serious category of offenses. He also filed a series of suits under the Freedom of Information Act, including one to force the CIA to reveal details of LSD tests it had conducted on unsuspecting subjects and another to force the Army to release details of some tests that showed that you could be just as good a soldier if you smoked as if you didn't.

Drug law was a new area, and Meyers worked to make NORML a clearinghouse for the latest information that could be of use to local defense lawyers. Sometimes NORML would formally enter a local case; more often, Meyers would give advice from the background. In other cases NORML would not be called in until a smoker, represented by a lawyer inexperienced in drug law, had been given a long jail sentence; then NORML's volunteer lawyers would help with the appeal. The suits were many and varied. Indiana's NORML chapter overturned a state law that made it a crime to possess smoking paraphernalia. In South Carolina a lawsuit forced the Citadel, a military college, to recognize a NORML chapter. In California, NORML joined in a suit that established that marijuana use was not a crime of "moral turpitude" for which a public-school teacher could be fired. In all this NORML was keeping pressure on the government, winning publicity, demonstrating that smokers had legal rights, and making itself the rallying point for a national effort by lawyers, many of whom were themselves smokers, to challenge the laws that defined smokers as criminals.

Another important staff addition at NORML came in the spring of 1974, when the long feud between NORML and Amorphia was at last resolved. The defeat of CMI had left Amorphia dispirited and all but bankrupt. Blair Newman left in the spring of 1973, and Gordon Brownell, Amorphia's political director, Mark Heutlinger, its business manager, and Mike Aldrich, its writer-philosopher, struggled to keep their reform lobby alive. In time they began to consider a merger with NORML. The feud, they decided, had been between Stroup and Newman; the others got along with Stroup well enough. Discussions were held, and the merger took place. Brownell stayed in San Francisco as NORML's West Coast coordinator. Heutlinger, a West Orange, New Jersey, lawyer's son who had a master's degree in business from George Washington University, came to Washington to be NORML's business manager. But Stroup could find no place for Mike Aldrich in his plans, and when Amorphia closed its doors, as LeMar had before it, Dr. Dope was abruptly an unemployed marijuana scholar, forced to collect unemployment insurance until he got back on his feet.

By the spring of 1974 it was clear that other states, rather than rushing to follow Oregon's example, were taking a wait-and-see attitude, and decriminalization bills were bogged down in a dozen states.

During this period of uncertainty the anti-marijuana forces launched a major counteroffensive. The leader of the counteroffensive was Sen. James Eastland, of Mississippi, already distinguished as a racist, a reactionary, and one of the world's leading anti-communists, but not as an expert on drugs.

Marijuana is often viewed simply as a health issue, but with the entry of Eastland into the debate, its essentially political nature becomes more clear. It was no coincidence that Ramsey Clark was the first important politician to encourage NORML, or that Eastland was the first important politician to oppose the fast-spreading reform movement. Both men were symbolic figures: Clark a champion of American liberalism and Eastland of American conservatism. For a time, when Clark was attorney general and Eastland was chairman of the Senate Judiciary Committee, they were poised in classic, public confrontation. They disagreed on voting rights, on legal aid for the poor, on capital punishment, on Vietnam—on almost everything—and it was therefore no surprise that their disagreement should extend to marijuana. Underlying the questions of whether people should use the drug or whether marijuana is a health hazard is the more basic issue of personal freedom versus governmental power. Eastland liked the marijuana laws for the same reason he had liked the Jim Crow laws: because they were a convenient way to put people in jail. Eastland represented political forces that were concerned with preserving the status quo and that rightly perceived marijuana as yet another threat to their authority. His hearings came at a time when Richard Nixon was about to be driven from office, when the war in Vietnam was about to be written off as a failure, and when gay rights and the women's movement and many other liberal causes were gathering momentum. Thanks to the Marijuana Commission and the Oregon legislature, the ban on drugs seemed to be crumbling. To Eastland, it must have seemed that the Bolsheviks were at the gates, and that his anti-marijuana hearings were the last opportunity to turn back the tide. Politically, the drug issue provided a way for Eastland to rally many people who did not share his views on economics and on race. If in the 1930s marijuana could be painted as a drug that turned black men into rapists, then marijuana laws could be passed and used to lock up black troublemakers. If in the 1970s marijuana could be portrayed as a serious health hazard, then that fact could be used to discredit all the liberals who smoked or defended the drug. It was with these larger political concerns in mind that Eastland opened hearings that were nothing less than an attempt to discredit the Marijuana Commission and to reverse the trend toward marijuana-law reform.

The forum for Eastland's anti-marijuana offensive was the Senate Sub-Committee on Internal Security of which he was chairman. Since his subcommittee had no jurisdiction over the drug issue, it was necessary for Eastland to argue that marijuana had become a threat to national security. The hearings were therefore called "Marijuana-Hashish Epidemic and Its Impact on United States Security," and Eastland argued first that marijuana was creating a generation of "semi-zombies" who would not or could not defend their country and second that "subversive forces" were behind this epidemic. The only subversive force he named was Dr. Timothy Leary.

Eastland's hearings opened on May 9 and continued for five more days. He called only anti-marijuana witnesses, mostly scientists and Pentagon officials, and he refused to let pro-marijuana scientists or other reform spokesmen testify. He made no pretense of objectivity, declaring at the outset, "We make no apology, therefore, for the one-sided nature of our hearings—they were deliberately planned this way."

It was Eastland's thesis that pro-marijuana scientists and their allies in the media had in recent years fostered a "myth of harmlessness" about marijuana. Moreover, he said that a "pro-marijuana cabal" had launched a program of "character assassination" against scientists who warned of the weed's dangers. Eastland did not attack the Marijuana Commission directly, but he and various witnesses stressed that important "new evidence" had made the dangers of marijuana more clear than they had been three years earlier, when the Marijuana Commission conducted its investigation.

A central charge, made by various witnesses, was that marijuana caused an "amotivational syndrome," one that led young people to become passive, to ignore their studies, to dislike work, and generally to drop out of society. Warned Eastland: "If this epidemic is not rolled back, our society may be largely taken over by a 'marijuana culture' —a culture motivated by a desire to escape from reality and a consuming lust for self-gratification, and lacking any moral guidance. Such a society could not long endure." Interestingly, the "amotivational syndrome" was the opposite of a major claim made by anti-marijuana spokesmen of the 1930s: that smoking made people violent.

Going beyond the amotivational syndrome, various witnesses at the hearings blamed marijuana for causing insanity, psychosis, homosexuality, promiscuity, impotence, deformed children, and violent crimes, including the "fragging" (murder by hand grenade) of U.S. Army officers by enlisted men in Vietnam. One scientist said moderate marijuana use caused chromosome damage similar to that suffered by survivors of the Hiroshima bombing. However, upon examination, most of this "new evidence" tended to be very tentative—this was "suspected"; that was "indicated"—and all parties called for more research grants.

One witness, a psychiatrist from the Tulane University medical school, had conducted experiments on monkeys. He pumped marijuana smoke into the lungs of ten monkeys and implanted electrodes in their brains to measure the results. Two of the monkeys died (of respiratory complications, he explained), and the other eight suffered changes in brain-wave patterns. His testimony resulted in national headlines along the order of "Marijuana Smoking Causes Brain Damage." A later witness at the hearings, a Nobel Prize winner, pointed out that the monkeys had been given dosages that were the equivalent of a human being's smoking one hundred strong marijuana cigarettes a day. But that sort of rebuttal didn't make headlines.

From a political point of view the Eastland hearings were extremely effective. Their purpose was to discredit the Marijuana Commission, and to a very great degree they succeeded, by publicizing the "new evidence" theory that could be used to sidestep the commission's findings. The underlying political reality was that the Marijuana Commission was a paper tiger politically, because millions of people wanted to disbelieve its findings and because it had no continuing institutional role. The scientists, both in and out of government, who set the tone for national drug policy did not look to the Marijuana

Commission for their budgets and research grants; they looked to Congress, and Congress reflected the mood of a nation still opposed to marijuana. Eastland, by stacking his hearings with anti-marijuana witnesses, was able to flood the country with anti-marijuana propaganda at a crucial time in the struggle for reform. His hearings had no legislative intent. They were purely a publicity barrage—part of the battle for the hearts and minds of the American people—and as such they succeeded brilliantly.

Some two years after the Eastland hearings, Dr. Norman Zinberg wrote an article for *Psychology Today* in which he examined the fine print in some of the "new evidence." He noted that the Tulane "brain damage" report had been based upon a dosage level equivalent to about a hundred joints a day. He noted also that a 1975 study that supposedly supported the "amotivational syndrome" theory was based on volunteers who received THC, the intoxicating agent in marijuana, equal to fifty to one hundred joints a day. He pointed out that one well-publicized study, used to suggest chromosome damage to smokers, was based on the examination of only three people. He said another study, used as evidence that marijuana caused brain damage, was based on the experience of ten subjects who had used LSD, heroin, barbiturates, and alcohol as well as marijuana. Of a study charging that marijuana caused psychosis, he wrote, "They cited the case of a 17-year-old boy seduced by a homosexual who also gave him marijuana; the youth became psychotic. But the insistence of these researchers that it was clearly the marijuana that was responsible for the psychosis hardly convinced other psychiatrists."

Time after time, upon examination, the new evidence against marijuana fell apart. Yet each new study received coast-to-coast headlines and reinforced the reefer-madness mythology. Reporters seemed to put aside their professional skepticism when dealing with people with "Dr." before their names, seemed never to suspect that some of them might be incompetent or publicity-seeking or politically motivated. This disinclination was a constant frustration to the reformers, as the new evidence slowly eroded the momentum that the Marijuana Commission had given their cause.

As Stroup traveled to various states in the summer and fall of 1974, he began to encounter a new mood. Previously, the reformers had gone to a state on the offensive, with the Marijuana Commission report as their Bible. Now their opponents had their own Bible: the green-jacketed, printed volume of the Eastland hearings, which had been sent to thousands of legislators and law-enforcement officials across America. (The volume became an underground best-seller among marijuana smokers because of the numerous marijuana recipes —for brownies, chili, meat loaf, banana bread, and the like—that were printed in its Appendix.)

Not only did opponents of reform have their answer to the Marijuana Commission report; they now often called Eastland's anti-marijuana scientists to testify at their state legislative hearings. Suddenly the reformers were on the defensive again, forced to rebut medical arguments that they thought meaningless but that laymen found alarming. The Eastland hearings may have been deliberately one-sided, but they carried the imprimatur of the U.S. Senate, and many state legislators took them very seriously.

By the fall of 1974 the reform movement was at a standstill. It was at that point that Stroup, in desperate need of new ammunition, looked for help to his new allies at the Drug Abuse Council.

By then, eighteen months after Stroup had won Tom Bryant's gratitude by briefing him for William Buckley's television show, the NORML–Drug Abuse Council alliance was in high gear. Tom Bryant was on NORML's advisory board, the Drug Abuse Council was giving up to $30,000 a year for NORML's nonpolitical activities, and Stroup was on close personal terms with several members of the council's staff. After the Eastland hearings Stroup went to his friend Bob Carr, the council's chief writer, and said he needed help. In state after state, reform bills were bogged down, and the Eastland hearings' scare stories were a major factor.

Carr suggested that Bryant might issue a statement. He checked with Bryant, who gave tentative approval to the idea. Carr and Stroup then stayed up all night drafting a tough statement that attacked the various "new evidence" studies. The next morning, somewhat to Stroup's and Carr's surprise, Bryant approved the statement as they'd written it. The UPI story that resulted, in which Dr. Thomas E. Bryant deplored the widespread publicity being given unreliable, misleading scientific data received wider coverage, and had far more credibility, than if Stroup had said the same thing.

Later, the council sponsored a conference at which two dozen leading scientists declared that there had been no significant new scientific findings on marijuana since the Marijuana Commission's report in 1972, another challenge to the "new evidence" argument.

Throughout the fall of 1974, Stroup and Carr searched for ways to challenge the Eastland committee and the wave of anti-marijuana publicity it had created. Stroup was badly worried, because in state after state reform bills were stalled and legislators were saying "Let's wait and see how it works in Oregon."

But how was Oregon's new law working? Smokers thought it was working fine, some law-enforcement officers grumbled about it, and no one really had any solid information on it. One night Stroup and Carr came up with the idea that the council would sponsor a survey of public attitudes toward the new law in Oregon. Carr took the idea back to the council and was given $10,000 for the survey, which was carried out by a Portland public-opinion firm.

The results of the survey, briefly, were that there had been no significant increase in marijuana use in Oregon after the new law, and that most people there approved of the law. That was exactly what Stroup and Carr had hoped the survey would say. Carr issued a press release on it that got national attention, on the order of "New Marijuana Law Works in Oregon." For a mere $10,000, it was the most publicity the Drug Abuse Council had ever received; it also underscored how politically effective surveys and analyses could be.

Politically, the Oregon survey could be used as proof that decriminalization worked. Just what the survey actually proved was debatable, but politicians like studies, surveys, statistics—evidence that makes it easier for them to justify doing what they already want to do. The following spring, Bryant and his staff often testified before state legislative hearings, reporting on the Oregon survey and other data. They could not lobby for decriminalization, of course; they were only non-political experts, providing their statistical data and their policy analysis. In fact, Stroup worked closely with Carr to coordinate the testimony of NORML witnesses and council witnesses—to divide it up so that NORML's people would make the key political points and the council witnesses would stress the scientific points.

The NORML–Drug Abuse Council alliance was politics as usual. If NORML's scruffy band of dope smokers and Tom Bryant's very respectable think tank were improbable allies, they only proved once again that politics makes strange bedfellows. And effective bedfellows, because their alliance, and particularly the Oregon survey, would contribute to the great political breakthroughs of 1975.

But before that happened, Stroup would become caught up in some extraordinary politics, politics that definitely were not being played as usual. The Nixon administration, in its final years, had been obsessed with an "enemies list" mentality, with finding ways to use the power of government to destroy its critics. One man who was high on Nixon's enemies list was Hugh Hefner, and in 1974 Stroup's friend Bobbie Arnstein would become tragically enmeshed in the Nixon administration's attempt to destroy her boss. She turned to Stroup for help, but there was precious little help that he, or anyone, could give her.

8

As 1974 began, Hugh Hefner was living what was, even by his own extravagant standards, a most enjoyable life.

In the 1960s Hefner had pushed himself hard to build and expand his publishing empire. He had not then learned to delegate authority, to trust others, and for a time he had used amphetamines to drive himself through the round-the-clock sessions in which he wrote his "Playboy Philosophy" series and chaired the marathon editorial meetings that had helped make him the rich and powerful publisher he was. But by the 1970s Hefner's life had started to change. He was learning to delegate authority. He was spending less and less time in Chicago, where his magazine was located, and more time at his new mansion in Los Angeles, where he could bask in the California sun and let the world come to him when he had need of it. Hefner was, moreover, deeply involved in the most intense romance of his life, with a vivacious, bright-eyed young woman named Barbi Benton, who had captivated him as had few of the thousands of women who had passed through his life. Finally, most amazingly, Hefner had discovered something that had enriched, indeed revolutionized, his already prodigious sex life: marijuana.

Hefner had grown up accepting the reefer-madness mythology. He thought of marijuana as something jazz musicians used, a drug like heroin that drove men to crime and violence. When Hefner began to build his own private world in the mid-1950s, he felt no need for drugs in it. Sex was Hefner's obsession—sex and his magazine. Even his drinking was moderate. He would sip a Scotch but he never got drunk, for Hefner hated to lose control.

Although Hefner had helped create the sexual revolution of the sixties, he missed that decade's drug revolution entirely. If anything, he was disdainful of drugs and people who abused them. (He did not think of amphetamines as drugs; they were an energizer, like coffee, that had helped him do his work.) As the seventies began, Hefner took only an occasional hit of marijuana, and did not allow marijuana use in his mansions, except by his closest friends in semiprivate situations. Still, as the decade progressed, there was more marijuana around, more talk of it; more joints were being circulated, and in time Hefner made a quite startling discovery: Smoking marijuana greatly enhanced his sexual pleasure.

It was, for Hefner, a stunning turn of events, and not without its ironies. He had for fifteen years been both America's leading sexual philosopher and its leading sexual practitioner. He had slept with hundreds, even thousands of beautiful young women, in a sexual odyssey unequaled in the Western world. But now, as he began to combine marijuana with lovemaking, he learned how much he had been missing. "I didn't know what making love was all about for all those years," he said in a three-hour interview in his Los Angeles mansion in the spring of 1980. "Smoking helped put me in touch with the realm of the senses. I discovered a whole other dimension to sex. I discovered the difference between fucking and making love."

Hefner's discovery was, to be sure, one that millions of other people had already made; in this instance Hefner was a follower, not a leader, in the nation's sexual exploration. Smokers had found that at best marijuana produced a state of receptivity, even of childlike wonder, that enabled them to experience anew, often with stunning intensity, things that they had come to take for granted. The experiences that could be so dramatically enhanced might include a meal, a movie, a

child, a song, a sunset, and in particular they included physical
contact. Certainly, one reason for marijuana's popularity, despite
official disapproval and repression, was the fact that millions of people
thought it made their sex lives even more enjoyable. That was the case
with Hugh Hefner.

Hefner had grown up, like most American men, thinking of sexual
success in terms of performance: Success was how many women you
took to bed, how long you kept your erection, how many orgasms you
managed. Now he began to see that performance was virtually the
opposite of what real lovemaking was all about. Erections were not the
point, you could have wonderful sex with or without an erection. Real
lovemaking was a sensual sharing of erotic pleasure with someone you
cared about. Marijuana, he found, helped him tune out distractions—
deadlines, corporate disputes—and focus all his energies and passions
on his pleasure and his partner's. As Hefner had earlier overcome his
repressions about the sexual act itself, he now began to overcome his
resistance to sensitivity, to sharing, to giving of himself. It was, for
him, a time of discovery, of opening up his life. Sometimes Hefner
wondered what America would have been like if hundreds of years
ago, in the Colonial days, we had adopted marijuana, not alcohol, as
our drug of choice. It puzzled and saddened him to think that
America's two favorite drugs—alcohol and tobacco—were killers, and
yet we put people in jail for using a drug that he found not only
harmless but liberating.

As 1974 began, the forty-six-year-old Hefner believed himself
truly a man who had everything. Indeed, if there was any small
irritation in Hefner's life, it was that so many people refused to believe
how happy he was. People who wrote about him, Hefner had
discovered, almost always wanted to believe there was a dark side to
his life, that he was lonely or unhappy or frustrated, that there had to
be trouble in his paradise. Time after time, to Hefner's growing
annoyance, interviewers demanded of him, "But are you *really*
happy?" To some extent, Hefner thought, the question was rooted in
the envy of men who needed to rationalize the frustrations of their
own mundane, monogamous lives. But he thought that in a larger
sense the question reflected America's lingering puritanism, which
would have it that all his wealth and fame and sexual indulgence could
not give him happiness, which indeed insisted that pleasure was sin
and sin must inevitably be punished. People thought that if you

danced, you had to pay the piper, but Hefner knew better. He lived precisely as he wanted to live, and he considered himself a truly happy man. He thought the only enemy he had was time, mortality, and sometimes he half believed that somehow even time might stand still for him.

He was wrong, of course. Hefner had enemies he didn't even know about, political enemies, powerful men who hated him and what he stood for and who wanted nothing more than to drag him from his flowered paradise and lock him in prison. Before 1974 was ended, Hefner would know fear, would spend sleepless nights, would face the possibility that his world could come crashing down around him. Ironically, the instrument his enemies would use to try to destroy him was a woman who would have died for him, Bobbie Arnstein.

In 1971 Keith Stroup and Bobbie Arnstein had become lovers; by 1974 they were friends. Stroup had in time realized that Bobbie was far less interested in sex than in friendship, in finding people who would flatter her, laugh with her, argue with her, be kind to her, and above all who would not use her, as so many people tried to, because of her status with Hefner. She had gone to work as a receptionist at *Playboy* soon after she graduated from a Chicago high school. She became one of Hefner's secretaries, and in time became his executive assistant, which meant she was one of two people who could grant access to the reclusive publisher. Hefner relied on her professionally, to screen out people and problems he did not wish to be bothered with, and he enjoyed her personally. She had a tough, challenging mind, and they had long dialogues on every possible subject. When Hefner was depressed, it was often Bobbie he would tell his troubles to. Hefner's girl friends came and went, but Bobbie had remained important in his life for a decade.

To Stroup, Bobbie's friendship was crucial as he struggled to get more money for NORML from the Playboy Foundation. With Bobbie's help he was able to establish a personal relationship with Hefner that enabled him, when there were problems, to bypass the foundation and take his case directly to the top. As Stroup saw it, Hefner was a very busy man who needed to be reminded from time to time just who Keith Stroup was and just what NORML was. But you didn't make appointments with Hefner. You hung out at the mansion and you talked to

Hefner when Hefner felt like talking. Thanks to Bobbie, Stroup had access to the mansion—he could simply stay with her when he was in Chicago—and, moreover, she could tell him when to approach Hef and when to leave him alone.

She gave him help, and she needed help, too. He was also coming to understand what her friends at *Playboy* had long known, that she was a woman with serious psychological problems. Her friends thought her problems came in part from the death of her father when she was a child, and in part from the fact that she was a twin, who like many twins had identity problems and somehow never got all the attention and affection she craved. One of her close women friends says, "Bobbie was one of the funniest, brightest people I ever knew. There was a robustness and a tenderness about her. But she was a desperate person, too. She had no sense of herself, no ego strength. She needed constant approval. She tried to act tough but she wasn't. There was something of a chameleon about her, something essentially parasitic. And in time it all focused on Hefner. He was daddy, the authority figure, the person she had to please."

For his part, Hefner was pained by the great gap between the talented, attractive person Bobbie was and the person she thought she was—for she was torn by insecurity, by a sense of inadequacy. She worried constantly about her looks, although most men found her highly attractive. She would spend hours getting ready for a party, and then leave it after ten minutes. She devoted herself to Hefner —she wanted to be available to him around the clock—and was never able to achieve a satisfactory personal life of her own. One way or another, her romances always seemed to end badly.

In 1963 Bobbie had fallen in love with a young man named Tom Lownes, the younger brother of a senior *Playboy* executive. While they were driving to Florida, with her at the wheel, there was an accident. She suffered a broken arm; he was killed instantly. She returned to the mansion to recuperate, and she was deeply depressed. She felt guilty about Lownes's death, she began to drink heavily, and she gained a great deal of weight. Eventually she went to a health resort, lost the weight, and stopped the excessive drinking, but by the time Stroup met her, in 1971, she was well into the uppers-downers cycle—amphetamines to get up in the morning and get through the day, barbiturates to come down at night. The uppers didn't interfere with her work—they helped her do her work—but

Stroup thought they were starting to take a toll on her. She was often depressed, insecure, erratic. Stroup came to see her in two quite different lights, almost as two people. On the one hand, she was one of the most exciting people he'd ever known. They liked to do drugs together—marijuana, sometimes cocaine or MDA—but he thought of her as someone who was high not on drugs but on ideas, laughter, life. She had a quick, bizarre sense of humor—she was a great fan of Lenny Bruce—and she loved to debate politics, philosophy, morality, anything. She was challenging and invigorating; he almost always left her feeling happy.

And yet Bobbie was clearly someone living at the edge. He saw, behind her exuberance, a hopelessness, a sense of despair, that her dark humor and her drug use only partly concealed. She had been in and out of analysis for years (she made bitter jokes about what fools psychiatrists were). She rarely left the mansion anymore, and some of her friends feared that she was losing touch with reality, that the sweet, pampered madness of the mansion had become her reality. Outside, in the real world, her jangled nerves could barely survive a rude cabdriver or an indifferent shopgirl. She had moved out of the mansion once, after the accident that killed Tom Lownes, and lived a few months in an apartment she never bothered to furnish; then she returned to her real home, the mansion, the womb.

She increasingly spoke of suicide. She would call her women friends in the middle of the night and say she was going to kill herself. At least one of her friends took these calls as self-pity, a cry for attention, and told her to stop calling, that she wouldn't play the game. This, then, was Bobbie Arnstein in 1972—bright, hardworking, insecure, isolated, often depressed, potentially suicidal—when the outside world, the real world, began to intrude on her fantasy life in ways more terrible than she could have imagined.

Her troubles started, inevitably, with a man. As she entered her thirties, Bobbie had begun to date younger men. One of them was a handsome twenty-four-year-old drug dealer named Ron Scharf, and in September of 1971 she had flown to Coral Gables, Florida, with Scharf and a friend of his named Ira Sapstein. They visited a thirty-five-year-old drug dealer named George Matthews, and Scharf bought a half-pound of cocaine from Matthews. Later the three of them flew back to Chicago together. Whether or not Bobbie knew about the cocaine purchase, and whether she or Sapstein carried the cocaine back from Florida, were questions that were later bitterly disputed.

It developed that Scharf's telephone was being tapped as part of a federal drug investigation. Some of the taped calls were between him and Bobbie, and often they talked about drugs.

Early in 1972 there were rumors that Scharf was about to be indicted and that Bobbie might be indicted along with him. She called Stroup in panic, and he flew to Chicago to see if he could help her. It turned out that she was not indicted, although Scharf, Sapstein, and Matthews were, for conspiracy, in the cocaine sale. But for some reason the case was not prosecuted.

Instead, the investigation continued. Bobbie was repeatedly called in for questioning. Sometimes the prosecutors played her the taped conversations in which she and Scharf discussed drugs. The implication was clear: She still faced possible prosecution. She and her lawyers began to hear reports that the prosecutors were divided, with some wanting to indict her and others insisting they had no case against her.

In the fall of 1973, amid this pressure and uncertainty, Bobbie tried to kill herself with an overdose of sleeping pills. A friend found her unconscious in her apartment in the Chicago mansion, and she was rushed to a hospital and her life saved. She later told Stroup, with bitter amusement, that there was no experience quite like waking up, thinking you were dead, only to find yourself strapped to a bed and surrounded by people who thought you were crazy.

After her suicide attempt, Bobbie was sent to a private psychiatric hospital. She called Stroup in hysterics. She was locked up with crazy people, she said. There was one man who kept pissing on the floor right next to her. He had to get her out of there, before she did go crazy. Stroup flew to Chicago and found that she had not been legally committed to the hospital. He therefore told Bobbie's doctor he wanted her freed.

"She shouldn't leave yet," the doctor protested. "You'll have to take the responsibility for what might happen."

"Wait a minute," Stroup replied. "You're the doctor. If you don't think she should leave, you have her committed. That's *your* responsibility. I'm her lawyer, and if she's not committed, then I want her out of here."

He took her back to the mansion, where he sensed that many people would have preferred that she stay in confinement longer.

"Listen, Bobbie," he told her, "if you kill yourself now, I'm really fucked."

She laughed and told him not to worry, that she wouldn't do a thing like that to him.

Then she was indicted.

At noon on March 23, 1974, two years after the first indictments in Scharf's case, Bobbie stepped briefly outside the mansion, on her way from one of its wings to the other. She was wearing a pantsuit and sunglasses and carrying some papers. A man stepped into her path and asked if she was Roberta Arnstein. When she said she was, he said he was a federal agent and she was under arrest. He produced handcuffs and snapped them onto her wrists. "But I haven't had lunch yet," she protested—a choice example of her deadpan humor, her friends thought. Newspaper photographers, alerted by the prosecutors, snapped pictures of her arrest; it was the first indication of the media extravaganza the government would make of her case.

Earlier that morning, before her arrest, new indictments had been handed down in the cocaine-conspiracy case, indictments that reflected a major change in the government's case. At the time of his arrest, Matthews had given a long statement to the authorities. It implicated Scharf and Sapstein in the cocaine deal and mentioned Arnstein only in passing. But now, after he had been convicted and sentenced to fifteen years in prison, Matthews changed his story to say he had seen Bobbie put the cocaine in her purse.

The new indictments were brought by a Justice Department anti-crime strike force, working in cooperation with the Drug Enforcement Agency and the U.S. attorney for the Chicago district, James Thompson, a Republican who had made his name prosecuting Democratic politicians and who would in time be elected governor of Illinois and be talked about as a future presidential candidate.

It was clear, throughout the case, that the government saw the prosecution of Arnstein as a first step toward making a major drug case against Hugh Hefner. The Nixon administration's law-and-order crusade was at its peak then. Narcotics agents were kicking down doors, often the wrong doors, on their no-knock raids, and undercover agents were sending hundreds of people to prison with testimony that would later be proved to be perjury. There seemed to be no restraints on what the government could do in its anti-drug crusade, and there

cannot have been many more inviting targets for ambitious prosecutors or publicity-hungry politicians than the publisher of *Playboy*.
Hefner was a champion of the "new morality," and as such he was
hated and feared by millions of Americans who still clung to the
verities of the old morality. To make it worse, he was a middle-aged
man who flaunted his sexual adventures with an endless stream of
young women. Small wonder, then, that the zealots of the Nixon
administration would put Hefner on their enemies list and would try to
make a drug case against the publisher that at the least would make
him sweat and at best might bring down his empire. It was Bobbie
Arnstein's misfortune to become an unwitting actor in this high-stakes
political drama.

That first afternoon, after her arrest, she was freed on bond, and
she called Stroup for help. He hurried to Chicago to advise her and to
help her select her lawyer. They eventually settled on a first-rate
criminal-defense lawyer named Tom Sullivan. Stroup agreed to serve
as unpaid cocounsel, primarily to mediate between Bobbie and
Sullivan, who was an excellent lawyer but also a very straight
middle-aged Catholic who did not relate with ease to his very hip,
nervous, demanding client.

From the first, the prosecutors made it clear to Bobbie and to her
lawyers that it was really Hefner they wanted, not her. Their
questions to her were invariably directed at alleged drug use by
Hefner and by others at his mansion. They were obsessed with the
idea that he passed around bowls of cocaine at his parties. Tell us about
Hefner, they said again and again, and you have nothing to worry
about. Perhaps the prosecutors did believe Hefner used and dispensed
cocaine, but the fact was that, so far as Hefner's closest friends knew,
he used no drugs except occasional alcohol and marijuana. He
disapproved of cocaine and hallucinogenic drugs, and people who used
them in his mansions did so behind his back.

As the trial drew near, Bobbie's lawyers had one great problem:
how to rebut George Matthews' testimony that he saw Bobbie put the
cocaine in her purse.

Ron Scharf, her codefendant, was not going to testify, lest he be
cross-examined about the drug deals he had discussed in the taped
phone calls. He told Bobbie's lawyers that if Bobbie could get a
separate trial, he would swear that she knew nothing about the drug
deal, but the judge denied Sullivan's motion for a separate trial.

Ira Sapstein, who had been named in the first indictments but not indicted the second time, was nowhere to be found.

There remained the possibility of Bobbie's testifying in her own behalf. She wanted to. Matthews was lying, she said, and she wanted to say so. But Stroup and Sullivan were agreed that she must not take the stand. For one thing, she would not be a witness with whom a working-class Chicago jury was likely to feel much sympathy. An even bigger problem was the tapes on which she and Scharf had discussed drugs. If she took the stand, she could be cross-examined about everything on the tapes. Stroup's fear was that under cross-examination she would either perjure herself or be forced to admit criminal acts, and that she might suffer a breakdown in the process.

The trial began on October 27 and lasted three days. Stroup and Bobbie would ride to the trial each day in a chauffeured Mercedes, listening to Beatles tapes and perhaps sharing a joint on the way. They always got out of the Mercedes a block away from the courthouse, however, lest the jury see Bobbie in her limousine. It was her only concession to convention. She rejected Stroup's suggestion that she "dress down" for the jury's benefit; instead she arrived at court each day in some expensive new outfit, perhaps featuring a flashy leather vest or knee-length boots. Worse, Bobbie and Ron Scharf would sometimes pass notes back and forth at the defense table, and one day Stroup noticed that one of the folded-up notes contained some drugs. Stroup was furious at Bobbie, but she only laughed.

The prosecution's star witness was George Matthews, the Florida drug dealer who now swore he had seen Bobbie put the cocaine in her purse. He was brought to the stand in handcuffs, for he was then serving the fifteen-year sentence on his own drug conviction.

With Bobbie not testifying, Sullivan had little defense to offer except to try to discredit Matthews and to call character witnesses, including *Playboy*'s editor, Arthur Kretchmer. It wasn't enough. The jury found both Bobbie and Scharf guilty. On November 26 the judge sentenced Scharf to a six-year prison term and Bobbie to a provisional fifteen-year term. She was to undergo ninety days of psychiatric testing and then be resentenced.

It seemed unlikely that the judge would let stand the fifteen-year sentence. But Bobbie could not be sure of that. It was as if the judge were helping the prosecutors put one more form of pressure on her.

Within days of her sentencing, subpoenas had gone out to past and present Playboy employees in a federal-grand-jury investigation of drug use in Hefner's mansion. A federal prosecutor told reporters, "Hefner's in a hell of a lot of trouble." Hefner agreed. He was in more trouble than he had ever dreamed possible. He had seen Bobbie convicted with what he believed to be perjured testimony, and he had to face the possibility that he, too, could be convicted. He had already seen how much harm the government could do to him even prior to any charges. They were brilliant at playing the media, at leaking stories about the investigation even before they had proved anything. The Playboy world was kept unsettled by rumors that there would be raids on the mansion, or that narcotics agents would try to plant drugs there. Two outside members of his board of directors resigned over the controversy, a major bank threatened to cut off Playboy's credit, and advertisers quit his magazine. The government could wear you down, make you suspect your friends, make you question everyone's motives. The government's best shot at Hefner still seemed to be Bobbie, if she, desperate to save herself from prison, would testify that she had supplied him with cocaine or other hard drugs. That seemed wildly improbable, but, in this situation, nothing was impossible.

Bobbie was, in fact, in a terrible condition as she awaited the outcome of her legal appeals. Her uncertainty and despair left her barely coherent at times. She was torn by guilt, by a sense that she, by her association with Scharf, had made it possible for the government to threaten Hefner and his empire. Stroup, who spoke with her daily, thought the government was putting truly inhuman pressure on her to turn against Hefner. He thought the prosecutors knew she was a fragile, disturbed woman who would do almost anything to escape prison. And they were right about that. Bobbie was desperately afraid of prison. She wasn't going there for fifteen minutes, much less fifteen years.

What the prosecutors did not seem to understand was that Bobbie would never harm Hefner. It was simply inconceivable, a nonalternative.

For Bobbie, there was another alternative: suicide. All Bobbie's friends understood that. Stroup thought the prosecutors understood it, too, and that they coldly gambled that Bobbie would turn against Hefner before she would kill herself.

She had, after all, tried to kill herself even before the trial. She had read *The Bell Jar* and *The Savage God* and other books about suicide. She liked to debate the subject, and as her trial neared, the discussions became more frequent and less academic. She asked Stroup whether, if she were convicted, he could guarantee her thirty days before she was imprisoned. He said he could.

After her conviction they continued to discuss suicide. For a while he made all the standard arguments against it, but she was unpersuaded. "Keith doesn't accept suicide as a legitimate alternative," she would say. In the end she persuaded him that her life was her own, to terminate when she wished.

Still, given the many legal appeals open to them, Stroup thought Bobbie was a long way from killing herself. He believed, as he stressed to her, that they had a good chance of overturning her conviction, perhaps because the judge had refused to sever her trial from Scharf's.

Then, in early December, the government played an unexpected card.

U.S. Attorney James Thompson called Bobbie to his office and told her he had information from two sources that there was a contract out on her life, that someone was offering to pay to have her killed. He refused to give names or specifics, but warned that if he were in her position, he'd trust neither friend nor foe.

The implication seemed clear enough to her: Hefner, or people close to him, would have her killed rather than face the possibility that she might testify against him.

Bobbie called Stroup in hysterics. He flew to Chicago, demanded a second meeting with the prosecutors, and furiously accused them of making up the contract story to put further pressure on Bobbie. Although she did not take seriously the idea that Hefner would harm her, Bobbie was further unsettled by the prosecutor's death-threat story. She began to have nightmares in which killers broke down her door. On December 16 she had Stroup draw up her will.

Throughout the trial Bobbie had remained on salary, and Hefner had paid her legal fees. He had also called her from time to time from Los Angeles to encourage her. He was in fact under pressure from his corporate advisers to put some distance between himself and Bobbie, and eventually he did take one step in that direction. It had been agreed that Bobbie would move to Los Angeles. She could work for Hefner in the mansion there, and her friends hoped the move would improve her state of mind. The compromise was that she wouldn't live in the mansion. Instead she would share a house with her friend Shirley Hillman and commute to work. Thus, the Playboy empire would be spared the embarrassment of constant newspaper stories saying that a convicted cocaine conspirator was living in Hefner's mansion, as well as the risk that she would again bring drugs into the mansion.

She was to fly to Los Angeles on Saturday, January 11. Instead she stayed in Chicago, called Stroup for a chat in the afternoon, had dinner with Shirley Hillman, went to a late movie, returned to the mansion at 1:30 A.M., then walked five blocks to the Hotel Maryland, where Lenny Bruce used to stay when he was in Chicago. She checked into a room on the seventeenth floor, then took enough sleeping pills and tranquilizers to kill herself several times. While she waited to die, she wrote a letter that she addressed to Stroup and Hillman.

It was important to her that her suicide cause minimal embarrassment to Hefner. That was why she had left the mansion to die. And in her letter, in addition to protesting her innocence on the cocaine charge, she insisted that Hefner was "a staunchly upright, rigorously moral man—I know him well and he had never been involved in the criminal activity which is being attributed to him now."

A cleaning woman found her body the next day, and the news of her death caused a great sensation. Hefner flew to Chicago for her funeral, and then he called a news conference at which he said, among other things, "It is difficult to describe the inquisitional atmosphere of the Bobbie Arnstein trial and related Playboy probe. In the infamous witchcraft trials of the Middle Ages, the inquisitors tortured the victims until they not only confessed to being witches but accused their own families and friends of sorcery as well. In similar fashion, narcotics agents frequently use our severe drug laws in an arbitrary and capricious manner to elicit the desired testimony for a trial.

"Testimony thus acquired is at best highly suspect, since the witness has good reason to provide whatever the prosecutor wants of him. This is the sort of testimony that was used to convict Bobbie Arnstein; this is the technique that was used in an attempt to force Bobbie Arnstein to falsely incriminate me.

William Safire, the Nixon speechwriter and then New York *Times* columnist, picked up Hefner's "inquisition" charge in his column: "If she had told the prosecutors what they wanted to hear—obviously by involving a prime publicity target—she would have been treated leniently. . . . Bobbie Arnstein committed suicide under the new torture."

Tom Fitzpatrick wrote in the Chicago *Sun-Times* about how Bobbie would be remembered in the Playboy mansion: "They'll remember that it was Bobbie who worried whether the butlers got overtime pay in their checks. They'll remember it was Bobbie who fought to get raises for secretaries whom everyone else overlooked.

"Yes, and they'll remember Bobbie in a new outfit with her hair freshly done. They'll remember her laughing both at herself and with everyone around her.

"She was a classy lady who never hurt anybody but herself, and who was crushed by a system that wasn't really out to get her, just her boss."

To Stroup, to Hefner and others in his world, and to many informed outsiders, like William Safire, the Arnstein case was a classic example of the government's power to use the drug laws selectively for political purposes. The prosecutors of course insisted that theirs was a solid case, and in fact they did obtain a jury conviction against Arnstein, but Stroup and others were absolutely convinced that the government's key witness, a convicted felon, had perjured himself in the hope of receiving favorable treatment, and in fact he did serve less than a year of his original fifteen-year sentence. Had Arnstein been stronger, she might in time have won her case on appeal. As it was, many people will remember her as the victim of a classic Nixon-era witch hunt.

In a way, Stroup thought Bobbie had had the last laugh. The prosecutors had set out to use her to get Hefner, and they had failed. She had quit the game at a time and in a manner of her own choosing. And they hadn't got Hefner, either. Some months later the Justice Department announced it had closed the investigation into his world, for lack of evidence.

9

After the unexpected victory in Oregon in the summer of 1973, the marijuana-law reformers waited anxiously for the walls of resistance to come tumbling down. For a long time they waited in vain. The rest of 1973 passed, and all of 1974, without another state following Oregon's example, although many states were considering decriminalization bills.

Then, in 1975, the dam broke. Five states—including two of the nation's largest, California and Ohio—passed decriminalization bills. The most obvious reason for this dramatic breakthrough was political: In August of 1974 Richard Nixon resigned from the presidency in disgrace. A month later, his hand-picked successor, Gerald Ford, granted Nixon pardon for whatever crimes he had committed in the Watergate affair. Two months after that, the voters of America took revenge on Nixon's political party by ousting Republican incumbents in Congress and in the state legislatures in record numbers.

There was a new, post-Watergate mood across the land. In Washington this new mood was most perfectly expressed in the person of Dr. Robert L. DuPont, the director of the White House Special Action Office for Drug Abuse Prevention (ODAP, to its friends), who delivered the keynote speech at NORML's third annual conference, in November of 1974, just three months after Nixon's resignation.

DuPont was a tall, handsome, sandy-haired man in his late thirties, a psychiatrist who was rapidly making a name for himself as a drug expert. He was an engaging, outgoing man, a natural politician who was quick to explain that he was not one of the rich chemical-company du Ponts. He was, however, blessed with aristocratic looks and self-confidence. He had gone to Emory University, in Atlanta, where he was a friend of both Tom Bryant and Peter Bourne, and from there to the Harvard medical school, where, in the early 1960s, he tried marijuana a few times but never managed to get high. By the early 1970s he was gaining a national reputation as the head of a methadone program in Washington, D.C., and in June of 1973, although he was a registered Democrat, he had been recruited by the Nixon White House to head its anti-drug program. He would later say that he had favored an end to jail penalties for possession of marijuana since 1970, but "knowing of the strong feelings of President Nixon opposing any move toward 'decriminalization,'" he "carefully avoided any comment on the issue until [Nixon] turned over the presidency to Gerald Ford."

With Nixon out and Ford in, DuPont gladly accepted an invitation to address the NORML conference and to declare that criminal penalties had not prevented marijuana use, had needlessly disrupted lives, and should be replaced by a noncriminal fine, perhaps twenty-five dollars or so. For NORML, to have the top White House drug-policy adviser endorsing its no-jail policy as DuPont's old friend Tom Bryant, another speaker at the conference, beamed his approval was dramatic proof both that the dope lobby had achieved respectability and that there was a thaw taking place after the long, cold winter of Nixon.

There was, to be sure, no national surge toward legal marijuana, but as the state legislatures convened in January of 1975, there was a growing sense that the existing laws were too harsh. Democrats in many states were in their strongest position in ten years, and many of the new Democratic legislators were young, had used marijuana and other drugs, and were committed to marijuana-law reform. The reformers sensed the stirrings, and their hopes were high, nowhere more so than in California.

When the new legislature convened in Sacramento, the Democrats held a fifty-five-to-twenty-five majority in the assembly and a twenty-five-to-fifteen majority in the senate. Moreover, Ronald Reagan, who had vetoed several marijuana-reform bills, had been succeeded as governor by Jerry Brown, who had said in his campaign that he favored a law based on the Oregon model. Also, the Democratic leader in the state senate, George Moscone, who was committed to reform and had sponsored several bills in years past, was determined to pass a decriminalization bill in 1975. Part of Moscone's motivation was that he was planning to run for mayor of San Francisco. It was a city that had voted decisively for the CMI proposal in 1972, and a decriminalization bill would obviously be popular there.

Moscone's closest ally, through six months of intense political conflict, was NORML's man in California, Gordon Brownell. Throughout the first half of the year, Brownell spent two or three days a week in Sacramento, working out of Moscone's spacious majority leader's office. There was no friction or suspicion to the relationship. Moscone regarded Brownell as he might a member of his own staff—except that his services came for free. Moreover, besides Brownell's help, NORML was willing to spend whatever had to be spent to fly in witnesses, get out mailings, and otherwise support the California effort.

Stroup largely stayed out of California, partly because he trusted Brownell's political judgment and partly because he had a dozen other states to worry about. But California was always number one in his thinking. It was the nation's most populous state, it was the scene of roughly a fifth of the nation's marijuana arrests (eighty-eight thousand in 1975), and it was an acknowledged political style-setter for the rest of the nation. Stroup went all over America that spring promising that decriminalization would soon pass in California. He put NORML's credibility on the line, and he came to think that if the reform bill didn't win in the Golden State, NORML would be wiped out politically.

By the time the new legislature convened early in January, Moscone and Brownell had agreed on the sort of bill Moscone would introduce. The original bill was more liberal than they thought would pass, in order to leave room for negotiation. Existing California law still made possession of any amount of marijuana a felony punishable by up to ten years in prison. The Moscone bill proposed to make possession of up to three ounces of marijuana an "infraction," punishable by a fine of up to $100. Existing felony penalties for sale or cultivation would remain unchanged.

It was not enough to satisfy the purists—it did not allow free backyard grass—but Moscone and Brownell thought it realistic. If their bill passed, 90 percent of the hundred thousand people who were being arrested in California on marijuana charges each year would not face jail, only a citation and possible fine. It was a start; cultivation could come later.

Hearings were scheduled for February in the senate judiciary committee, a graveyard for past reform bills. Seven votes were needed for passage there—a majority of the committee's twelve members—and those seven were by no means certain. As it developed, the decisive vote belonged to a newly elected Democrat named Robert Presley, who had previously been the undersheriff of Riverside County. Moscone had campaigned for Presley, and Presley wanted to support Moscone's bill, but he and others on the committee thought up to three ounces of marijuana was too large an amount to decriminalize. Also, they didn't like calling possession an infraction; they wanted to call it a misdemeanor, even if only a fine was provided as punishment.

Presley was supported in these concerns by the lobbyist for the District Attorneys Association, who said many DAs would oppose the "infraction" terminology but might not oppose the bill that called possession a misdemeanor. Brownell and Moscone agreed to fall back to one ounce, but they were more concerned by the infraction/misdemeanor issue. In one sense, it was only face-saving terminology for the law-enforcement people, but in another sense it went to the heart of the question of whether or not smoking was a crime.

Finally, knowing that without Presley's vote the bill might die in committee, they agreed to the "misdemeanor" terminology, but they extracted some concessions in return, notably a provision calling for the destruction of the felony records of more than half a million people who had been arrested in California in past years for simple possession.

When the bill thus amended, hearings began. Tom Bryant came to testify and brought with him a new, politically important survey of attitudes toward marijuana in California. The poll had been conducted by the respected Field Research Organization and paid for by the Drug Abuse Council. It showed that 46 percent of those questioned favored a civil-fine approach to marijuana use. It also showed that only 9 percent of Californians were regular marijuana users—a figure that could be used to counter Senator Eastland's claim of a marijuana epidemic. To legislators the survey strongly suggested that a vote for reform was politically safe in California. Pat Horton, Steve Kafoury, and Stafford Hansell came from Oregon and attested to the success of decriminalization in their state. NORML paid for the expenses of their trip.

The bill was not without opposition. A lady from the Women's Christian Temperance Union asked if NORML might not be a Communist front. Dr. Hardin Jones, of the University of California, a star of the Eastland hearings, claimed that regular marijuana use could cause loss of memory, sterility, and chromosome damage equal to that of survivors of the Hiroshima blast. Another outspoken opponent of reform was Los Angeles police chief Ed Davis, an unannounced candidate for governor, who warned an American Legion convention that marijuana use was probably responsible for poor test scores in California schools and added that George Moscone was becoming the Marie Antoinette of California—one who said "Let them smoke pot" instead of "Let them eat cake."

The bill cleared the judiciary committee with the bare seven votes required, and went next to the full senate.

Twenty-one votes were needed in the senate, a majority of its forty members, and those twenty-one were by no means certain. Everything depended on Moscone's personal leadership. He was the Democratic leader, he was popular, and he was calling in his IOUs on the marijuana bill. He was able to win the vote of the conservative, seventy-five-year-old dean of the senate who had opposed previous reform bills. He swung the vote of a Chicano senator who had strong anti-drug feelings. It was an intense, all-out effort by a first-rate politician—Moscone the Magnificent, Brownell would call him in later years—and even so, his bill cleared the senate on March 20 with only the minimum twenty-one votes it needed, and that included the support of two liberal Republicans.

The reformers celebrated that night. The senate had traditionally been the more conservative of the California legislature's two houses.

The assembly, with its more than two-to-one Democratic majority, and with several Republicans favoring reform, seemed to pose no problem. Brownell, in a memo to Stroup, predicted smooth sailing there.

He was wrong.

The reform bill's sponsor in the assembly was Alan Sieroty, who represented Beverly Hills and had worked for reform in the past, but the two key actors in the drama there proved to be the Democratic speaker, Leo McCarthy, and a conservative Republican gadfly named John Briggs. In early May, as a vote neared, Brownell began to hear rumors that conservative Republicans, led by Briggs, would try to evoke unit rule on the marijuana bill. This meant that if two-thirds of the Republican caucus opposed the bill, they could require the other third to oppose it, or at least abstain from voting, or else lose all party rank and privileges. However, unit rule had almost never been invoked in the assembly, so Brownell hoped the talk of its invocation was some sort of bluff.

It wasn't. On the morning of May 8, the day the vote was scheduled, the Republicans caucused, and John Briggs argued forcefully for unit rule. The Republican leaders opposed his proposal; several of them planned to support the reform bill. Briggs was, in effect, leading a conservative rebellion against his party's more liberal leaders. But there was more than factional hostility here. Briggs, an outspoken, publicity-prone politician who later allied himself with Anita Bryant's anti-homosexual crusade, had a very clear strategy in mind.

As he and many Republicans saw it, their party had been decimated the previous year by an issue that had nothing to do with them: the sins of Richard Nixon. They were fighting for survival, and if the Democrats wanted to go out on a limb on the marijuana issue, why give them a free ride? If every Republican in the assembly opposed the bill, several things would happen. For one, they could probably defeat the bill and thereby embarrass Moscone and other Democrats who had put their prestige on the line. Moreover, if every Republican opposed reform, a clear-cut issue would be raised for the 1976 elections: The Democrats would be the pro-pot party. In particular, a pro-marijuana vote might be enough to defeat several of the first-term Democrats who had been elected in 1974 in traditionally Republican districts.

The Republican caucus did invoke unit rule, outraging Republican liberals who had planned to vote for the reform bill and sending into panic several Democrats who had hoped their votes would not be needed to pass it.

There was a further complication that hectic Thursday morning. Assemblyman Willie Brown's "consenting-adults bill" was voted on and passed narrowly; it removed criminal penalties for homosexuality and was sometimes called the "gay bill of rights." The timing was terrible: It was very hard for many Democrats to vote for both gay rights and marijuana reform on the same day.

Worried Democrats started streaming into Speaker McCarthy's office, particularly the first-termers from conservative southern California districts. His advice: Don't walk into the trap. Don't support the marijuana bill. McCarthy wanted to postpone the vote. He knew that one pro-reform legislator was in Europe, and that a vacant assembly seat would soon be filled by a pro-reform liberal. McCarthy had his majority to think about. Why should young Democrats risk their careers on a pro-marijuana vote when, in a month or two, the bill might pass without their votes' being needed?

To wait, or to vote? Moscone, Sieroty, and Brownell debated the issue, amid much confusion. Sieroty wanted to wait, but Moscone and Brownell wanted to go ahead, despite the speaker's recommendation. They thought they could still count forty-one votes, even without Republican support.

They were wrong.

The vote was thirty-eight to thirty-four, a majority of those voting, but still three votes short of the forty-one needed. Three first-term assemblymen the reformers had counted on had backed away, apparently at the urging of Speaker McCarthy.

Brownell called Stroup in Washington to break the news. Brownell was outraged, furious. He had been waiting five years for this vote, waiting since the days when he worked for Ronald Reagan, and now all his hopes and efforts seemed down the drain.

Stroup, hearing the news, could only mutter, "Oh, my God." So much was riding on California—not only NORML's credibility but perhaps the fate of reform bills in five or ten other states. Stroup was soon on his way to California, not because he had a plan to save the day but because he didn't know what else to do.

The reformers were furious. Moscone spoke bitterly to reporters about legislators whose only concern was self-preservation. It was not clear, in the immediate aftermath, whether there would be a second vote, or whether the bill would pass if there was. Brownell was more angry at Speaker McCarthy than at anyone else. He started calling FM radio stations, asking announcers to tell their listeners to call Leo McCarthy if they didn't like what the assembly had done. Within hours McCarthy's lines were tied up by hundreds of calls, and that afternoon he took the extraordinary step of calling Brownell, asking him to call off his troops, and giving his personal assurance that the bill would pass when it came up for a second vote.

The question had become one of timing. In retrospect, the reformers had been wrong to push for the first vote, and it was imperative they not make the same mistake twice. There had been several reasons Brownell and Moscone had ignored McCarthy's advice and demanded the first vote. One was that political crusades take on a certain momentum; they are easier to start than to stop. Passions are aroused; hopes are high. To stop becomes a kind of political *coitus interruptus:* easier said than done.

Also, the marijuana reformers lived in fear that some sudden development might swing public opinion against them. Senator Eastland might hold new hearings, or some scientist might claim that marijuana caused cancer, or some Manson-type atrocity might be blamed on drugs. (Later, in Michigan, after a reform bill had narrowly passed, its sponsor was bitterly denounced by another legislator, who said his son had smoked marijuana and it had led him to heroin and to death. With passions thus aroused, another legislator attacked the bill's sponsor with an ashtray, and when the dust settled, a second vote was taken and the bill was defeated.)

Perhaps most important, California was the keystone of NORML's national strategy. In California itself it didn't matter if the bill passed in May or November; it would still go into effect on the first day of 1976. But NORML was counting on early passage of the California bill to have a domino effect, to blast loose the passage of bills in perhaps five or ten other states. It was imperative that those bills pass in 1975, because the next year, 1976, was a national-election year, a time when many legislators might not risk a pro-reform vote. It was now or never, or so it seemed.

When Stroup arrived in Sacramento, Brownell took him around to meet several Democratic assemblymen, one of whom took him for an outside agitator and threw him out of his office, whereupon Stroup carried his lobbying campaign to Beverly Hills, where he rallied rich liberals to contact their assemblymen. The Playboy mansion was made available for lobbying efforts, a fact that reflected Hefner's intense interest in the legislation.

The second vote came on June 24. The Republicans invoked unit rule again. During two hours of emotional debate, Assemblyman Willie Brown, a black liberal, waved a hand-rolled cigarette and declared that people who smoked a few joints were not criminals. (He later said the joint was made of tobacco). John Briggs, the anti-gay, anti-pot leader, gave the Democrats a candid summary of his political strategy: "It's quite possible that in 1976 your platform will be 'Grass, Gays, and Godlessness.' "

The bill needed forty-one votes, and it got forty-two. In Brownell's eyes the heroes of the second vote were two first-term Democrats from conservative districts who voted no the first time but switched to yes on the second vote. One of them was Floyd Mori, a Mormon who neither smoked nor drank. The reformers had succeeded in convincing him that a vote against jail penalties did not amount to an endorsement of marijuana. The other convert was Richard Robinson, a former Marine officer in Vietnam who decided that as a matter of conscience he could not oppose reform, even if his vote was not needed and might harm him politically.

The bill's passage was denounced by Ed Davis, who said the legislature was favoring "pansies and potheads" and urged Governor Brown to veto it. In fact, Brown postponed action on the bill until it was within hours of becoming law without his signature; then he signed it with a minimum of ceremony. Still, he signed it, and on the first day of 1976, California stopped putting people in jail for smoking marijuana.

A state agency later conducted a survey of the results of the new law in its first year. It found that arrests dropped from about eighty-eight thousand in 1975 to about ten thousand in 1976 (these were for possession of more than an ounce), and about forty thousand citations were issued for possession of less than an ounce. An estimated $25 million in police and court costs was saved.

Finally, in the 1976 elections, there was a political footnote: None of the Democrats who supported the reform bill was defeated.

That spring, as the battle raged on in California, strange things were happening in Alaska.

The Alaska saga actually began in 1972, with two young lawyers sitting around one evening smoking marijuana and grumbling about the marijuana laws. The two lawyers in Alaska were about thirty years old, and their names were Robert Wagstaff and Irwin Ravin. Wagstaff was a native of Kansas City who had done his undergraduate work at Dartmouth. It was there, in 1961, that he first smoked. Marijuana was not readily available in those days, but Wagstaff was a jazz fan, and some black jazz musicians introduced him to the weed. He returned to the University of Kansas law school, then moved to Fairbanks, Alaska, where he became an assistant district attorney. It was in Fairbanks that he met Ravin, a native of Newark, New Jersey, and a graduate of Rutgers. Later they moved to Anchorage and practiced law together.

They also smoked marijuana, and as they talked that night in 1972, they agreed the legal and political climate in Alaska was such that a good test case, with the right client, could overturn the marijuana laws. But who would be that client?

That question was left unresolved. Then, a couple of nights later, fate intervened in the person of a Fairbanks policeman who stopped Ravin because a taillight was out on his car. It was a routine traffic violation. All Ravin had to do was sign the citation and go on his way. But Ravin decided the time had come to take a stand. Knowing he had a couple of joints in his pocket, he refused to sign the citation. That left the arresting officer no choice but to take him to the station. There he was routinely searched, the two joints were found, and the case of *Ravin* v. *Alaska* came to be.

Wagstaff and another lawyer, R. C. Middleton, filed a motion to dismiss the charges before trial, arguing that the state law prohibiting possession of marijuana was unconstitutional because it violated the right of privacy guaranteed by both the U.S. and the Alaska constitutions. In a sense, the issue was not so much legal as political. Reformers in other states had made the same right-of-privacy arguments and had always been turned down. But Alaska was not like other states. It was a frontier. People went there for privacy, for freedom; for Alaskans the right of privacy came near to being sacred. That, at least, is how Wagstaff hoped the courts would see things, and he was aware that the Alaska supreme court was the youngest and most liberal in the nation.

Lengthy hearings were held in district court on the constitutional question. Wagstaff was a member of the national board of the ACLU and he had legal and financial help from it. He also had help from NORML, who paid the expenses for Drs. Thomas Ungerleider, Joel Fort, and Lester Grinspoon to go to Alaska to testify. The district court denied Wagstaff's motion to dismiss, and he appealed the constitutional question to the Alaska supreme court. By the spring of 1975 the court was near a decision, and Wagstaff was increasingly optimistic that it would be a favorable one.

Meanwhile, things were happening in the state legislature. State Senator Terry Miller, a clean-cut Republican in his early thirties, had introduced a decriminalization bill similar to Oregon's. Stroup never went to Alaska, but he kept in touch with the situation there through Wagstaff, who had agreed to be NORML's state representative. As legislative hearings drew near, an unexpected conflict arose between Stroup and Wagstaff. Wagstaff was convinced there was a very good chance that the supreme court would make smoking legal in Alaska. For that reason he was very skeptical about the decriminalization bill. It provided for $100 fines for private possession and $1000 fines for public smoking or possessing while driving. As far as Stroup was concerned, it was a good bill, but Wagstaff feared that if the bill passed, it would take the pressure off the supreme court to rule in favor of Ravin. Thus, Alaska might settle for a system of fines when it could have had full legalization of private possession. He therefore announced to Stroup that he intended to go testify *against* the bill.

Stroup couldn't believe it. Wagstaff was the kind of smart, able lawyer he dreamed of finding to be a NORML state coordinator—and now he said he was going to testify against decriminalization. Stroup thought it made him and NORML look like idiots. A transcontinental shouting match ensued.

"Bob," Stroup insisted, "we can't have NORML opposing a decriminalization bill. It may not be a perfect bill, but we've only been able to pass one in America so far."

Wagstaff was not moved, and he did in fact testify against the bill. It didn't matter. On May 16 the Alaska bill passed, and the state's new Republican governor, Jay Hammond, keeping the promise he had earlier made, did not veto it. The bill became law without his signature.

That made Alaska the second state, after Oregon, to adopt decriminalization. Then, eleven days after the legislature acted, the state supreme court, in a stunning decision, ruled five to none that possession of marijuana by adults at home for personal use was constitutionally protected by the right-of-privacy provision in the state constitution.

In its fifty-four page opinion the court said there was "no firm evidence" that marijuana was harmful to the user or to society, and that "mere scientific doubts" could not justify government intrusion into the privacy of the home. The court added, "It appears that the use of marijuana, as it is presently used in the United States today, does not constitute a public health problem. . . . It appears that effects of marijuana on the individual are not serious enough to justify wide-spread concern, at least as compared with the far more dangerous effects of alcohol, barbiturates and amphetamines."

The ruling stuck down the legislature's new system of fines for marijuana use. Private cultivation of marijuana was not mentioned by the court, but later the state attorney general ruled that the right of privacy included cultivation. It was as legal to grow marijuana in Alaska as it was to grow tomatoes. Only sale remained illegal.

On June 16 Maine became the third state, after Oregon and Alaska, to decriminalize marijuana use. The main reason marijuana-law reform passed easily in Maine was that it was part of a new state criminal-code revision that had been recommended by a high-level commission after several years of study. The commission concluded that far too much time and money were being spent on victimless crimes, such as marijuana use and prostitution, and the legislature accepted the view.

In Maine, as in several other states, it was not until after decriminalization passed that its opponents, particularly law-enforcement officials, began to speak out strongly against it. Pressure from police officials, who claimed the new law was causing increased smuggling activity in the state, led to new hearings the next year. A repeal bill was introduced, and anti-marijuana scientists, veterans of the Eastland hearings, were brought in to testify. But now the pro-reform legislators were in the unusual but enjoyable position of defending the status quo, and they saw to it that the repeal bill never got out of committee.

In 1974 Stroup had found himself part of an unlikely scheme to legalize marijuana use in Colorado. While visiting the state, he had met a handsome, Yale-educated rancher and politician named Michael Strang, who was a liberal Republican and a member of the state senate. One day, as they discussed the marijuana laws, Strang declared, "Hell, why don't we just legalize the stuff, tax it, and put the money in the old folks' pension fund?" Strang introduced a bill to that effect, and Stroup testified in support of it, along with Dr. Dorothy Whipple and Ed Brecher, the author of the Consumers' Union report on drugs. Stroup never expected the bill to pass, but the hearings drew plenty of publicity, and it was all part of the consciousness-raising process.

In 1975, however, a decriminalization bill was introduced that had a serious chance of passage. NORML's man in Colorado then was James Moore, a tough-talking cowboy lawyer in his mid-forties who was the deputy district attorney for Pitkin County, which includes Aspen. Perhaps the turning point in Colorado came when Moore, as a middle-aged, whiskey-drinking law-enforcement official, was able to persuade the state senate's Republican majority leader, a Denver lawyer named Richard Plock, to be the floor manager for the decriminalization bill.

Certainly the bill could not have passed without the Republican leader's support, and even with his support it passed the senate by only one vote, and after two days of intense debate. Moore's impression was that the most effective argument in Colorado, an essentially conservative state, was that millions of dollars were being wasted needlessly on enforcement of the marijuana laws.

In May, as the states began to move, the reformers got an unexpected boost from Washington. Sen. Birch Bayh, of Indiana, held hearings before his Juvenile Delinquency Sub-committee on a federal decriminalization bill sponsored by Sens. Jacob Javits, Ed Brooke, Alan Cranston, and Gaylord Nelson. Bayh's support of decriminalization was a personal turnabout and one that many people assumed was intended to win support for him among the young when he ran for president in the next year. The witnesses included Stroup, Pat Horton, of Oregon, and Richard Bonnie, of the Marijuana Commission staff, but the dramatic highlight of the hearings came when Sen. Philip Hart, of Michigan, one of the most respected members of the Senate, explained that he had changed his mind on marijuana after his son was arrested. "I knew then we had a topsy-turvy operation here. He spent twenty days in jail for a stub this big. I'm from the older generation who thought taking marijuana on Tuesday meant heroin on Friday. His arrest was all the education I needed."

On August 22 Republican governor James Rhodes, of Ohio, signed a bill that made Ohio the sixth state, and the fifth since May, to decriminalize marijuana use. It was a remarkable victory for the reform movement. Oregon, Alaska, California, and Colorado were all Western states with a pioneer tradition that government should leave people alone. Maine was a flinty, no-nonsense New England state, proud to go its own way. But Ohio? Ohio was the heartland, one of the most conservative states in the union. It made no sense at all that Ohio would pass the nation's most liberal marijuana law—not, that is, unless one understands the unique role played there by a Republican businessman and civic leader named Richard M. Wolfe.

Dick Wolfe's grandfather was a shoemaker. He and his brother, in the best Horatio Alger tradition, became successful shoe manufacturers and went on to found an Ohio dynasty. By the 1970s the Wolfe family owned among other things, the Columbus *Dispatch*, television stations in Columbus and Indianapolis, hotels, radio stations, and a major interest in the state's largest bank. The Wolfes were rich, Republican, and ultra-respectable, and Dick Wolfe was very much in that tradition.

In 1975, at age forty-two, he was president of WBNS, the CBS affiliate in Columbus, president of the local symphony, chairman of the Franklin County Mental Health and Retardation Board, and involved in more civic affairs than he could keep track of. A graduate of Ohio State and the Harvard Business School, he was a tall, good-looking

man, balding, always elegantly dressed, who had a wife and two
daughters, a beautiful home, and a taste for expensive sports cars and
stereo equipment. He was the very epitome of the Midwestern
Establishment, the public-spirited citizen who can work behind the
scenes to get things done in his community.

In the late 1960s, while he was chairman of the Columbus Area
Community Mental Health Center, Wolfe became concerned about
drug use at Ohio State University, and he helped set up a drug clinic,
the Open Door Clinic, near the campus. He came to the drug issue as a
hard-liner, but as he got to know the doctors and the patients at the
clinic, he began, as he later said, to see what was myth and what was
reality. He decided that the drug problem was in large part a political
problem—that the need was to change the laws so that drug use was
seen as a health problem, not a law-enforcement problem. It happened
that at about the same time, one of the state's most powerful
politicians had reached a different conclusion.

Ohio's attorney general was an ambitious young Democrat named
William J. Brown, who wanted very much to be governor and had
decided that to sponsor a tough new drug law would help him toward
that goal. In 1973 he introduced a bill that was modeled after the
Rockefeller law in New York. His bill passed the state house and
senate easily, but was defeated in conference committee, not because
it was too harsh, but because Republicans didn't want to see Brown
get credit for what they knew would be a popular measure.

It was then that moderates began to meet and consider how to cope
with Brown's bill the next time around. A series of meetings at Wolfe's
home, with civic leaders and legislators attending, led to a model bill,
one that called for the decriminalization of marijuana and increased
treatment facilities for drug addicts. These moderates assumed that
Brown's bill would pass, in some form; their strategy was to amend his
bill so they could live with it, all the while giving Brown credit for
having sponsored a tough new law. Wolfe liked to say there was a train
coming down the tracks and all he wanted to do was change a few of its
boxcars.

He had immediate access to any legislator or state official, and he
used it effectively. He approached them not as a marijuana advocate
(although he had smoked) but as a concerned civic leader and a
mental-health expert. He found it was often quite easy to convince
legislators that young people shouldn't be jailed for marijuana use;

they knew that their children and their friends' children smoked. Their concern was whether they could support marijuana-law reform without getting burned politically. And it was there, as a member of a family that controlled a newspaper and radio and television stations, that Dick Wolfe could play a crucial role.

Wolfe thought, throughout his lobbying effort, that legislators overestimated his influence on his family's media empire. He knew that he could not dictate the news or editorial policies of his television station, even as its president, and he certainly had no editorial control over the Columbus *Dispatch*. He knew, in fact, that most of the members of his family did not share his views on drug policy. They were mostly hard-liners, as he had been. Still, the fact that he was lobbying on behalf of the drug bill had an impact. Reporters tended to assume the bill had the Wolfe family's endorsement. Certainly his family's newspaper and radio and television stations were unlikely to criticize the bill; to a very large extent, Wolfe's involvement protected the progressive aspects of the bill from right-wing attack.

Wolfe and other supporters of reform were careful always to speak of the new bill as a very tough law, and in part it was. Penalties for the sale of heroin, for instance, were strengthened. But nestled among the hard-line provisions was the decriminalization of up to 100 grams (about three and a half ounces) of marijuana, and also of up to five grams of hashish and one gram of hashish oil. Three and a half ounces was far more than any other state had decriminalized, and no other state had included hashish and hashish oil in its reform package.

The bill's first legislative hurdle was the house judiciary committee, and it was there that Wolfe staged a dramatic political coup: He arranged for Art Linkletter to testify.

In thirty years as a radio and television personality, Art Linkletter had become one of the most beloved men in America. He was a man, like Lawrence Welk and Arthur Godfrey, with whom Middle America could be at ease. Art Linkletter was as American as could be. And then one day drugs tore his life apart.

In 1969 his daughter fell to her death, apparently while under the influence of LSD. Linkletter's first response was anger, outrage. Drugs had killed his daughter; therefore he would use his influence to combat the drug menace. But he could not speak out on the evils of drugs until he knew more about them, and the more he studied the issue, the more he came to see that harsh laws were not the answer. In time, his views on drugs were not greatly different from Dick Wolfe's or NORML's.

Wolfe met Linkletter at a meeting of the Young Presidents Organization in Florida. As they talked, Wolfe felt that Linkletter's transition from hard-liner to reformer was much like his own. He asked if the entertainer would come to Ohio and testify before the legislature. Linkletter said he would. To make the trip as convenient as possible, Wolfe sent his plane to pick up Linkletter. Speaking before the house judiciary committee, Linkletter said that after his daughter's death he had viewed the drug problem as a vengeful parent, but later he had changed his mind. "I don't think any law is going to solve the drug-abuse problem," he said. "I don't think hiring more policemen or devoting more money or building bigger walls is going to be the answer. We've sent far too many young people to jail.

"I'm soft on people," Linkletter concluded, "not soft on drugs."

It was a moving statement, and immensely effective politically. Dick Wolfe, anticipating this, had it filmed. Thus, when Wolfe himself testified before the senate judiciary committee, he took with him a film that featured highlights of Linkletter's testimony and concluded with an even more dramatic segment from the television program *60 Minutes*. The segment concerned a young marijuana smoker in Pennsylvania named Billy Nester. Billy's parents found some marijuana in his room. Horrified that their son was using a dangerous drug, they called the police and said they wanted him arrested and sent to prison, if that was the only way to save him from drugs. He was in fact convicted and sent to prison. Soon after his arrival he was gang-raped. Shortly thereafter he hanged himself in his cell.

By the end of Wolfe's presentation, many people in the hearing room were in tears. The bill cleared the judiciary committee without difficulty.

A final obstacle to the reform elements of the bill arose when opponents tried to lower the amount of marijuana to be decriminalized from three and a half ounces to one ounce. The reformers might have compromised—to decriminalize one ounce would have been a victory —but they chose to fight. Wolfe was able to call for help from labor-union lobbyists he'd worked with in the past on mental-health legislation, particularly with regard to alcoholism, a major concern to union leaders. The labor lobbyists weren't greatly concerned with the hundred-grams-versus-one-ounce issue, but they owed some favors to the mental-health people and they believed in paying their debts.

Finally, when a vote came on the question, Lt. Gov. Richard Celeste, a liberal who was presiding over the state senate, arranged for the question to be settled on a voice vote—one in which individual members' positions were not recorded. The three-and-a-half-ounces provision won easily.

NORML's Ohio coordinator was David Weiner, a friend of Stroup's from law school who had joined a leading Cleveland law firm. Weiner attended some meetings at Wolfe's house and worked with student groups seeking reform, but he recognized that NORML was very much the outsider in Ohio politics and Wolfe was the insider who could get things done. So although Stroup and Wolfe had become friends, and Stroup gave Wolfe long-distance advice on strategy and on what outside witnesses could be most helpful with the legislature, NORML stayed in the background. As Stroup saw it, he had created a sort of drug-law supermarket, where reformers like Wolfe could pick and choose the best strategies and witnesses to suit their local needs.

When the bill became law in August, newspaper headlines in Ohio declared, "Ohio Gets Tough New Drug Law," which was true in part, although it was equally true that Ohio had got the nation's most liberal marijuana law. For Attorney General Brown, the bill was a politician's dream come true: He was able to reap immediate credit for a tough drug law, and later, when decriminalization was seen as a success, he could claim credit for it, too. But, politics aside, supporters of reform knew who deserved credit for the progressive elements of Ohio's new law: Richard Wolfe, the very respectable Republican who had provided a textbook example of how a conservative can bring about the reform that liberals wanted but could almost never achieve on their own.

The political victories of 1975 had given NORML new respectability. Decriminalization seemed no longer a fringe issue but the wave of the future, and Stroup had made NORML central to the movement. If a reporter wanted to write about the issue, if a state legislator wanted advice on how best to write and present a reform bill, if reform-minded citizens wanted to know how they could help, NORML was the starting point, the central clearinghouse for all of them. NORML thus became the national organization it had always claimed to be. Stroup had coordinators, most of them first-rate lawyers, in almost every state, and in many states there was also a network of volunteers to raise money, gain publicity, lobby the legislature, and help individual defendants. As his Washington staff grew, along with his national organization, Stroup traveled more, and increasingly focused his talents on the things he did best. One was publicity, his role as celebrity-spokesman, Mr. NORML. Another was simultaneously expanding and holding together his burgeoning coalition. Another, perhaps the most urgent, was the endless battle to keep NORML afloat financially.

10

One afternoon in the spring of 1974 a bearded, disheveled young man wandered into Stroup's office. Stroup took him for a street person and silently cursed his receptionist for letting him slip past her. If he spent five minutes with every hippie who wanted to talk about the glories of staying stoned all day, he'd never have time to run NORML. Still, they had a pleasant chat, and when the boy got up to go, he said he had a present for Stroup in his car. He returned a moment later, not with the ounce of grass Stroup had expected but with a handsome set of antique scales.

A few days later the boy returned again, and this time he brought an even more welcome gift: a $500 donation to NORML. He said he'd once attended the University of Maryland, and Stroup took him for a small-time dealer who wanted to contribute to the cause. The third time he came to call he was treated as an honored guest; he and Stroup shared a joint, and in time their talk turned to the NORML ads that appeared twice a year in *Playboy*.

"Those ads are great," the young man said, "but why do you only have them in *Playboy*?"

"Because they give us free space," Stroup explained.

"Why not run one in the *Reader's Digest*?"

"In the first place, because we can't afford it," Stroup said. "Besides, the people who read the *Digest* aren't going to send us contributions. The right and the left already have their minds made up. We need to go after the middle. What I'd really like to do is run ads in *Time* and *Newsweek*."

"Why don't you?"

"We can't afford it."

"What would it cost?"

Stroup shrugged. "Let's find out," he said, and grabbed his phone. He found someone in *Time*'s advertising department who said that a full-page ad would cost about $10,000.

"I'll give you that," the young man said, to Stroup's astonishment. It developed that he was the heir to a major American fortune.

With the $10,000 promised, Stroup burst into action. He knew the ad he wanted to run: the Queen Victoria ad, which had already appeared in *Playboy*. It featured a humorous portrait of Queen Victoria puffing a joint, and it asked why people should be jailed for smoking a weed that Queen Victoria used to relieve pain from menstrual cramps.

In truth, the ad rested on an uncertain historical foundation. It was a fact that Queen Victoria's doctor advocated the use of marijuana to relieve menstrual pain, but it was not known whether his royal patient had followed his advice. However, Stroup was willing, as he put it, to make the leap of faith necessary to assume she had.

Stroup submitted the Queen Victoria ad to *Time*, only to be informed by phone that *Time*'s copy-acceptance committee had rejected it. Stroup flew into a rage, shouting at the caller that it was discrimination against marijuana smokers, that it showed the hypocrisy of the Establishment, that they were happy enough to print cigarette ads, and so on.

However, later in the evening, as he and Schott got high and analyzed the matter, Stroup realized two things: First, the situation was bizarre: He had $10,000 cash and *Time* magazine wouldn't take it. Second, he had an issue. He had *Time* on the defensive, and there was both fun and publicity to be reaped from the situation.

His next move was to submit the ad to *Newsweek*, who also rejected it. He then began writing indignant letters to executives of both magazines, pointing out that they ran alcohol and tobacco ads, declaring that NORML wanted only to keep people out of jail, and warning that legal action would follow if this discrimination did not stop.

Ms. magazine also refused the ad, and Stroup wrote its advertising director that he was pained that she failed to see the parallel between discrimination against women and against smokers.

Along with writing indignant letters, Stroup was leaking the story to friendly reporters and getting a good deal of mileage out of it. Eventually he had a call from Hedley Donovan, an elder statesman at *Time*, who said the real problem was that the ad concerned menstruation. Give us an ad without that, Donovan said, and we'll print it.

"What's this, a secret we're letting out?" Stroup demanded. "Half the people in the world do it every month, and you can't tell your readers?"

"It's a matter of taste," opined the *Time* executive.

Stroup thought it over. He felt he'd won a moral victory, since *Time* had agreed to print a NORML ad. He'd already got more free publicity than the ad would bring him for $10,000. Most important, he desperately needed money to pay NORML's bills. So he called his young benefactor, explained the situation, and asked if he would simply donate the money. The young man agreed, and *Time*'s readers were spared NORML's importunings.

Fund-raising was not always so easy.

NORML existed in a state of permanent financial crisis. This was true despite the fact that its income increased each year that Stroup directed it, from $87,000 in 1972 to $520,000 in 1978. The problem was Stroup's habit of always spending about 10 percent more than he took in, which meant he was under constant pressure to find new sources of money.

The ideal was a smoker-financed lobby. If a hundred thousand smokers had contributed $10 a year, NORML would have been on easy street. Alas, NORML never had much more than ten thousand dues-paying members, and even with direct mailings and the sale of T-shirts and lapel pins, individual smokers never paid more than half of NORML's expenses. For the rest NORML had to look to rich liberals, foundations, and sympathetic magazines.

The Drug Abuse Council donated some $55,000 over a three-year period. Stewart Mott, the General Motors heir and philanthropist, contributed some $120,000 over the decade. Max Palevsky donated about $25,000. And then there was Playboy. The Playboy Foundation had at the outset viewed its contributions as seed money to get NORML started. But Stroup, because of the personal ties he forged with Hugh Hefner and people close to him, was able to keep its funding between $50,000 and $100,000 a year, so that over the decade Playboy's seed money became more than half a million dollars.

Still, by the mid-1970s, as NORML's expenses soared, more money was desperately needed, and Stroup found it in the person of a man he once called, with affection, "the craziest, most drugged-out mother-fucker I ever met": Tom Forcade.

One evening in the fall of 1976 an attractive, sixtyish woman with impeccable social credentials gave a fund-raising party for NORML at her elegant Park Avenue apartment in New York. She had become interested in the marijuana laws because her granddaughter had been arrested, and she had invited more than a hundred of her friends, at $25 each, to come meet Stroup and Frank Fioramonti. Stroup was glad enough to shake hands and make small talk for an hour, if it meant several thousand dollars for the cause, but he feared the party would be deadly dull, so he invited his friend Tom Forcade to drop by.

The party was indeed dull, but Stroup was playing Mr. NORML, all solemn and statesmanlike, hoping a few big donations might be forthcoming, when Fioramonti whispered the bad news in his ear: Tom Forcade had arrived and was causing trouble.

Forcade had indeed arrived, along with Jack Coombs—his body-guard, pilot, and closest friend—and several of his employees from *High Times* magazine. Forcade was a small, pale man with a wispy black beard who was wearing a dirty trench coat and who was, it happened, in the midst of a nervous breakdown. It had been one of those days at *High Times* when he grabbed a knife and cut the telephone lines and, when the office was still too noisy to suit him, fired his entire staff.

Forcade and Coombs, a big man in black leather who looked like a
biker, plopped themselves down in a small sitting room, put their boots
up on an antique table, pulled out a bag of prime Colombian, and
started rolling joints.

Stroup, arriving upon this scene, could only pray that no one else
would notice the intruders. Alas, the butler, a small black man, spied
them and ran to alert the hostess, who in turn took Stroup aside.

"There are some strange men in the next room," she said. "I'm sure
they can't have been invited. My butler says they're smoking
marijuana."

Stroup promised to investigate. Hurrying back to the sitting room,
he found that Forcade had lit all the candles in an ornate candelabrum,
the better to light his joints.

"Tom, you crazy fucker, cool it," Stroup pleaded.

"What the hell?" Forcade said with a growl. "It's a dope party, isn't
it?" He took a hit and passed the joint to Stroup, who sighed and
followed suit. He decided this wasn't his problem; he was the guest of
honor, not the bouncer.

The hostess ordered her butler to eject the intruders. The butler
gamely tried to usher Forcade out, whereupon Coombs lifted him
howling into the air. Stroup tried to persuade Forcade to go peaceably,
but Forcade muttered incoherently and stood his ground. Guests
began to peer in the doorway, thinking perhaps this was some sort of
skit. Finally, Forcade shuffled reluctantly toward the elevator. When
the elevator door opened, Forcade still wasn't sure he wanted to leave,
and his irate hostess gave him a shove. Forcade shoved back, and the
butler began struggling to force him into the elevator, whereupon
Forcade grabbed a large vase and flung it at the troublesome black
man. It struck a guest who had ventured too close to the melee, and
left him sitting on the marble floor of the hallway with a bleeding scalp.
At that point Stroup and Fioramonti were able to push Forcade and
Coombs into the elevator, and they all descended to the relative safety
of Park Avenue, with Forcade still puffing on a joint and muttering
darkly about capitalist pigs.

A few days later Stroup wrote the lady and apologized for the
"unfortunate incident." That did not stop her from resigning her new
membership in NORML. Stroup was sorry about the incident
—Fioramonti was furious with him—but the cold fact was that he

could afford to lose a lot of Park Avenue matrons so long as he kept the support of Tom Forcade, whose good will was bringing NORML upward of $50,000 a year.

Tom Forcade, Yippie, drug smuggler, and founder of *High Times* magazine, was described by his closest friends as a paranoiac and manic depressive, and even Stroup, who had grown tolerant of eccentric behavior, viewed him as clearly over the line. Yet Stroup also regarded Forcade as a genius of sorts, perhaps the most creative figure the drug culture had produced, a man, like Hefner, with a sense of where things were going. Vicky Horn, who worked for Forcade at *High Times*, said, "He had so much energy it was spooky. He was like a man who has lived many lives. He'd walk into a room and you'd feel him before you saw him." Craig Copetas, Forcade's friend and star reporter, says, "He was the King of the Smokers. He was the most generous, idealistic person I ever met. He was a Renaissance man in an age with no renaissance."

Forcade was variously a writer, editor, publisher, pilot, smuggler, political activist, filmmaker, and bookstore owner, and he was success- ful at all those things. He created an underground news service, produced the annual Yippie smoke-in across from the White House, and founded a spectacularly successful magazine. And yet, as with any Renaissance man, his sum was greater than his parts: Forcade's greatest creation was himself.

He was born Kenneth Gary Goodson, in Phoenix. His father was an engineer and political conservative who had once been a celebrated football hero in Arizona and who died in an automobile crash when his son was about ten. The young Goodson went to high school in Phoenix, and there began his smuggling career. At first, he and his friends would bring a few pounds of marijuana hidden in their car back from Mexico. The border searches were a threat, however, so they started throwing sacksful over the fence that ran along the border, then going to pick them up later. In time Forcade became a pilot and would fly across the border at night in small planes filled with grass. He found time to enroll in the University of Utah and get his degree in business administration in two years. Threatened by the draft in the mid-1960s, he joined the Air Force, then decided he wanted out and acted crazy enough to make the Air Force agree. He grew his hair long, lived for a while in a commune in Arizona, and became politically active after the police raided it and arrested some people for possession of LSD. He started a radical literary magazine called *Orpheus*, operating it from a 1946 Chevy school bus he drove around the state to avoid police harassment. By then he called himself Thomas King Forcade; he changed his name to spare his family embarrassment at his radical antics, and the name he chose, Forcade, was a deliberate play on "façade."

In 1969 he drove his bus to New York's Lower East Side and helped start the Underground Press Syndicate, a left-wing wire service providing news to college and underground papers that didn't trust the Establishment media. Forcade had worked with Students for a Democratic Society (SDS) in the 1960s, and some say he had ties to its terrorist faction, the Weathermen. By 1970 he emerged as a Yippie.

Most Americans who opposed the war in Vietnam did it in a law-abiding manner. A few became anti-war guerrillas, and many of those ended up in prison or dead. The Yippies chose a third means of protest: ridicule. They dressed in Uncle Sam suits, threw pies instead of bombs, and in 1968 ran a pig for president, on the theory that he was a better man than Nixon or Humphrey. The Yippies were, among other things, brilliant media manipulators who understood that if you threw a brick at a politician you would be put in jail, but if you threw a pie at him you would be put on the evening news.

Forcade first won national attention in 1970, when he testified on behalf of the Underground Press Syndicate before a congressional commission on pornography. Dressed in black, as a priest, he accused the commission of "a blatant McCarthyesque witchhunt." When a commissioner objected, Forcade shouted, "The only obscenity is censorship," and threw a pie in his face, thus inaugurating the Yippie custom of pieing political antagonists.

Stroup first met Forcade in Miami Beach in 1972, where the Yippies were demonstrating against both Nixon and McGovern. Besides leading an anti-Nixon piss-in and assorted riots, Forcade was engaged in an intra-Yippie power struggle. He denounced the Yippie's founding fathers, Abbie Hoffman and Jerry Rubin, as too old, and they in turn denounced Forcade as a government agent. In Yippiedom no proof was needed, only an interesting allegation, and the charge haunted Forcade for years, even after he was indicted for conspiracy to firebomb the Republican convention.

In the summer of 1974, after the conspiracy charge was dropped, Forcade pulled together $12,000, from friends and from a drug deal, and put out the first issue of *High Times*. Twenty-five thousand copies were sold in a week. Like Hefner before him, Forcade had seen a magazine audience that no one else knew existed: hard-core drug users, in Forcade's case. His magazine soon became slick and well edited. New York *Times* reporters sometimes wrote for it under pseudonyms. Its model was *Playboy*, but its obsession was not sex and its centerfolds featured ripe marijuana plants instead of ripe young women. Soon several hundred thousand copies were being sold each month and advertising was pouring in, mostly from the drug-paraphernalia industry. The magazine's success came about despite the fact that for most of its first year, Forcade was running it from his hideout in a flophouse, where he was avoiding a subpoena in a drug case. But having a fugitive publisher could not stop *High Times*: It was a magazine whose time had come.

Forcade called Stroup when he was starting *High Times* and asked if it might be possible to get an interview with John Finlator. Stroup arranged an interview and later, when he was in New York, went by the *High Times* offices to meet its editors. They arranged for him to visit Forcade in the flophouse. He found Forcade in a tiny room with no phone or electricity, but, typically, the publisher had several ounces of the finest Colombian, which he was eager to share.

"I never met a drug I didn't like," Forcade liked to say, and in truth he was a prodigious drug user. He once described the early days at his magazine thusly: "Walking through the offices of *High Times* was like going through the midway in a sleazy carnival. There were people with pills in one room, grass in another, coke in another room, nitrous in the next room, glue in another room, and so on down the hall."

One of Forcade's favorite drugs was nitrous oxide. This is the "laughing gas" that dentists give their patients, but dentists limit its strength and Forcade did not. He usually had a tank of it at hand, and at his parties people would fill *High Times* balloons with the gas and walk about inhaling it. It is a drug that takes people deep into themselves—an astral high, Stroup calls it—and it contributed to Forcade's habit of sitting alone with his thoughts at parties, ignoring everyone and everything around him. He also loved marijuana, which he saw as a kind of vitamin. "Most people walk around with a marijuana deficiency," he would say. He didn't much like cocaine, but kept it around for his friends, and he took Quāāludes when he was depressed, which was often, because Forcade saw DEA and CIA plots everywhere. He was never able to reconcile his paranoia with the fact that he was getting rich publishing a pro-drug magazine.

Even after he became a publisher, he remained a smuggler, so his basic editorial philosophy was pro-smuggling. Just as Stroup believed that smokers had a right to smoke in peace, Forcade believed smugglers had a right to smuggle in peace. He was proud of being a smuggler, and he was fond of saying "There are only two kinds of dealers, those who need forklifts and those who don't." Forcade needed a forklift.

His friend Craig Copetas viewed Forcade as an honest, righteous smuggler in a business turning increasingly dishonest and violent. Copetas has said of Forcade, "Not a seed entered this country without Tom knowing about it," and he tells a story that suggests how close the publisher kept to the smuggling scene.

Copetas was at the *High Times* offices and was in touch by ham radio with some smugglers who were loading three freighters on a beach in Colombia. Coast Guard planes zoomed down from the sky and began firing. The smugglers fired back. Over the ham-radio hookup, Copetas, safe in New York, could hear the crackle of gunfire and his friend's desperate cry: "They're still firing. . . . We're carrying our wounded into the jungle. . . . We need help. . . ."

Copetas rushed into Forcade's office to tell him what was happening. "There were tears in his eyes," Copetas recalls. "He said, 'Craig, hire a plane—I don't care what it costs—and get our people off that beach.' "

It was a scene from a John Wayne movie, *Fighting Leathernecks*, perhaps. "Come on, Marines, we've got to get those men out of there"—except that John Wayne was a pale, intense little man with long hair and dark glasses, dressed all in black, who believed that the CIA and DEA were trying to destroy him.

Stroup liked Forcade—he admired his creativity and enjoyed his craziness—and Forcade respected Stroup's political efforts on behalf of the drug culture. They became friends, and Forcade agreed to publish a free NORML ad each month. Soon those ads were bringing in donations of about $1000 a week. Twelve *High Times* ads a year brought in about as much money as the two ads *Playboy* was running each year, and Stroup always told Forcade he was doing more for NORML than Hefner was. That was not necessarily true—it depended on how you figured it—but he knew how it pleased Forcade, who liked to see himself as the new Hefner.

Stroup was criticized by conservative members of NORML's board for his alliance with *High Times,* but he didn't see how he could turn down $50,000 a year just because it came from a magazine for dopers. Stroup's friendship with Forcade meant that Forcade's Yippie friends sometimes showed up at NORML's office. Stroup would try to talk politics with them, but a political discussion with Yippies always began with conspiracy theories and ended with everyone stoned. Stroup was glad to have the good will of the Yips. Previously they had denounced him, called him a government agent, and picketed television stations where he was being interviewed, on the theory that they were the true spokesmen for America's marijuana smokers. As Stroup saw it, it was better to have them inside his office getting stoned than outside denouncing him.

Forcade never asked for anything in return for his support. Sometimes he would grumble that NORML should champion the marijuana smuggler as well as the smoker, but Stroup insisted that he couldn't function politically if his opponents could accuse him of being a front for smugglers, which they did anyway, as NORML's ties to *High Times* became known.

The question of accepting money from smugglers came up in 1975 when a San Francisco lawyer told Stroup he had clients, major marijuana growers, who wanted to donate several hundred thousand dollars a year to NORML. Stroup was suspicious. On the one hand, he feared it might be some kind of government effort to entrap him. On the other hand, he feared that if he took the money and it really was from dealers, the dealers might turn up at his office one day armed with baseball bats and announce they were NORML's new policy committee. So, reluctantly, he turned down the money.

He did not always turn down mysterious donations. In the summer of 1976 he was given $10,000 in cash. A note attached to the money said it came from "The Confederation," an alliance of marijuana growers and distributors. Forcade's friends said later that Forcade, knowing NORML needed money, made the donation in hopes of shaming other drug dealers into supporting NORML.

Stroup, with the $10,000 in hand, might have simply put it into the bank, but he decided instead to turn the windfall into a media event. He called reporters in, spread the money out across his desk for photographers, and declared that the money might be some sort of government setup and he had therefore summoned the media to show he had nothing to hide. It didn't make much sense, but it was a slow news day and Stroup wound up with $10,000 and national publicity as well.

Forcade was the mastermind behind the annual Fourth of July Yippie smoke-in in Lafayette Park, across from the White House. Stroup had for years refused invitations to speak at the smoke-in. It was the sort of crazy hippie stunt he thought not in keeping with NORML's middle-class image. Forcade loved the smoke-in, however, and in time he changed Stroup's thinking on it. If there were several thousand people in America who worshipped marijuana, who smoked it constantly, and who were willing to travel to Washington at their own expense to demonstrate for its legalization, Stroup reasoned, then perhaps he should not ignore them. Stroup thus agreed to speak at the 1977 smoke-in, and also to handle the negotiations leading up to it. The Yippies had never bothered to get a permit, but Stroup decided that if he was to speak, the demonstration should at least be legal. He therefore met with representatives of the Park Police, the Secret Service, and the District of Columbia police.

"Is there going to be marijuana-smoking at this thing?" a Park Police official demanded indignantly.

"Jesus Christ, man, it's a smoke-in," Stroup said. "What do you think they're going to do?"

The smoke-in went off uneventfully. Stroup and others spoke, bands played, joints circulated, and the only way a Yippie could get himself arrested was to scale the White House fence, which some did. Stroup felt he'd helped legitimize the smoke-in, and he was glad to do that favor for Forcade. He took some heat inside NORML for being involved, but he thought it was well worth it in exchange for Forcade's continued support.

To Stroup, it was all part of the coalition-building process. He worked with Tom Bryant on the right and with Tom Forcade on the left. As far as the Yips were concerned, he agreed with Lyndon Johnson that it's better to have people "inside the tent pissing out than outside the tent pissing in." What Stroup did not fully appreciate was that the Yippies, let inside the tent, might keep right on pissing in. He would learn this later, and it would be a costly lesson.

By the mid-1970s Stroup could relax a bit. NORML's early struggles were over; the pot lobby was increasingly solvent and respected, and its founder ("the John L. Lewis of the marijuana movement," *New Times* called him) enjoyed ever-growing celebrity. The reform movement's successes had transformed Stroup from a political curiosity to a political star. He was on the Tom Snyder show, the Phil Donahue show, the Geraldo Rivera show (Rivera joined NORML's advisory board), and he was the subject of countless newspaper and magazine articles, even a *Playboy* interview. Stroup liked running NORML, heading a national organization, playing political chess with all of America as his chessboard. He had taken up the smokers' cause because he was looking for an issue, a good horse to ride; it could have been jail reform or saving the whales. But as the years passed, he had come to take the issue very seriously, very personally. He defined himself as a smoker, a member of an oppressed minority. Since childhood he had sought social acceptance, and it outraged him that boozers passed laws against smokers, treated them as second-class citizens. He identified, in this regard, with the gay activists; for Stroup, it wasn't enough for the larger society to say "Okay, we'll stop putting you characters in jail." He wanted to force society to say "Yes, your life-style is just as good as ours." And of course that was what America would never say.

He had, over the decade, become more and more candid about his own smoking. He had come out of the closet, so to speak. In the early days he minimized the emphasis on his smoking, but by mid-decade Stroup would confront a hostile legislature by saying, "Gentlemen, I've been a daily marijuana smoker for years," as if defying his opponents to match wits with him, if they really believed the weed rotted men's brains.

The mid-1970s was a good time for Stroup and NORML. The paranoia of the early 1970s was gone, and the anti-marijuana reaction of the late 1970s was still to come, unforeseen. There were still many arrests, still many outrages, still many battles to fight, but the new national mood that had begun with Nixon's banishment seemed to have taken root across the land. Reform was popular; reformers were respectable. There were endless signs of this. Down in Louisiana, the NORML chapter had rented billboards outside New Orleans to put across its message: SHOULD PEOPLE WHO USE MARIJUANA GO TO JAIL? CALL YOUR STATE LEGISLATOR! In Washington, Bob DuPont was saying that cultivation of marijuana for personal use should be decriminalized and that alcohol and tobacco were without question bigger health hazards than marijuana. The opposition seemed mostly to be cranks, bitter-enders like Ed Davis, who was warning that cultivation would lead to "two-year-old addicts" who would become hooked by eating leaves off the marijuana plants their parents were growing.

In Washington, Sens. Phil Hart and Jacob Javits had joined NORML's advisory board, along with Sheriff Richard Hongisto, of San Francisco, and one representative said that if smokers were disqualified from membership in Congress, "they wouldn't be able to raise a quorum." John Denver and Mary Tyler Moore, perhaps the most wholesome man and woman in America, had declared that they smoked; Moore said she considered marijuana no more dangerous than her pre-dinner martini. The bar association of Baton Rouge, Louisiana, and Little Rock, Arkansas, went on record for decriminalization, as did the Democratic party of New Mexico, and a government report acknowledged that alcohol was the most serious drug problem in the U.S. Army. Throughout the spring of 1976, Stroup kept busy flying to the fund-raising parties that NORML chapters were giving around the country: a showing of *Reefer Madness* in Phoenix, a dinner dance in Philadelphia, concerts in Atlanta and Milwaukee—events that were almost as decorous as Jaycees banquets. Smoking and smokers were out of the closet and into the mainstream, or so it seemed.

Stroup rushed about America, buoyed by the new national mood, higher on the sweet wine of political success than he would ever be on drugs, fighting the good fight and having plenty of good times in the process. Craig Copetas, his frequent companion in those days, recalled, "There was a great intensity to our lives then. It was a time of serious work and serious play. Keith's commitment was fantastic. To get some kid out of jail he'd go for three days without sleep, calling reporters, hounding judges, yelling at cops, whatever it took. But the work was so depressing that you had to go out and blow your mind sometimes."

Copetas recalls a time when he and Stroup were flying first-class and built themselves a tent of blankets to smoke under, explaining to the stewardess that they wanted privacy as she passed food into their smoky cave. (Stroup eventually began smoking openly when he flew, and no one seemed to know or care, except for an occasional stewardess who would say, "I can't *believe* you're doing that!" and then smile and ignore him.) There was another time, at a NORML conference, when Copetas and Hunter Thompson were on a hotel balcony shooting Secret Service flares at cats down in the alley, and another time when Forcade poured long lines of cocaine around the tile floor of his hotel bathroom and some people were crawling around on all fours, snorting madly, like dogs following a scent. Forcade's parties were the most insane of all. He would rent a nightclub and invite hundreds of people—the *High Times* crowd, the dealers, the Yippies, the punk-rock crowd, the Andy Warhol crowd, the transvestites, every freak in New York—and the ballroom would be filled with tanks of nitrous oxide and stoned people wandering around breathing in and out of balloons.

It was at Forcade's party in New York in July of 1976, during the Democratic convention that nominated Jimmy Carter, that Stroup first met Margo St. James, the head of COYOTE (Cast Off Your Old Tired Ethics), the prostitutes' lobby, and several of her young activists, and a NORML-COYOTE alliance was proclaimed and vigorously consummated.

High times, indeed, but there was an irony to all this that escaped the revelers. They had rejected their Middle American roots. They scorned the whiskey culture they had left behind, and yet as they fired flares from hotel windows and cavorted with prostitutes, they resembled nothing so much as drunken Legionnaires at a convention, the only difference being that their drug of choice was the Killer Weed, whereas the Legionnaires were true to the Demon Rum.

Still, there was always work, serious work. Stroup's life sometimes seemed poised between the chemical madness of the drug culture and the legal madness of the world outside. One morning in July of 1976 he took a call from a young man who said his name was Jerry Mitchell and that he was in jail in Missouri.

"I called *Playboy* and they told me to call you," Mitchell said. "I

want you to be my lawyer. You've got to help me. The judge sentenced
me to twelve years for selling a guy five dollars' worth of marijuana.
My parents are blind and they need me."

"Don't you have a lawyer?" Stroup asked.

"He told me to plead guilty. I want NORML to represent me."

"I'll be there tomorrow," Stroup promised, and thus began NORML's
most publicized case.

Jerry Mitchell had just graduated from high school, where he'd been
a member of the student council, in the little southwestern Missouri
town of West Plains, not far from the Arkansas border. He was a
somewhat unusual young man for West Plains. He read a lot, was
interested in philosophy, wore his hair shoulder-length, had been
opposed to the war in Vietnam, liked rock music, and planned to go to
college and study political science and then become a lawyer. He was
also a marijuana smoker. That fact had come to the community's
attention a few months earlier when he'd been arrested for possession.
He'd gone before Circuit Judge Winston Buford and been given a
suspended sentence. Unfortunately, he'd continued to smoke, and one
night in August of 1975 an old friend had come by with another man, a
man Mitchell didn't know. They drove around and smoked three joints,
and at the end of the evening the stranger asked Mitchell if he could
buy the rest of his marijuana. Mitchell gave him a third of an ounce for
$5. Later, the man came back and asked if Mitchell could sell him a
pound. Mitchell didn't have a pound, but he took the man to meet
someone else who did.

The stranger turned out to be a highway-patrol undercover agent,
and Mitchell was arrested on two charges: one for selling the third of
an ounce, one for selling the pound. Mitchell hired a lawyer from St.
Louis, who entered into plea-bargaining with the prosecutor. As a
result, Mitchell pleaded guilty to the lesser charge, and the larger one
was dropped. Two months later Mitchell went before Judge Buford for
sentencing. His St. Louis lawyer did not attend; he sent another
lawyer who was unfamiliar with the case. Mitchell was not too
worried. All the courthouse regulars told him he'd get probation or
maybe a few weekends in jail. When the judge asked Mitchell if he had
anything to say for himself, Mitchell said he did not. The judge then
declared, "A pusher of an unlawful substance has the means to poison
the whole community," and sentenced Mitchell to twelve years in
prison.

The nineteen-year-old Mitchell, stunned, broke into tears. His blind parents wept, too, as they heard the sentence. Betty Mitchell had been blind since birth, and Roy Mitchell had been blind for six years.

Mitchell begged for mercy, saying his parents needed him. Judge Buford said he should have thought of his parents before he became a drug dealer. His lawyer didn't ask for bond, so Mitchell was taken off to jail. A few days later, realizing that the media might be his court of last resort, Mitchell called *Playboy, Rolling Stone*, and *High Times*, asking for help. Someone at *Playboy* told him to call NORML.

Stroup flew to St. Louis, where he was joined by Mike Stepanian, from San Francisco, whom he'd called for help because he considered him one of the best drug lawyers in America. They were joined by Bill Helmer, who edited the *Playboy* feature called "Forum," which often publicized particularly outrageous drug sentences. The lawyers' first step was to talk to Mitchell's original lawyer and to read the record of the case. They wanted to find out what had gone wrong, why a judge had given such a sentence. Obviously, Mitchell's involvement in the sale of a pound of marijuana was a factor. In theory, that case was not before the court. In reality, both the judge and the community were very aware of it. Mitchell's was the first case of a drug pusher in the county's history. A reading of the record made another problem clear: Mitchell had stood mute, saying nothing in his own defense, not even prior to sentencing.

Stroup and Stepanian went to see Mitchell in the county jail and asked him why he hadn't said he was sorry and asked for mercy. Because his lawyer had told him to remain silent, he said. He'd been scared and confused, and so he'd said nothing, and in the process had made the judge think he was hostile, unrepentant. He was a soft-spoken, intelligent boy who would have made a good witness in his own behalf.

The lawyers next went to see the prosecutor, who was sympathetic and said he would not resist a reduction in the sentence.

Finally, Stroup and Stepanian went to see the judge in his chambers. It was a delicate confrontation. Judge Buford was not the ignorant hillbilly they had expected—he was articulate and intelligent—but he was indignant. "Who are you people and where did you come from and who's paying you?" he demanded. They explained that they were from an organization that believed marijuana smokers should not go to jail, that they were representing Mitchell, and that they would receive no pay for their efforts. An hour-and-a-half meeting followed, one in which several things were happening. While Stroup and Stepanian were trying to make friends with the judge, to persuade him they were sincere, well-intentioned people, they were also trying to intimidate him, to make him think they represented powerful forces that were coming to the aid of Jerry Mitchell. In fact, as they became friendly, the judge confessed that the presence of the *Playboy* reporter in West Plains had started rumors that Hugh Hefner was going to fly in *Playboy*'s lawyers in the *Big Bunny*.

The judge also told them, as the talk grew candid, that they should not try to paint Mitchell as an innocent lad—that he knew Mitchell was a pusher. "Judge, I know he's a smoker," Stroup said. "I'm a smoker, too. But someone who sells an ounce to a friend for no profit is not what most people consider a pusher." The judge also said that the possible sentence for drug dealing was five years to life, and many members of the community felt he'd been too soft, not too hard, on this young drug dealer. But he hinted that he might consider a reduction in the sentence, and then the three of them left his chambers and went to court.

The NORML lawyers said they wished to enter a motion for a reduction of sentence. The judge said he would entertain such a motion. Mitchell was brought in and given a chance to speak. He said he'd been confused before, that he was sorry for what he'd done and the pain he'd caused his parents, and that he appealed to the court for mercy.

Judge Buford declared that he now saw a "ray of hope" for the boy, and he would therefore reduce his sentence from twelve years to seven.

Overjoyed, the NORML lawyers asked that Mitchell be released on bond, pending appeal, and the judge agreed. The bond was set at what it had been before the conviction. (Mitchell's parents had mortgaged their small house as surety that their son would not flee from justice.)

Stroup and Stepanian went to the jail and personally escorted Mitchell out. It was exhilarating for them both, to have come into a small rural community, to have established contact with the prosecutor and the judge, and to have freed the boy from jail and got five years taken off his sentence. Still, they knew there was a long fight ahead. Stroup's next move was to contact a first-rate lawyer in Kansas City, Howard Eisberg, who was a member of NORML's national legal committee, and to arrange for him to handle Mitchell's appeal. Eisberg took the case *pro bono*—NORML and the Playboy Foundation paid his travel expenses—and while the appeals dragged on, Mitchell enrolled in Southeastern Missouri State College. It would be two years before his case burst into public view once more.

Despite all the successes, all the celebrity, all the parties and the glitter, there was another, darker side of Stroup's life. He was broke, uncertain of his future—his home a tiny room above his office—living under constant pressure, both emotional and financial. Money was an endless concern. His salary went down instead of up, as he and others at NORML took pay cuts during financial crises. In 1976, when the government tried to collect some $15,000 Stroup owed it for college loans, he filed bankruptcy, and the government was forced to settle for his watch and his bicycle—his only assets—which it then sold back to him for half price.

Money was a source of constant friction between him and Kelly. After their separation she had got a Montessori teaching degree. Then she decided she didn't want to teach—that, once more, she was only doing what society said women should do—and she returned to college to study filmmaking. After he filed for bankruptcy, Stroup sought a reduction in his child-support payments, but a woman judge not only ruled in Kelly's favor but gave him a dressing down in the process. Furious, Stroup walked the twenty blocks back to his office, trying to work off his anger. But, soon after he arrived, Kelly came to pick up Lindsey. It seemed to Stroup that she was gloating, rubbing it in, and he went berserk, grabbed her by the throat, pushed her up against a wall, and was brought to his senses only by his daughter's horrified screams.

Another time, he went to National Airport to fly to a lecture date, but the airline ticket agent informed him that his credit card had been canceled, so he had no choice but to return to his office. He encountered a friend there, and they chatted casually enough, but when he got a call through to his lecture agent, whom he blamed for his humiliation, he began screaming at him, cursing wildly, red-faced, out of control. It was the other side of Stroup's cool, confident pose—the pent-up frustration of a man who was living at the edge.

Besides the financial and political worries, there was the constant pressure of being at the cutting edge of an issue that aroused violent passions. He was often in hostile situations, confronting anti-reform legislators, parents who thought he wanted to destroy their children, anti-marijuana scientists who felt he had slandered their professional achievements. For every smoker who thought Stroup was a hero, there was a mother somewhere who thought he was the devil incarnate. Dealing with his enemies was exhausting, and so, too, in a different way, was dealing with his supporters. He traveled about the country, appearing at fund-raisers, speaking at colleges, meeting with local chapters, and he was always expected to be the star, to provide energy that he didn't always have.

Stroup sought relief from the pressure in several ways. His closest friend was his daughter, Lindsey, who spent some weekends with him. She was all the family he had, and he was never happier than when they could get away together, perhaps to take his van and camp out at a country-music festival for a weekend. When he was depressed, he would tell her she must be ashamed of him, that her friends must think he was some kind of criminal, and she would hug him and tell him it was all right. In fact, he knew she had been upset when she was younger, had feared the police would take him away, but as she grew older, she came to accept his work, and he was never more proud than when at age ten or so, she told him she wanted him to come to her school and tell the other kids about his work. "About being a lawyer?" he asked. "No," she said, "about NORML."

There were women, of course, but for most of the decade his relationships with women were more distinguished for quantity than for quality.

One evening Stroup was making love with a woman in the Jacuzzi at the Playboy mansion in Los Angeles. It was in a kind of cove or grotto, designed to be one of the most erotic spots in the world. You swam in under a waterfall; there were jets of warm water, colored lights, gentle music, and a ledge equipped with soft cushions, thick towels, an assortment of body oils. It was also supposed to be private, but Stroup noticed someone appear briefly at the entrance. Stroup thought it was Hefner, and, sure enough, when he saw Hefner back inside the mansion a little later, playing backgammon with his cronies, the publisher called out, "Well, Keith, I'm glad to know you're hetero-sexual."

It was a joke of sorts. Hefner knew of Stroup's affairs with several women in the Playboy world. Still, by the standards of the mansion, Stroup was rather puritanical. While other men were trying to hit on the Bunnies, Stroup was trying to hit on potential contributors to NORML.

Throughout his years at NORML, Stroup avoided entanglements with women. Although this was due in part to his obsession with his work, it had mostly to do with his fear of being hurt. When he separated from his wife, he cried for days and avoided women for months, resenting them, fearing them. And a bitter divorce added to his determination not to let himself be vulnerable again. Sex was fine, but nothing more. Typically, he would work at his office until nine or ten o'clock, then call some woman, perhaps one he'd just met, and ask if she wanted to come smoke a joint. If she came, the chances were they'd wind up upstairs in his little bedroom; then, when the sex was over, he'd go back down to his office and return to work, leaving the woman to get the hint and go home. Or, if Stroup had gone to the woman's place, he would leave after the lovemaking. He didn't like to wake up with women; the morning-after scenes were too seductive. Better to have your fun, then hurry back to the safety of work. Once, in the mid-1970s, he was seeing a tall, sophisticated blonde who shared his fascination with sex, drugs, and politics. He started spending a lot of time at her Georgetown apartment, and one night she asked if he'd like to move in. She might as well have put a gun to his head. He soon stopped seeing her.

Finally, there were drugs.

Stroup smoked more or less constantly. There were certain important things he would not do high: go to court, give an important interview. But he believed he could do routine office work just as well high as not. He felt that marijuana focused his attention, energized him, and provided a certain valuable introspection. When he was under pressure, he sometimes smoked his first joint upon arising, and some mornings, when he was irritable and ill-humored, his secretaries wished he *would* hurry and smoke his first one. He disliked comparing his drug use with other people's alcohol use, but after appearing before a hostile legislative panel, he would unwind with a joint or two the way another lobbyist might unwind with a couple of stiff drinks.

He had tried almost every drug, but marijuana remained his favorite. He viewed it as a drug you could integrate with a productive life, in a way that you could not alcohol or cocaine or hallucinogens. He used a good deal of cocaine in the latter part of the decade, and he thought that in moderation it was a fine drug, with a fascinating high. But moderation was not his strongest point, and he knew that too much cocaine left you jumpy and depressed. He remained a marijuana smoker, as other men are committed to beer or wine or dry martinis.

Stroup always insisted that he used drugs for fun, not because he was addicted to them or to meet any deep personal needs. "I can do without drugs," he would say. "I just don't want to." Still, it was difficult to know Stroup and not think he had at least a psychological addiction to drugs. They clearly had become essential to his self-image, and they were also a kind of sedation, a way he dealt with the pressures of his life, both from without and within. For all his talent and success, Stroup seemed to have, very near his core, a large measure of insecurity. He needed the constant activity, the phone calls, the publicity, the one-night stands, the Mr. NORML persona, to give him constant reassurance of his own worth. It is not an uncommon symptom in Washington, of course; insecurity, a desire to prove himself, to show those bastards back home, has driven many a man to political success, even to the White House.

There was also in him an uncertainty as to whether he wanted to be outsider or insider, rebel or respectable citizen. His Jekyll-and-Hyde quality contributed to his success at NORML, made it possible for him to move between the drug culture and the corridors of power, but it was a difficult balancing act to maintain. All politicians want to be all things to all men, but at some point you have to come down on one side or another.

Stroup came down, was forced to define himself, when the Carter administration came to power. It had been easy enough to deal with the Nixon administration: You opposed it, which took courage, anger, audacity, but not great subtlety. But with the coming of Carter the game became more complicated, because it was a game, played by experts, with the prospect of winning some points and losing others. He had cheered Carter's march to the White House, and not only because Carter supported decriminalization. It was more than policy; it was cultural. Carter and his people were from small towns, were Baptists, were hillbillies. Fine, so was he. The younger ones liked to smoke dope and listen to Willie Nelson. Fine, so did he.

Stroup, like a lot of people, let his guard down, let himself expect too much of the smiling Georgian. Soon he would think he had been wrong, tricked, that Carter, too, had rejected him. Predictably, he took the rebuff very personally, lashed back angrily, hurt himself and others, and in the process defined himself, permanently, as an outsider.

11

One frigid February morning in 1977, soon after Jimmy Carter was inaugurated, Keith Stroup came in from the cold.

Or so he thought.

He walked the dozen blocks from NORML's office to the White House, but it was more like a walk through time, from one life to another. Six years earlier, when he started NORML, Stroup had been a freak, an outlaw lobbyist who dealt with the White House only via angry letters and defiant gestures. Now, incredibly enough, he was the leader of a respected national lobby, and he was on his way to see his friend Dr. Peter Bourne.

Two months earlier, during the postelection transition period, when every lobbyist in Washington was scrambling to get a handle on these unknown Georgians, Stroup had persuaded Bourne to be the keynote speaker at NORML's annual conference. That had been an impressive show of the dope lobby's intimacy with the new administration, but today's visit was what counted: Stroup was going to the White House to talk policy, to try to define how NORML and the Carter administration could work together toward common goals.

He marched up briskly to the guardhouse outside the West Wing and announced that Mr. Stroup had arrived to see Dr. Bourne. There was a brief delay, as there always is, but that was all right. The trick was to be cool, as if you came to the White House every day, and not to notice the tourists who gawked and wondered who you were. Stroup was wearing jeans and a blue blazer with his gold marijuana-leaf pin in its lapel. He had thought it over and decided he couldn't *not* wear it just because he was going to the White House. After a moment the guard gave Stroup a pass and pointed him up the driveway to the West Wing door.

For all his professional cool, Stroup felt his heart beat faster when he stepped inside the White House. You couldn't deny it: There was something awe-inspiring about the place. If you were a power groupie, this was your Mecca, your Rome, your rainbow's end. Stroup did a double-take as he started down the stairs to Bourne's office. James Schlesinger had passed by, puffing on his pipe. Stroup thought about lighting a joint, and laughed.

In truth, Stroup was already high, but not on drugs. No more would he have to do battle with hostile, faceless bureaucrats. He would be dealing with friends now, with Peter Bourne and with Mathea Falco, from the Drug Abuse Council, whom Peter had put in the top drug-policy job at State. These were people who knew the score, people now with the power to pick up the phone and make the bureaucrats snap to.

And it was more than Peter and Mathea. A new generation of political activists, smokers, had come to power. He'd heard plenty of stories about people using drugs in the Carter campaign. Hunter Thompson had found himself doing so many drugs with Carter staff that he'd pulled back, gone home, because he'd become one of them instead of a journalist. And it didn't stop with the staff. Carter's three sons had all smoked—their mother told a reporter this during the campaign—and the oldest one, Jack, was booted out of the Navy for smoking.

Bourne's was a windowless office in the White House basement (the Ground Floor, its occupants called it). Bourne was waiting there, and he seemed stiff at first, uncomfortable. Stroup wasn't surprised. That was the purpose of this meeting, really, to clear the air. Stroup had some specific points to discuss, but mainly he wanted to say to Peter, in so many words, Okay, what are the rules? How do we play this game? Are we the outsiders rattling your cage, or are we insiders?

The meeting stayed stiff until the door burst open and Bob McNeally ran in the started shooting pictures and yelling, "Blackmail! Blackmail! I've got you now, Bourne!"

McNeally was a friend of Stroup's who'd signed on as a White House photographer. His office was next to Bourne's, and this was his idea of a joke—busting in, as in a raid on a motel room, and photographing the dope lobbyist and the drug-policy czar.

After that the meeting loosened up. Stroup thought Bourne was pleased that he hadn't made any demands, hadn't set any deadlines, had only set out NORML's agenda and his hopes of working cooperatively. Bourne must have been pleased, because he suggested that Stroup stay for lunch in the White House mess.

Ellen Metsky joined them. She was Peter's assistant from the campaign, a plump, pleasant young woman with dark hair, a sly smile, and oddly slanted, feline eyes. The mess was subdued and elegant, with dark walls and red leather furnishings, and it offered excellent food at ridiculously low prices. Stroup tried not to rubber-neck as he ate, but it was difficult. He saw Jody Powell across the room, and Stu Eisenstat, and once or twice someone had a phone plugged in beside his table so he could solve some crisis while he ate.

Stroup believed there was no such thing as a free lunch—certainly not in the White House—and he wondered why Peter had brought him here. Perhaps he wanted to show off his hip friend to his White House colleagues, to show he wasn't as stuffy as they thought. Or perhaps —and this bothered Stroup—he was trying to co-opt him, trying to "stroke" him, as the Nixonites put it. It worried Stroup because he saw how seductive this whole White House routine could be. It was hard not to start thinking in terms of "we happy few who run the world."

Still, Stroup left the White House that afternoon feeling that everything had gone just as it should. They had spoken frankly, neither side had made demands, and they had opened communications. It was clear that Peter would deal with him as an insider, as the spokesman for a legitimate and important constituency. Stroup was jubilant as he walked back to his office. He liked the view from the inside.

The honeymoon was soon over. Within a week Stroup had managed, quite deliberately, to outrage Peter Bourne, Jimmy Carter, Rosalynn

Carter, Chip Carter, Jody Powell, and Hamilton Jordan, among others, and in the process to make himself *persona non grata* at the White House.

It was quite a remarkable performance, and to understand how it could have happened, it is necessary to consider not only Stroup's volatile, very personal view of drug politics but also Peter Bourne's ambiguous, even precarious position in the Carter circle.

Peter Bourne's father, Dr. Geoffrey Bourne, was a distinguished Australian scientist whose career took him first to England, where Peter was born, in Oxford in 1939, and then in 1957 to Atlanta's Emory University, where he became the director of the internationally known Yerkes Primate Research Center. From the first, Peter Bourne seemed destined for a career as distinguished as his father's. He earned his medical degree at Emory, studied psychiatry, and in the mid-1960s served his adopted country as a U.S. Army doctor in Vietnam. He was shocked by the violence and human misery there, so much so that when another Army doctor, Howard Levy, was court-martialed for refusing to train Green Berets, Bourne agreed to testify in his behalf. It was a courageous act for Bourne, a rather shy, diffident young man, quick to blush, anxious to please, and having thus outraged his military superiors, he proceeded, soon after his release from the Army, to help organize Vietnam Veterans Against the War.

He returned to Atlanta to teach at the Emory medical school, and he might have proceeded to a quietly distinguished academic career had he not happened to catch the eye of the state's new governor, Jimmy Carter, and thus make his way into the world of politics. Heroin use was increasing in Georgia, particularly among blacks in Atlanta, and the local newspapers had declared a state of emergency. At Carter's invitation, Bourne set up a program that soon converted several thousand drug addicts from heroin to methadone. The program was hailed a success, and Bourne began advising Governor and Mrs. Carter on ways to improve the state's mental-health program. Bourne began to develop a national reputation, and in 1973 he took a job in the Nixon White House's drug-policy office, which was encouraging methadone-maintenance programs across America. But Bourne, with his English accent and his liberal views, was an outsider in the Nixon White House, and he stayed less than a year. By then, his friend

Jimmy Carter was planning to run for president, and Bourne intended to help him.

Tom Bryant was an old friend of Bourne's from the Emory medical school, and he made Bourne a consultant to the Drug Abuse Council, with plenty of free time for politics. Bourne, with his knowledge of medical and health matters, was in effect Carter's first issues adviser. In mid-December of 1974, only days after Carter amused the political world by announcing he would run for president, he spoke at a drug conference in San Francisco. Bourne wrote Carter a statement in which, without really committing himself, he said it bothered him for young people to go to jail for using marijuana, and he would be watching the results of the Oregon law with interest. Later, Chip Carter would push his father toward outright endorsement of decriminalization.

Bourne's job, for all of 1975 and half of 1976, was to be Jimmy Carter's man in Washington. He arranged Carter's meetings with reporters and courted the local political establishment, and when the candidate came to town, Bourne gave him a bed in his Capitol Hill town house. Bourne's was a thankless task—trying to sell an anti-Washington candidate to Washington—and he probably did it as well as anyone could. Certainly the candidate had nothing but praise for him; in the early days, when reporters would challenge Carter to name someone of importance who supported him, he would often mention his good friend Dr. Peter Bourne, the distinguished psychiatrist and former White House adviser. But even as Bourne was pleasing the candidate, he was running afoul of the two big, tough, shrewd young South Georgians who were his closest advisers, Jody Powell, the press secretary, and Hamilton Jordan, the political strategist.

It was possible to distinguish between Powell and Jordan on a personal level—Powell's hair was light and Jordan's was dark, and Powell was the more intelligent and stable of the two—but politically they were indivisible. They had learned, back when Carter was governor, that if they stuck together, they could rule Jimmy Carter's world, Powell as Mr. Outside, managing the media, and Jordan as Mr. Inside, controlling politics and patronage. They were indispensable to Carter because they could see people he didn't want to see and do the dirty work he didn't want to do. To win their favor, via loyalty and humility, was to rise in Carter's world; to lose it was to twist slowly in the wind. They were proud, cynical men, and it was Peter Bourne's misfortune that they came to view him with what was, even for them, a high degree of scorn.

Graham Greene wrote of a character in one of his novels, "There are men whom one has an irresistible desire to tease, men whose virtues one doesn't share." Peter Bourne was like that, as he tried to find his place among Carter's cadre of Georgians. He was so different from them, and particularly from Powell and Jordan. They were tough as nails, battle-hardened veterans of the political wars, and Bourne was a soft, uncertain man, a political amateur. They were hard-drinking, rough-talking, boots-and-jeans South Georgia shitkickers, and he was an effete Englishman with a flaky accent who drank sherry and wore fancy tweed coats and striped ties, like the Harvards. They had no ideology except winning, and Bourne had liberal ideas that annoyed them, intellectual concerns that wasted their time.

Most of all, Jordan and Powell didn't like the fact that Bourne fancied himself their peer. Their annoyance reached a peak on the morning of June 21, 1976, when a long article about Bourne appeared in the Washington *Post*. Its headline proclaimed Bourne as Carter's "closest friend," and its first sentence read, "Peter Bourne was the first person to tell Jimmy Carter four years ago he should run for President."

Powell and Jordan happened to disagree with both those assertions, and soon after that story appeared Bourne's star went into rapid decline.

Little items began to appear in various newspapers and magazines, items that were critical of Bourne's performance in the Carter campaign. Peter Bourne was losing influence with Jimmy Carter, the items would say. The candidate and his top advisers felt Bourne was getting too much publicity for himself, or was becoming too fond of Georgetown cocktail parties, or wasn't a shrewd enough politician, or whatever. The criticisms were anonymous, or vaguely attributed to "top campaign aides," so that when Bourne went to Powell and Jordan, to ask what he was doing wrong, they could of course tell him he wasn't doing anything wrong, and commiserate with him about what horseshit those goddamn columnists would print. Still, within a month of the *Post* story, Bourne was out as Carter's Washington representative.

Peter Bourne was thus one of the first people to be taught a lesson in humility by Powell and Jordan. Later they would give the same treatment to many others: Jack Watson, a talented Atlanta lawyer who seemed to challenge Jordan during the postelection period; Midge Costanza, Carter's first adviser on women's issues; independent-minded Cabinet members such as Califano and Blumenthal; even Vice-President Mondale, when he once or twice got out of line. The treatment was always the same: critical, sometimes humiliating leaks to the press until the troublemaker repented, resigned, or was driven out. It was a foolproof system. The reporters went along with Jordan and Powell's anonymous quotes because they would continue to be important sources, whereas the people they were humiliating or driving from government might soon be nobodies. It worked nicely for Carter, too, for he could remain everyone's dear friend while Powell and Jordan attended to the necessary unpleasantries.

Thus, as Peter Bourne entered the White House in January of 1977, he was not the powerful figure he seemed to outsiders. He had spent the final months of the campaign in agonizing limbo, and he was very much on probation as he started his new job. Jordan had not granted him the top-level title of assistant to the president but rather the second-level title of special assistant to the president. Jordan had not assigned him one of the choice offices upstairs in the White House but rather a windowless office in the basement. Bourne did not even have the job he wanted. He was special assistant on mental health and drug abuse, and he had not wanted to work on the drug issue at all. He wanted to advise Carter on broader issues, on world hunger and national health insurance, but over the years Carter had come to think of Bourne as his drug-policy man, and Bourne was stuck with it. Still, he hoped that he would be able to spend less than 10 percent of his time in the White House on drug-related matters. That wish would not come true, in part because of his friend Keith Stroup.

One of the questions Stroup raised with Bourne that February morning was how the White House could help the passage of decriminalization bills in state legislatures across the country. Stroup had a specific suggestion. There would be a hearing in New Mexico in a few weeks. The vote was expected to be close. Why didn't Chip Carter, the president's son, go testify on behalf of the bill?

The proposal had a certain logic. Carter *had* said, in his campaign, that he favored decriminalization. And Chip, the second of his three sons, was the most politically active of them, an attractive and articulate young man who would make an excellent spokesman for reform. Bourne promised Stroup that he would take it up with Chip.

He did, and Chip rather liked the idea. Chip Carter was very much a part of the 1960s generation: He had smoked dope, worshipped Bob Dylan, opposed the war, and the idea of speaking for marijuana-law reform appealed to him. However, when he took the proposal to Powell and Jordan, they suggested, in the gentle, roundabout way they used with their employer's family, that maybe it was not such a good idea, not just yet.

It was, of course, a crazy idea. Jordan and Powell knew that in an instant. Send Chip to testify for marijuana? Sure, and why not send Rosalynn to testify for abortion too? That'd be swell on the evening news. The fact that Bourne would even take such an insane proposal to Chip was an example of why Powell and Jordan held him in such scorn. Anyone who understood anything about Jimmy Carter would know there was no way in hell that he would ever let Chip do such a thing.

After a few days, still thinking he was about to bring off a great political coup, Stroup called Bourne's office to find out what had happened. Bourne was out, but Ellen Metsky called back with the bad news: Hamilton had advised Chip that to testify in New Mexico would not be a good use of his time.

Stroup might have taken this news philosophically. He might have said, "Well, win a few, lose a few," and reasoned that the White House would owe him one the next time around. That would have been the reasonable thing for a Washington lobbyist to do.

Instead, Stroup exploded. Those bastards had campaigned as pro-decriminalization, and now they were backing away. The fucking hypocrites! They all smoked dope, knowing they'd never be busted, but they wouldn't lift a finger to keep kids out of jail in New Mexico. But it wasn't just the kids in New Mexico. This was a personal rebuff to Stroup. He had spent six years being treated as a political outcast, and he had trusted the Carter people; they were his contemporaries, his peers, they were *smokers*. But now, in Stroup's very personal view of the world, they had betrayed him. Hamilton Jordan may not think the marijuana issue is important, Stroup raged, but it's my whole fucking life!

So he decided if he could not get Chip Carter to testify, he could at least get some mileage out of the episode. He would show those bastards that they couldn't play games with him, that he couldn't be bought off with lunch in the White House mess.

He began calling reporters, telling them how Hamilton Jordan had refused to let Chip Carter testify in New Mexico. He added his own allegation that senior Carter staff figures had smoked marijuana during the campaign. "Maybe the police ought to make some arrests closer to Sixteen hundred Pennsylvania Avenue," he declared.

The newspapers were delighted with the story; the White House was not. Rosalynn Carter in particular was outraged, and blamed Bourne for getting her son into this controversy. Bourne was stunned by Stroup's political bomb-throwing, and he did not invite Stroup back for lunch in the White House mess a second time. Mr. NORML was out in the cold again.

It was the first of a series of events that would prove that Stroup was better prepared, by temperament and training, to function as an outsider than as an insider. Stroup had let himself expect too much from the Carter administration. His mistake was in thinking that the change in administrations meant that the White House was suddenly populated with his friends instead of his enemies. The Carter people were closer to the drug culture than were their Republican predecessors, but that didn't mean they would let it cause them any political problems. To Stroup, that was outrageous hypocrisy. To Jordan and Powell, who had shed a lot of blood to get where they were, it was elementary, Politics 101. It was Stroup's misfortune to have let his hopes rise too high. It was Bourne's misfortune to be caught between Powell and Jordan and the political realities they embodied, on the one hand, and the angry zeal of Stroup and the smokers on the other. There was no way to win, not for Bourne, not for anyone.

On March 14 the House Select Committee on Narcotics opened two days of hearings on marijuana decriminalization.

Peter Bourne, the first witness, declared that the Carter administration wanted to discourage all drug use, including alcohol and tobacco, but it didn't believe that putting people in jail was the answer to the marijuana problem. He said the administration favored the decriminalization approach, and he cited the success of the Oregon law, as proved by the Drug Abuse Council surveys. He noted that moderate marijuana smoking caused no known health problems. Finally he stressed that the Carter administration opposed the legalization of marijuana, and would vigorously enforce the laws against smugglers.

Another administration witness was Dr. Robert L. DuPont, director of the National Institute for Drug Abuse, who supported decriminalization and noted that the laws seemed to have little effect on people's decisions to use or not use marijuana. Other pro-decriminalization witnesses included two black political leaders, Mayor Richard Hatcher, of Gary, Indiana, and California representative Yvonne Braithwaite Burke, as well as spokesmen for the American Bar Association and the ACLU.

Bourne's was the most progressive statement any senior government official had ever made about marijuana. The reefer-madness mythology seemed finally dead and buried. A new era of drug policy seemed at hand—an era of humanism, Bourne liked to call it.

All of which did not make Stroup any happier when he arrived to testify the next day. Stroup felt vast frustration as he took his place at the witness table and looked up at the congressmen seated before him. In particular, he resented the roles that two of them, Paul Rogers, of Florida, and Lester Wolff, of New York, had played in blocking marijuana-law reform.

Rogers was the chairman of the House Sub-Committee on Health, which had authority over marijuana legislation, and for years Rogers had refused even to hold hearings on a decriminalization bill. Stroup found this particularly galling because Rogers, who was a doctor, had been a member of the Marijuana Commission.

With Rogers refusing to act, the initiative had passed to Lester Wolff, the chairman of this "select committee." Stroup viewed Wolff as a lightweight who wanted to use the marijuana issue only to gain all the publicity and round-the-world junkets he could. The cold fact was that this select committee had no legislative authority over marijuana, and these hearings were only Lester Wolff's publicity circus. It was the ultimate congressional Catch-22: The committee that could legislate wouldn't hold hearings, and the committee that would hold hearings couldn't legislate.

Adding to Stroup's anger was the fact that he had clashed several times with the select committee's chief counsel, Joseph Nellis, during the negotiations that led up to his testimony. First, Nellis wanted him to testify along with Peter Lawford, the actor. Stroup refused. He thought it would make him look silly to be paired with an aging English movie star. Nellis, a heavyset man with slicked-back hair, warned that if Stroup wasn't careful, he might not get to testify at all.

"Joe, you don't have to let me testify," Stroup shot back, "but if you don't, I'll testify in the hallway outside your hearing room, and I'll get more press than you will."

Stroup got to testify inside, and after his opening statement, he was delighted to find his nemesis Paul Rogers questioning him. They parried on whether or not decriminalization caused increased smoking, and then, when Rogers finished and started to leave, Stroup turned the tables by demanding to be told why Rogers had never held hearings on decriminalization bills. Rogers answered rather lamely that his committee had more important health issues to consider. Stroup shot back: "We feel that elected officials should by this time be willing to take a position. Either you favor criminal penalties for us or you do not. Right now you are not voting; you are ducking."

It was a sweet moment for Stroup. For years he'd dreamed of having a chance to put Paul Rogers on the spot, and to get a shot at him in a public hearing was almost too good to be true. Their exchange was the day's dramatic highlight—lobbyists do not often put important congressmen on the defensive—and it made the day's news. The Washington *Post*'s headline was "Angry Marijuana Backer Tells Hill: 'You're Ducking.'"

Once again Stroup had won the battle for the headlines, but his opponents in Congress were still winning the war. And of course he had done himself no good with Congressmen Rogers and Wolff, or with Chief Counsel Joe Nellis, by upstaging them at their own hearing. Nellis, in particular, would be heard from again. Later that year he would play a role in a slapstick, pie-in-the-face comedy that, as much as anything, would lead to Stroup's downfall.

The good news that spring was mostly from the states.

In 1976 only one state, Minnesota, had passed a decriminalization bill, becoming the seventh state to do so. But that was an election year, always a slow time for reform, so NORML had high hopes for 1977, particularly with the new administration supporting reform.

In April, Mississippi became the first Southern state to decriminalize. It seemed quite a dramatic breakthrough, but Stroup had mixed feelings about it. The $250 fine for first-offense possession was part of an otherwise harsh, Rockefeller-style omnibus drug law. Stroup was increasingly concerned that in these legislative trade-offs the reformers were "only trading prisoners for prisoners." He thought NORML's Mississippi coordinator, a handsome, thirty-year-old insurance executive named Doug Tims, had been too quick to make deals with the law-enforcement officials who opposed reform. At one point Stroup and Tims had clashed because of some pro-cocaine statement Stroup had made on television. It was another example of the difficulty of holding together a national coalition that stretched from a Mississippi insurance man on the right to Tom Forcade on the left. More and more Stroup wondered when the whole damn thing was going to explode.

As Mississippi took a small step forward, South Dakota took a big step back. In the spring of 1976 its legislature enacted the lowest fine in the nation, $20 for simple possession. Unfortunately the new law did not take effect until 1977, and by then a more conservative legislature had been elected. It amended the new law, before it even took effect, to allow a $100 criminal fine and thirty days in jail for possession. It was a blunt reminder of how fragile reform could be.

In June, after a bitter political struggle, New York became the ninth state to decriminalize. Reform efforts had been under way since the Rockefeller law passed in 1973. NORML's Frank Fioramonti had journeyed to Albany almost every week to meet with legislators and lobbyists and, like Brownell in California, had made himself central to the reform campaign. A bill was introduced in 1977 with support from the state's new Democratic governor, Hugh Carey, but worried Democrats, along with the state's Conservative party, killed the bill in May. There could be another vote, however, and pressures for reform came from many directions.

William F. Buckley, Jr., wrote a column headed "A Cry from the Heart," warning that the conservatives were writing off young voters by their anti-marijuana stand. Governor Carey declared he would personally campaign for any legislator who needed help because of a pro-reform vote. In time a compromise bill passed that provided a $100 fine for possession of an ounce, twice that for a second conviction, and fifteen days in jail for a third conviction.

North Carolina was next, the tenth state, with a bill providing a $100 fine for possession of an ounce and up to six months in jail for second offenders. With bills passed in Mississippi, New York and North Carolina by summer, it seemed that the dam was finally breaking, that five or even ten more states might act before 1977 was over. They did not. The surge of reform that began in Oregon in 1973 was almost over. No more bills passed in 1977 and only one, in Nebraska, in 1978. Increasingly, a new issue would preoccupy both the reformers and the government and bring them into sharp conflict: paraquat, a herbicide that was used to kill marijuana plants in Mexico and that, NORML feared, was also killing marijuana smokers in America.

In 1971 the Nixon administration, anxious to stop marijuana from entering the U.S., offered helicopters and airplanes to the Mexican government for a program to defoliate marijuana fields. That was at a time, however, when much of the world disapproved of the U.S. defoliation of forests and rice fields in Southeast Asia, and the Mexican government indignantly rejected the offer. "Mexico will never allow itself to be used as a proving ground for herbicides nor to suffer damage to the ecology of our country," declared the Mexican attorney general.

By 1975 the situation had changed. There was a new government in Mexico, and it was concerned about the hundreds of thousands of acres in the Sierra Madre that were being used to grow marijuana, as well as poppies from which heroin was made. Their concern had little to do with the health or welfare of American drug users and much to do with Mexican politics. Mexico was then supplying some 90 percent of America's marijuana and receiving in return some $2 billion a year. But who was getting that money? The Sierra Madre was a twenty-three-thousand-square-mile region that had never been under effective government control. Promises of land reform there had been made but not kept, and peasants were starting to take over large farms by force. There were revolutionary stirrings in the region, and the millions of dollars pouring in could only aid potential revolutionaries. That was the ultimate fear: that American drug users might unwittingly finance a Mexican revolution.

The Mexican government therefore decided to carry out a major program to eradicate poppy and marijuana fields, and it wanted American money and technical assistance. The Americans were glad to oblige, for a number of reasons. For the DEA and the White House, it would be part of the war on drugs. For the CIA and the State Department, who didn't want a Mexican revolution any more than the Mexicans did, it was an excellent excuse to have Americans keeping a

close eye on what happened in the Sierra Madre. Finally, there was
the new factor that had revolutionized U. S.-Mexican relations: oil.
The discovery in 1972 of vast new oil and gas deposits in Mexico, at a
time when the U.S. had a desperate need for new energy sources, had
changed everything. U.S. presidents and secretaries of state, after
years of giving orders to Mexican governments, were now forced to go
to them, hat in hand, in hopes of winning favorable oil agreements. If
the Mexican government wanted a few million dollars and a few dozen
helicopters to spray marijuana fields, the U.S. government would be
glad to oblige.

John D. Ford, an aviation-services adviser to the Agency for
International Development, was one of the Americans who went to
Mexico in the fall of 1975 to help set up the spraying program. During
test-spraying in October of that year he noticed, and reported to his
superiors, something quite unexpected when he returned one day to a
marijuana field he had sprayed. "Upon landing, we discovered that a
large portion of the field had been harvested after it was sprayed."

What Ford did not understand, but what was quickly apparent to
the Mexican peasants, was this: If they harvested the sprayed plants
quickly, before the herbicide turned the leaves brittle and the taste
bitter, the contaminated plants could still be sold to the Yankee drug
dealers. Just what might happen to people who smoked that
herbicide-drenched marijuana was not of great concern to the peasants, for whom a marijuana crop could mean, by one estimate, the
difference between an income of $200 a year and $5000 a year.

Thus, aided by $15 million a year in U.S. money, the spraying
program began and some unknown amount of contaminated marijuana
began making its way back across the border into the U.S.

It was well known at this time that paraquat would kill people who
swallowed it. Scientists say that more than two hundred cases of fatal
paraquat poisoning have been reported in medical journals. A single
mouthful will kill an adult, and even a taste will kill a child. There have
been several cases in which adults put paraquat in a cola bottle to pour
on weeds and then left the bottle in a garage or tool shed; a child,
thinking it a bottle of soda, would drink it and die a horrible death.
Paraquat, if swallowed, gravitates to the lungs and causes slow
suffocation. There is no antidote.

All this was known. What was not known was what would happen to
people who smoked marijuana that had been sprayed with paraquat.

Stroup first heard reports of the spraying program from drug dealers who attended the NORML conference in December of 1976. Craig Copetas, of *High Times*, said he had been hearing the same thing. Stroup, at his meeting with Peter Bourne early in February, asked if there was some sort of herbicide-spraying program going on, and Bourne promised to check into it. On February 16, after his leak about Chip Carter had angered Bourne, Stroup wrote Bourne and formally asked how extensive the program was and what was known about the effects on people who smoked marijuana that had been sprayed with a herbicide.

It was a month before Bourne replied. He said it was true that the Mexican government was using herbicides to eliminate illegal opium-poppy and marijuana crops. The U.S. government, he said, "has nothing to do with the selection, procurement, payment or reimbursement in regard to the herbicides." He added that the experts he had consulted did not know the effect, if any, the poisoned marijuana might have on the health of people who smoked it.

Stroup, at that point, was at a dead end. He didn't know anything about the spraying program, and having outraged Bourne and the White House, he couldn't look for much cooperation there. And yet if what he feared was true, millions of Americans were smoking contaminated marijuana.

Fortunately, as he pondered the paraquat problem, Stroup was able to turn to a powerful ally: Stuart Statler, his friend since they were young lawyers at the Product Safety Commission a decade before and who had gone on to Sen. Charles Percy's staff, eventually to become chief counsel for the Republican members of the Senate Permanent Investigations Sub-committee, which oversaw, among other agencies, the DEA. It had been in large part because of Statler that Senator Percy had held hearings, back in 1973, into ODALE's no-knock drug raids, and now, in 1977, Statler would become an important ally for NORML on the paraquat issue.

Stu Statler was a short man with a thatch of unruly reddish-brown hair. Despite the conservative way he dressed and the careful way he spoke, he had a certain aura of the leprechaun about him. He liked Stroup and admired the work he'd done at NORML. He felt he'd kept the reform movement from being taken over by the crazies, whose work would only be counterproductive. As a lawyer Statler was concerned by what Stroup told him about the spraying program. One of the basic principles of law, Statler felt, was foreseeability. If you could foresee that your action would harm someone, then you had an obligation not to take that action. It seemed clear to Statler, therefore, that if the U.S. government's support of the Mexican spraying program was foreseeably harming American citizens, then that support should stop. The first step, however, was to learn more about the program, and to that end he persuaded his boss, Senator Percy, to write to Peter Bourne and request information.

Prodded by Senator Percy, and by his own concerns, Bourne then took two steps that indicated his determination to get the facts on the Mexican spraying program. First, he and Mathea Falco flew to Ixtepec, Mexico, for a first-hand look at the spraying program. They walked through fields of ten-foot-high marijuana plants and examined them before and after spraying. Everything Bourne saw, and everything the U.S. and Mexican officials told him, indicated that the sprayed plants would turn brittle and wither away before they could be harvested and shipped back to the U.S.

Pursuing the matter, Bourne next called a meeting in his office, on May 27, of representatives of the DEA, the Food and Drug Administration, the Environmental Protection Agency, the State Department, and the National Institute for Drug Abuse (NIDA), all to discuss the facts and implications of the spraying program.

For Peter Bourne, at that time, the trip to Mexico and the meeting were just further examples of how drug-related issues were taking more and more of his time.

Unexpected controversies kept arising. The president had caused one of them. Bourne went to his office one evening to review his work. Carter asked if there was anything more he should be doing about drugs. Bourne was not caught unprepared. "One thing we could do is take barbiturates off the market," he said. He explained how barbiturates were overprescribed, and how more people died from their misuse each year than from heroin. Bourne was pleased by Carter's keen interest in what he said, but he was stunned at what Carter did the next day. Carter had his first radio call-in program that afternoon, and when someone asked him what he was going to do about the drug problem, he declared that he was going to ban the sale of barbiturates.

It was an example of Carter's habit of shooting from the hip, and Bourne was kept busy for several days picking up the pieces, explaining what the president really meant and meeting with the drug industry and the AMA and the FDA to work out a compromise whereby the drug industry could "voluntarily" phase out barbiturates.

There were other controversies. Just a few days before the May 27 meeting in his office, Bourne had testified before a Senate committee, and someone had asked if he'd ever smoked marijuana himself. He admitted that he had, with some friends, when he was an Army medical officer stationed in Vietnam, and to his amazement that became the day's big story, in newspapers across the nation. It was incredible, he thought, that so much attention would be paid to one man's admission that he'd smoked.

And there were the mothers. All over America, it seemed, community anti-marijuana groups were springing up. They wrote letters to the president, hundreds of them. Sometimes they came to see the president. "How can we control our children when you're talking about making marijuana legal?" they would demand. There was one group in Decatur, Georgia, that had direct access to Carter. They would send their delegations, and often he would send them down to talk with his expert on drugs. Bourne would have to listen to their outraged complaints. They didn't want to hear about the Marijuana Commission report, or scientific findings that suggested marijuana was not harmful, or the arguments for decriminalization. All they knew was that they didn't want their children smoking the stuff. Their passions were as intense as those of the right-to-lifers during the campaign. "You're destroying our children!" they would cry. And Peter Bourne, a gentle man who did not want to destroy anyone's children, would smile and take the heat.

And now there was paraquat.

The meeting in Bourne's office that day happened to include, in addition to the people from State, DEA, FDA, and other executive agencies, a young man named Daryl Dodson, who was a $125-a-week intern on the Senate Permanent Investigations Sub-Committee staff and who was present representing Stuart Statler. More than a year later, when paraquat had exploded into a national controversy, Dodson described the meeting in Bourne's office to Jesse Kornbluth, who was writing an article about the issue for *The New York Times Magazine:*

"The opinion of almost everyone there was that people didn't want to spend resources testing for paraquat poisoning. 'This may be the biggest breakthrough in drug abuse yet,' someone said. There were jokes like, 'Well, we've finally found a way to stop pot smokers.' Richard Dugstad [of the State Department] continued to say there was no evidence contaminated marijuana was being harvested—yet he had forwarded the Ford memos, which directly contradicted him, to us. Over and over, people asked, 'Why are we even concerned about this?' until Peter Bourne said, 'Because we have a responsibility.'"

It was Dodson's impression that Bourne alone, of those at the meeting, was seriously concerned about the possibility that the spraying might present a health hazard to American smokers. Bourne's subsequent action suggests that. He ordered DEA to provide NIDA with samples of marijuana confiscated at the Mexican border, and NIDA to test them for paraquat contamination. Because of his own observations in Mexico, Bourne doubted that any contaminated marijuana would be found, but he wanted to find out, if only to settle the matter once and for all.

The meeting in Bourne's office, as described by Dodson, first revealed the attitude that would be taken time and again by federal bureaucrats, which was that marijuana smokers simply had no rights. If paraquat had been accidentally sprayed on a tobacco field in North Carolina, or spilled at the Lem Motlow distillery in Tennessee, the U.S. government would have moved heaven and earth to be sure that no cigarette smoker or whiskey drinker was harmed. But because marijuana was illegal, the bureaucrats reasoned, it was all right for the government to take actions that might harm them. To Stroup, who for years had resented the idea that he and other smokers were second-class citizens, it was the ultimate indignity: The government thought it could poison them with impunity.

Despite his clash with the White House in February, Stroup was dealing socially with members of the White House staff more and more as 1977 progressed. In part this was because of his friendship with two young entrepreneurs, Fred Moore and Billy Paley. Moore was slender and bearded, a lawyer turned restaurateur in his mid-thirties. Paley, still in his twenties, was the son of CBS founder William S. Paley and Babe Paley, a legendary figure in American fashion and society. Billy Paley was a tall, handsome, broad-shouldered man with a jet-black beard, one earring, and a taste for beautiful women, flashy sports cars, and fancy night life. Together Moore and Paley opened a restaurant on Capitol Hill called the Gandy Dancer, which they hoped to make the sort of hip, fashionable spot that would attract media figures and the younger Carter crowd.

To that end, Moore appeared in Stroup's office one day early in 1977 and said he admired the work NORML had done and hoped Stroup would patronize the Gandy Dancer. In fact, Moore said, Stroup could have a "tab," which meant that his food and drinks would be free. Stroup appreciated the offer and frequently took advantage of it. Moore and Paley were equally successful in attracting some of the Carter people, and Stroup began to meet them at the Gandy. Bill Dixon, who'd run Wisconsin for Carter in 1976, was often there, as were Stroup's photographer friend Bob McNeally and Tim Kraft, Carter's appointments secretary. A lot of people from Capitol Hill and the D.C. government hung out there, too, and entertainers, like Jimmy Buffet, would drop by when they were in town. For a time the Gandy Dancer was the in spot for Washington's younger political crowd, much as Duke Ziebert's restaurant had been for the older political generation. For Stroup it became a social headquarters, a place to entertain, to see and be seen, and Moore and Paley became, in effect, NORML's social chairmen, most notably when he entrusted to them the planning of the NORML conference parties in 1977 and 1978.

If drugs were one of the common denominators that united Washington's younger political crowd, another was rock music. When Willie Nelson or Jimmy Buffet or the Eagles or Fleetwood Mac came to town for a concert, it was important to be there, to be backstage, to be at the postconcert parties, and it was at these concerts that Stroup met many of the Carter people. Often, when a favorite rock group was coming—usually to the huge Capital Centre, a long ride out from downtown Washington—Fred Moore would get tickets, organize a party, and the Gandy Dancer crowd would all ride out together. The first time Stroup rode on a bus with some White House people, he was very straight. Beer was being passed around, and he took one and sipped it. Then a Carter aide yelled across the aisle, "Hey, Stroup, don't you have any dope?" Stroup shrugged, pulled out a joint, and shared it with the more adventurous Carterites.

In July, Fleetwood Mac played a concert in Washington. They were trying to get approval for a tour of Russia, and they attended a party at a Washington hotel that was mainly for members of the White

House staff. Stroup was one of the few outsiders to attend. He saw Chip Carter there and was about to introduce himself and to say he was sorry about the incident in February, but one of his other White House friends advised him against it. Before he left he chatted with Pat Caddell, the president's pollster, and Barry Jagoda, Carter's television adviser; the next day he wrote them both letters and enclosed NORML brochures. That was the point with Stroup: The others were playing, but he was working.

As it happened, the biggest favor Stroup got from the White House that year didn't come from one of his friends at the Gandy Dancer but from a little-known presidential speechwriter named Griffin Smith, who had been assigned to draft a presidential message to Congress on drug abuse.

Smith was a plumpish, soft-spoken man in his early thirties who in 1972–73, as a legislative aide in Texas, had been a key figure in the passage of that state's reform bill. Stroup had known and admired Smith back then and had been delighted when he'd emerged as a member of Carter's speechwriting staff. They talked a few times in early 1977, and in the summer Smith called and asked Stroup to send him ideas for the president's drug statement. Stroup quickly did so, and Smith later called again and invited Stroup to come by his apartment to make suggestions as he wrote a final draft of the statement.

By that point Griffin Smith was a very demoralized, discouraged man. He had come to Washington quite by accident, because of his friendship with Jim Fallows, Carter's senior speechwriter, and he had not expected to be such a small frog in such a large pond. It sounded impressive to say you were one of the president's speechwriters, but the truth was he'd met Carter only once, and he'd soon learned that speechwriters were supposed to keep quiet and write what they were told to write. This drug message was typical of the frustrations of his job. He kept writing good, strong drafts of the message and sending them to Peter Bourne, and Bourne kept watering them down and sending them back.

He invited Stroup over for moral support, and also just for the hell of it. What Smith wanted to do was to write the strongest possible message, yet consistent with the president's policy as he understood it. But that left room for a good deal of rhetorical flourish, and as the evening progressed, Smith and Stroup inserted into the proposed message such statements as "Marijuana has become an established fact throughout our society and the sky has not fallen," and "States should repeal criminal penalties, thus bringing to a close an unhappy and misguided chapter in our history."

A few days later this draft reached the desk of Stu Eisenstat, Carter's top domestic adviser, a cautious man, who was shocked at what he read. In a memo to Carter, Eisenstat said, "I am very concerned about the marijuana section of this message." He warned that the section on marijuana was "written in an almost laudatory tone," and that some of the statements almost seemed "to be a positive recommendation of the drug."

Eisenstat's analysis was perceptive, and Carter, heeding the advice, personally edited out the most blatantly pro-pot rhetoric. Still, even as edited, Carter's message called for decriminalization and was excellent from NORML's point of view.

For Stroup it was yet another lobbyist's dream come true: to help the president's speechwriter write the presidential message to Congress in the area of his concern. And of course it also made a nice, self-serving story to drop to his friends at the Gandy Dancer. Stroup seemed to be riding high as the summer ended. The paraquat issue was at least temporarily on the back burner, as both sides awaited the results of the tests Bourne had ordered. Meanwhile, Stroup partied with the Carter crowd and helped write Carter's drug message. He had intimacy with the people in power, and yet he remained his own man.

In fact, Stroup was riding for a fall, and when it came, the only real surprise was that it happened in Canada instead of in Washington.

12

One afternoon in mid-October of 1977, Stroup was airborne, about to land in Calgary, Alberta, Canada, his last stop on a three-night lecture tour. He was tired and in a lousy mood, because he didn't like flying and he didn't much like lecturing either. He did it because it brought in several thousand dollars a year to NORML. The first stop on this swing had been a small college in Ohio, where the turnout was small and the kids apathetic. "When will marijuana be legal?" one boy finally asked, and Stroup wanted to say, "When you turkeys get off your asses and help change the laws!" The late 1970s' apathy infuriated him. These kids could get all the dope they wanted and weren't likely to be busted, so what did they care about political action?

The next night, in Denver, was better. The audience were mostly law students, and they asked good questions. After the lecture Stroup stayed up late getting high with local NORML backers. So he had slept most of the way to Canada. He hadn't wanted to go to Canada at all, but an American named George Baker, a fugitive from a drug charge in Arizona, had joined with four Vancouver lawyers to start Canada

NORML, and on this visit, besides lecturing, Stroup would meet his new international allies.

As he waited in the line at customs, Stroup was unconcerned about the border crossing. He had a joint on him, some good Hawaiian grass he'd brought for a get-acquainted smoke with George Baker, but he could see at a glance that customs was a formality. He gave the routine answers to the first agent he came to—he was in Canada on business; he would be there two days—and then he stepped to the second, final checkpoint.

The agent there was a pinch-faced man in his forties who gave Stroup a cold stare. With his shoulder-length hair, designer jeans, open collar, and sunglasses, Stroup wasn't the typical American businessman.

"What's that pin?" he asked.

As always, Stroup was wearing his gold-plated marijuana-leaf pin. He loved those little pins. NORML raised thousands of dollars selling them, and reporters almost always mentioned them in stories about him. Once, in Texas years before, Stroup had been stopped for speeding and the trooper had asked about his pin, and Stroup had said it was his garden-club pin. This time he was more candid.

"It's a marijuana leaf," he said. "I'm a public-interest lawyer, and I work for the decriminalization of marijuana in the United States."

"What are you doing in Canada?"

"I'm here to give a lecture."

"Open your briefcase."

Stroup opened his briefcase, somewhat amused, since it contained mostly NORML brochures. The agent examined the pro-pot literature, then noticed the pile of marijuana-leaf pins, just like the one Stroup was wearing.

"You can't bring jewelry into Canada without paying a tax," he said. "I'm going to confiscate these."

"Come on," Stroup protested. "Those are worthless. They cost a dime each to make and I give them away."

"They're still jewelry."

"No, they're not," Stroup shot back. "They're trinkets, and you know it."

"Open your suitcase," the agent said.

Stroup did as he was told, knowing there was nothing illegal in the suitcase. But he didn't like the pleasure the agent and a second agent took in slowly going through every item in his suitcase, and he didn't like the disdainful looks he was getting from the other airlines passengers who were clearing customs without incident. He glared back at them, trying to keep his temper.

A third agent, in civilian clothes, appeared and ordered Stroup to follow him. He led him through an unmarked door into a small, windowless room. Stroup felt a shiver of fear. The plainclothesman flashed his badge and said they would perform a body search. Another agent came in and told Stroup he would have to take off every item of clothing, one at a time, and when he was naked, he would have to submit to an anal inspection. Stroup thought of a lot of wisecracks he could make, but instead he quietly began taking off his clothes. The agents were deadly serious, and he was scared. All his life he had hated and feared authority, people who had power over his life, and now he was naked in a windowless room in a foreign country with two policemen who clearly hated his guts.

Still, he thought he had outbluffed them. The dope was in his coat pocket, and they'd already checked the coat once. It was so obvious they were going to miss it.

Then one of the agents began to reexamine the coat, and after a moment he pulled out the stick of Maui grass from the vest pocket.

"What's this? Marijuana?"

"Come on. Surely you don't care about that small an amount."

"Importation of marijuana is a seven-year felony."

"Bullshit. Possession is a misdemeanor. What do you care if I have a joint or not?" There was no use denying he had the marijuana. His only hope was to bluff them out of pursuing such a minor case.

"How much more do you have?" one of the agents asked.

"That's all," Stroup said. "Just one joint to share with a friend."

The agents left the room. He hoped they were going to consult their superiors. Surely they wouldn't prosecute for one joint. But he could hear the agents laughing outside, as they told their colleagues of their big bust. He had made their day.

The agents returned and told him the Royal Canadian Mounted Police were coming to take him to jail. Stroup wondered if they'd come on horseback. The agents left him alone again. They guffawed outside while Stroup got dressed.

The three Mounties who came for him were young and hip-looking

—probably smokers, Stroup thought. As they led him out of the airport, Stroup heard someone calling his name.

"Keith? Is that you? What's happened? I'm Baker."

"That's my friend," Stroup told the Mounties. "I've got to explain to him."

"Keep walking," one of the Mounties said.

"They busted me," Stroup yelled over his shoulder. "They're taking me to jail."

By 7:00 P.M., three hours after his plane landed, Stroup was locked in a cell in the Calgary jail. He had been questioned, fingerprinted, and relieved of his shoes, his belt, and the $26 he'd been carrying. It didn't look like he'd make his eight-o'clock lecture. Probably he'd be held overnight, although one of the Mounties said it might be possible to get a magistrate to set bail tonight.

To his delight, George Baker arrived at eight with the student lecture-board representatives, a magistrate, and a check drawn on the student-activity fund to cover the $350 bail. Stroup was a free man again. He had never been so happy in his life. On the drive to the university, he shared a joint with his hosts and laughed until he almost cried.

As he mounted the stage at the university auditorium, an hour late, a thousand students stood and cheered. He was a hero. When the cheering stopped, Stroup cracked, "Why'd they search me? Do they think I *smoke* the stuff?" The crowd roared with delight, and soon he had them in the palm of his hand. They'd have stormed City Hall if he'd given the order. During the part of the lecture when scenes from *Reefer Madness* were shown, Stroup stood in the back of the auditorium taking hits from the joints and hash pipes that the Canadian students kept handing him. He felt wonderful. It was worth an hour in jail to win this sort of acclaim.

His high continued the next day when he flew to Vancouver. He gave some interviews there, denouncing a law that would arrest a man for possessing one joint of marijuana. That night he ate dinner in an elegant French restaurant with some of the lawyers who'd started Canadian NORML. After dinner someone lit a joint and proposed a toast to the chef. They smoked openly, and no one seemed to mind.

His only remaining concern was how the media would handle his bust, and when he got back to Washington, he found it was fine. The

Washington *Star* had put its story on the front page and played it
tongue in cheek. Other papers had put it in "personality" columns
—dope lobbyist busted for dope. Stroup was pleased. There was only
one remaining question. Would he return to Canada for his trial? He
didn't have to. He could simply forfeit bail. The problem was that his
new friends in Canada wanted him to come back and be a test case. For
Canada NORML that would mean a million dollars' worth of free
publicity. Stroup was undecided, but his trial was not until the next
spring, so he could worry about it later. In the meantime the 1977
NORML conference was coming up, the first to be held during the
Carter administration, and Stroup wanted to make sure that it was the
biggest and best ever. In particular, he wanted to make sure the
Saturday-night party was a sensation, the party of the year.

On Friday, December 9, the day the NORML conference began, the
White House press office issued a release on behalf of the Office of
Drug Abuse Policy, Peter Bourne's office. Its key paragraphs were
these:

> In response to recent concern that Mexican marijuana plants
> which have been sprayed with Paraquat might be harvested and
> imported into the U.S., the Office of Drug Abuse Policy has
> issued the following statement.
>
> While we do not at present time see any major health hazard
> associated with Paraquat-treated marijuana, we have directed
> the National Institute for Drug Abuse to conduct research to
> determine if marijuana contaminated with Paraquat is being
> imported and, if so, whether its use could cause injury to the
> marijuana user.
>
> Samples of marijuana confiscated in the Southwest Region of
> the United States by the Drug Enforcement Administration
> were analyzed by the National Institute for Drug Abuse. Out of
> 45 samples, six were found to be contaminated with Paraquat.

In other words, the government's own tests showed that 13 percent
of the marijuana coming into the U.S. from Mexico was contaminated.
Peter Bourne was disturbed. Seven months earlier, when he'd

toured the Mexican marijuana fields, the DEA officials had told him this couldn't happen. But it had, and now Bourne had medical concerns and political concerns as well. He had come to understand how committed the State Department was to the spraying program, and he knew, too, how bitterly opposed to the program NORML was. Bourne was caught in the middle. He knew how troublesome Stroup could be, how he delighted in running to the press. Bourne was not only caught in the middle between NORML and the State Department; he was increasingly feeling political pressure from organized anti-marijuana groups. On a recent trip to Atlanta he'd met with an intelligent, determined woman named Sue Rusche who was outraged by teenage drug use and by the proliferation of head shops that sold drug paraphernalia to minors. Rusche had organized a group called Families in Action, others like it were springing up around the nation, and they were furious at Jimmy Carter for endorsing decriminalization, which seemed to them to be the same as telling young people it was all right to smoke marijuana.

But NORML was the immediate problem. Clearly the government's admission that poisoned marijuana was coming into the country would outrage the scientists and reform activists who were arriving in Washington for the NORML conference that weekend. That concern was one reason Bourne decided to drop by NORML's party the next night, Saturday night, December 10. Some good people were associated with NORML, and if this paraquat issue heated up, he didn't want them denouncing him and the president. So he would make an appearance at the party, shake hands, mend his fences, play politician for an evening, build up his personal contacts. Peter Bourne considered himself a rather skillful politician, and he knew that, in politics, the personal touch is everything.

The planning of the 1977 conference was in the hands of a talented and ambitious NORML activist named Marc Kurzman, who had worked hard to make the conference outstanding. Kurzman was a wiry, intense man with bright brown eyes and a neatly trimmed black beard. He had unusual credentials for drug-law reform, in that he was both a lawyer and a pharmacist. He had been active in the anti-war movement, and then he had started a drug-education program at the University of Minnesota. His program became a huge success, receiving several million dollars in state and federal funds and earning Kurzman a national reputation. He had also become involved with

NORML, becoming its Minnesota coordinator, then its Midwest coordinator, and playing a central role in bringing about Minnesota's 1976 decriminalization bill. Stroup admired Kurzman's talents and viewed him as someone who might in time succeed him as NORML's national director. He suspected Kurzman had the same thought.

Much of Saturday, the first day of the conference, was devoted to an impressive series of workshops that Kurzman had assembled. There was a workshop, for example, on marijuana and science, featuring a NIDA official, and one on research and regulation that included Drs. Zinberg and Ungerleider and three FDA officials. Six women participated in a panel on marijuana and women, including Linda Lucks, a feminist and political activist who was NORML's Los Angeles coordinator; Lucks's complaints had prodded Stroup toward some improvement in the male domination of NORML.

One highlight of the conference was a legal seminar attended by some seventy drug lawyers from around the country. Many of them were members of NORML's new legal-defense committee and took constitutional cases *pro bono*, with Peter Meyers providing backup assistance from Washington. Meyers outlined to them some of the cases NORML had been involved in that year. One case involved twenty-one-year-old Brian Kincaid, who had been decorated for valor in Vietnam before returning to the University of Idaho, where he was student-body vice-president when he was one of thirty students arrested during a crackdown on drugs. Police broke into his apartment, with guns drawn, handcuffed him, and found less than an ounce of marijuana. Kincaid pleaded guilty of possession, the prosecutor recommended a fine, but the judge said he was a danger to society and sentenced him to nine months in jail. NORML entered the case, raising constitutional right-of-privacy questions. (Eventually the Idaho supreme court upheld the conviction, and Kincaid served several months in jail.)

In New York, NORML had mounted a major constitutional challenge in the case of Dr. Martin Shepard. Police forced their way into Shepard's house when he was away, found several marijuana plants growing in a window box, and interrogated Shepard's babysitter and his twelve-year-old son. Rather than plead guilty to a misdemeanor charge, Shepard decided to raise a right-of-privacy defense, aided by Michael Kennedy and Gerald Lefcourt, NORML lawyers who worked on the case without charge.

Meyers could report some victories that year. At NORML's urging the governor of Pennsylvania ordered the release of a man who had served seven months of a three-year sentence for selling an ounce of marijuana to a friend for $15. Also that year, Judd Golden, NORML's Iowa coordinator, won a suit to stop random searches of people entering rock concerts.

There was one other important development at the legal seminar. NORML's national legal committee adopted a resolution that its members would not represent informants. The resolution said it was "inherently inconsistent" for a NORML lawyer to fight the marijuana laws and at the same time to help enforce those laws by representing informants. The resolution reflected the scorn the drug culture felt for people who would use drugs and then betray other drug users. It became more significant a few months later when some people at NORML felt that Stroup had, in effect, informed on Peter Bourne.

One of Stroup's guests at the 1977 conference was a young man who knew all too much about informants, Jerry Mitchell, then a college student in Missouri, awaiting the appeal of his seven-year sentence. Another of the delegates was a tall, thin man from New Mexico named Lynn Pierson, who was dying of cancer and had come to the conference to learn what he could do to force the government to let cancer patients use marijuana legally to ease the agonies of chemotherapy.

The conferences were like that, reflecting the issue itself, largely serious, but always with an undercurrent of craziness. Some of the craziness was seen at the luncheon that Saturday. Stroup had arranged for Christie Hefner, Hunter Thompson, and Craig Copetas to address the luncheon. Copetas was to give a slide show on the paraquat-spraying program, which he'd been investigating for *High Times*. As they waited for lunch, Thompson grumbled that he couldn't get a drink, and they all agreed they were wiped out from partying the night before.

There had indeed been quite a party in Stroup's suite the night before. It had been like the stateroom scene in one Marx Brothers movie, with more and more guests crowding into the suite, with someone always ordering more food and champagne from room service, with various people turning up with excellent cocaine. Some of the guests who had come and gone, in addition to Stroup, Copetas, Thompson, and Hefner, had included Tom Forcade; Gerry Goldstein;

Vicky Horn, from *High Times*; and a Washington rock singer named
Root Boy Slim and his Sex Change Band.

So they were all wasted, not entirely sure they could survive the
luncheon, and then one of Thompson's fans came forward, gulped a
hello, and slipped his hero a bit of cocaine, which everyone agreed was
just the pick-me-up they needed. Copetas produced a New York
Times, which he held up in front of them, and Christie Hefner sighed
and looked away while the three crazies snorted coke in more or less
full view of three hundred luncheon guests.

The luncheon antics were only a prelude, it turned out, to the
greater madness that evening, for that was the night that Peter
Bourne shocked so many people by making his way to the little room
on the top floor of the S Street town house and, as various witnesses would later attest, using cocaine with Stroup, Copetas, and
the others.

Stroup slept late Sunday morning, almost till noon, and he awoke
feeling guilty, for he was supposed to be seen at the conferences. He
was concerned, too, about the Bourne incident, wondering how much
gossip there was, wondering if the media might get wind of it. So he
dressed quickly and went downstairs to the hotel's conference area to
see what he could learn. It was then that he became caught up in the
infamous Yippie pie-kill.

A few days before the conference Marc Kurzman learned that a
delegation of Yippies wanted to attend. He didn't want them and
proposed to keep them out by insisting that each pay the full $50
registration fee; Yippies, of course, never paid for anything. When
Stroup heard of this problem, he felt that Kurzman didn't fully
appreciate the politics of the matter. The Yippies were Tom Forcade's
people, and Tom Forcade was one of NORML's most important backers.
In the end, a compromise was reached: Forcade paid the fees, and the
Yippies turned out en masse.

One of the Yippies whom Stroup had got to know was Aaron Kaye, a
big, bearded, bearlike man, usually dirty and disheveled, who was
America's foremost pie-thrower. Tom Forcade had invented political
pieing, but Kaye had popularized it, with Sen. Daniel P. Moynihan,
Mayor Abe Beame, and anti-gay activist Anita Bryant among his
targets.

Stroup was on friendly terms with Kaye, but he was never entirely comfortable around him, because he feared his Yippie friend might decide to pie *him*. When Stroup saw Kaye at the hotel on the opening night of the conference, he said, in a friendly way, "Aaron, if you're here, there's bound to be trouble."

Kaye replied seriously, "Is there gonna be anybody here worth pieing?"

Stroup laughed. "Maybe Joe Nellis," he said.

Kaye frowned. He thought he knew all the pie-worthy figures in America. "Who's he?"

"Oh, he's one of the real bad guys on the Hill. He's chief counsel for Lester Wolff's subcommittee, and they keep screwing us."

"Then what's he doing here?"

"He's on a panel on Sunday. Come to speak to the crazies."

Aaron Kaye nodded thoughtfully and went off to meet his friends.

But the next day, Saturday, he approached Stroup again and asked if he really thought this guy Nellis was pie-worthy. Stroup laughed and told him that was his decision.

Thus it happened that Sunday morning, when Stroup went downstairs, with Peter Bourne very much on his mind and Aaron Kaye not at all, the first person he saw was the mad pie-thrower.

"You still think I should pie that guy Nellis?"

"Oh, shit, Aaron, you decide."

"But whadda *you* think?"

What Stroup thought was fairly complex. His friendship with Tom Forcade had given him more sympathy for the Yippie world view than was prudent for a Washington lobbyist. He had come to see pieing as a legitimate form of protest, so long as the pie-thrower was willing to pay the legal consequences. And Stroup thought that most of Kaye's victims richly deserved a pie in the face. Moreover, Stroup's feelings about Joe Nellis were not entirely rational. He resented the way Nellis (and his boss, Congressman Wolff) had treated him politically, and he had developed a personal loathing for Nellis. The truth was that Nellis reminded Stroup of his father: Physically he was the same sort of short, stocky figure, and his behavior struck Stroup as gruff, humorless, and oppressive. The comparison may not have been fair either to Nellis or to the elder Stroup, but it was there in Stroup's subconscious and it was part of the reason for his gut response to Aaron Kaye's question.

"Aaron, if you want my honest opinion, I can't think of anybody who deserves a pie more than Joe Nellis."

The Yippie beamed, then looked worried. "But where can I find a pie on Sunday, Keith?"

"You mean the world's greatest pie-thrower can't find a pie?"

Kaye looked pained. Pieing was an art, no laughing matter. "You know I don't know Washington, Keith. Help me out."

Stroup sighed and told Kaye where there was a bakery, a few blocks away. But there was one more problem.

"Keith, could you loan me some money to buy the pie with?"

"For Christ' sake, Aaron, do I have to throw the fucking pie for you?"

But he gave Kaye six dollars to be rid of him.

Then he began to look around the conference, and what he found was that the Yippies were out of control. They'd been disrupting workshops all morning, asking hostile questions, grabbing the microphones and making speeches, and eventually they focused their attentions on the afternoon workshop on international control of marijuana. Its panelists included Joe Nellis; Richard Bonnie, from the University of Virginia law school; and Robert Angarola, the chief counsel of Peter Bourne's Office of Drug Abuse Policy in the White House.

Stroup watched for a while from the hallway as the panelists tried to answer questions over the jeers of the Yippies. He saw Aaron Kaye enter the room with a white box under his arm. Then, a moment later, Mark Heutlinger and Marc Kurzman rushed up to Stroup. Kurzman had heard about the planned pieing, and he was furious. Stroup quickly agreed that Kurzman was right, and Heutlinger went into the conference room and brought Kaye out. With Stroup and Kurzman looking on, Heutlinger read Kaye the riot act.

"Aaron, the pieing is off! There can't be any pieing. You can't screw up our conference. No pie-kill—do you understand?"

Kaye seemed to agree, and he shuffled back into the conference room. He did not, however, surrender the lemon cream pie he had purchased. Instead, he produced a knife and cut off several slices of the pie and shared them with his friends. For a time all seemed peaceful, with the Yippies eating lemon pie while the discussion droned on.

What no one realized was that Kaye was sitting next to a San Francisco doctor named Eugene Schoenfeld, who wrote a medical column under the name Dr. Hip. And Dr. Hip was doing his best to persuade Aaron Kaye that Stroup and Heutlinger hadn't really meant it, that of course they wanted him to pie Joe Nellis; that was what everyone was waiting for.

Meanwhile, a Yippie named Dana Beal was giving Joe Nellis a hard time. Beal was an aging Yippie with long brown hair and a drooping mustache, an urban desperado in his black shirt, white tie, and leather vest. He was making a speech to the effect that Americans have a God-given right to smoke dope. Nellis countered with something called the Single Convention, an international anti-drug treaty that in theory makes legal marijuana impossible in the U.S.

"It's the law of the land," Joe Nellis declared. "As long as we're a signatory of the Single Convention, no legalization is possible."

"Justice, justice," cried the Yippies.

Just then, Aaron Kaye slouched forward, a burly man in a tweed coat and a black hat, with half a lemon cream pie in his hand.

Joe Nellis, seeing the assassin lurch toward him, rose to defend himself. He was a husky man and was wearing a dark suit and a dark shirt, open at the neck, and he had a cigarette in one hand. He looked rather like Edward G. Robinson in a gangster movie, and he also looked like a man who could take care of himself.

The pie sailed through the air—and plopped harmlessly on the floor. There were both jeers and cheers from the startled audience. Aaron Kaye raced away, crying, "Yip, yip, yip!" Joe Nellis was outraged. The pie had missed, but in the confusion a water pitcher had been knocked over, soaking his pants.

A moment later Mark Heutlinger escorted Joe Nellis out of the room, trying to convince him that it was actually an honor to be pied by Aaron Kaye.

The angriest man in the room was not Joe Nellis but Marc Kurzman. He had worked hard for months to put together an outstanding conference, and now, as he saw it, Stroup had sabotaged him, humiliated him. It had been Stroup who'd let the Yippies come to the conference, and it might as well have been Stroup throwing the pie himself. Moments after the pie was thrown, Kurzman grabbed the microphone and began to denounce Stroup. One man was responsible for this outrage, he said. "I ask you all to join me in condemning the actions of the national director of NORML for this individual, immature act," he said furiously.

Craig Copetas, who was enjoying the scene hugely, began a straight-faced interrogation of Kurzman. "Sir, do you mean to suggest that Keith Stroup, the national director of NORML, would be a party to a vicious pie-kill?" For a time Kurzman was too angry to realize his leg was being pulled.

Down the hall, Heutlinger raced up to Stroup.

"Aaron just pied Joe Nellis," he said. "People are really pissed. You better disappear until it cools down."

Stroup agreed, and went up to Hunter Thompson's room, where he found Thompson and Michael Stepanian, the San Francisco drug lawyer. The three of them watched a football game and smoked a few joints, and then Dr. Hip joined them and brought a tape recording of the pieing and Kurzman's denunciation of Stroup.

"This is an outrage, Stroup," Hunter Thompson declared. "You've been up here getting high all morning. I want you to march down there and say, 'What pie? I don't know anything about any pie.'"

They discussed the "What pie?" defense, but at length Stroup decided the best strategy was to stay in Thompson's room getting high the rest of the evening.

But the pie incident was not so easily ignored. The next morning Stroup was awakened by Gordon Brownell, who was banging on his door, wanting to talk about it. There were other complaints, and in the weeks ahead Stroup began getting reports that Kurzman was telling everyone that he was irresponsible, that he was doing too many drugs, that he was no longer fit to run NORML.

In late December, hoping to put the pie incident to rest, Stroup wrote a memo to NORML's staff and advisers in which he detailed his role in the matter. He admitted he had been unwise to encourage Kaye, but he added that the affair was insignificant and that they should all forget it and get on with their work.

Stroup was wrong, for the pie affair was significant in two ways. First, it was another in a series of incidents that showed he was not taking his work as seriously as he should. Stroup loved NORML—it had been his life for seven years—but he was also bored with it. He was ready to move on to something else, but he didn't know what. He could practice law, but he still viewed that as "selling out." He thought vaguely of some other public-interest project, some other issue, but its nature eluded him. So, while he pondered the future, he enjoyed himself. He had paid his dues for a long time, he thought, and he deserved some fun. Which was fine, except that his bad-boy antics were starting to detract from NORML's serious work.

The pieing was significant, too, because it would come back to haunt Stroup. After he wrote his memo, he thought the issue was closed, just as he thought the Peter Bourne incident was closed. In a strange, maddening way the pie-throwing, the Bourne incident, and the paraquat issue had become linked. It was an ungodly mixture —cocaine, lemon cream pie, and a deadly herbicide—a witches' brew that in 1978 proved fatal to several people.

There was a final footnote to the fun and games of 1977. FBI statistics, later compiled and made public, said that 458,000 people were arrested on marijuana charges that year, the most ever. Despite changing attitudes, despite reform laws in a dozen states, the arrests continued to mount, lives continued to be damaged, and the war continued to escalate.

13

During the first week of 1978, Stroup was in New York for three days of fun and fund-raising at the drug-paraphernalia industry's annual boutique show. He had got to know many of the industry people through Tom Forcade. By some estimates, paraphernalia was close to being a billion-dollar-a-year business, and Stroup hoped that some of its leaders could be persuaded to support NORML. In his travels Stroup had sought out local head-shop proprietors and often persuaded them to sell NORML T-shirts, distribute its literature, and even put DONATE-TO-NORML jars on their counters. He found most head shop operators to be politically naïve, but he hoped that would change as they took more and more political heat. Local officials and legislators who could not otherwise discourage marijuana-smoking were trying to do so by passing laws against head shops and the paraphernalia they sold. The laws they passed were often struck down by the courts as unconstitutional and they did little to stop drug use, but they made the politicians look boldly anti-drug, and they caused people in the business some inconvenience—enough, Stroup hoped, to make them organize and be more politically active.

In addition to thousands of generally unsophisticated head-shop operators the industry had created six or eight tycoons, marijuana millionaires, and Stroup had found some of them to be more politically aware. Two examples were Don Levin and Burt Rubin. Levin had been a General Motors management trainee in the late 1960s when he saw the potential in the paraphernalia business. He opened a head shop and in time started Adams Apple, Inc., which became the largest distributor of rolling papers in the U.S. Burt Rubin, who had been a trader in precious metals, noticed how many smokers would stick two standard-sized cigarette papers together so they could roll a good, fat joint. He had the inspiration to market a double-sized paper with a punny name, E-Z Wider and thereby parlayed a $6500 investment into a $9-million business.

Stroup had become friendly with Levin and Rubin, and both had begun contributing $5000 or $10,000 a year to NORML. It was Stroup's hope that as he cultivated others in the industry, many more would be moved to do the same. During the January boutique show a rolling-paper distributor named Ralph Kaplan gave a benefit reception for NORML. There was an art auction featuring originals of *High Times* covers, and by prearrangement some of Stroup's friends pushed up the bidding, challenging others to support NORML, and pledges of $40,000 were made. It was for Stroup a good night's work, a step toward what he hoped could be an important new source of funding for NORML.

On January 25 Peter Bourne wrote an unusual "To Whom It May Concern" letter to the provincial court in Calgary, Canada. He began by saying he was writing on behalf of Keith Stroup, who was facing criminal marijuana charges in Canada. "I have known Mr. Stroup in a professional capacity for several years, and I can attest to the seriousness of his work," he said. "I have always found his conduct to meet the highest standards of professionalism." He suggested that "Mr. Stroup be accorded whatever diversion programs" might be available so that "he not have his career needlessly blemished by a criminal conviction."

Peter Bourne had not wanted to write this letter. He knew that it was a tricky, potentially explosive act for an assistant to the president of the United States to give even the appearance of meddling in the

judicial affairs of another nation. It was always possible that the judge
or the prosecutor might protest the intrusion. International incidents
had erupted from less. To minimize that risk, Bourne wrote his letter
on his personal stationery and signed himself simply "Peter G. Bourne,
M.D." There was no mention of his official role. Still, he disliked
writing the letter, and he resented Stroup's requesting it.

That summer, when reports of Bourne's cocaine use at the NORML
party were published, columnist Michael Novak charged that Stroup
had, in effect, acquired blackmail power over Bourne—that Bourne
had, for example, no choice but to write the letter Stroup wanted.
Stroup resented the suggestion. As he saw it, when his lawyer
suggested that character references might help with the Canadian
court, he'd naturally turned to Peter Bourne and Stuart Statler, two
men who were both his friends and his professional associates. Still,
the potential for blackmail was there, and before another month had
passed, Stroup would wield it like a bludgeon against his friend Peter
Bourne.

On January 26, the day after Peter Bourne wrote his letter, Stroup
sent a "Dear Sirs" letter to Cyrus Vance, the secretary of state, and
Peter Bensinger, the head of the Drug Enforcement Administration, a
letter that was NORML's declaration of war on the paraquat-spraying
program in Mexico.

Stroup's letter was, in legal terms, a "demand letter." It demanded
that the State Department file an environmental-impact statement on
the spraying program and that it halt all U.S. participation in the
program until that statement was completed. As all parties involved
understood, the demand letter was only a formality, a prelude to a
lawsuit. And although the letter was signed by Stroup and was largely
written by Peter Meyers, the prime mover of NORML's anti-paraquat
campaign was a twenty-three-year-old law student named George
Farnham, who was having the time of his life.

George Farnham, unlike Stroup and Schott and most of NORML's
senior staff, did not come from a middle-class or working-class
background. His father, a conservative Republican, was a senior
partner in a leading New York law firm, and Farnham grew up in very
comfortable circumstances in Scarsdale, New York. After graduating

from Scarsdale High, he went off to Washington University, in St. Louis, to study political science, and it was there that he became a marijuana smoker and a great fan of Hunter Thompson's writings. He wrote a three-hundred-page term paper that argued that Thompson's was by far the best coverage of the 1972 presidential campaign. Later, when he attended the 1976 Democratic convention, Farnham persuaded one delegate, a friend of his, to cast her vote for Thompson for vice-president.

Farnham decided to attend law school at George Washington University, in Washington, D.C., and when he learned he could receive credit for working as an intern for some public-interest program, he quickly made his way to NORML. He chose NORML in part because Hunter Thompson was on its advisory board and in part because he had been impressed with what he'd heard about Stroup. Farnham began working as an aide to Meyers in July of 1977 and was immediately assigned to the paraquat issue. At that point not much had happened, except that Peter Bourne, in response to Stroup's and Senator Percy's inquiries, had ordered DEA and NIDA to investigate the matter. That fall, Farnham filed Freedom of Information Act requests with State, DEA, and NIDA asking for information on their roles in the spraying program in Mexico. He was spurred in part by rumors that the government planned to expand the program to Colombia and other countries. The DEA never turned over any information, but in January of 1978 the State Department did surrender some 150 pages of material. Most of it was quite innocuous —it had obviously been carefully edited—but there were references to memoranda written by John Ford, who'd set up the spraying program for the Mexicans in the fall of 1975. It seemed to Farnham and Meyers that if they could get Ford's reports, they might get at the truth about U.S. involvement in the spraying program. Officials at State refused to hand over the Ford memos, but NORML was given copies by a friend on Capitol Hill, and after that the pot lobby was no longer working in the dark on the paraquat issue.

What the Ford memos did was to document the full extent of U.S. involvement in the program and thus contradict the government's claims that it was entirely a Mexican program over which the U.S. had no control. The memos showed, among other things, that Ford had personally set up the program; that the stress from the first was on spraying marijuana fields, not poppy fields; and that contrary to official claims, DEA was deeply involved in the program.

With this information in hand, Farnham began to meet with State Department officials. First he talked to an environmental specialist who laughed aloud when Farnham suggested State should file an environmental-impact statement on the spraying program. The National Environmental Policy Act, the official explained, applied only to domestic programs, not to the overseas activities of the State Department. When Farnham suggested that the spraying program was poisoning marijuana smokers, the official laughed again and said that maybe all the marijuana smokers would die, and then the problem would be solved.

Another meeting, the next day, made it clear that State would release no more data on the spraying program, would concede no U.S. control over the program, and had no intention of filing an environmental-impact statement. The State Department was completely committed to the paraquat program, and there was nothing left to do but to sue.

It happened that NORML could make a good legal case for the government's obligation to file an impact statement on the program. The 1969 Environmental Policy Act required impact statements on "major federal actions significantly affecting the quality of the human environment," and the courts had liberally interpreted this requirement. Stroup's letter to Vance and Bensinger noted, for example, that the Law Enforcement Assistance Administration had been required to file an impact statement when it made a $3000 grant to spray herbicides on marijuana plants in Indiana in 1972. As for State's argument that no impact statement was required, because the spraying program was outside the United States, the NORML letter cited two precedents. In one, the Agency for International Development (AID), when sued by an environmentalist group, agreed to file an impact statement on its pesticide-spraying programs. In another, after the Sierra Club brought suit, a U.S. district court held that an impact statement was required for the construction of a highway through Panama and Colombia.

In short, NORML was about to bring a lawsuit that had a good chance of forcing the Department of State to stop a program that it did not wish to stop. NORML had ceased to be a mildly amusing bunch of crazies and had become a major annoyance, a problem to be dealt with.

All this was a prelude to the remarkable letter that Stroup received from the White House on February 4, just nine days after his letter to the secretary of state.

On the first of February, Gordon Brownell called Stroup with a puzzling report: He had heard that Stroup was about to receive a "stinging" letter of rebuke from the White House on the pie incident. Brownell had heard this from Roger Roffman, the University of Washington professor who was NORML's Washington State coordinator, who in turn had heard it from Wes Pomeroy, a former California law-enforcement official who had joined Peter Bourne's staff in the White House.

Stroup didn't know what the stinging rebuke might prove to be, but he did know that the two-month-old pie incident was far from dead. Joe Nellis had sent word to the Playboy Foundation that he was displeased that it would support an organization that allowed pies to be thrown at its conference guests. More important, Stroup continued to get reports that Marc Kurzman was calling NORML's state coordinators, saying that Stroup had to go and apparently offering himself as successor. Stroup had decided to fire Kurzman as his Midwest coordinator. He was not going to pay someone to organize a coup against him.

The White House letter arrived. It was on White House stationery and was signed by Robert Angarola, general counsel for the Office of Drug Abuse Policy. It was a very curious document, one that makes sense, if at all, only in the hothouse of high-level Washington politics. It was headed "Dear Keith," and began by noting that Angarola was a panelist at the NORML conference when "the unfortunate pie incident" occurred. Angarola said he had considered the matter closed until he was sent a copy of Stroup's memo on it to the NORML staff, which caused him and others to be concerned about his "apparent absence of regret regarding this incident." Angarola then praised NORML's work and Stroup's "patient and able leadership," but added, "I was therefore upset to learn that its National Director condoned, and in a sense encouraged, such an irresponsible act against one of the organization's invitees. This can only prove counterproductive to your and NORML's most worthwhile efforts. It also must call into question the advisability of participating in future conferences which you sponsor." He said he had discussed the matter with Peter Bourne, Marc Kurzman, and others, all of whom shared his concerns. He concluded: "Although it will inevitably have a negative impact, I sincerely hope that it will not seriously affect your future activities and that NORML will be able to maintain support and continue the fine work it has done in the past."

The letter, signed "Bob," noted at the bottom that copies were going to Bourne, Bonnie, Kurzman, Nellis, and Pomeroy.

It was not exactly a stinging letter, but it was one Stroup read with mounting outrage. He was not interested in Angarola's compliments, only in certain negative phrases: "call into question the advisability of participating in future conferences," "inevitably have a negative impact," and most of all the question of whether "NORML will be able to maintain support."

As Stroup saw it, this letter was nothing less than an effort to destroy him.

He assumed, first, that the real purpose of the letter was not for a minor White House functionary to express concern over a two-month-old pie-throwing. He assumed, second, that Angarola would not have written the letter without Peter Bourne's approval. No, Stroup thought that now that NORML had challenged the State Department over paraquat, the White House was looking for a way to oust him and encourage more docile leadership at NORML.

He took the letter to be a threat that the White House would not work with NORML so long as he remained its director. He thought, by way of analogy, that if the president's top energy adviser had sent word to Exxon that he no longer wished to deal with its senior Washington lobbyist, Exxon would have rather quickly replaced that lobbyist, and the White House was gambling that the dope lobby would do the same. Stroup feared the letter might put him on the defensive, and he might even lose control of the organization he had created.

Whether Stroup's analysis of the Angarola letter reflected paranoia or political realism is debatable but not relevant. Another, more secure man might have shrugged it off as an ambiguous letter from a minor official, but Stroup, attuned to the byzantine ways of Washington, took it as a deliberate attempt by Peter Bourne to destroy him. He responded in kind.

He called Bourne but could not reach him. He talked instead to Wes

Pomeroy, an aide to Bourne who was a respected and quite remarkable law-enforcement officer. After serving as undersheriff in California for many years, Pomeroy had been a special assistant to Ramsey Clark at the Justice Department in 1968 and then was chief of security for the Woodstock rock festival in 1969. Stroup had met him when Pomeroy was a fellow at the Drug Abuse Council in the early 1970s. Stroup respected the older man, but now he shouted his outrage over the Angarola letter, and Pomeroy protested that it was intended only as constructive criticism.

"Bullshit!" Stroup raged. "Listen, Peter is crazy. What does he think he's doing? You guys are all vulnerable as hell. Do you want to play hardball?"

"You can't threaten me," Pomeroy shot back.

Stroup hung up.

To make sure his message got through, Stroup next called two people who were both his friends and Bourne's, Bob Carr at the Drug Abuse Council and Mathea Falco at the State Department. He gave both the same message: "My constituents know I use drugs. Do Peter's know he uses drugs? You tell Dr. Bourne he'd better repudiate that letter!"

Bob Carr, who understood the threat and was shaken by it, quickly talked to his boss, Tom Bryant, who in turn talked to his friend Peter Bourne. Still, days passed and Stroup heard nothing from Bourne. When he tried to call him, he could only reach Ellen Metsky, who asked what he wanted. "I want that letter repudiated," Stroup said. Metsky said Bourne was extremely busy, and asked if it would wait a few days. Stroup assumed that Bourne simply wanted time to decide what to do. He told Metsky that it would wait only until the next Monday.

Then, as if to prove his resolve, Stroup took what proved to be a fateful step: He called Gary Cohn, a friend of his who was a writer on Jack Anderson's staff.

Gary Cohn was twenty-six years old, an ambitious and aggressive young reporter. One day in 1976, when he needed a story, he'd noticed a NORML poster on the wall over another reporter's desk. On impulse he called Stroup, and came away with a nice item about an expensive government study that had proved only that marijuana makes monkeys hungry. After that, Cohn dropped by Stroup's office from time to time to smoke a joint and poke around for news.

Cohn attended the 1977 NORML party, heard the rumors of Bourne's cocaine use there, and had several times asked Stroup to confirm them. Each time, however, Stroup brushed his questions aside. Now, however, the situation had changed. Stroup asked Cohn to come by his office. Cohn arrived and found him furious. Stroup told Cohn about Bourne's cocaine use at the party and gave him the names of two other witnesses. He stressed, however, that the information was off the record. He said that if Bourne sent him the letter of apology he wanted, it would stay off the record; if not, Cohn could go with the story.

On Monday, February 11, eight days after Angarola sent his letter, Bourne called Stroup and asked what the problem was.

"The problem is that you fuckers are trying to blow me out of the water," Stroup shouted. "I don't like it, Peter. I don't understand it. You've gone out of bounds. That letter was like an official White House reprimand."

Bourne protested that Angarola was only expressing his personal opinion, not White House policy.

"Then why did he write it on White House stationery?" Stroup demanded.

"Keith, I assure you I did not approve the letter," Bourne said. "I understood he was writing some letter of protest, but I didn't see it before it went out."

"Peter, the White House has no right to inject itself into NORML's internal affairs, and that's what that letter did."

"You're probably right," Bourne conceded. "What can I do to put this right?"

"You can write me a letter on the same White House stationery and repudiate Angarola."

"I can't repudiate him, but I'll write a letter saying he doesn't express the White House position, and that I've always held you in the highest regard."

"I wish you'd do that," Stroup said bitterly. "And I wish you'd have it hand-delivered to me today."

Bourne said he would, and then he added, "Keith, I hope this won't harm our personal relationship."

Stroup sighed. "Peter," he said, "after this, I really don't know if I can trust you."

Bourne's letter arrived that afternoon. It began by saying that

Bourne was sure Angarola's letter was intended to be "constructive and helpful," and then concluded, "I want you to know of the very high personal regard in which I hold you and the remarkable leadership that you have provided to NORML under conditions that I know have not always been easy. I will look forward to continuing to work closely with you in the future."

It was all Stroup could have asked. If anyone tried to say he was in disfavor at the White House, he had Bourne's glowing letter to disprove the charge. But of course Bourne's letter meant nothing; if anything, it meant the opposite of what it said, for it was written under a clearly implied threat. Neither Bourne nor Stroup would ever trust the other again, and in the small world of drug policy a good many people knew why.

Once Stroup received Bourne's letter, he called Gary Cohn and told him the cocaine story would have to remain off the record. Cohn took this news with mixed emotions. In part, he was relieved. Cohn had smoked dope and used cocaine, and he had misgivings about this story. Was it fair? Was it legitimate? He was also concerned because he assumed the story would cost Bourne his job, and he thought Bourne was a good man to have as the president's adviser on drugs.

Still, Cohn was ambitious, and he knew it was a hell of a story, the sort of exposé that helped make a young reporter's reputation. Part of him lusted for the Bourne story, the part that could rationalize that reporters don't make moral judgments but only report the facts. In the weeks ahead Cohn several times asked Stroup if he wouldn't put the Bourne story on the record. Each time, Stroup refused. Still, the cat was halfway out of the bag. When Stroup gave Cohn the names of the two witnesses, he all but guaranteed the story would come out eventually. The only question was when.

But first, late in February, while Stroup was preoccupied with paraquat and Peter Bourne, NORML scored a dramatic victory in a battle it had been waging for years: the effort to gain recognition for the medical uses of marijuana.

14

During the NORML conference in December of 1977, as other delegates variously attended workshops, snorted cocaine, and threw pies, two men and a woman huddled together for hours talking earnestly about politics, medicine, and marijuana.

One of the men, twenty-six-year-old Lynn Pierson, who had come to the conference from New Mexico, was six feet two, weighed less than 130 pounds, and was entirely bald because of the chemotherapy treatments he was undergoing for lung cancer. The other man, Bob Randall, was twenty-nine years old and lived in Washington, D.C. He was solidly built, with dark, curly hair and a drooping mustache, and he wore thick glasses because glaucoma had damaged his vision and would probably blind him someday. The two men both found that smoking marijuana helped them medically. It stabilized Bob Randall's glaucoma and thus held off blindness, and it enabled Lynn Pierson to endure the chemotherapy treatments that were keeping him alive.

The woman, Alice O'Leary, was dark-haired, heavyset, and had a determined look about her. She and Randall had met as college students, and she had shared Randall's long battle against both glaucoma and the federal government, which had bitterly resisted giving him legal access to marijuana. Now Lynn Pierson had come up from New Mexico to ask Randall what he could do in the remaining months of his life to aid in the battle for medical use of marijuana.

Incredibly, on February 21, 1978, less than three months after Pierson, Randall, and O'Leary met at the NORML conference, New Mexico enacted the nation's first medical-use bill, making possible legal access to marijuana for persons suffering from cancer, glaucoma, and other life-threatening diseases. New Mexico's example, along with NORML's new "medical-reclassification project," which O'Leary direct- ed, would soon spark medical-use legislation in twenty other states. This dramatic breakthrough was a tribute to the efforts of Pierson, the cancer victim, and Randall, the glaucoma victim, and it was also a milestone in NORMAL's longtime effort to force the federal government to admit what scientists have long known: that marijuana has legitimate medical uses.

Marijuana has for centuries been used as medicine throughout the world. In the United States in the nineteenth century it was routinely prescribed as a pain reliever and anti-convulsant. Its medical use was severely restricted, however, by laws passed during Harry Anslin- ger's anti-marijuana campaign in the 1930s. The virtual end to its medical use came when the Nixon administration, in writing the Controlled Substances Act of 1970, chose for symbolic purposes to classify marijuana as a "schedule-one" drug, along with, among others, heroin and LSD. This meant that marijuana was officially defined as having a high potential for abuse and no known medical value. That was blatantly untrue, but it was politically expedient, and it became the law.

NORML petitioned DEA in 1972 to reclassify marijuana, but DEA and other government agencies bitterly resisted the request and NORML's subsequent lawsuit. That was the situation—legal stalemate —when Bob Randall walked into Stroup's office one day in September of 1975 and said he'd been busted for growing marijuana.

Bob Randall grew up in Sarasota, Florida, where his father owned a furniture store (and where, to the endless delight of Randall and his friends, the Ringling Brothers Circus spent the winter months). In 1967, when he was an undergraduate at the University of South Florida, majoring in speech and political science, Randall began to have trouble with his eyes. In the evenings his vision would become hazy, and there would be tricolored circles, halos, around lights. Doctors told him it was eyestrain.

In June of 1971 he received a master's degree in speech and went up to Washington, D.C., where he hoped to find a job as a political speechwriter. When that didn't work out, he shrugged off his disappointment and started driving a cab. He also continued to have problems with his eyes. One evening near the end of the summer of 1972, he was reading, and when he closed one eye, he suddenly couldn't see the words. Then he couldn't see the book. He went to an ophthalmologist the next day and finally learned he had glaucoma.

Glaucoma occurs when fluid within the eye fails to drain properly and pressure builds on the optic nerve; in time the pressure destroys the nerve and causes blindness. Randall was given the standard treatment—eyedrops and pills—but it didn't work for him. He had already lost 85 percent of his optic nerve, and his doctor predicted he'd be blind in three to five years; his 20/400 vision made him already legally blind in his right eye. The only possible treatment was surgery, but the operation was a dangerous one and might cause immediate blindness. Then, one evening in 1973, Bob Randall discovered that marijuana helped him.

He was spending a quiet evening in his apartment in Virginia. He smoked a couple of joints and was feeling quite mellow when suddenly he realized that the tricolored halos around lights had gone away. He was stunned. In college he'd sometimes had a vague sense that smoking somehow relieved his chronic eyestrain, but he'd never made a direct, cause-and-effect connection. Now he did. He had no doubt about it. Smoking marijuana improved his vision. He felt a great euphoria. He knew at once, instinctively, that the marijuana laws would no longer apply to him.

When he awoke the next morning, his euphoria was gone. He laughed bitterly at his illusions. How could he have been so self-deluding as to think *smoking dope* would save his sight? That was childish, true reefer madness. Still, he experimented. He smoked every evening, testing what effect different amounts of marijuana had on his sight. After a few months he knew it was true. His condition was supposed to be one of irreversible deterioration, but marijuana stabilized, perhaps improved, his vision.

But what should he do with his discovery? He thought long and hard about telling his doctor, and finally decided against it, for fear his doctor might not treat him if he knew of his illegal self-treatment. Nor did he have any inclination to tell the government or the scientific world of his discovery. He knew how the government felt about marijuana; at best he would be laughed at, and at worst he might be arrested. It was not Randall's nature to be a gadfly, a troublemaker. He was an easygoing, good-humored, intelligent young man who feared he had only a few years of sight left and didn't want to spend those years being hassled by the government. So he kept buying illegal marijuana on the street, but it was expensive ($25 or so for the ounce he smoked each week), and the quality was inconsistent. In the spring of 1975 he decided to grow his own.

He had by then got a job teaching speech at Prince George's Community College, in Maryland. He and Alice O'Leary were sharing a comfortable second-floor apartment on Capitol Hill with several cats and a great many books, classical recordings, and hanging plants. Randall began growing four marijuana plants in what he thought was a secluded spot on his back porch. But when he and O'Leary returned home from a trip to Florida one Sunday evening that August, they found their apartment ransacked. They also found a summons order- ing the occupant of the apartment to report to the nearby police station. Randall dutifully turned himself in and learned he was charged with possession of marijuana. Police, investigating an unrelated incident, had climbed a fire escape and spotted his plants.

"It was a gentle bust," Randall recalls. "I wasn't handcuffed or anything. Yet I felt psychological abuse. It made me feel very insecure to realize the government could walk into my house, tear my things apart, and take away what to me was medication. It made me insecure; then it made me mad as hell."

Randall went to a lawyer. He had a growing sense that he should not be charged with a crime for using what was, to him, medicine. The lawyer was skeptical. It might be easier to pay a fine and forget it. At the least, Randall would need more scientific evidence, so he wouldn't be laughed out of court.

His search for information took him to Stroup and NORML. He was impressed that he could walk right in and see Stroup, but he was not much encouraged by what Stroup told him: that NORML was in the fourth year of a legal battle to force the government to reclassify marijuana for medical use and the government was bitterly resisting any change. Stroup didn't see how one young teacher could take on the government. He assumed that the battle would be won, if at all, by NORML's suit. At that point, Stroup had seen a great many angry young men charge into his office, vowing to sue the government for this or that injustice. What he could not foresee was how determined Randall was, and what a potent symbol of the medical-use issue he could become.

Stroup gave Randall some clippings and the names of several government scientists who might give him information. The scientists all told Randall the same thing: Recent studies demonstrated that marijuana was useful in treating glaucoma.

That news, although it confirmed Randall's own discovery, made him furious. The government *knew* that marijuana could help glaucoma victims, and it was doing nothing about it. His anger was not just for himself. From two to four million Americans suffer from glaucoma. About 90 percent of them can be helped by the standard medications. The other ten percent, two hundred thousand to four hundred thousand people, have no alternative but dangerous surgery. Those were the people, Randall among them, whom marijuana might help.

Randall flew to Los Angeles in December for thirteen days of testing with Dr. Robert Hepler of UCLA, who in 1970 had conducted a pioneering study on marijuana and glaucoma. The tests confirmed Randall's own self-testing, and he returned to Washington in early 1976 to begin planning a two-pronged challenge to the government. In the first place, he would challenge the criminal charges that were pending against him. Second, he would demand that the government provide him with marijuana to meet his medical needs. During his visit with Dr. Hepler he had learned that the government grew marijuana, rolled it into joints, and provided it to the few scientists who had obtained permission to conduct marijuana research. He had smoked those nicely prerolled government joints while he was with Dr. Hepler, and he thought the government should continue to provide him with them. At his lawyer's suggestion, Randall obtained a sworn statement from Dr. Hepler that said that marijuana helped Randall's vision, that without it he would face either blindness or a dangerous operation, and that he would recommend that Randall be given marijuana by prescription.

With this evidence in hand Randall on May 20 petitioned DEA to give him immediate access to government marijuana. DEA's first reaction was to do nothing. Randall assumed they thought he was some nut who would go away if ignored. He didn't. After a few weeks he went to reporters for the Washington *Post* and UPI and told them about his petition. Randall wanted the publicity, not only for himself but for all those other people who were going blind and had no idea that marijuana could help them. Friendly reporters told Randall DEA's unofficial comment on his case: Mr. Randall was a criminal.

Next came his trial, in the D.C. superior court in late July. Randall raised the very rare defense of "medical necessity." He was saying that it was no crime for him to use marijuana, because he needed it for medical purposes. The government said the only issue was whether Randall had in fact possessed marijuana. The prosecutor added gratuitously that Mr. Randall had no constitutional right to his eyesight. The judge was a black man named James A. Washington, Jr., formerly a professor of constitutional law at the Howard University law school. After two days of testimony he took the case under advisement. It was against this backdrop that Randall continued to negotiate with the government for legal access to marijuana.

First the government, through a middle-level bureaucrat at NIDA, said it would give him all the marijuana he wanted if he would agree to be hospitalized for the duration. Randall declined. Then the government said Randall could have marijuana if he would go to a hospital to smoke it. Randall said that reminded him of the churches in the Middle Ages that kept their Bibles chained to the wall for use on the premises only. Next the government said it might give him marijuana to take home if he would purchase a 750-pound safe to protect it. Randall replied that no one had ever stolen his marijuana except the D.C. police. Finally the government said it might let Randall take its marijuana home if he would agree not to tell anyone about it.

No way, Randall said. No way.

Finally, in October, the government proposed to establish a special "research program" for Randall. His doctor would be authorized to receive government marijuana, give it to Randall, and conduct tests on him. Randall was uncertain. He wanted a more general ruling that would apply to all glaucoma victims. But his lawyers urged him to accept the offer. It was a start, and in theory others could do the same.

Randall accepted the offer. The doctor he found after a six-month search was John Merritt, of the Howard University medical school, a black man who had a special interest in the matter, since black males suffer disproportionately from glaucoma. In November, Randall's first government-issue joints began arriving: seventy a week, ten a day, decent stuff. At about the same time, Judge Washington announced his verdict. Randall was not guilty, because of medical necessity. Randall assumed that it was the threat of such a verdict that had forced the government to offer the deal it had: better for a government agency to set the terms of his legal marijuana than for a judge to do it.

Throughout 1977, in defiance of the government's wishes, Randall began to speak out. He attended drug conferences and testified on behalf of decriminalization in New Mexico (at the hearings Chip Carter declined to address); he gave newspaper interviews and appeared on Tom Snyder's *Tomorrow* show and even on *To Tell the Truth*. Sometimes he became annoyed at the questions reporters asked. "They always ask, 'Do you still get high?' and not 'Can you still see?'" he says. Still, he realized it was the controversy surrounding marijuana that got his medical issue on the front pages.

All that year, Randall and his doctor were subjected to what they regarded as increasing harassment from the government, and he believed it was in direct retaliation for his speaking out. First, in March, when he asked DEA for a letter stating that his marijuana was legal, in case he was ever stopped by police, the DEA replied that he had no immunity from prosecution. Randall took that as an attempt at intimidation, discouraging his travels. Next, in May, after he spoke at a drug-abuse conference in San Francisco, the FDA said he must start receiving his marijuana daily instead of weekly. That would have effectively stopped Randall's travels, but he and Dr. Merritt refused to accept the change, and FDA backed down. Next, FDA ordered him to stop smoking for two months, as a "test"; again he refused, and the government backed down. Next, FDA demanded that he sign a previously unmentioned "consent form," one he feared would make him subject to its "research" whims; he signed, but noted on the document that he did so under duress.

Late in May, Randall wrote to Peter Bourne, protesting what he viewed as the harassment of him by the various agencies. He hoped that Bourne would intervene and force the bureaucrats to leave him alone. That was not to be. Bourne, taking the side of the bureaucrats, bluntly replied to Randall on June 6: "Publicity in the case has forced consideration of tightening up the dispensing of your supplies." He added, "We do not want to interfere with your rights, but as a patient taking part in a research study you have a certain responsibility to assure its success."

After that, Randall had no more illusions about Bourne or the Carter administration. He was surprised only that Bourne would put on paper what he viewed as a crude threat. Randall filed away Bourne's letter for use in the lawsuit he expected to bring against the government. He gave a copy to Stroup, however, who mentioned it to his friend Gary Cohn, and Jack Anderson quickly broke the story of White House indifference to a man who was going blind.

It was not long after the Jack Anderson story that Bourne made public a letter he had written to officials at the Department of Health, Education and Welfare requesting a study of possible medical uses of marijuana and heroin. Bourne's action was well publicized and seemed to express the White House's concern for the Bob Randalls of the world. Unfortunately, his letter led only to a series of meetings, which led to a report calling for more study.

The government's position throughout the medical-use controversy had been to minimize the medical value of marijuana and to stress the need for more research. In effect, when the Bob Randalls and Lynn Piersons had asked for legal marijuana to treat urgent medical needs, the government had told them to come back in a few years. The government insisted this was necessary scientific caution, because smoking might prove to have harmful side effects, although it is difficult for the layman to see what side effects would be worse than going blind or dying of cancer. Another explanation is that the bureaucrats were simply afraid of the political controversy surrounding marijuana, afraid that Congress or the White House might think them "soft" on the drug, and they therefore sidestepped the issue by endless calls for more research.

To NORML, Randall was a near-perfect personification of the medical-use issue, and the government's treatment of him was an incredible show of stupidity and/or malevolence. Stroup could never quite believe that the government could be so dumb as to deny medicine to people who were going blind. Medical use was a humanitarian issue, but it was also a wonderful political issue. It put a friendly face on marijuana; the Killer Weed became the Helpful Weed. It also attracted a new pro-marijuana constituency of old people and the ill. Randall had been quick to organize more than sixty cancer and glaucoma victims to join in NORML's medical-reclassification suit against the government.

As 1977 progressed, Randall became absolutely convinced that the research program the government had set up for him was a sham. As he saw it, the government had decided to give him marijuana to shut him up, but when he insisted on speaking out—saying others should be allowed medical use of marijuana—the government would threaten to cut off his medicine. He saw it as medical blackmail, and he became increasingly outraged.

The climax came in January of 1978 when Dr. Merritt left Washington for a teaching post in North Carolina. A year earlier NIDA had helped Randall find Dr. Merritt. Now the government said he must find his new doctor on his own, and until he did, and his new doctor received government authorization to handle marijuana (which could take months or years), he would be given no more marijuana. Randall thought the government was gambling that he would give up the struggle and return to illegal marijuana. (Time after time, bureaucrats had told him it would be simpler for everybody if he would only buy his dope on the street.) Randall searched for a new doctor and found several who were willing to take him as a patient but none who was willing to become involved with government paperwork at best and government harassment at worst.

Desperate, Randall again wrote Peter Bourne, who replied, "That issue should be resolved between you and Dr. Merritt." Randall took this to mean he was supposed to persuade Dr. Merritt not to leave Washington for his new job.

At length Randall decided his only hope was to sue the government, but he already owed $12,000 in legal fees, and several lawyers told him a new suit could cost $10,000 at the outset and perhaps much more. Then he got a break. A leading Washington law firm, Steptoe and Johnson, agreed to represent him *pro bono*. His case was given to a young lawyer named Thomas Collier, who tried to persuade FDA to give Randall a "compassionate IND," or "investigational-new-drug exemption." The negotiations dragged on for months, and finally, on a Monday afternoon, May 6, Collier filed suit against FDA, DEA, and NIDA. He argued in his brief that the government cannot pass laws that impinge upon a person's constitutional right to maintain his or her health. Moreover, Collier declared that freedom of speech was at issue in the Randall case: "During his participation in Dr. Merritt's program, repeated efforts were made to limit Mr. Randall's access to marijuana in retaliation for his exercise of First Amendment rights. Mr. Randall should not again be placed in a position where he would have to choose between his right to protect his eyesight and the exercise of his First Amendment rights."

The day after the suit was filed, the government agreed to a settlement. It stipulated that Randall would get his marijuana allowance immediately, directly from a federal pharmacy, and that no research requirements would be made of him without his and his doctor's approval.

The settlement was a total victory for Randall, and yet he accepted it reluctantly, because he knew it was unlikely that other glaucoma patients would benefit from it. In theory, they could do what he had done and force the government to grant them legal marijuana. In reality, Randall had won his victory because of three special circumstances: the fact that he had won his criminal trial with a medical-necessity plea, and thus gained some legal leverage over the government; the fact that he lived in Washington and could thus keep after the government when it gave him the runaround; and the fact that a major Washington law firm had taken his case *pro bono*. He had won his case, but he also felt he had reached a dead end in his crusade to help other glaucoma victims. It was then that he met Lynn Pierson, who was able to build on Randall's achievement and to carry the medical-use issue into a new forum: state legislatures all over America.

Lynn Pierson grew up in Grants, New Mexico, the son of an accountant. He planned to study accounting, then perhaps go to law school. He served a two-year stint in the Army, returned to the University of New Mexico, and was married. One day in October of 1975 he noticed he had a swollen testicle. He feared it might be venereal disease. A doctor informed him it was testicular cancer and he might die within six months. He underwent surgery, and after that chemotherapy.

In chemotherapy a cancer patient's body is injected with a great amount of poison; the hope is that the poison will kill the cancer before it kills the patient. Its side effects are excruciating: nausea, vomiting, loss of hair, convulsions, depression. Hubert Humphrey called it "living hell." After Pierson's first chemotherapy, and convulsions that left him trembling, he did what many others have done: He told his doctor he would not undergo that treatment again. In response, the doctor gave him a medical-journal article about recent studies showing that marijuana-smoking often reduced the side effects of chemotherapy.

Pierson tried the chemotherapy once more, this time smoking marijuana; it reduced his vomiting and convulsions and enabled him to take solid food and liquid during the treatment. Within a few months Pierson's cancer went into remission. By then he was becoming interested in the politics of the marijuana issue. He attended the New Mexico legislative hearing that Randall addressed early in 1977, but the two did not meet. In October, Pierson's cancer returned, this time in his lungs, inoperable and terminal. He began chemotherapy again, smoking along with it, to prolong his life. He bought his marijuana illegally, of course, and in November he heard about paraquat and realized that even his marijuana might be poisoned, and by the very government that would not allow him legal marijuana. It was too much. The government was truly monstrous, offering him a choice between illegal, poisoned marijuana on the one hand and the agonies of chemotherapy on the other. And he wasn't alone. He'd had a friend in the Veterans Hospital, a middle-aged man who refused to smoke, because it was illegal, and Pierson had watched his friend die an unnecessarily agonizing death. Lynn Pierson wanted to act, to do something that would give meaning to his death. He wasn't sure what, but something. It was then, early in December of 1977, that he went to the NORML conference and met Bob Randall and Alice O'Leary.

Randall and Pierson felt close from the first, peers in a select fraternity. Randall felt as if he'd been waiting for a long time to find Lynn Pierson. He'd fought his fight, taken it as far as he could alone, and now he thought Pierson could take it further. Pierson felt the same way. He confessed that he had clippings about Randall at home on the wall beside his desk. "If you hadn't done it first, I would have," he told Randall.

At first Randall wondered if Pierson would have the strength for political action. He'd met other cancer victims who wanted to fight the government but who lacked the physical or psychological resources.

But he soon saw that Pierson was a fighter, a hell raiser, as determined a man as he'd ever met. "Lynn had the critical element, a sense of rage," Randall said. "Rage that he was forced to smoke illegally and that other people didn't even know it would help them."

As they talked that weekend at the conference, Randall told Pierson he faced a choice. He could petition DEA, as Randall had, for legal access to marijuana, or he could take the issue to his state legislature. The latter was what Randall hoped Pierson would do, because if he succeeded, he would help not only himself but many others. Pierson agreed to go the legislative route.

He already had allies in the New Mexico legislature. He had come to the conference with two legislators, Tom Rutherford and Manny Aragon, who had worked with NORML on decriminalization. When he returned to New Mexico, legislative aides drafted a medical-use bill. Randall and Pierson then rewrote it, in the long-distance phone conversations they had almost every night. They made sure that the bill's language was open-ended, allowing treatment to others whom marijuana might help, not just cancer and glaucoma victims, and they made sure it was defined as a program primarily to help people, not a research program.

When the bill was ready, Pierson stalked the halls of the state capitol, personally talking to each of the nearly one hundred legislators. "Don't play politics with my life," he told them. He stressed that he was asking only for medical use, not for recreational drug use. The bill won widespread media support. The state AMA backed it. It passed easily, thirty to one in the state senate and forty-four to sixteen in the house. Gov. Jerry Apodaca signed it into law on February 21, 1978, with Pierson looking on. "Okay, Lynn, you can start smoking it legally now," the governor said jokingly.

It was not that easy. The New Mexico program still had to obtain federal approval, and that approval was very slow in coming. Pierson, who had been so successful in dealing with the legislature, learned the frustrations of dealing with the bureaucracy. He and Randall continued to talk by phone almost every night. That was in the period when Randall's legal marijuana had been cut off, after Dr. Merritt left Washington, and they would joke about which of them would get his legal dope first. But it was not a joke. Pierson couldn't understand how the will of his state legislature could be thwarted by federal bureaucrats.

"Lynn became more aggressive that summer," Randall recalled. "He began growing marijuana in his backyard, and he invited a television crew to come film it. He wanted to demonstrate that he could grow marijuana faster than the government would provide it for him. Near the end of July, he was on the *Tomorrow* show. He looked a little better—his hair had grown back—but he was obviously in terrible pain. I called him after the show and he told me he was bleeding internally but he felt it was important to do the show and let the country know what the government was doing to people.

"In the last conversation I had with Lynn, his state was beatific. I had bad news that I decided not to give him: I'd learned of another delay on the New Mexico proposal. But he felt good. He felt he had changed things. This was August, and the Florida medical-use bill had passed by then. Lynn felt a sense of personal reward. He felt very satisfied with what he'd done. He died three days later."

Three hours after Pierson's death, Randall added, an FDA official called the New Mexico health department and said its medical-use plan had finally been approved. Then, three months later, FDA withdrew its approval. To Randall, this runaround was all too familiar. "They decided that New Mexico was a small state and they'd try to stop medical use there," he said. Finally, nearly a year after the bill was passed, and after state officials had angrily denounced FDA for the delays, the New Mexico program was given federal approval. State officials named it the Lynn Pierson Therapeutic Research Program.

15

By early March of 1978, Peter Meyers was ready to proceed with NORML's lawsuit against the government on the paraquat spraying program. Stroup set Monday, March 13, as the day they would file the suit and hold a conference to explain it.

At that point NORML knew that the U.S. was deeply involved in the Mexican spraying program, and it also knew (by the government's own admission) that contaminated marijuana was being harvested and returned to the U.S. What it could not prove was that the sprayed marijuana harmed people who smoked it. That seemed a reasonable assumption, but there was no proof, because no one had ever studied the question.

Then, the week before NORML's scheduled news conference, NIDA finally completed its long-awaited study of the effects of smoking paraquat-contaminated marijuana. The study was devastating to all the government's optimistic forecasts. It concluded that a person who smoked even moderate amounts of the sprayed marijuana could suffer permanent lung damage.

A debate raged within the government over who should be the bearer of this bad news. Peter Bourne's office had announced that the study would take place, but the White House did not wish to associate itself with government-supported lung damage. Nor did NIDA, which had carried out the study. Finally, the buck was passed to Joe Califano, the secretary of Health, Education and Welfare, who was already in White House disfavor.

The NIDA report reached Califano's office on Wednesday, March 8. That day Stroup got a call from a NIDA official, who summarized its findings for him. The official said he feared the report "would never see the light of day" and promised that if the government didn't release the findings soon, he would send NORML a copy to release itself.

Stroup would have loved to break the lung-damage story at his Monday news conference and thus be able to suggest a government cover-up. The government, for its part, needed to get the news out first, so it could at least claim credit for honesty. By Thursday, Stroup was telling reporters about the report but asking them to hold the story until his Monday news conference. Someone at the Senate broke the story on Friday morning, and on Friday afternoon Califano's office rushed out a press release, one that made no effort to understate the danger of paraquat-contaminated marijuana. Its first paragraph warned that smoking it "could lead to permanent lung damage for regular and heavy users of marijuana and conceivably for other users as well," and concluded that "paraquat contamination may pose a serious risk to marijuana users."

"Permanent lung damage": It was enough to strike fear into the hearts of even casual marijuana smokers. "Pot Kills," screamed the headlines. For days NORML's telephone lines were backed up with calls from smokers wanting to know how they could test their marijuana for paraquat and how they would know if they were poisoned. (Various entrepreneurs were quick to market "paraquat-testing kits," which sold like hotcakes and were entirely worthless.)

That Friday night the story made the network news shows. As Stroup and Farnham watched the news, Stroup was shocked to see that the person defending the spraying program on behalf of the State Department was a *friend* of his, someone he had smoked with in her pregovernment days. Now, there she was, on the evening news, calmly declaring that marijuana was illegal and the government had a perfect right to spray it. Stroup jumped to his feet, screaming abuse at the woman on the television screen, until Farnham feared he might attack the television set.

At his crowded Monday news conference, Stroup presented himself as a pro-consumer David challenging the pro-lung-damage Goliath of the Carter administration. About the only reporters who weren't interested in what Stroup had to say were those from *High Times* and the *Yipster Times*. They sat in the back of the room, puffing on joints and yelling that the paraquat scare was all a hoax being perpetrated by DEA. This theory came from Tom Forcade, whose paranoia, combined with his pro-smuggling bias, had convinced him that the paraquat menace had been invented to scare people out of smoking.

Stroup called him that afternoon. "Forcade, you crazy fucker," Stroup yelled, "you're just like every other businessman. All you care about is your profits, and you don't care if people die!" Forcade responded by offering Stroup $1000 if he could produce a single ounce of paraquat-contaminated marijuana.

Forcade aside, NORML's anti-paraquat crusade quickly found support across the nation. The New York *Times*, the Chicago *Sun-Times*, the Seattle *Times*, the San Francisco *Examiner*, and many other newspapers called for an end to the spraying program. Fifteen members of the California congressional delegation urged President Carter to end U.S. participation immediately. New York lieutenant governor Mary Anne Krupsak wrote to Secretary Vance that the spraying was "unconscionable." The Michigan state legislature passed an anti-paraquat resolution. When a Los Angeles disc jockey suggested that smokers call Jimmy Carter to protest the spraying program, and helpfully gave out the White House phone number, thousands of calls jammed the White House switchboard.

All of which mattered not at all. The State Department was determined to continue the program, President Carter backed the decision, and Peter Bourne had become its outspoken defender. Some of Bourne's friends assumed that he knew better but had simply bowed to the State Department's determination to play oil politics. In any event, he spoke out vigorously, minimizing the NIDA report, suggesting that Califano had just been after headlines, saying there was more evidence that marijuana was harmful than that paraquat-sprayed marijuana was harmful, warning of a "heroin epidemic" if the program was stopped, and declaring, "If the risk exists, the guy has the option not to smoke the grass to begin with." (To which NORML replied that the people most likely to smoke Mexican marijuana were teenagers, blacks, Chicanos, soldiers—the people least likely to be informed of its dangers.)

Bourne also argued that Stroup was only seizing on the paraquat issue as a way to revive NORML's fading political fortunes at a time when reform legislation was stalled all over America and money was increasingly hard to come by.

On that, at least, Bourne and Stroup could agree. Stroup saw paraquat as a legitimate health hazard to American smokers, but he also saw it as the most potent political issue he had ever got his hands on. He was constantly amazed that the government would be so stupid as to continue a program that would threaten millions of Americans. It was the first time NORML had found a truly national issue, one that would move millions of smokers to action. For although relatively few smokers were ever arrested, every smoker had to wonder if his or her marijuana was poisoned by paraquat. Stroup was soon crisscrossing the country, appearing on countless television shows, accusing the government, among other things, of "cultural genocide." When Tom Snyder asked Stroup what the contaminated marijuana looked like, Stroup said, "Tom, I happen to have some here," and pulled out a bagful for the cameras.

Stroup had another dramatic issue he was publicizing that spring: Jerry Mitchell, who was in prison, starting to serve his seven-year sentence.

It had been almost two years since Stroup and Mike Stepanian had gone to West Plains, Missouri, and persuaded Judge Winston Buford to reduce Mitchell's sentence from twelve years to seven. Howard Eisberg, the NORML lawyer who was representing Mitchell, raised several constitutional challenges to the state's marijuana law, but in March of 1978 the Missouri supreme court rejected the appeal.

Within hours, Mitchell was taken in handcuffs from his apartment near the Southeastern Missouri State University campus to start his sentence.

For NORML it was a classic case: the college student with blind parents, hauled from the campus to prison. The question was whether publicity, however much it might help the reform movement, would help or hurt Mitchell. His only chance of freedom was either a pardon from Gov. Joseph Teasdale or an early parole, and publicity might anger either the governor or the parole board. Stroup talked it over with Eisberg, Mitchell, and Mitchell's parents, and they agreed that NORML should bring whatever pressure it could on the governor for a pardon. Mitchell, at that point, faced at least two years in prison, and he and his family decided he really didn't have much to lose.

Stroup therefore orchestrated the biggest publicity campaign in NORML's history on behalf of Mitchell. *Playboy* carried several articles on the case, as did *Rolling Stone, High Times,* and other youth-oriented magazines. NORML sent a mailing to all its members urging letters to Governor Teasdale. Stroup appeared on Phil Donahue's television show, and Donahue showed a taped interview with Mitchell in prison, discussing what his sentence had done to him and his parents. By the time he finished, Stroup was in tears, Donahue was shaken, and apparently many viewers were moved, because thousands of letters of protest soon flooded NORML and the governor's office.

Most dramatically, on April 27, Stroup, Eisberg, and Betty and Roy Mitchell went to the Missouri state capitol to ask the governor to release Jerry from prison and to require from him a year of alternative service in a drug-rehabilitation program. They carried with them petitions with ten thousand signatures, mostly from people in Mitchell's hometown and students at his college, asking the governor to lessen his punishment. The governor did not see the visitors, but they spoke with his legal counsel, who was polite but noncommittal. After the meeting the Mitchells and the lawyers held a news conference at the capitol—scores of reporters and photographers were there, from all over the state—and then they proceeded to the nearby prison farm where Mitchell was confined, and *he* held a news conference, flanked by his blind parents.

The entire day was incredible political theater. The coverage was necessarily one-sided, with all the attention and sympathy going to the slender, soft-spoken young prisoner and to his blind parents, with their canes and dark glasses, simple, decent country people who tried haltingly to express what the loss of their only son meant to them. Time after time, as he watched, Stroup asked himself, How can the state of Missouri be so fucking dumb as to let me be the champion of these two blind people?

As a consciousness-raising exercise, the Mitchell case was a success. Thousands of people were moved to write Governor Teasdale to express their revulsion over the sentence given Mitchell. Dozens of Missouri newspapers supported Mitchell editorially. The St. Louis *Post-Dispatch* contrasted Mitchell's case with that of an older Missouri man who pleaded guilty to selling five pounds of marijuana and was given unsupervised probation.

As a means of freeing Jerry Mitchell, however, the publicity blitz was a failure. In July, after three months of deliberation, Governor Teasdale, a forty-two-year-old former prosecutor, said he would not intervene in the Mitchell case and didn't believe he should grant pardons except "in the most extreme cases." (The New York *Times* commented that perhaps the governor would have considered it an extreme case if Mitchell had been sentenced to hang.)

So Mitchell stayed in prison, awaiting a parole hearing the next year, while NORML took his appeal into the federal courts and also tried to persuade prison officials to transfer him to a minimum-security facility where college courses were available.

For Stroup, with both the Mitchell case and the paraquat issue to publicize, the spring of 1978 was a busy season. If he was genuinely outraged, he was exhilarated, too. Then he made a mistake. He went back to Canada.

He went reluctantly, and only at the urging of his new friends at Canada NORML, who of course wanted the publicity his trial would attract. It would not be a "test case"—you could hardly have a worse case to test the marijuana laws than that of someone caught red-handed at a border crossing—but Stroup felt he could argue that his possession of the marijuana was not morally wrong and thus raise the Canadian consciousness a bit. In mapping his legal strategy he turned to a man who was his close friend and also, in Stroup's opinion, the best drug lawyer in America, Gerald Goldstein.

Gerry Goldstein's great-grandfather, whose name was Solomon Solomon, was the first rabbi in San Antonio, Texas, and his father, Eli Goldstein, was a successful lawyer there. Gerry Goldstein graduated from Tulane University and then from the University of Texas law school in 1968. He entered his father's law firm and was soon very bored. More than bored, he felt guilty, because he had escaped the military by medical deferment and now was making a lot of money practicing law while other men his age were dying in Vietnam.

One of Goldstein's heroes since childhood was Maury Maverick, Jr., a San Antonio lawyer who, like his father before him, was a liberal leader in Texas politics. (The family name became the common noun denoting a stubborn or independent person.) Maverick, it happened, was representing a great many draft resisters. They were relatively easy cases to win, but most Texas lawyers were pro-war hawks who wouldn't touch them. Goldstein began taking some of Maverick's overflow, and in time the draft cases led him into taking drug cases. It seemed to Goldstein that the drug cases were usually a form of discrimination, that the kids were actually being arrested because they had long hair, because the police saw them as outsiders, hippies, troublemakers. When he heard about NORML in 1972, he quickly contacted Stroup, who began referring Texas cases to him. In time, Goldstein worked on Frank Demolli's appeal and on the Piedras Negras jailbreak case, and in the process he came to have great respect for Stroup and what he had done.

As Goldstein saw it, Stroup had paid his dues, had paid the dues for a lot of them. While he and a lot of young lawyers had been getting rich off drug cases, Stroup had been killing himself for almost no money at all. He thought that what Stroup had done at NORML was amazing, and it was amazing, too, to think of all that energy pouring through one man's body. Keith gave us all balls, he thought; we owe him for that. It gave courage to lawyers all over America who wanted to take on the drug laws to see Keith standing up and being honest about a subject that very few people were honest about.

Goldstein was living a very good life in San Antonio. He had a tall, beautiful, English-born wife (and a right-hand-drive Bentley for her to buzz about in), a stately Victorian home, a pool, a sauna, and the freedom to do what he pleased, personally or professionally. He'd taken the case of an unemployed young man who'd taken a job as a movie projectionist and been arrested for showing *Deep Throat*; he won that one before the Supreme Court. He was an aggressive, commanding figure, a husky, dark-haired Texan in boots and a hand-tooled cowboy belt, and he tended to dominate any courtroom he entered.

This was the lawyer Stroup asked to defend him in his Canada trial, and in addition to mapping their defense strategy, Goldstein several times stressed to Stroup an extralegal factor: He must check his clothes and luggage carefully and make damn sure he was clean this time. Stroup was amused by Goldstein's concern, but he did as he was told. He even looked in all ten zipper pockets of his shoulder bag and turned it upside down and shook it. The search uncovered one old "roach" and twenty-odd seeds that he guessed he'd been carrying around for years.

In Montreal, Stroup cleared customs routinely (he didn't wear his marijuana-leaf pin this time) and then flew on to Calgary, where he went to his hotel to wait for Goldstein. Soon he had a call from Sheldon Schumer, a law professor who was his local counsel. To Stroup's surprise, Schumer reported that the prosecutor in his case wanted to have dinner with him that night.

Stroup exploded. "Does the fucker want my autograph, too, before he tries to send me to jail?"

Stroup and his Canadian lawyer were totally at odds. Schumer said the prosecutor was a nice guy, only doing his job, and it couldn't hurt to be on friendly terms with him. Stroup saw it quite differently. He had lived for a long time in a black-and-white world in which police and prosecutors were enemies. If they were such good guys, they should get in another line of work. Stroup didn't want to fraternize with the enemy, and didn't see how other people could do it. No, Stroup would not have dinner with the prosecutor, and at length he convinced Schumer of that fact and ate alone in the hotel dining room.

The next morning, when Stroup and Goldstein marched into the courthouse in Calgary, they were trailed by a CBC film crew. When they got inside, the reporter said something had been wrong with the camera. Would they please go out and come in again? They did, of course, because that was what this trip was all about: publicity. Stroup was amazed at the amount of coverage he was getting over one joint. This was, he thought, virgin territory as far as marijuana politics was concerned.

Forty or fifty of NORML's Canadian supporters had crowded into the courtroom, and quite a few reporters. There were a number of other marijuana cases that morning, all routine, with the defendants pleading guilty and the judge giving them a fine. When Stroup's name was called, he stepped forward and pleaded not guilty.

The judge granted permission for Goldstein to represent Stroup. Goldstein immediately called his client to the stand.

"Why do you plead not guilty?" Goldstein asked.

"Because a plea of guilty connotes moral turpitude, and marijuana-smoking is not immoral," Stroup replied.

"Did you, as charged, bring approximately two grams of marijuana into this country?"

"I did."

"Why do you not consider this immoral?"

"Because marijuana-smoking is what is called in Latin *malum prohibitum* rather than *malum in se*." It was, he went on to say, prohibited by the law, like speeding or double-parking, but not immoral. That was the political point Stroup was trying to make, the lead he wanted on the next day's news stories. By admitting he'd brought in the marijuana, Stroup had guaranteed that he would be convicted, but he had also silenced the prosecutor. He would be fined, but his side would get all the publicity. And, as it happened, Stroup and Goldstein had another trick to play.

Goldstein held up a sheet of paper. "Mr. Stroup, I hand you a copy of a news article from the Washington *Post*, which I'd like for you to read to the court."

Stroup took the paper. "Yes," he said gravely, "this is an article I read recently, quoting Prime Minister Trudeau as follows: 'Those who come to Canada with a joint or two won't get hassled by us. But those who come with quantities to sell will likely get their asses kicked.'"

"Mr. Stroup, did you in any way base your conduct in coming to Canada on Prime Minister Trudeau's statement?"

Stroup said he certainly had, that he'd never dreamed he'd be arrested for one joint, and that he had no intent of confronting Canadian law.

As Stroup stepped down, the judge asked to see the clipping of the Trudeau statement. Goldstein then declared that his client was an important American lawyer, dedicated to social justice, and he read into the records the letters from Peter Bourne and Stuart Statler. With that, the defense rested. The prosecutor also rested his case: Stroup had already admitted his guilt. The judge said he found the defendant guilty and assessed the standard fine, about $100. Stroup and Goldstein exchanged a wink. It had all gone perfectly.

When Stroup went upstairs to pay his fine, he encountered the prosecutor, a man named Smith. Stroup had refused dinner with Smith the night before, but now he was feeling expansive, and he invited the prosecutor to have coffee with him, Goldstein, and George Baker. They went down to the coffee shop and had a pleasant-enough chat. Smith admitted he'd be happy if he never had to prosecute another marijuana case. Then Stroup and Goldstein left for the airport. Stroup was going to fly down to San Antonio for a few days' rest. Among other attractions, Goldstein's wife, Chris, had a beautiful friend she wanted him to meet.

At customs the agents knew who Stroup was. "Didn't I hear something about you on the radio?" one of them asked. "Didn't you just have a trial for marijuana?"

Stroup grinned. "Yes, we did have a discussion of marijuana with one of your fine Canadian judges."

Stroup was feeling good, cocky, and the agent seemed to enjoy the exchange, but some other agents gathered around, and they didn't seem amused. They started searching Stroup's suitcase, and one of them asked to see his shoulder bag.

Stroup handed over his shoulder bag, the one he had so carefully searched in Washington. He was getting a little nervous, not because of the bag but because of the time. Goldstein had gone on ahead, and the last thing Stroup wanted was to miss his plane.

Suddenly one of the agents jerked something out of the bag. "What's this, Mr. Stroup?" he said. "I do believe it's a bit of marijuana."

"*What?*" Stroup said. What was happening? There couldn't be a joint in that bag.

"And what's this?" the agent continued. "It looks like a vial of cocaine." It was indeed a small vial with traces of white powder inside it.

Stroup was too stunned to speak. The agents were suddenly surrounding him. "I don't believe you'll be making your plane, Mr. Stroup," one of them said. "You may not be leaving Canada for quite some time."

Stroup could see Goldstein trying to fight his way back through the crowd, but before he could get there, the agents had led Stroup back into the windowless search room. "We've had enough of your shit, fellow," one of them said, and they shoved him up against the wall to frisk him. "All right, give me one piece of clothing at a time," another said, and when Stroup handed over both his socks at once, the agent snapped, "One at a time, motherfucker. Listen, the joke's over. You're going to jail." They seemed furious, ready to hit him if given the slightest excuse. Stroup still couldn't focus. Where had the joint come from? Fuck the joint: It was the cocaine that would kill him. Cocaine meant jail, period. Had they planted it on him? Or had he been stupid enough to miss it somehow? What did it matter? He'd been crazy ever to come back to Canada in the first place. What was wrong with him? His crazy grandstanding had finally caught up with him. He was headed for a Canadian prison, and for no good reason at all. He was confused. It was as if he were going crazy, or having a bad trip on acid. Things were happening too fast, were out of control.

Three Mounties came to get him. Two of them had done the same thing six months earlier. They looked at Stroup and burst out laughing.

"Not you again," one said. "You've got to be kidding."

"It's me," Stroup said.

"Well, it won't take so long this time," the Mountie said. "You've already been fingerprinted."

"That's great," Stroup said. He tried to smile. At least these guys were friendly. Already he was a con, clutching at straws.

On the ride to the jail, one of the Mounties asked, "Did you do this on purpose? Get yourself busted again for the publicity?"

Stroup shook his head and said no, that really hadn't been his plan at all.

They put Stroup in a large cell with four or five other prisoners. The Mounties had told him that Goldstein was trying to arrange bail but that it was very unlikely he'd get a hearing before morning. That meant a night in jail, and Stroup was terrified by the prospect. Too many marijuana prisoners had told him about homosexual rape in jails and prisons; the idea made him physically weak. Whatever his faults, Stroup thought, he was not a violent person, and he was horrified at the idea of other men attacking him. So when the other prisoners tried to make conversation, to be friendly, Stroup cowered in a corner, giving simple yes and no answers, trying for the first time in his life to make himself invisible.

Still, he had to talk. For all he knew he would offend the others by keeping to himself, and he got to know a man of twenty-eight who'd spent the past eight years in prison for armed robbery. He was in this jail overnight waiting to be transferred from one prison to another. Stroup bummed a cigarette from the man. He hadn't smoked in ten years—he hated cigarettes—but he thought a cigarette might give him a buzz, make him a little high, and he was desperate for anything that would relieve his gloom. It worked, sort of. He felt a little light-headed, so he smoked a second one, but it made him feel sick to his stomach, so he gave up on cigarettes. He tried to read a copy of the novel *Shogun* that he'd brought along, partly as a joke, in case he got any jail time. He couldn't concentrate. Then he talked to a man in his forties, an alcoholic who was doing sixty days for drunken driving. Finally someone produced a battered deck of cards, and Stroup and three other men played an erratic game of bridge. Stroup hadn't played since college, and one of the men had never played, but it made the time pass.

It was late afternoon when Goldstein arrived, along with a Canadian lawyer named Webster MacDonald, Jr., who was experienced in drug cases. They were on their way to a bond hearing, the lawyers explained, but the prospects did not look good. Smith, the prosecutor, was furious. As he saw it, he'd been friendly to Stroup and Stroup had tried to make a fool of him by deliberately getting himself arrested a second time. He wanted to throw the book at Stroup. He had spoken of a six-week jail term.

The magistrate was young, skinny, and bewigged, and he seemed to be in the prosecutor's pocket.

"I see Mr. Stroup is unemployed," he began.

"No, Your Honor," Stroup said. "I'm an attorney in Washington, D.C., and have been for ten years."

"But you're unemployed in Calgary."

Stroup could not resist a touch of sarcasm. "By that definition, two hundred million Americans are unemployed in Calgary."

The prosecutor jumped to his feet. "Your Honor, it should be pointed out that this man was apprehended at the airport, fleeing the country."

Stroup couldn't believe it. "Your Honor," he protested, "I was at the airport because I was going home. I'd just finished a trial, one I had no legal obligation to attend, and I was catching my plane back to the U.S."

Goldstein and MacDonald pleaded for bond, no matter how high. Their client had returned for his first trial, they argued, and he would return for a second.

The magistrate said it seemed to him that the prisoner might flee.

Bond was denied. That meant Stroup would await his second trial in jail.

Stroup turned to Goldstein. There were tears in his eyes. "I wish you'd call Lindsey and tell her not to worry."

"I've already talked to her," Goldstein said.

The bailiff was coming to handcuff Stroup and lead him away. "See you in the morning," Stroup said.

"I'm sorry," Goldstein said.

"So am I."

Back in his cell, facing his first night in jail, Stroup was more terrified than ever.

At 7:00 P.M. a jailer came to take the men to their evening showers. The men were to strip naked and be marched to the shower room. Stroup held back as long as he could, fearing the indignity, the vulnerability. Finally he took his shower and, still naked, was given a towel and led down the hall to a row of little six-foot-by-three-foot cells. They were one-man cells that were being used by two men. The jailer told Stroup to pick his cell. They were all occupied, so he had to pick a companion for the night. He held back, afraid, not knowing what to do. It was like Russian roulette. What if he picked the wrong cellmate? Was this some kind of setup, some initiation?

"Make up your mind fast," the jailer said.

Stroup stepped into the cell with the twenty-eight-year-old who'd given him the cigarettes. It proved a good decision. The fellow went quickly to sleep, and Stroup spent the night staring at the dark ceiling and listening to the two men in the next cell noisily engage in sex. He kept thinking, Six weeks, I can't handle six weeks of this.

The next morning two Mounties took Stroup to a holding cell near the courtroom where Goldstein was waiting. He quickly outlined Stroup's alternatives. He could plead not guilty and go to trial, but if the judge did not grant him bond, it meant he would have to await trial in jail, perhaps for several weeks. Or he could plead guilty to a marijuana-possession charge. The prosecutor had reluctantly dropped the cocaine charge, after flying in an expert who had advised him that the traces of cocaine on the vial were not enough to make a case. Goldstein had been talking to the prosecutor, trying to convince him Stroup had made a stupid mistake but hadn't got himself arrested just for publicity. The prosecutor had calmed down to the point that he said he would be neutral on the question of a jail term. They had to face the possibility that the judge would give him a jail term, but Goldstein had been watching the judge in court that morning, and his instinct was that he would be reasonable. Goldstein said he thought they should gamble on a guilty plea. Stroup agreed.

Goldstein left, and a man from the U.S. counsel's office came with the helpful news that if Stroup got a sentence of more than six months, he could serve it in the U.S. under a U.S.-Canada prisoner-exchange program.

In midafternoon two Mounties escorted Stroup into the courtroom. It was the same courtroom he'd been tried in the day before, but not the same judge. As Stroup entered, his Canadian lawyer whispered to him, "Don't say a word!" Stroup did as he was told.

Goldstein entered a guilty plea. The prosecutor quickly said, "Your honor, The Crown notes that Mr. Stroup was before this same court only twenty-four hours ago, for the same charge, and believes that should be considered in determining sentence."

MacDonald reminded the judge of a recent, somewhat similar case in which a California doctor had been arrested in Canada for marijuana possession a second time but was given probation.

"I see Mr. Stroup in a different situation," the judge said. "His profession is dedicated to changing the marijuana laws. He must have been aware of the legal repercussions of his action."

Stroup sagged. That was it. He would get jail time. The only question was whether they could get him out on bond pending appeal.

Then, to his astonishment, the judge said that he was fining Stroup $300. There was no jail sentence. Stroup almost ran from the courtroom, lest the judge change his mind.

That night he and Goldstein and Chris and Chris's beautiful friend sat by the pool under the star-spangled Texas sky, and the Canadian jail seemed a million miles away. Canada was behind him. He could not go back there, and he never wanted to go back there. And yet it was not entirely behind him. When he got back to Washington, back to NORML, he could sense the impatience of Schott and Meyers and people on his board. The first Canadian bust had been a joke, more or less. (When he returned to Canada for his first trial, NORML's staff had organized an office pool on how big his fine would be.) Then there had been the pie-throwing incident, which wasn't a joke. And now this second Canadian bust, which made him and NORML both look crazy as hell. Stroup wrote a detailed account of the Canadian episode—as he had, a few months earlier, of the pie-throwing episode—and sent it to all NORML staff and advisers. He raised the possibility that he might have been set up by the Canadian customs agents, but he admitted it was just as likely that he'd simply been careless. That was what worried him most. Was he getting too careless? At some level, did he want out of NORML, so much so that he was trying to self-destruct? He didn't know, and as the spring progressed, he didn't have much time for soul-searching. For one thing, the paraquat issue was still hot, and he was still speaking out against it all over the country. For another, his socializing with the Carter administration and his anti-paraquat campaign were about to merge, as he became friendly with Chip Carter and tried to recruit him for some high-level lobbying against the Mexican spraying.

16

Early in 1977 Stroup wrote Phil Walden, the burly young president of Georgia-based Capricorn Records, asking for a chance to tell him about NORML's work. Walden, the manager of the Allman Brothers Band and an early financial supporter of Jimmy Carter, was known as an intelligent, politically astute man. Stroup hoped that Walden, having seen the Allman Brothers Band destroyed by drugs and a drug trial, would understand the need for drug-law reform and thus would support NORML. Stroup especially hoped that Walden would help him persuade some rock groups to give benefit performances for NORML.

Since the first days of NORML, Stroup had sought help from the entertainment world, and with some success. He'd got benefits or public-service tapes from Kris Kristofferson, before he was a superstar, and from the Nitty Gritty Dirt Band, blues singer Jimmy Witherspoon, and comedian George Carlin. But the biggest names, the ones who could produce the most money, had eluded him. Increasingly, by 1977, he was courting stars like Willie Nelson, Jimmy Buffet, and the Eagles, hanging out backstage with them, playing groupie, but always pressing them to do a NORML benefit. Many promises were made, many drugs were consumed, but the concerts never seemed to happen. The stars were always agreeable, but not the managers and lawyers who advised them. Stroup guessed it was because the musicians were all so vulnerable to arrest, and they or their managers feared that support of NORML might anger the police or prosecutors who could bust them almost at will. Still, Stroup kept trying. His dream was a big NORML benefit concert in the South, with the proceeds going to open a Southern regional office in Atlanta, and in time he came to think of Walden as the man who could make that dream come true.

Walden responded to Stroup's letter with an invitation to come down to Capricorn's annual picnic that summer. Stroup did, rubbed elbows with a lot of musicians, and hit it off well with Walden, who agreed to join NORML's advisory board. Stroup knew it could not hurt him, in status-conscious Washington, to have such a close friend of the president on his advisory board, and it was always possible that he could use Walden to bypass Peter Bourne and put his case directly to Carter, on paraquat and other issues.

On April 11, 1978, Stroup wrote Walden and urged him to discuss the paraquat issue with President Carter if he had the opportunity. Stroup still believed that Carter was being misled by his advisers, and that if he knew the truth about the spraying program he would see that it was both morally wrong and politically insane. He added, in his letter to Walden, that he would himself be glad to discuss the paraquat issue with Chip Carter. That seemed unlikely, however, given the way he had embarrassed Chip fourteen months earlier over his decision not to testify in New Mexico. But one afternoon a few days later, Walden called and told Stroup he was just leaving the White House and he would drop by NORML in a few minutes and bring Chip Carter with him.

Stroup warned Lesyle Williams, NORML's receptionist, that if some men with guns arrived, it wasn't a raid, only the Secret Service. Moments later, Walden, Carter, and two men with bulges on their hips arrived. Walden left Carter in the outer office while he went into Stroup's office; this wasn't rudeness but a way of protecting the president's son if Walden and Stroup wanted to share a joint. Meanwhile, the Secret Service men, not sure what den of iniquity they'd been brought to, locked the front and back doors and announced that no one was to enter or leave without their approval.

Lesyle Williams, a vivacious, dark-haired woman, soon engaged the two agents in conversation and was pressing NORML brochures on them. Across the room, George Farnham was trying, with much less enthusiasm, to make conversation with Chip Carter. Farnham's work on the paraquat issue had given him a vast disdain for the Carter administration, presidential sons included, but to make the best of the situation he tried to tell Chip about paraquat. It didn't go well. Chip seemed uninformed about the issue and not eager to learn. When Farnham tried to give Carter a copy of NORML's legal brief, he refused it, as if he were being served with some sort of summons.

Just then, Walden called Carter into Stroup's office, and the three of them settled down to talk. Stroup was all charm that afternoon. He told Carter that he regretted his leak to Jack Anderson the previous year, that he'd feared the Carter administration was backing away from decriminalization, but he'd later seen he was wrong. He went on to outline NORML's current political priorities: medical reclassification, a federal decriminalization bill, and, most of all, stopping the paraquat spraying. Chip listened politely, asked some questions, and said he'd like to know more. Soon, Walden said he and Chip had better be going. It had been only a get-acquainted call, a favor Walden was doing for his friends at NORML. After that, it would be up to Stroup to follow through.

Stroup saw young Carter's visit as purely business. Chip was the Carter administration's unofficial ambassador to the youth culture, and Stroup assumed that he therefore saw the pot lobby as part of his political responsibility. As Stroup saw it, he wanted things from the Carter administration and the Carter administration wanted things from him: You make me; I make you. Certainly he was excited at the prospect of using the president's son as a way to bypass Peter Bourne and the bureaucrats and to present the anti-paraquat case directly to the president.

At the same time, on a personal level, Stroup liked Chip, and thought they had a lot in common. Both were small-town boys who were fascinated with politics and who also enjoyed parties, celebrities, life in the fast lane. Stroup saw Chip as much like himself five years earlier, a young man determined to make a name for himself in the political world, except that when Stroup was starting out, he had been spared the burden of a father who was president. When Chip left NORML's office that first afternoon, Stroup intended to send him data on paraquat and to request another, more formal meeting. As it turned out, he soon had an unexpected chance to lobby Chip in an informal setting.

One of Stroup's friends was John Walsh, an editor with the Washington *Post*'s "Style" section. Walsh was a plump white-haired man of thirty or so, an albino, who had previously been an editor with *Rolling Stone*. He maintained his contacts in the music world, and when Waylon Jennings and Willie Nelson played the Capital Centre that month, he got tickets and chartered a bus to take a party of journalists and political people to the concert. Stroup managed to miss the bus, but when he arrived, Walsh came over and gave him a backstage pass and whispered that Willie wanted to talk to him after the concert. That was good news: Stroup had been after Willie Nelson for months to do a NORML concert.

Stroup made his way backstage and spent some time hanging out with the band. He had some cocaine and good Colombian marijuana with him, for it was rock-world protocol that you always offered drugs to the musicians, although they usually had better drugs than you did. He noticed that Jody Powell and some other White House people were backstage, and after a while he was pleased to have his new friend Chip Carter come over and join him. They watched the show together for a while, and when the concert was over, Carter asked Stroup what was happening next. Stroup said he was going over to Willie's motel to party for a while. Chip asked directions and said he'd meet him there.

When the postconcert party assembled, in a Holiday Inn near the Capital Centre, there were a dozen or so people present: Willie and Waylon; two or three members of the band; Chip Carter and his wife, Caron; the actor Jan-Michael Vincent; Stroup's friend Fred Moore; and Stroup and a friend from Atlanta, Marlene Gaskill.

Stroup had met Marlene back in the early days of NORML. She was married then, and she smoked. Then she heard on the radio about a meeting to organize a NORML chapter, and she reasoned that if she was going to smoke, she should at least be trying to change the laws. So she went to the meeting, and met Stroup, and after that he would stay at her house when he was in Atlanta. Marlene would drive him around to interviews, and she could remember times when radio stations weren't sure they should let him on the air, for fear he was some kind of drug dealer. But Marlene liked him, and what he stood for, and she became a NORML volunteer. She spoke at colleges and to PTAs, and she thought it was wonderful how polite people were to her, even parents who strongly disagreed with her. She guessed it was because she was herself a mother and a businesswoman and a Southerner. In time, Marlene separated from her husband and quit her job. She had some money, she was forty years old, and she decided she wanted to enjoy life. This trip to Washington was certainly an example: partying with Keith and Willie and Waylon, plus Chip and Caron Carter. Marlene had to laugh. Keith had certainly come up in the world since the days when he slept on her sofa.

The party was in a typical Holiday Inn room, with two beds and only two chairs in it. Chip was sitting in one of the chairs, and Paul, Willie's drummer and close friend, was slouched in the other. Paul always dressed in black and stared coldly at people and rarely spoke. Everyone else stood or sat on the beds. They had some soft drinks, but they couldn't find any ice. Marlene thought it was about as relaxed, down-home a party as she'd ever been to. There was a lot of talk and laughter, and a few dirty jokes, but nothing *too* dirty. Marlene was wearing her Coca-Cola T-shirt, which was a patriotic act if you were from Atlanta, but it gave rise to a lot of cocaine jokes. Chip and Caron had on jeans, and Willie had on his jeans and red bandanna. Keith was huddled with Chip and Willie, talking politics the way he always did, talking to Chip about rock concerts he'd helped organize for the president's campaign, asking if Chip could help persuade any groups to play a NORML benefit. When Keith urged Willie to do a NORML benefit in Austin, Willie's adopted home, unless that would cause him any problems there, Willie growled, "There ain't nothing I can do that would be unpopular in Austin."

Keith was rolling joints and passing them around, and that had bothered Marlene, until she realized that Chip's Secret Service men were out in the hall to protect them, not to hassle anybody. At first someone had locked the door, but an agent had banged on it and told them, "Look, we don't care what you do in there, but just don't lock the door." That was when Chip had said, "Keith, for God's sake put that dope away." Marlene talked mostly to Caron Carter, a slender, vivacious young woman with dark hair and bright brown eyes, who she thought was one of the most attractive people she'd ever met. Caron seemed so happy to be here. The White House could be so stuffy, she said, so formal, and it was so rare for her and Chip to get a chance to wear jeans and sit cross-legged on a bed and talk to people without any political pressures. Caron talked about the 1976 campaign and how exhausting it had been, and Willie broke in and said he knew what she meant, that he and the boys had been touring in their bus since December with only fourteen days off.

Caron told how she sometimes saw the president at breakfast and he would say how his advisers were always urging him to do the expedient thing, the political thing, but he wanted to know what was the *right* thing. Keith chimed in, half joking, and said he hoped that the next time Chip was having breakfast with his dad, he'd urge him to do the right thing about paraquat. Chip said he understood that it was a Mexican program, not a U.S. program, and there was no evidence that it was hurting anybody, and Keith said that might be what Peter Bourne told him, but it wasn't true. Willie spoke up and said he'd heard of this marijuana-spraying down in Mexico and didn't like it worth a damn. There was some more talk about paraquat, all very friendly and relaxed, and finally Chip and Caron said they'd better be going.

Stroup was jubilant. Talk about doing it with mirrors! Willie had come away thinking Stroup always hung out with the president's son, and Chip had come away thinking Stroup always hung out with Willie Nelson. He hadn't pinned Willie down on a NORML concert, not yet. Willie had reached that level of celebrity at which you had to move slowly, to cultivate his entourage, to study his moods. It was like dealing with Hefner. And Chip's stopping by had been a great bonus: It was good for Chip to see how seriously Willie took the paraquat issue. Those bastards at State might think paraquat was a joke, but in Willie Nelson's world, poisoned marijuana was deadly serious. Stroup thought the evening had gone perfectly. He hadn't pushed Chip, hadn't embarrassed him, had kept it friendly. Stroup was increasingly impressed with Chip Carter, with how effortlessly political he was. The more he thought about it, the more Stroup regretted that Chip hadn't testified in New Mexico the year before. The kid was so damn smooth he might have got the bill through.

On June 1 Stroup's friends Fred Moore and Billy Paley had the grand opening of their new restaurant-nightclub, the Biltmore Ballroom. It was on Columbia Road, a racially mixed neighborhood in Northwest Washington, in what had once been a ballroom on the second floor of an old building. Stroup arrived at the club around nine and found it packed with media and political people. He sipped a glass of champagne and from time to time stepped into the men's room to snort cocaine with someone. He chatted for a while with John Walsh, and with Ed Bradley, the talented CBS correspondent, and then to his surprise he found himself face to face with a slender black man named Sterling Tucker, the chairman of the D.C. city council, who was running for mayor.

Stroup grumbled a hello; Sterling Tucker was not one of his favorite politicians.

"Well, Keith, I hope you'll support my candidacy," Tucker said.

"I don't think so," Stroup shot back. "You sold us out on the decrim bill."

"No, no," Tucker protested. "I supported that bill. You stick with me."

The defeat of the D.C. bill a year earlier had hurt, because it meant that Stroup continued to be officially a criminal in his hometown. Still, he was enjoying the exchange because a Washington *Post* reporter was watching, and it was fun to see Tucker squirm as he wondered what she might write.

Tucker made his escape, Stroup laughed and sipped his champagne, and then someone spoke to him. He turned and saw Chip Carter, whom he hadn't seen since the night of the Willie-Waylon concert, although they'd talked by phone. Stroup's lobbying effort had thus far been unsuccessful. Chip had talked to Peter Bourne, who'd given him the official line about the spraying's being entirely a Mexican program. But Stroup's exchanges with Carter had been friendly, and they'd talked about the NORML–White House softball game that was coming up and about taking Chip's sister, Amy, and Stroup's daughter, Lindsey, who attended public school together, to the premiere of *International Velvet* at the Kennedy Center. Stroup continued to be impressed by Chip and to like him. He thought of theirs as a political friendship, a relationship often seen in Washington, in which personal regard existed but was never entirely innocent of political motivation, on either side.

Chip was uncomfortable because he didn't know many of the people there in the Biltmore Ballroom. Stroup, who knew most of them, moved quickly to turn the situation to his advantage.

"Let me introduce you around," he said, and led the president's son along the bar that divided the ballroom. He made introductions and gave Carter whispered explanations of who was what. It was the sort of assistance that presidents and their families expect when they make public appearances, and of course Stroup gloried in the role of Carter-administration insider and power broker. He was impressed, once again, by how smooth, how professional, Chip was. Still, it was work, and soon Chip had shaken all the hands he cared to. "Let's get out of here," he said. Stroup asked where he wanted to go. Carter said he didn't care. "Let's go to my place, then," Stroup said.

Stroup had moved from the room over his office to a $126-a-month efficiency apartment in an ancient apartment house called the Marcheta, which was on New Hampshire Avenue, a few blocks from NORML. The apartment was perhaps twenty by twenty and featured a sagging sofa, lots of dirty clothes and paperback books tossed about, a stereo, and plenty of Willie Nelson and Delbert McClinton albums.

Stroup and his guests drove to the Marcheta in separate cars. Chip arrived with his friend Kevin Smith and two Secret Service agents. The agents agreed to wait in the lobby while Stroup, Carter, and Smith took the elevator to Stroup's apartment on the seventh floor. There they proceeded to put on some records and, for the most part, talk about paraquat. There was some talk of other subjects—of politics, of music, of women—but Stroup kept turning the conversation back to paraquat, because for him this was one more priceless opportunity to enlist the president's son in his cause. Chip seemed interested, concerned, but he also seemed to have bought the Peter Bourne–State Department line, and Stroup was determined to make sure he understood NORML's view, both as to the physical harm that poisoned paraquat was doing to Americans and the political harm it was doing to the Carter administration.

The key, Stroup insisted, was to get the facts to the president. Chip agreed, but stressed that he would have to talk to Bourne again, would have to make sure he had the facts straight, so he could not be accused of meddling. Stroup said he understood that, and he was delighted at how seriously Chip took the issue and at his promise that he would talk to his father about it. When Chip finally left the Marcheta, sometime past midnight, to return to his more elegant lodgings in the White House, Stroup counted it a good night's work.

By the time Stroup and Chip Carter were becoming friendly, in the late spring of 1978, Stroup had already, among other things, leaked an embarrassing story about Chip to Jack Anderson, threatened to expose Peter Bourne's drug use in retaliation for the Angarola letter, and filed a major lawsuit against the government over paraquat. Moreover, Stroup was a controversial figure whose use of various illegal drugs was well known. Given all that, it might be asked what the president's son, as well as many lesser administration figures, were doing associating with Stroup.

The answer is part political, part personal. Politically, Stroup was there, a force to be reckoned with. If you were Peter Bourne, or anyone in government who was concerned with the drug issue, you would have to deal with Stroup. He had a large constituency, he was well plugged into the media, and he could help you or hurt you. But it was more than political.

Official Washington is a very dull place, and it was fun to drop by NORML's office, to listen to some music, to hear the latest gossip, to get high. If people didn't always understand that while they were playing, Stroup was working—that turning people on was part of a pot lobbyist's job—then that was their problem.

Ten days after Chip Carter came by Stroup's apartment, the long-awaited softball game between NORML's staff and the White House staff was played. The game came about after Tim Kraft arranged for several members of NORML to tour the White House. As NORML's people wandered wide-eyed through the West Wing, someone asked if they played softball. Sure we play softball, the dopers declared, and a challenge was made and accepted.

NORML's people prepared for the game with practice sessions, new T-shirts (featuring a softball with a garland of marijuana leaves), and some new cheers written by Eric Sirulnik, a law professor who was working on the paraquat suit. As it turned out, the game was played on a cold, windy day; the dope lobbyists showed little aptitude for softball; the White House team won easily; and the day's best moment for the NORML team was one of Professor Sirulnik's cheers:

> Paraquat
> Paraquat
> Spray our dope;
> White House team
> Ain't got
> No hope!

The summer was starting off well for the marijuana lobby. Even when Chip Carter called to report that his father would not be moved on the paraquat issue, that he believed the spraying to be necessary and just, Stroup was not greatly upset. For one thing, no lobbyist could ask for more than to have his case put directly to the president, by his own son, even if the decision went against him. No, for Stroup, the important thing was that he and NORML finally had acceptance, respectability, lines of communication to the highest levels of government. If you had that kind of status, you would win more battles than you lost. What Stroup could not foresee, as July arrived, was that within weeks all that hard-won status and respectability would be gone, destroyed by a senseless drug scandal, and the White House door would be slammed in his face for good.

17

On June 8, 1978, U.S. district court judge Joseph Waddy denied NORML's request for an injunction to stop U.S. funding of the spraying program in Mexico. NORML was then forced to turn to a new anti-paraquat strategy. First it had tried to persuade the Carter administration to stop the program. Then it had gone to court. Now NORML set out to persuade Congress to stop the spraying, and a key figure in this effort was Stroup's friend Stuart Statler, who continued to be troubled by U.S. support of a program that he viewed as a serious health hazard to Americans. Statler outlined his concerns to his boss, who shared them, and thus was born the Percy Amendment.

The amendment was quite simple. If approved by Congress, it would prohibit U.S. financial support for the spraying of marijuana in Mexico. By July a vote was drawing near in both houses of Congress, and a key factor was what position the Carter administration would take. Statler was first told that the administration would not oppose the Percy Amendment, but then he heard that Mathea Falco, of State, was lobbying actively against it. He passed that news along to Stroup, who was moved to have his first talk in some time with Peter Bourne.

Bourne's public support of the spraying program had been so outspoken that Stroup had quit trying to discuss the issue with him. But now, on Friday, July 14, he called Bourne and, as he later recalled it, said, "Peter, we're in a fight. Do you want to move? *Can* you move? Because if you can't, let me know and we'll go on lobbing grenades but we won't try to kill you."

He meant that he wanted to know how Bourne really felt about the paraquat issue, whether he truly opposed the amendment or was simply bowing to top-level pressure. Bourne's reply seemed encouraging: Stroup could tell senators that, unofficially, the White House had no objection to the Percy Amendment.

Stroup was elated. He had the impression that Bourne's hands were tied, because of the president or the State Department, but he still might give them some help, seek some sort of compromise, when he could. He passed on that good news to a friend of his on Sen. Birch Bayh's staff. "Keith, that's not what Peter's telling the senator," his friend replied, and went on to say that Bourne had asked Senator Bayh to rally opposition to the Percy Amendment.

Once again, Stroup was furious with Peter Bourne. And it was the next morning, Wednesday, July 19, that the political equation was dramatically changed, as all Washington was stunned by a Washington *Post* headline:

CARTER AIDE SIGNED FAKE QUAALUDE PRESCRIPTION

What Stroup could not know when he talked to Peter Bourne the previous Friday was that Bourne had far more serious problems on his mind than the Percy Amendment. Bourne's difficulties had begun the Friday before that, July 7, when, as he would later reconstruct the story, Ellen Metsky came to him for help. Metsky was nervous, upset. The pressures of the job were getting to her. Worse, she was breaking up with the young man she'd been involved with for two years, since the campaign. She was tense, unable to sleep. If she could just get some rest this weekend, she said, she might snap out of it. Bourne was familiar with her problems. Once before he'd suggested she talk to a psychiatrist, but she had not, explaining that she feared any history of psychiatric treatment might make it difficult for her to get government jobs in the future.

Bourne wrote her a prescription for fifteen Quaaludes, a tranquilizer that can be used as a "downer" and is often used in the drug culture to enhance sex. Bourne wrote the prescription on one of his own prescription forms, with his name on it, but he did not write it for Ellen Metsky. Instead he wrote in a fictitious name: Sarah Brown.

He thought no more about the prescription until Sunday, when he saw Metsky at a party. She said she hadn't got the prescription filled; she'd gone to a Washington drugstore, waited two hours, and finally given up. She added that she felt better, and she didn't think she'd get it filled at all.

"Ellen, you should get it filled," Bourne told her. "You'll be back at work on Monday and all the same pressures will be there again."

Metsky followed his advice, but she didn't take the prescription to a crowded Washington drugstore again. Instead she gave it to a friend, Toby Long, who took it to a People's Drugstore in suburban Woodbridge, Virginia. But there was a new problem. A state-pharmacy-board inspector happened to be in the drugstore. She asked for Long's identification. She had none, of course, in the name of Sarah Brown. The inspector called the police, and Long was arrested.

It seemed possible that, at least technically, both Bourne and Long had broken the law. Because of Bourne's position, Virginia authorities notified the U.S. attorney general's office in Washington. By the end of the week, Bourne was talking to a lawyer, his old friend Charles Morgan, who had gained a national reputation battling for civil rights in the South and then as an ACLU lawyer in Washington.

While all this was happening, President Carter and his top advisers were in Germany for what was billed as an economic summit conference. On Friday, the fourteenth, the day Bourne was assuring Stroup he would not oppose the Percy Amendment, a Justice Department official called Jody Powell in Germany and told him there was a problem concerning Bourne and a prescription. On Tuesday, the eighteenth, back at the White House, Powell checked on the problem and was told that Bourne was discussing it with Bob Lipshutz, the White House counsel. Powell somehow remained ignorant of the fact that the Washington *Post* was on to the story and was trying unsuccessfully to reach Bourne for comment.

It was the next morning, Wednesday, that the *Post* broke the Quaalude story, and for the rest of the week there was chaos in the White House, as the Carter administration, the press corps, and

NORML were caught up in an unfolding drama that lurched between tragedy and farce.

Peter Bourne went to the White House that morning with a proposal: He would issue a statement explaining his action, but he would give up his role as the president's drug adviser (which of course he wanted to be rid of anyway) and continue only as a health adviser until the official investigation of his action was complete.

The men who mattered, Jody Powell and Ham Jordan, were not sure that was enough. They were faced with a crisis, and they were starting from scratch. They had to have facts, they had to talk to lawyers, before they could decide what the president should do about Bourne. For Bourne, that Wednesday became an agonizing day of waiting for Powell and Jordan to settle his fate. As he saw it, if they'd only let him issue his statement that morning, it would have ended the story right there. Instead, by midafternoon the reporters were in a frenzy, tasting blood, and Ham and Jody's inaction had turned his minor error in judgment into another Bert Lance affair.

As Jordan and Powell saw it, the Lance analogy applied quite differently. A year earlier, when Lance's financial dealings had come into question, they and Carter had defended Lance month after month, revelation after revelation, until by the time he finally resigned, the Carter administration had been bled white. Powell and Jordan could not let that happen again. Peter Bourne was not Bert Lance, a South Georgian, to be protected to the bitter end.

There had to be a quick decision. Hovering in the background of their deliberations was a furious Jimmy Carter, who had just returned from the economic conference, who was trying to demonstrate his global leadership, and who had a news conference scheduled the next evening. The last thing he needed was a drug scandal involving a man he had often called one of his closest friends.

Late in the day, at a tense meeting in Jordan's big corner office in the West Wing, Jordan announced the verdict: Bourne must take a leave of absence, continuing to draw his $51,000-a-year salary, until the matter was cleared up. That news was given to the waiting reporters, along with statements by Bourne and Metsky.

Those statements differed in their explanations of why the prescription had been written to the fictitious Sarah Brown. Bourne's statement stressed Metsky's desire for confidentiality. But Metsky's raised the specter of sinister forces lurking in the background: "I know of the controversies in which Dr. Bourne becomes engaged regarding drug policy. His prescription number and name, as well as my name, are well known in the area of drug law enforcement. Consequently, I feared that my name would become known to those who might attempt to influence that policy."

There, at the end of that long, agonizing Wednesday, the matter rested: Bourne was on leave with pay until it was clear what the legal repercussions of the false prescription might be. If (as proved to be the case) no charges were brought against him, he might have quietly returned to the White House in a few months. Metsky's statement had already laid the groundwork for a portrayal of him not as a man who had done something stupid but as a liberal martyr who was somehow being persecuted by nameless drug-law-enforcement officials in retaliation for his enlightened policies. Whether Bourne would have been reinstated will never be known, for the next day, Thursday, for the second straight morning, Bourne woke up to a devastating body blow: Shortly after 7:00 A.M., Jack Anderson charged on ABC's *Good Morning America* that Bourne had used cocaine at the NORML party eight months before.

On Wednesday morning when the *Post* broke the Quaaludes story, Stroup got a call from Gary Cohn, his friend on Jack Anderson's staff, who said he had to see him at once. Stroup told him to come by his office.

"We've got to go with the story about Bourne using cocaine," Cohn said when he arrived. "I've kept it off the record, but it's going to break now. Somebody will break it. Can I go with it?"

Stroup knew that question was coming, but he did not know how important his answer would prove to be. "I won't tell you not to use it," he said. "But you can't use me as a source."

"I don't need you as a source," Cohn said, and left quickly, lest Stroup change his mind.

By the rules of Washington journalism Stroup could have forbidden Cohn to use the story. Cohn had two other sources, but they were two people whose names Stroup had given him back in February, when Stroup was angry at Bourne about the Angarola letter. Stroup was still the source of Cohn's information, and he could have stopped Cohn, or tried to, but he didn't. It was the most important decision of his career, and he made it quickly, on the basis of his anger at Bourne over the paraquat issue.

Gary Cohn hurried back to his office and called the two people at *High Times* whose names Stroup had given him back in February as witnesses to the cocaine incident. Both of them, before responding, called Stroup for guidance. They were torn between anger at Bourne's paraquat policy and a strong sense that people who used drugs shouldn't burn other people for using drugs. They looked to Stroup for guidance, but Stroup was still playing God. "Do whatever you want to do," he told them. "As head of NORML I can't be a source, but I think Bourne deserves it."

So the two witnesses confirmed the story of Bourne's cocaine use, and that evening, as Bourne left the White House, his leave of absence announced, his ordeal seemingly over, Gary Cohn was a few blocks away, banging out the story that would cause the scandal to explode anew the next morning.

It may be that if Stroup had not given Cohn the story about Bourne, it would never have been published. A Washington *Post* columnist later revealed there were three *Post* reporters in the room when Bourne used cocaine, but they had decided not to report the incident, as had Craig Copetas of *High Times*. There were difficult questions involved for the young reporters. Not the least was that some of them were using drugs, too, as were hundreds of other people at the party. Was Bourne to be singled out for exposure? Or were certain social situations implicitly off the record? There were no clear-cut rules to follow. Cohn, driven by his fear that someone would beat him to the story, made the rules for everyone else. He got the exclusive, and the *Post* reporters got criticism from their superiors for sitting on what the editors considered a legitimate story.

As Cohn was writing his story, Stroup was at the Biltmore Ballroom meeting Lynn Darling, a tall, slender, twenty-six-year-old reporter for the *Post*. When the Quaalude story broke that morning, Darling's editor assigned her to do a piece on drug use in Washington, and she called Stroup and asked for an interview. When Stroup arrived at the Biltmore, Tim Kraft and some other White House people were there, and he joined them at the bar and sipped a mimosa as they gloomily discussed the Bourne affair. One young woman, Missy Mandel, who was a friend of both Bourne and Metsky, was close to tears. Stroup began to see that this was not only a policy dispute but was also a personal tragedy. As the talk went on, Stroup grew increasingly depressed. He knew something his White House friends did not—that Jack Anderson was going to break an even worse story the next morning—and he began to realize that he should have said nothing to Gary Cohn, that he'd blundered badly, that this might be the last time he'd be seeing some of his White House friends for a long time.

That midnight Stroup was asleep in his room at the Marcheta when the phone awoke him. It was Gary Cohn, who told Stroup he wanted to read the story to him. Stroup was hesitant. He was still not a source on the story. Cohn told him he didn't want him to be a source, only to warn him if there was anything seriously wrong with his account of the cocaine incident. "I can't stop the story now," Cohn explained, "not unless there's something terribly wrong with it. But I want to double-check." Gary Cohn was scared, scared by what this story would do to Bourne and scared by the uncertain ethics of it. He read it over the phone and then Stroup was scared too, as he realized the finality of what he had done. "It's accurate," he told Cohn. It took him a long time to get back to sleep.

Jack Anderson, a Mormon who used no drug stronger than coffee, had no trouble sleeping that night. He arose early Thursday morning, and broke the cocaine story as scheduled on *Good Morning America*. Soon thereafter, Peter Bourne had reporters and photographers banging on his door, camping on his lawn, as they had on the lawns of Dean and Magruder and Haldeman in the heyday of Watergate. Bourne hurried to the White House, where he nervously told his version of the cocaine incident. Yes, he had gone to the NORML party. Yes, he had gone to the private room on the top floor of the town house. Yes, Stroup and Copetas and others had been passing around vials of cocaine. Yes, he had held them, examined them, joked about them. But no, he had not actually *used* the cocaine. The distinction was more political than legal, since federal law prohibited possession of cocaine, not use.

Bourne's superiors at the White House later told reporters that they did not find his denials entirely convincing, but at that point whether or not he actually inhaled the cocaine hardly mattered. For Jimmy Carter's chief adviser on drug policy to admit he had knowingly attended a party where cocaine was used was politically devastating. Possibly Bourne might have survived that revelation alone. Possibly he might have survived the fake prescription alone. But he could not survive both. "Things were out of control," one of his White House colleagues told a reporter. "There was no way he could stay on."

The Bourne affair had to be resolved before the president's 7:00 P.M. news conference, and it could only be resolved by Bourne's resignation. Hamilton Jordan persuaded Chuck Morgan, Bourne's friend and lawyer, of that fact, and by midafternoon Morgan had persuaded Bourne. With tears in his eyes, Bourne sat in his windowless office in the White House basement, writing a letter of resignation to his friend Jimmy Carter.

It was an emotional letter, written by a man under enormous strain. He said, "Though I make mistakes, they are of the heart and not of the mind." He twice noted that "law enforcement officers" had been the source of the "grossest innuendo" against him. "I have never intended to do anyone harm," Bourne said. And he concluded, "I fear for the future of the nation far more than I do for the future of, Your friend, Peter."

With Bourne's resignation in hand, the president's next problem was his news conference that night. He faced a no-win situation. There was nothing Carter could say about Bourne, either to defend him or deplore him, that would do Carter any good. He therefore announced at the outset of the news conference that he would not answer questions about Bourne. It was a stunning gambit—for a president to open a news conference by saying he would not talk about the biggest news story of the month—and to their credit some reporters would not stand for it. Daniel Schorr asked if Bourne had ever written prescriptions for Carter or his family. Carter said he had not. Sam Donelson asked if he agreed with Bourne that the attacks on him were really attacks on Carter. Carter said grimly that he would prefer not to answer that question.

Then Craig Copetas had his chance.

Twenty reporters were on their feet, waving their arms, shouting for the president's attention, but Craig Copetas shouted the loudest. He was a man with a mission, an avenger. Copetas had waited for this moment for a long time. He passionately believed that the government was deliberately poisoning marijuana smokers. He had been working on the story for almost two years; he had gone to Mexico; he had interviewed people who thought paraquat had damaged their lungs.

That morning he had talked to a woman who'd had an abortion because she feared that smoking contaminated marijuana had damaged her unborn child.

All things considered, Copetas asked his first question to the president fairly calmly. He noted that the NIDA report had warned of lung fibrosis to American marijuana smokers. He outlined the Percy Amendment and asked if Carter would support it.

Carter replied, "I am not familiar with the bill. My understanding is that American money is not used to purchase the paraquat. I think Mexico buys this material from other countries and they use their own personnel to spray it with. My preference is that marijuana not be grown or smoked. It is illegal."

Craig Copetas went berserk. He knew he was going berserk, right there on national television, and he didn't care. He's lying, Copetas thought. The president of the United States is lying to the American people. Wild-eyed, barely coherent, he shouted out a follow-up question.

"What about the thirteen million dollars a year that is being channeled into Mexico now, that is being used with the helicopters to go out spraying the fields, or DEA, Drug Enforcement Administration, intelligence that goes out to help eradicate these fields?"

Copetas's outburst was the best thing that had happened to Carter all day. Confronted on national television by a bearded, shouting, pro-pot journalist, Carter could play the role of the patient statesman who was protecting America from the international drug conspiracy.

"I favor this relationship with Mexico," Carter said smoothly. "When I came into office, about seventy-five percent, for instance, of all the heroin used in our country was coming from Mexico. Because of the work of Dr. Bourne and the officials of the DEA, the Drug Enforcement Agency, we and the new president and officials of Mexico, President López Portillo, we have mounted a very successful campaign, and now we have almost stopped the flow of heroin, for instance, from Mexico to our country. Marijuana happens to be an illicit drug that is included under the overall drug-control program, and I favor this program very strongly."

With that ringing endorsement of the paraquat-spraying program, Jimmy Carter concluded one of the more difficult days of his administration.

It had not been a good day for Keith Stroup, either. Dozens of reporters were calling, wanting him to confirm Jack Anderson's story of Bourne's cocaine use. Stroup tried to tell them the issue should be paraquat, not Bourne's personal drug use, but of course that wasn't the issue anymore. And when he was pushed, Stroup told reporters he would not confirm Anderson's story but would not deny it, either. A *Post* reporter, aware that he had denied the cocaine story several times in months past, asked if his new nondenial was significant. Yes, Stroup said, it was significant. It was one last bit of grandstanding for the media, and it would soon come back to haunt him.

The next morning's newspapers carried front-page accounts of Bourne's resignation, and the *Post* also carried Stroup's remark that it was "significant" that he no longer denied the reports of Bourne's cocaine use. It was not a comment that meant much to the world at large, but it meant a great deal to the staff and supporters of NORML. Stroup had not been named in the Jack Anderson story, but now he had linked himself, by name, to Bourne's downfall. Now it was no longer a matter of Bourne's bringing himself down; the head of NORML had helped destroy him. NORML supporters were troubled by a question of ethics: Should Stroup in any way have contributed to Bourne's downfall, paraquat or no paraquat? Wasn't that playing DEA's game? Wasn't it dangerously close to informing, which NORML's legal committee had officially denounced? There was a question of practical politics: Would this make it impossible for NORML to work with the Carter administration? And finally there was a personal question that many scientists and lawyers and political activists were asking themselves. Many of the people who supported NORML used illicit drugs to one degree or another, and many of them could not afford to admit it. Now they had to ask themselves, If Keith would get mad and blow the whistle on Peter Bourne, when might he blow the whistle on me?

Finally, as the calls poured in, from people who were angry, from people who were worried, from people who were disbelieving, Stroup realized how disastrously he had blundered. By evening, he wanted nothing more than to escape the controversy. It was then that the drama moved toward comic relief. It happened that Willie Nelson was back in town, playing a concert at the Meriwether Post Pavillion. Someone in Nelson's entourage had sent thirty complimentary tickets to the White House, and one of Stroup's friends there had sent several of them to NORML. Stroup decided to go to the concert, get high, listen to Willie, and get his mind off his troubles. He and Fred Moore, Billy

Paley, George Farnham, and a few others piled in a car and drove out to the concert in Columbia, Maryland. They arrived late, and slipped into their seats after Emmylou Harris, who opened the show, had started singing. Stroup noticed a couple of Secret Service men as he entered, but he took that to mean that Chip or perhaps Jeff was around somewhere. When they were settled in their seats, Fred Moore lit a joint and passed it to Billy Paley, who had a hit and passed it to Stroup, who had a hit and passed it back to Moore. Just then, someone spoke to Stroup from the row behind.

"Do you really want to smoke that?" the voice demanded.

Stroup was indignant. Of course he would smoke a joint. Everyone smoked at concerts. "Why not?" he snapped.

"Because the president is right behind you," the man said.

Stroup turned and saw, to his horror, that it was true. Jimmy Carter was sitting in the row behind him, about five seats to the right. Stroup turned to Moore.

"Fred, put that fucking thing out!"

"What?"

"Carter's behind us."

Seeking to escape from Jimmy Carter, Stroup and his friends got up and went backstage. A few minutes later, Carter and his entourage also went backstage. Stroup was starting to panic: *He couldn't get away from Jimmy Carter.* As it happened, one of Stroup's friends didn't want to escape the president. His name was Stuart Levitan and he was a long-haired underground reporter. Without identifying himself as a reporter, Levitan buttonholed Carter and asked him about Peter Bourne's remark, printed in that morning's New York *Times*, that there was a "high incidence" of marijuana use among the White House staff, and "occasional" cocaine use. That was true enough, but politically harmful, and no one was sure if Bourne had just blurted it out in a moment of candor or was deliberately embarrassing the White House for what he saw as shoddy treatment of him in his hour of need. In any event, Carter, according to Levitan, replied, "I'm sure many people smoke marijuana, but I'm not going to ask them about it."

The interview was soon terminated by Carter aides Jody Powell and Frank Moore, who dragged Levitan away, but the damage was done. Levitan wrote a story, which appeared on the front page of the

Washington *Star*, in which Carter's remark was used to suggest that Carter condoned marijuana use by his staff.

Meanwhile, Stroup and Paley had sat down on two empty chairs at the edge of the stage and were sharing a joint and watching the show. Someone tapped on Stroup's shoulder. He turned and saw a Secret Service agent. "Sorry, sir, those chairs are for President and Mrs. Carter," he said. Sure enough, there were the Carters, waiting to claim their seats. Stroup and Paley fled to the other side of the stage, where they joined Emmylou Harris and were finally able to smoke in peace. They were watching contentedly a few minutes later when a grinning Jimmy Carter skipped out onto the stage and joined Willie Nelson in a duet of "Georgia on My Mind."

The fiasco continued over the weekend. When reporters interpreted Carter's "I'm not going to ask them about it" comment to Levitan as presidential approval of pot-smoking, Jody Powell denounced Levitan as "a nut," a "bongo," and "spacy," and also accused reporters of a "witch-hunt" and "cheap shots" in their efforts to document drug use by people in the White House. Powell also denounced the media for hypocrisy, noting in particular that Jack Anderson's account of the cocaine episode had not revealed that his reporter, Gary Cohn, was a guest at the party. There was some merit in what Powell said, but it was too late to matter. The Bourne affair, plus Bourne's charges of both marijuana and cocaine use among the White House staff, had raised the specter of reefer madness surrounding the born-again president, and in the weeks ahead political commentators had a field day. Editorial cartoonists, in particular, conjured up visions of presidential aides smoking joints, popping pills, snorting powder, bouncing around the ceilings of the West Wing. All of which, if unfair, was also politically devastating.

People at NORML were also feeling devastated that weekend, and not only Stroup. One example was Mark Heutlinger, whose work in the reform movement went back to Amorphia in 1972. Heutlinger had been worried ever since Wednesday morning, the day the Quāāludes story broke, when he saw Gary Cohn go into Stroup's office. He knew why Cohn was there. Heutlinger had been afraid this would happen ever since the party. Keith's knowledge of Bourne's drug use was like a rock he had clenched in his fist, Heutlinger thought, and he knew Stroup's temper and knew his loathing of Bourne, and so he had thought it inevitable that Keith would throw that rock sometime. The only question was when.

Heutlinger, like all the NORML staff, had for a long time coexisted uneasily with Stroup's temper, his underlying anger. His anger had fueled his tireless work at NORML, had enabled him to create the pot lobby and finance it and publicize it. No one on the staff imagined he could have done those things half as well as Stroup had. But they had also seen the times when Stroup felt wronged or rejected and his anger would explode into wild, irrational rages. Stroup's anger had been like a time bomb, ticking away, and this time Heutlinger feared the explosion was coming and the whole house of cards would come tumbling down.

The next morning, Thursday morning, when the cocaine story broke and press calls were pouring in, Keith had handed him the phone when a *Post* reporter wanted details of the NORML party. "Was there cocaine use at the party?" the reporter asked. Heutlinger thought that was the dumbest question he'd ever heard. "Sure there was cocaine use," he said. "What do you expect when you have six hundred people at a party?" So the next morning, Friday morning, in the same story that had Stroup saying his nondenial was "significant," there was Mark Heutlinger saying sure there was cocaine use at the NORML party, and suddenly he realized, My God, I am in the middle of this disaster. As soon as he could, Heutlinger left town for a weekend at Rehoboth Beach.

Running away didn't help. At the beach on Saturday he couldn't get Peter Bourne out of his mind. Finally he called Gordon Brownell in California and Larry Schott and Peter Meyers in Washington to see what they thought. They were concerned, troubled about the morality of what Keith had done, but they seemed to think the crisis would pass. Heutlinger was not so sure. As he saw it, Keith had thrown the rock into the pond and the ripples had started flowing outward and no one could say how huge they might become or what damage they might do. Everything was out of control. Heutlinger was worried, and he was ashamed, too, because he had made his career in the reform movement and he had made sacrifices, but he had always thought that changing the drug laws was right, was good for the country, was patriotic. Now he feared the movement had done something that hurt the country, hurt the political process, something that could not be defended. Finally, as he sat on the sandy beach staring out at the ocean, Mark Heutlinger knew what bothered him most. It was his fear that when he got back to NORML the next week, and he and Keith sat down to talk it all over, Keith would never admit he had been wrong.

18

Stroup knew he was wrong, but he didn't know what to do about it.

He had plunged the world of drug policy into turmoil. Calls were pouring in from NORML supporters who feared Stroup had killed any hope that the Carter administration would support drug-law reform. Tom Bryant resigned from NORML's advisory board, calling Stroup's actions with regard to Bourne "unconscionable." Roger Roffman, NORML's Washington State coordinator, had also resigned. Stroup had Larry Schott take most of the calls; he wasn't ready to talk to anyone. Schott and Brownell were urging him to issue yet another statement of explanation and apology, but Stroup wanted more time to evaluate the damage. Would he have to resign? Or could he ride out the storm?

He alternated between defiance and despair. Sometimes he tried to justify himself. He'd been battle weary, he would say. But that wouldn't wash. Everyone is battle weary. That's what battles are all about. Or he would say that Bourne had deserved it, because of paraquat. But that didn't hold water either. Paraquat was Carter's policy, not Bourne's, and Stroup wasn't going to get a better policy by destroying Bourne. No, the truth was that Stroup had done something stupid, and now he, as well as Bourne, was paying for his mistake.

Stroup had spent eight years constructing his own little world, one in which he was admired and respected, and now it was collapsing. Tom Bryant was outraged, people like Norman Zinberg were upset, and many on Stroup's own staff were barely speaking to him, for they had made NORML their world, and it was falling down around their heads, too. For the next several weeks Stroup would reach out in many directions for support and encouragement. He called Kelly the day the cocaine story broke and asked if he could come by and see Lindsey that night. Kelly had seen the papers, and she had to say to him, "Keith, you really did it this time. Instead of waving the gun you pulled the trigger." In Kelly's mind his lashing out at Bourne was much like his lashing out at her, after their separation, wanting to punish her. He came by that night and they smoked a few joints and talked. It was the first time in a long time she could remember their having talked without fighting, and he had seemed to listen to what she had to say. Finally he went and kissed Lindsey good night and left. Kelly thought she had never seen him so unsure of himself. She felt sorry for him.

Stroup decided the best thing was to get out of Washington for a while, to give himself time to think and for things to cool down. Willie Nelson had invited him to join him and the band on the road, and Stroup decided to accept the invitation.

Before catching up with Willie Nelson in Las Vegas, Stroup flew first to Albuquerque to visit his brother, Larry, and his family. He called Larry that morning and said he was coming west to hide out for a few days, to get away from a problem back in Washington. When he arrived in Albuquerque, the two brothers, and Larry's wife, Pat, went to dinner at a Mexican restaurant and then returned to Larry's home. It was a pleasant evening, in part because the brothers were careful to avoid any political discussion: Larry Stroup regarded Barry Goldwater as a dangerous liberal.

At breakfast the next morning Stroup read a Joseph Kraft column in the local paper that was critical of his role in the Bourne affair. Stroup had planned to see his brother later in the day, but once he saw the Kraft column he packed his bag, said hurried good-byes, jumped into his rented car, and headed farther west, still trying to escape.

Driving through the desert that morning, Stroup smoked two joints and managed to miss the turn to Santa Fe. Doubling back, he was stopped at a police roadblock. A state trooper smelled marijuana smoke in his car, forced him to open his suitcase, and found two ounces of marijuana. Stroup guessed that was it, the last straw. To be busted in New Mexico, on top of everything else, would be the end. He'd have to quit NORML or be thrown out. He'd be a laughingstock, a fool. But the trooper, a Chicano, let him go with a lecture.

Stroup stopped in Santa Fe to visit Louise Dubois, the former wife of his friend Larry Dubois. Louise was a petite blonde, blessed with patrician beauty and a serene nature. She loved animals and had moved to Santa Fe, where she was working for a veterinarian and living in an adobe farmhouse on a ranch outside of town. Stroup tripped on MDA his first night with Louise, and stayed up late, listening to dogs howl out on the desert, content at last, the fiasco in Washington finally blown from his mind. Then the phone rang. It was Larry Dubois, calling to warn that Stroup was in deep trouble.

NORML's board of directors consisted of Stroup, Schott, Brownell, Fioramonti, and Dubois. The only way Stroup could have been forced out of NORML would have been by a majority vote of the board. Dubois had for several years been an inactive member of the board, but now his phone was ringing. Stroup's critics were asking Dubois if he thought it might be time for a change in NORML's leadership. Stroup could count on Dubois's vote, come what may, but Dubois nonetheless urged him to return to Washington and issue a statement of apology to quiet the critics. Stroup refused. He was on his way to see Willie Nelson, and that was that.

He spent three days in Las Vegas, partying with Nelson and his band and entourage. Nelson's traveling party amounted to a big extended family, and that of course was what Stroup was seeking in his journey west. NORML had been his family for several years, but he was in disfavor there, and so he had turned for approval and moral support to Nelson, who was a kind of father figure and guru to many people.

When Stroup returned to Washington, Larry Schott said he thought it necessary for the board of directors to censure Stroup for his role in the Bourne affair. That was done in a statement that stressed NORML's belief in every person's right to privacy with regard to his or her drug use, regardless of politics. After that, Stroup issued a statement of apology. By then, he seemed to have ridden out the storm.

Thus assured, Stroup was off to Miami in mid-August for the long-awaited Jimmy Buffet benefit for NORML. Stroup had been working on this one for more than a year. He had partied with Buffet, traveled with him, gone to his wedding, got to know his parents. One concert at the Kennedy Center in Washington had been canceled when Buffet's new manager decided he was overexposed in the Washington area. But Stroup persisted and enlisted the help of Hunter Thompson and friends of Buffet's in the Carter administration, and finally he had pinned down Buffet and, more important, his manager. Buffet was going to play three concerts in Miami, during which a live album would be recorded, and the proceeds, after expenses, would go to NORML. Considering the size of the hall and the price of the tickets, Stroup estimated that NORML would receive a minimum of $25,000.

Just as important as the money, of course, was the demonstration that despite the Bourne affair, he was still Mr. NORML, was still alive and well in the world of rock-and-roll celebrity. He invited many of his friends to Miami for a week of partying: Tom Forcade and Craig Copetas came from New York, Fred Moore and Billy Paley from Washington, Marlene Gaskill from Atlanta. (Forcade wanted Stroup to fly to Colombia with him after the concerts. "Are you crazy?" Stroup said. "After I've been busted in Canada, do you think I'm going to Colombia with *you*?" "Don't worry," Forcade told him. "In Colombia the cops are on our side.") Everyone stayed at the Coconut Grove Hotel, a rock-and-roll hangout, and for five days and nights Miami had *its* party of the year. Dealers came and gave away cocaine. Women came and gave away themselves. There were so many women, going from room to room, wanting only anonymous sex with anyone who smacked of stardom, that in time the men were turning them away. It was a level of rock-and-roll craziness that shocked even Stroup; he didn't see how people could live at that pace and survive.

Somehow the three concerts were held, all sellouts, and after the last one Stroup rented a house and hired a band and gave a party for Buffet and the band and everyone. But there was a problem. All week the promoter of the concert had treated Stroup rudely. He'd given Stroup and his friends lousy tickets for the concerts. And now, when Stroup gave his farewell party, Buffet didn't bother to come. It seemed possible that the word was out that Stroup was no longer the man with big White House connections, that perhaps he was something of a political pariah.

The next afternoon, Stroup, Paley, and Moore were racing through the Miami airport to catch their plane back to Washington when two security men stopped them. Stroup guessed their dark glasses and modish clothes had triggered a spot check. He began protesting, talking very fast, because he was carrying both marijuana and cocaine, and images of the windowless search room in Canada were flashing through his mind when one security guard told the other, "I think these are the wrong ones," and let them go.

Back in Washington, there was another unexpected complication in Stroup's life. For the first time since his marriage he was becoming seriously involved with a woman.

She was Lynn Darling, the Washington *Post* reporter who'd interviewed him back in July on the day the Quāāludes story broke. Darling was a tall, slender woman with brown hair, high cheekbones, and huge brown eyes that made her look even younger than her twenty-six years. She and Stroup were, in fact, a great deal alike: smart, nervous, fast-talking, fast-thinking people, people who savored the limelight. Darling's father was an Army colonel, and her mother was the daughter of Polish immigrants; she had been pushed since childhood to excel. She entered Harvard at sixteen, discovered the joys of drugs, journalism, and radical politics, and by the time she graduated she was an editor of the *Crimson* and an ex-Maoist.

Stroup and Darling had met and had a brief affair in 1974 when she was a free-lance writer. She remained interested in him, and when they met again in 1978, she was older and more sure of herself, and he was in urgent need of comfort and support. He called her when he returned from Las Vegas to tell her he'd admired the long front-page article she'd written on drug use in Washington. Using the Bourne affair as a starting point, Darling had pointed out that drug use was part of the life-style of many young people in the political world. She mentioned in passing that she was herself not unfamiliar with drugs, and she commented on the generation gap at her newspaper, where, she said, older journalists compared cocaine to heroin while younger ones compared it to coffee.

Stroup was soon spending most of his free time with Darling. He was still unsure of his future, still feeling hostility from many quarters, and he talked for hours about his uncertainties. Darling found him confused, torn by Calvinist guilt, uncertain of his identity, fearful that he was at bottom self-destructive. One night he would regret what he had done in the Bourne affair, the next night he would justify his actions and declare that the bastards would never force him out. He knew he couldn't stay at NORML, and yet he feared being stripped of his Mr. NORML persona and becoming just another lawyer.

Despite Stroup's problems, or because of them, the romance blossomed. Eventually, after much hesitation and soul-searching, Stroup moved into Darling's apartment. He did so a step at a time, like a man getting into a cold bath, keeping his clothes in his own apartment for several weeks, keeping his apartment for several months after he'd quit using it, finding it very difficult to admit, even to himself, that he'd finally surrendered his hard-won independence.

As autumn began, Stroup knew he had to leave NORML, the question was when. He could hang on, but he could never be as effective as he was before the Bourne episode. For one thing, he had lost his White House connections; Peter Bourne's successors in the Office of Drug Abuse Policy understandably wanted nothing to do with him. An even worse problem was criticism within NORML. Important allies were wondering if he'd outlived his usefulness. In mid-September, he told the staff he would leave NORML sometime the next spring.

Early in October, Stroup got an unexpected call from his friend Mike Stepanian, the San Francisco drug lawyer. Several of NORML's leading scientific advisers had been to San Francisco for a drug conference, Stepanian said, and they'd had a long talk about NORML, and they felt they could no longer work with the organization if Stroup stayed on as its director.

Stroup exploded. "I've already said I'm leaving," he shouted at Stepanian.

That wasn't good enough, Stepanian said. The scientists wanted a firm date for his departure.

Stroup declared that he'd leave when he was ready and the scientists could go fuck themselves. He interpreted the scientists' threats as another example of White House pressure. By some reports, the scientists had been told they must choose between working with NORML and the government contracts and consultant positions that were so important to them.

He remained resolute for a week, declaring that nobody could force him out; then, abruptly, he realized that practicing law looked a great deal more attractive than struggling to rebuild NORML's coalition. He called Gerry Goldstein and asked if he'd be interested in forming a law partnership. Goldstein said he would, and Stroup announced he would leave NORML by the end of the year.

In November, Stroup flew to Los Angeles for a NORML fund-raiser at the Playboy mansion. Two hundred fifty guests were invited, at $100 apiece, and Hugh Hefner picked up all the expenses. There was no easier or more pleasant way to raise $25,000. And NORML needed the money, all the more so because the Jimmy Buffet benefit had ended in disaster. After waiting a couple of months, Stroup called Buffet's accountant and was told that expenses for the Miami concerts had been higher than expected. In fact, instead of the $25,000 or more Stroup was expecting, NORML wouldn't get anything. It was only when Stroup threatened to tell reporters that Buffet's manager had ripped off NORML that the manager agreed to send $10,000.

Soon after Stroup arrived at his hotel in Los Angeles for the Playboy fund-raiser, he received stunning news from New York: Tom Forcade had shot and killed himself.

Forcade had been deeply depressed by the death a few weeks earlier of his friend Jack Coombs in a plane crash in Colombia. The crash had apparently been accidental, but Forcade believed the DEA was responsible. After Coombs's death Forcade had been using a lot of Quāāludes, a drug that only added to his depression. His wife, Gabrielle Schang, an attractive Briarcliff dropout turned Yippie, later said, "Tom was really gifted and a little unbalanced. I think he was clinically a manic depressive. On his highs he had boundless energy, but he'd fall into lapses of despondency and be like a zucchini. I think it was hard for him to be a radical leftist and a successful capitalist, too." As soon as the Playboy party was over, Stroup flew to New York for a wake Schang was holding for Forcade on the top floor of the World Trade Center—because, she explained, it was the highest place in New York.

Stroup spent the evening of Saturday, December 2, getting very, very high. That afternoon, the second day of the 1978 NORML conference, he'd delivered his farewell speech to the delegates. He'd been a bit nervous as he began his speech, for there was a rumor that the Yippies were going to pie him, a prospect Stroup found distinctly unsettling. But no pie throwers appeared, and Stroup began by paying tribute to two allies of NORML who had died in recent weeks: Tom Forcade and George Moscone, the mayor of San Francisco, who'd been shot by an assassin. He went on to regret the rise of an anti-reform New Right, to denounce the DEA as an American Gestapo and call for its abolition, to advocate the legalization but not the commercialization of marijuana, to challenge President Carter to provide action instead of rhetoric on drug-law reform, and to declare that the fate of people imprisoned on drug charges concerned him far more than the fate of Peter Bourne. As if to dramatize that point, the audience included Stroup's special guests for the weekend, Roy and Betty Mitchell, the blind couple from West Plains, Missouri, whose son, Jerry, had then been in prison about eight months and would remain there for another six months before he was paroled. Stroup tried to keep in touch with people like the Mitchells; they were a kind of extended family for him. He had heard recently from Frank Demolli; after getting out of prison in Texas, Demolli had got his college degree in Colorado and gone to work for the state prison system there, with the intention of making his career in prison reform.

As he warmed up to his speech, Stroup had some kind words for the nation's drug smugglers. "They're not criminals," he declared. "They're our friends and we have to support them." It was both something he believed and a reminder that his new law firm would be specializing in drug cases, smugglers included. As Stroup saw it, that was the new cutting edge of the marijuana issue. The battle for the smokers was almost won—few of them went to jail anymore—but lots of dealers went to jail, and in Stroup's view they were simply businessmen, performing a necessary function, whom society unjustly defined as criminals.

As he ended his speech, Stroup made only modest claims for the reform lobby he had created: They had demonstrated that smokers were a legitimate constituency, he said, a political force, and the government would have to listen to them when it made its drug policies.

The delegates gave Stroup a standing ovation as he stepped down, and it was deserved. To have conceived NORML in 1970, to have brought it into being, and to have made it the formidable national organization it became were quite remarkable achievements. In the process Stroup had helped a lot of people no one else had the talent or inclination to help. A lot of people were not in jail who would have been if NORML had not existed. Whatever his shortcomings, Stroup had made NORML about as effective and as respectable as any marijuana lobby could expect to be, and he had associated it with people who represented excellence in many fields: with Ramsey Clark and Phil Hart, with Kris Kristofferson and Willie Nelson, with Hunter Thompson and Garry Trudeau, with Norman Zinberg and Dorothy Whipple, with Hugh Hefner of *Playboy* and Tom Bryant of the Drug Abuse Council. He had made at least his share of mistakes, but it was impossible to say that anyone else could have done as well, or even come close. Stroup's critics might not consider him a proper model for the young, but he had fought effectively for what he believed, and history teaches that the people who step forward to lead unpopular causes are not often perfect gentlemen.

The speech was Stroup's official farewell; then the unofficial farewell began, as Stroup began to unwind and make the rounds of the suites at the Hyatt Regency. It was a warm, sentimental evening. Stroup's friends had forgiven him the Bourne affair and were remembering the good times. There were many handshakes, embraces, jokes, memories to be exchanged, and there were also many offers for Stroup to take a hit of this, a snort of that. For a while the party stopped in his and Lynn Darling's suite, where Gerry Goldstein kept ordering bottles of Dom Pérignon from room service. The party moved on to Hunter Thompson's suite, where Stroup noticed that Thompson had torn off the door between his two rooms and had also crashed a serving tray into the wall. "Jesus Christ, Hunter, I'm liable for all this," Stroup protested, for NORML picked up the tab each year when Thompson came to its conferences. While they were in Thompson's suite, Stroup sampled some methamphetamine—speed—that had been mixed with cocaine. Stroup was getting higher and higher, but he was still in reasonably good shape at eleven o'clock when the party moved a few blocks away to a huge old Elks Club building, where the official NORML conference party was being held.

Billy Paley and Fred Moore had been in charge of planning the 1978 conference party, as they had the previous year's party at the town house on S Street. This year, however, because of NORML's financial plight, a money-making party was given. Invitations were sent to all NORML members in the Washington area to attend at $10 apiece. And they had come, many hundreds of them, seemingly every long-haired freak within a hundred miles of Washington, to pack the Elks Club hall, smoke dope, drink beer, eat chili, and listen to records and a rock band. For a while someone kept playing a depressing rock song called "Christmas at the K-Mart." Quite a number of Washington reporters were present, perhaps hoping for a repeat of the previous year's cocaine scandal, but they were disappointed, for it would have been easier to locate a two-headed cow than a Carter administration official at the 1978 NORML conference.

Moore and Paley had set aside one room for NORML's elite. The door to that inner sanctum was being guarded by several large black men who were rumored to be black-belt karate experts. These doormen were admitting only people who displayed little paper stars that Larry Schott and others were giving to special friends of NORML. Inside the private room thirty or so people were smoking dope, snorting cocaine, sipping champagne, and generally having a fine time.

Outside, however, an angry group of activist lawyers were confronting the doormen. They were dues-paying members of NORML, they declared, and there could be no private party, no elitism, no discrimination: They demanded admission. The reputed karate champions were unmoved. No star, no entry. The NORML populists were outraged, but push did not come to shove. Such was the situation when Stroup arrived. "Let 'em in," he commanded, and NORML's elite were soon engulfed by a tidal wave of public-interest lawyers and ponytailed dopers.

Stroup didn't care. He felt great. With Lynn Darling at his side he moved about the Elks Club, shaking hands, laughing, greeting old friends, savoring his last hurrah. The trouble was that like many an old grad back for his class reunion, he was consuming more stimulants than was wise. He might have been able to handle the champagne, the marijuana, the speed, and the cocaine, but the problem was the Quaaludes that people kept pressing on him.

He downed them, half a Quaalude here, another half there, because he thought that Quaāludes combined with cocaine produced a nice high, and also because too much cocaine made you tense, wired, jittery, and the Quaāludes would bring you down, take the edge off the coke. All of which was fine, except that too many Quaāludes can kill you, and Stroup was past counting.

From the Elks Club the party returned to the Hyatt Regency, to the suite of a big, rich Texan who'd recently become an enthusiastic NORML supporter. Sometimes, for fun, the Texan would toss handfuls of Quaāludes into the air, as if they were candy or flowers. Stroup was saying something to Lynn Darling, was quite rational, and the next moment he sank to the floor, unconscious.

Darling was scared. Most of the people were higher than she was, and no one seemed too worried about Keith. People gathered around and began comparing notes, and as best they could calculate he had taken four or five Quaāludes, enough, some feared, to kill him. They tried to take him back to his own room, but no one could find the key, so they took him instead to Mark Heutlinger's room. Then there was conflicting medical advice. Someone said the best thing was to let him sleep, but someone else said no, the important thing was *not* to let him sleep, because he might go into a coma. The Texan thought a cold bath might revive him, so they put him in the tub, and it revived him enough that he mumbled that champagne and Quaāludes taken together were synergistic, and all the people gathered around the tub cheered that sign of improvement.

But he kept falling back to sleep, and they kept slapping him and talking to him and trying to awaken him. A young NORML aide had promised Darling he would find a doctor, but no doctor ever appeared. The Texan announced he had an ambulance standing by downstairs in case Stroup got worse. At one point the Texan demanded that room service send up some coffee and food, thinking that might revive Stroup, but the switchboard operator insisted room service was closed. The Texan went downstairs and broke into the kitchen and brought back cheese and crackers, but Stroup wouldn't eat them. It went on like that for hours—bizarre, chaotic, funny, or tragic, depending on the outcome. Darling, with a journalist's double vision, could see the headlines: "Mr. NORML Delivers Farewell Address; O.D.'s." From time to time Stroup would open his eyes and mutter some lewd sexual suggestion to her and then pass out again. Finally, around dawn, he opened his eyes and seemed to have some awareness of where he was. He squinted at Darling, then at the other people clustered around the bed.

"What the fuck are all these people doing in my room?" he demanded. "Can't you see I'm trying to sleep?"

With that, they knew he was all right.

19

Early in November of 1979, Rep. Lester Wolff's Select Committee on Narcotics held a busy day of hearings on the drug-paraphernalia industry. It was, inevitably, a media event, and the day's star witness was a plump teenager from New York City who told how she'd become a drug user at eleven and who, for the benefit of photographers, demonstrated how various pipes and bongs were used, while the lawmakers scrambled to get within camera range.

The teenager was the day's most photographed witness, but she was not the most politically important witness. That honor belonged to an attractive, fortyish Atlanta woman named Sue Rusche, who spoke as the president of DeKalb County Families in Action. For Sue Rusche, symbolically if not personally, had politicians and bureaucrats across America shaking in their boots. She was an outraged mother, speaking for millions of parents who did not want their children exposed to drugs. The organization she headed had already shut down most of the head shops in Georgia and helped pass anti-paraphernalia laws across the nation, and she and the anti-drug passions she embodied had become a significant force in the national drug-policy debate.

Rusche is a handsome, sad-eyed woman who wears her long brown hair loose at her shoulders. She is, in person, charming, witty, soft-spoken, and very feminine, but the message she delivered to the congressional committee that afternoon was a grim and powerful one. She was furious about the increase in drug use by adolescents, the growth of the smuggling and paraphernalia industries, and the activities of NORML. As Rusche saw it, those events were all interrelated, were in effect a conspiracy wherein NORML had become a lobby for smugglers and paraphernalia sellers. She cited as evidence the fact that NORML received money from *High Times* and that Stroup's new law firm represented the paraphernalia industry and accused smugglers. Declared Rusche: "We call upon Congress to conduct a full-scale, criminal investigation of the drug-paraphernalia industry, *High Times* magazine, and NORML."

That was not all Rusche wanted. Concluding her testimony, she said, "Mr. Chairman, we call upon the Congress to allocate funds for a national Adolescent Drug Information Center and to establish small grants to aid the hundreds of parent, family, and community groups that have formed across the country to stop drug use among children and teenagers." If that center came to be—and Rusche was seeking foundation money as well as federal funds—it would be in Atlanta, where Rusche lived, and she would be its director. Sue Rusche was adding insult to injury: She not only wanted to send Keith Stroup to jail; she wanted to become the Keith Stroup of the anti-marijuana movement.

Sue Rusche grew up in Ohio, studied art in New York, and worked in advertising before she and her husband, Henry Rusche, moved in 1962 to Atlanta, where he was to teach literature at Emory University. They arrived in Atlanta at a time when the civil-rights revolution was exploding across the South, and Sue Rusche wanted to be part of it. Most of all she dreamed of working for Dr. Martin Luther King, Jr. One day she started to look up the number of his Southern Christian Leadership Conference. But she hesitated. Passions were high in the South then, and she and her husband were newcomers, and she didn't know how his new colleagues at Emory would feel about her working for the controversial civil-rights leader. Then she noticed, just below the SCLC listing, one for the Southern Regional Council's voter-education project. She reasoned that no one could be against people voting, so she called SRC instead of SCLC, and she became a research assistant there, one whose job was to collect information on voting patterns that could be used to prove discrimination against blacks. She learned how facts, carefully assembled and properly used, could become the levers for political change, and in time she applied that understanding to her anti-paraphernalia crusade.

Rusche worked for SRC for a few years, then for Project Head Start, then opened her own graphic-design studio, designing corporate logos and the like. One reason she later became so outraged at the paraphernalia industry was that their graphics were so slick. They were so damn *good* at selling their drug-related products to kids.

One evening in August of 1976 some friends of the Rusches' were giving a thirteenth-birthday party for their daughter, a girl who sometimes baby-sat with the Rusches' two sons. It was to be a festive backyard affair, but when the parents went out to get things started, they found their daughter and her friends behaving strangely, giggling, stumbling about, evasive. Questioning brought forth the shocking truth: The kids were high on marijuana.

The girl's parents called a meeting of other parents, which the Rusches attended. The group sent off to Washington for information on marijuana, but at the time they were not thinking in terms of any citywide or national anti-drug campaign, only of how they could keep their own children off drugs.

A year later, in August of 1977, Rusche and other Atlantans received a second shock. An Emory student named Robert Topping, the son of a former co-owner of the New York Yankees and the stepson of a wealthy Atlantan named Rankin Smith, was stabbed to death in Miami. A police investigation revealed that he had flown to Miami with $47,000 cash to buy cocaine and that he had been selling drugs on and around the Emory campus.

Sue Rusche was not a prude. She'd tried marijuana a few times, and she drank socially. But now it seemed to her that the world had gone mad. Her baby-sitter was smoking marijuana. An Emory student had been murdered. The last straw came when she and other parents became aware of the head shops that had proliferated around Atlanta and that sold, among other items, marijuana pipes designed as *Star Wars* space guns and comic books that introduced young people to the logistics of rolling joints and snorting cocaine. Out of the accumulated outrage of Sue Rusche and other parents sprang DeKalb County Families in Action.

It was not the first or only anti-marijuana group, of course. At about the same time several of the leading anti-marijuana scientists formed the American Council on Marijuana, with offices in New York, to hold anti-drug conferences and to be a forum for their views. But what Families in Action and other parents' groups around the country brought to the anti-drug cause were the foot soldiers without which no political movement can succeed: in this case concerned parents who were willing to attend city-council meetings, buttonhole state legislators, and otherwise inject themselves into the political process.

Families in Action made a crucial political decision when it made the paraphernalia industry its prime target. No one has been able to stop marijuana from coming into this country, or to stop people from smoking it, but, politically speaking, the head shops were sitting ducks, and FIA opened up on them with both barrels. Soon its members had persuaded the Georgia legislature to pass three anti-paraphernalia laws that were designed to close down all the head shops in Georgia. There were, however, various legal appeals open to the head-shop operators, despite the new laws, so they remained in business for a time. Then the angry parents demanded action from local officials, and the result was a series of police raids that, Rusche says, closed down all but three of the thirty-odd head shops in Atlanta.

Families in Action had become the catalyst for hundreds of community groups that were springing up all over America. One result was that scores of communities, and four states besides Georgia, passed anti-paraphernalia laws. Sue Rusche was well aware that closing head shops was not going to stop young people from smoking marijuana. But, she said, "It's part of the process." Every political movement needs early victories to give it momentum. Parents who had involved themselves in the political process, who had driven the hated head shops from their midst, would only be emboldened by that initial victory to move on to larger political goals. By the spring of 1980 Rusche and other leaders of the new movement were meeting in

Washington to organize a national political alliance that they hoped
could help turn the tide against marijuana use in America.

The new movement already had considerable political power. Its
first stirrings had been in 1977, when some of its leaders would come to
Washington to protest to Peter Bourne about the Carter administration's support of decriminalization. At that point, the smokers,
through NORML, were a better-organized and more vocal political
force, and it was to them that Bourne and other officials were most
responsive. In retrospect, the Bourne affair in the summer of 1978 was
a turning point, symbolically and to a degree politically, in the
marijuana debate, for it discredited NORML, removed Bourne from
government, and put the Carter administration on the defensive on
the drug issue. Bourne's successor in the White House, Lee Dogoloff,
wanted nothing to do with NORML and was soon busy catering to the
wishes of the increasingly well-organized and vocal parents' movement.

Politically, President Carter was on record as favoring decriminalization, he was almost certain to run in 1980 against a Republican who
opposed it, and the last thing he needed was thousands of angry
anti-marijuana mothers marching against him. Thus, Lee Dogoloff
cultivated Sue Rusche, spoke to parents' groups around the country,
and invited their leaders to White House seminars on drugs. Besides
this conventional political stroking, the White House took one step
that was important to the anti-marijuana movement both as a symbol
and in practical terms: It had prodded the Justice Department into
producing a model anti-paraphernalia law that state legislatures could
use to outlaw head shops. This model law was of dubious constitutionality, but it was dramatic proof to the anti-marijuana parents of
America that their crusade had the blessing of the Carter administration.

By 1980 Sue Rusche had access to the White House, was sought after
after by the media, and was often invited to testify before congressional
committees. She had not yet got the federal or foundation money
she wanted for Families in Action, but the DeKalb County government
had given FIA $15,000 to teach teachers about drug abuse, and there
was the prospect of more money on the way. Sue Rusche had, in fact,
only one problem: She had political power, but she didn't know what
her political goals were. "I know what I don't want," she admitted,

"but not what I want." In that, as in many things, she was emblematic of the movement she had helped create.

The parents' movement came into existence because it was not only college students and Vietnam veterans and young professionals who took up marijuana smoking in the 1960s and 1970s. More and more teenagers, and even preteenagers, were smoking. A 1978 government survey reported that one high-school senior in nine was smoking every day, and about half smoked occasionally. Moreover, the survey said that 8 percent of the nation's sixth- and seventh-graders had at least tried marijuana, and 29 percent of the eighth- and ninth-graders. Without question, more adolescents were smoking, were smoking at an earlier age, were smoking more often, and were smoking the increasingly stronger marijuana that was becoming available.

Parents, although increasingly alarmed by their children's smoking, were by and large less politically sophisticated than the young lawyers who had started the reform movement and had been less quick to organize for political action. At first, many parents felt guilt or shame that their children were smoking, and felt theirs was a family problem. But in time many of them came to think in political terms and to feel that the reform movement was their enemy, that the removal of criminal penalties for adult marijuana use would lead inevitably to increased teenage use. So, in Atlanta and elsewhere, the parents began to organize, and their movement was aided by the fact that its rise coincided with the disintegration of the reform coalition.

As the 1980s began, NORML, demoralized and discredited by Stroup's role in the Bourne affair, was struggling to stay afloat, financially and politically. Both the political and the judicial tides were running against the pro-marijuana activists. No decriminalization bill had passed since Nebraska's in 1978. NORML's long battle to stop the paraquat spraying in Mexico had failed. A federal court rejected their right-of-privacy challenge to the federal marijuana law, and there seemed no point in even attempting an appeal to the Supreme Court. Similarly, a challenge to the California law had been rejected, as had those in ten other states, and the 1975 Alaska supreme-court decision increasingly looked like a fluke rather than the wave of the future. The U.S. Supreme Court, in response to an appeal by the state of Virginia, ruled that Roger Davis's forty-year term for selling marijuana was not cruel and unusual punishment, and ordered Davis back to prison.

Virtually the only bright spot was on the medical-use issue. In only two years twenty other states had followed New Mexico's example and passed medical-use laws, although the federal government continued to drag its bureaucratic feet and call for more research.

During the summer of 1980 the Food and Drug Administration, responding to increasing pressure from the scientific community, cancer patients, and the twenty-odd states that had approved medical use of marijuana, took a small step forward on the medical-use issue. FDA approved the use of THC pills by cancer patients if other forms of medicine had failed to relieve their nausea during chemotherapy treatments. Bob Randall and Alice O'Leary, who were working full time on the issue, Randall as president and O'Leary as director of a new group called Alliance for Cannibus Therapeutics (begun with a $5000 grant from the Playboy Foundation, after several other foundations had turned them down), criticized the FDA action for not going far enough. For one thing, the new program did not permit glaucoma patients to use the THC pill. Randall believes this was simply because the plight of cancer patients is more dramatic and therefore created greater political pressures. "Cancer patients vomit in their doctors' offices and die in great pain," he says. "People with glaucoma just quietly go blind." Even for cancer patients, the THC pill is considered unsatisfactory, by Randall and O'Leary and many scientists, because it simply is not as effective in reducing nausea as smoking marijuana. Ironically, while less effective, the THC pill is actually stronger and causes some patients to hallucinate. Patients say they can control the dosage when they smoke, by inhaling the marijuana smoke as needed, but the pill has unpredictable results. Randall and O'Leary say the pill should be available for people who object to marijuana-smoking, but that government-produced marijuana should also be available for those patients whom the pill does not help. O'Leary and Randall, and many others who have followed the issue, think that the FDA was simply afraid, for political reasons, to permit government-approved smoking. A marijuana pill is all right—Americans approve of pill-taking—but smoking is still too controversial. As a practical matter, many cancer patients will prefer illegal street marijuana to legal but ineffective THC pills, but the bureaucrats can now claim to have done something to help them.

Many people who had contributed in one way or another to the reform movement in the seventies were gone by the 1980s. The Drug Abuse Council was out of business. Peter Bourne had been appointed to a United Nations post and was not concerned with the drug issue. Dr. Robert DuPont, a champion of decriminalization in 1974–76 as the Ford administration's top drug expert, had recanted, and was speaking out against decriminalization. Mike Aldrich, the veteran of LeMar and Amorphia, was a director of the Fitz Hugh Ludlow Memorial Library in San Francisco and was writing a book on cocaine. Blair Newman, Amorphia's founder, had graduated from the Harvard School of Business and opened a computer consulting firm.

Stroup was no longer involved in NORML's day-to-day activities, but he continued as the chairman of its board of directors, and in the spring of 1980 he became concerned that his successor, Larry Schott, was not giving the pot lobby the aggressive leadership it needed. He therefore engineered action by the board that led to Schott's resignation. A search then began for a new national director for NORML, and Stroup's hope was that someone young and aggressive could be found, someone, indeed, much like himself ten years before.

Stroup, in starting his new law firm, had advanced from championing the cause of drug users to championing that of drug dealers. Many law firms took drug-smuggling cases reluctantly, if at all, glad to have the fees but not really approving of their clients. Stroup's firm—his partners were Gerald Goldstein, of San Antonio; James Jenkins, of Atlanta; and Michael Pritzker, of Chicago—not only defended drug dealers but unabashedly declared that the laws against them were wrong and should be repealed. The firm observed certain limits. Stroup said he would not represent PCP or heroin dealers, any more than he would represent someone accused of a crime of violence; nor would the firm represent clients who intended to turn on their fellow dealers to win leniency for themselves. But Stroup defended marijuana and cocaine dealers with all the zeal he had once brought to getting smokers out of jail. ("Convicted drug dealers," he declared, "were actually political prisoners.") He numbered many drug dealers among his friends, and he felt that in defending them he was in effect defending himself and everyone in the drug culture. As he saw it, everyone who used drugs was indebted to the people who took risks to supply them. "None of us is free until they're free," he would declare.

Clearly, Stroup was once more at the cutting edge of the drug issue, which was precisely where he wanted to be, and, it seemed, where he had some deep emotional need to be. His new role provided him with a more expensive life-style than he had enjoyed as head of NORML, but he also felt that he was in far more danger as an outspoken drug lawyer than he had been as a pot lobbyist. Stroup and his partners were well aware that the government was bringing more and more cases against drug lawyers, whom they most often charged either with bankrolling drug deals or with putting one dealer in touch with another and thus becoming party to a drug conspiracy. Drug lawyers saw this as a government effort to harass them and thus to discourage vigorous defense of drug dealers. Often, the defense lawyers charged, the prosecutors in effect said to a convicted drug dealer, "Give us your lawyer and you can go free," and the dealer would give perjured testimony against his lawyer rather than go to prison himself. "We view this as a war," one federal prosecutor said of the cases against drug lawyers, and the lawyers involved could only agree.

Stroup savored the controversy and combat, genuinely liked most of his clients, but necessarily moved warily, never sure if a fast-talking would-be client might turn out to be a DEA agent. In his private life he was, if not mellowing with age, at least growing more cautious. He no longer traveled with drugs, and he kept only small amounts on hand for his personal use. He was still living with Lynn Darling, in a luxury apartment near his Georgetown law office, and though marijuana was still very much a part of his life-style, he was also becoming something of a connoisseur of wine.

Another pro-reform spokesman of the 1970s who was retiring from the battle was Dr. Norman Zinberg, one of the nation's most serious and sophisticated students of the drug issue. Zinberg had never advocated legalization of marijuana, only decriminalization, and he felt that further research into its possible harm was needed. But he also believed, as a matter of scientific fact, that the new evidence had proved nothing that seriously challenged the Marijuana Commission's 1972 verdict on marijuana. He became an important spokesman for decriminalization, both in his writings and as a witness before legislative committees, and was closely associated with NORML. For his troubles he had been insulted by right-wing congressmen during legislative testimony, and by 1979 several of them were demanding his resignation from a prestigious advisory committee to the National

Institutes of Health, on the grounds that anyone who was associated with NORML was unfit to advise the government. It was classic guilt by association, what Zinberg's colleague Dr. Lester Grinspoon calls "psychopharmacological McCarthyism." The political pressure was accompanied by what Zinberg regarded as attacks on him in the press. Early in 1980 Zinberg responded to a reporter's inquiries about the government's latest anti-marijuana pronouncements only to find himself portrayed as a pro-marijuana crazy. Soon thereafter he told me, "I'm afraid your book will have to have an unhappy ending. I'll give you one example. I'm getting out, not giving any more interviews on marijuana, and so are a lot of other scientists I know. The sad part is there's no one to take our place. But we've been burned. I think I'm a rational person, but now I've been set up as a radical straw man to be ridiculed."

Such was the state of affairs as Sue Rusche and others in the anti-marijuana movement tried to determine just what their positive political goals should be.

Sue Rusche had started out being disturbed by teenage marijuana use, but the more she thought about it, the more she found to be concerned about. She was worried about adult drug use, and the example it set for children, and the possibility that America was becoming a drug-dependent society. She was (as one who had tried for years to kick the cigarette habit) concerned about the health hazards of cigarettes. She would say, only partly in jest, that they should be outlawed too. She disapproved of rock concerts, because of all the drug use that went on, but she wasn't sure what to do about them. It disturbed her that more and more mothers worked, and thus more and more children came home from school, had no parent at home, resented that fact, and acted out their anger with drugs. It concerned her that more and more children in their early teens were drinking, having unchaperoned parties, and engaging in sex. She was fearful that decriminalization would not only lead to more marijuana use but would have a domino effect and lead to social approval and perhaps legalization of cocaine, hallucinogens, and even heroin. She loathed NORML, and she once refused to sign a National Institute of Drug Abuse–sponsored letter condemning teenage drug use, because

Stroup had signed it and she was unwilling to make alliance with the devil. She was concerned about groceries' and drugstores' selling cigarette papers that could be used to smoke marijuana, and by rock groups that sang pro-drug lyrics and by disc jockeys who made joking references to drug use and by supermarkets that sold beer to minors. The list of her concerns was all but endless.

She felt strongly about all these social problems, she was a leader of a potent national political movement, and the question was what she and that movement could do to set things right. What are you for if you are against marijuana? The fact was that Sue Rusche, an intelligent and well-intentioned person, wasn't sure. She wasn't even sure how she stood on decriminalization. On the one hand, she didn't want to see anyone go to jail simply for smoking, but on the other hand, she thought it best to keep criminal penalties so the young understood that society was serious about discouraging marijuana. In a larger sense, Rusche and the anti-marijuana movement, for all their activity and early successes, had really not settled on their long-range goal. Was it to stop young people from using drugs? Or was it to stop everyone, minors and adults, from using drugs? Was the latter goal necessary, to achieve the former? Or would the latter goal, by being too ambitious, make even the former goal unattainable? Sue Rusche wasn't sure. In the meantime, her immediate political goals, beyond the closing of head shops, are stiffer penalties for drug smugglers, including fines to be used for drug education, and more public money to be used for drug education, including of course those that would be directed by Families in Action.

Rusche has given a good deal of thought to the pro-legalization argument that is advanced by many responsible people and runs like this:

Marijuana is here to stay; therefore we must make the best of the situation. We should begin by recognizing that adult use and adolescent use are separate issues. We should legalize and regulate marijuana for adults, just as we do alcohol, and enforce the laws against sales to minors. Legalization would end a great deal of crime and corruption, and it would also bring in billions of dollars in tax revenues, which could be used for, among other things, drug education. While legalizing adult use, we would make every effort to educate the young to the dangers of drug abuse and to point them toward responsible drug use, if they must indeed use drugs as adults.

This argument, Rusche admits, is "tempting," particularly the parts about ending crime and providing money for drug education. But on balance she rejects it because she is not willing to accept the idea that marijuana is here to stay and because she thinks that the adult-use and adolescent-use issues are indivisible. If you accept adult use, she thinks, you will inevitably encourage adolescent use.

But how are people to be stopped from using marijuana? Not by law enforcement, certainly, for the DEA and other agencies are spending hundreds of millions of dollars each year and only stopping some 10 percent of the marijuana that is imported into the country or grown domestically. The hope, Rusche thinks, lies in changing attitudes. She accepts the new evidence on marijuana, of course, and thus thinks it is at least as dangerous as alcohol or tobacco, and she hopes young people can be persuaded of that. Moreover, her experience in dealing with other parents all across America gives her hope that millions of people share her concerns and want to cut back on alcohol and tobacco, to set better examples for their children, and to change society by changing themselves. Drawing on her experience in the civil-rights movement, she says, "People used to say that segregation had been with us for four hundred years and we couldn't change. But the civil-rights movement taught us that we can change social attitudes, and I think we can change them on marijuana as well."

One of Sue Rusche's allies in the new anti-marijuana movement is Dr. Robert DuPont, the tall, handsome young psychiatrist who was a senior drug-policy official during the Nixon and Ford administrations. As we have noted, DuPont kept quiet about his pro-decriminalization views during the Nixon years, but once Gerald Ford became president and the mood began to change in Washington, DuPont began speaking out in favor of no-jail laws, and even attended NORML conferences to endorse marijuana-law reform.

But in 1977 the Democrats came to power, and DuPont lost his government post. He started the Institute for Behavior and Health, Inc., in Bethesda, Maryland, which conducts research and demonstration programs intended to prevent drug and alcohol abuse. Soon thereafter, DuPont reversed himself on decriminalization. This is how he explained his change of heart in one talk:

I for years supported decriminalization. Only within the last two years have I realized to my chagrin ("horror" is the better way to describe my feeling) that decriminalization is an issue that is not and cannot be dealt with on the basis of the substance of the issue. On the substantive merits of the issue, everybody is for decriminalization. But the real issue is symbolic. Nobody wants to have anyone, young or old, go to jail for possession of small amounts of marijuana. But being in favor of decriminalization is seen by the majority of the public as being in favor of pot. I have tried for five years to make clear that I oppose the use of marijuana and that I oppose the use of jail for pot smokers.

You must think about things and communicate them in such simple terms that you are either for or against them. If you are for decriminalization, you are, in the public mind, for pot. That process has forced me to retreat on my earlier position on decriminalization. . . . It is possible to eliminate jail as a threat for simple possession of marijuana without favoring decriminalization. That is the way out! In fact, as a nation we have already done that: Nowhere in his nation today are people in jail for possession of small amounts of marijuana. Those who now go to jail are the sellers of marijuana, and—in my opinion—too few of them are behind bars!

What this rather tortured language reflects is the fact that decriminalization has become a symbol, a political code word. If NORML is for it, decent people must be against it. Sue Rusche told me, "I'm for decriminalization, but I don't like to use that word, because that's what NORML's for," and there are people in the anti-marijuana movement who are starting to talk about "recriminalization." Jail or no jail, at this late date, is still an issue.

Dr. DuPont argues that to be anti-marijuana you must be anti-decriminalization. But because he isn't comfortable seeming pro-jail, he is forced to make the extremely dubious claim, "Nowhere in this nation today are people in jail for possession of small amounts of marijuana." Hundreds of people are arrested for possession of marijuana each day, and as long as criminal penalties are on the books, some judges will apply them, and most often against people who are poor, black, or politically unpopular. In an interview DuPont went even further and argued not only that no one went to jail anymore but also that jail had never been a serious threat to marijuana smokers: That was only NORML propaganda. "I misunderstood the issue," he said. "My heart was going out to the people who were arrested, and I missed the boat. So did the Shafer [the Marijuana] Commission and so have many judges. Decriminalization is a symbolic issue, a red herring. I have a hunch that not many people ever went to jail, and I think the influence on their lives has been exaggerated."

DuPont's change of heart on decriminalization is not without political benefit to him. He achieved national prominence during the Nixon and Ford administrations, and when some future Republican administration comes to office, he would be an obvious choice for a senior position in the health field. But his prospects of appointment would be greatly reduced if the vocal anti-marijuana groups—the Sue Rusches of America—opposed him because he was pro-decriminalization and thus seen as pro-drug. Thus, DuPont's *mea culpa* is a useful political device for him, one that puts him on the safe side of an explosive issue.

DuPont argues that both decriminalization and medical use are irrelevant issues. (The state legislatures, he says, are a "poor forum" to settle the medical-use question.) The real issue, he says, is public health. The use of marijuana and other drugs must be discouraged for the same reason, if not in quite the same ways, that alcohol and tobacco must be discouraged, because of the danger to people's health. DuPont believes, much as Sue Rusche does, that the nation is ready to reform itself, to turn away from the excesses of the past. He notes that as public awareness of the dangers of tobacco has grown, cigarette-smoking has declined. He notes that the use of certain types of prescription drugs, such as barbiturates, has declined. He thinks Americans are ready to use less alcohol and marijuana, as they know the dangers of them. The renewed interest in diet and exercise is one sign of the new attitudes. The challenge is to use various forms of social and cultural pressure to turn more and more people away from drugs. The ban on cigarette-smoking in restaurants and public buildings in one example, he says, and higher insurance premiums for people who smoke are another.

DuPont, like Rusche, recognizes the attractions of a system of legal, regulated marijuana, but rejects it because he also thinks adult and adolescent smoking can't be separated. "Regulation didn't work with teenage alcohol and tobacco use," he says, "and it won't work with marijuana." DuPont of course accepts the various new-evidence reports and argues strongly that marijuana is more dangerous than alcohol or tobacco. "I'll bet that in five years no one will dispute the dangers of marijuana," he says. "By then the pro-marijuana people will be like the pro-tobacco people: They'll concede the dangers but argue the right to smoke. They'll ask, 'Do you have a right to punish me for what I choose to do?' And the answer to that is yes. No man is an island. Society has a right to protect itself. I think the future holds more regulation on alcohol and tobacco. We don't want to increase the freedom of people to use drugs. Drug use is not an inalienable right under the U.S. Constitution."

Doctors are, of course, not always the best interpreters of the Constitution. Indeed, it is arguments of social engineers like DuPont that drive conservatives like William Buckley and James Kilpatrick to the defense of marijuana. For who can be sure that if Big Brother, acting in the name of public health, decides to prohibit one man's marijuana today, he may not decide to prohibit another man's predinner cocktail or postdinner cigar tomorrow? Our society has traditionally believed that once a person reaches maturity, he is in control of his own life. Knowing all the terrible costs of alcohol and tobacco, we tax them and warn people against them, but we do not use criminal penalties to prohibit them. We tried that once, with alcohol, and the experiment was a colossal failure.

The degree of danger involved in an activity is, of course, a major factor in determining if that activity should be restricted. That is why the new evidence is so important to the anti-marijuana movement. If marijuana is as nearly harmless as Drs. Zinberg and Grinspoon think, then it should be legal. If, by contrast, it is as harmful as Dr. DuPont thinks, there is a case to be made for its prohibition. It is difficult for the layman to form an opinion when distinguished scientists are in such total disagreement. But the consensus of the scientific community is still what the Marijuana Commission found in 1972: that marijuana, used in moderation, is in effect harmless. The new evidence time and again, on examination, proves to be tentative or inconclusive. Often, highly technical disputes arise about whether a particular dosage level to monkeys or rats is the equivalent of a few joints a day in a human or dozens of joints. A related dispute arises over whether feeding animals pure THC, the active ingredient in marijuana, can be equated with humans' smoking marijuana. One much-publicized study showed that men who were heavy marijuana smokers had lowered levels of the male hormone testosterone and reduced sperm production, but (the small print) even those lowered levels were still in the normal range, and other studies showed no lowering of testosterone at all. A UCLA researcher charged that a controversial NBC television documentary on marijuana had distorted his findings on possible lung damage by equating the smoking of five joints with the smoking of five packs of cigarettes.

The federal government has since 1967 spent more than $35 million to conduct more than a thousand marijuana-research projects. In the summer of 1979 Dr. William Pollin, director of the National Institute on Drug Abuse, gave detailed testimony on the government's findings on marijuana to a congressional committee. Dr. Pollin stressed that marijuana was not "safe." He stressed that young people should not smoke it. But time after time, in his highly technical testimony, though he pointed out possible dangers of marijuana, he also said that actual harm had not been proved. Here are some selections from Dr. Pollin's testimony:

Effects on the heart: "Acute effects of marijuana use on heart function in healthy young male volunteers have been viewed as benign."

On lung damage: "One study has found that smoking four or more 'joints' per week decreases vital capacity—the amount of air the lungs can move following a deep breath—as much as smoking nearly a pack of cigarettes a day. This comparison, while widely quoted, needs confirmation by independent studies. As yet, there is no direct clinical evidence that marijuana-smoking causes lung cancer."

Effects on the body's natural defenses against infection and disease: "Taking the body of animal and human evidence as a whole, the results to date are far from clear-cut in establishing whether or not the human immune response is impaired by marijuana."

Brain-damage research: "A British research report, which original-ly appeared in 1971, attributed brain atrophy to cannabis use in a group of young male users. It continues to be widely cited, particular-ly in the mass media. . . . This research was faulted on several grounds: All of the patients had used other drugs, making the causal connection with marijuana use questionable, and the appropriateness of the comparison group and diagnostic technique was questionable."

On studies suggesting brain damage to monkeys: "While both these experiments demonstrate the possibility that more subtle changes in brain functioning or structure may occur as a result of marijuana-smoking, at least in animals, the implications of these changes for subsequent human or animal behavior are at present unknown."

Psychological effects: "The question of whether or not enduring psychological effects occur in chronic users remains to be resolved. While three more carefully controlled studies of heavy users in Jamaica, Greece, and Costa Rica failed to find evidence of marijuana-related psychological impairment, it is possible that the mode of use there differed from American use."

Effects on female reproductive function: "One recently completed study of 26 females who used 'street' marijuana three times a week or more for six months or more found that these women had three times as many defective monthly cycles as nonusing women. By 'defective' was meant a failure to produce a ripened egg during the cycle or a possible shortened period of fertility. Unfortunately, since the marijuana-using women also used more alcohol it cannot be assumed that the effects observed were necessarily the result of marijuana use. . . . These and other studies using higher doses of marijuana or THC all underscore the undesirability of use, especially during pregnancy. Research directly concerning effects on human reproduction is, however, very limited. We know of no clinical reports directly linking marijuana use and birth abnormality."

Chromosome damage: "While there were earlier reports of increases in chromosomal breaks and abnormalities in human cell cultures, more recent results have been inconclusive. . . . Overall, there continues to be no convincing evidence that marijuana use causes clinically significant chromosome damage."

The hazards of marijuana versus other drugs: "Thus, any attempt to compare the health impact of marijuana with that of alcohol and tobacco at *current levels* of use is certain to minimize the hazards of marijuana."

And so it goes. Many dangers are hinted at, but few if any are actually proved. Indeed, many scientists are amazed that any drug, under such intense scrutiny, could prove to do such little physical damage to humans. This is not to say that marijuana is entirely harmless. There is obviously a case to be made that it is harmful to inhale hot smoke into the lungs, that no one should drive a car when high, that a person who is stoned cannot function in society, that the excessive use of marijuana should be avoided, that young people should be discouraged from smoking it, and that research into its possible ill effects should be continued. But there is also a case to be made that the anti-marijuana forces have tried, perhaps with the noblest of intentions, to use very tentative, inconclusive scientific data as a new, more sophisticated version of the reefer-madness campaign of the 1930s. Then, the anti-marijuana crusaders warned that marijuana would turn its users into violent criminals. Now the opponents of marijuana say, "It may make you feel good, but it is actually giving you cancer and/or damaging your brain and/or making you impotent and/or crippling your unborn children."

The problem is that the opponents of marijuana overstate their case. Every indication is that they scare more nonsmokers than smokers. To take one example, one of the more colorful and widely publicized new evidence allegations is that smoking marijuana causes young men to grow breasts. Dr. DuPont sometimes cites this alarming possibility in his talks to young people. But Sue Rusche has quit using that example, because she's had too many teenagers laugh in her face. The danger is that if young people don't believe the scare stories about marijuana, they're likely not to believe valid warnings about genuinely dangerous drugs like PCP, LSD, and heroin.

Still, whatever one thinks of the scientific merit of the "new evidence," it has without doubt been politically effective. The new allegations have effectively discredited the Marijuana Commission's 1972 findings. In the real world millions of people continue to smoke—marijuana is *de facto* legal—but in the political world there is stalemate. The reform movement is not likely to pass decriminalization bills in any more states soon, but neither is the anti-marijuana movement likely to "recriminalize" any states. The prospects for a clear-cut national policy, for legalization on the one hand or for the elimination of marijuana on the other, seem very dim.

Presidential leadership might end the political deadlock, of course, but the question is in what direction the leadership might lead. As I write this, it appears that either Jimmy Carter or Ronald Reagan will be elected president for the 1981–85 term. The difference between them would likely be considerable. Reagan had a staunchly anti-marijuana record as governor of California, and, campaigning in 1980, he embraced the new evidence and repeatedly warned that marijuana was the most dangerous drug in America. He apparently believes what he says, and his election could only be a disaster for those who hope to see reform of the drug laws.

Carter, by contrast, is a moderate on the issue. He knows that his sons and many of the people around him have smoked, and he knows all too well that America has many more urgent problems than marijuana. He has, moreover, witnessed as president dramatic examples of the injustice of the drug laws, in the Peter Bourne and Hamilton Jordan affairs. Both men may have acted most unwisely—Bourne to go to the NORML party and Jordan to go to Studio 54—but neither man, in any reasonable world, deserves to have his career destroyed or to be treated as a criminal. Whatever one may think of Hamilton Jordan personally, it is outrageous that he had to spend tens of thousands of dollars to defend himself against a federal investigation of a charge that he used cocaine. The point is not Jordan but that the same McCarthyist tactics could be used against hundreds of the most able young people in government, and by people whose motivations would have everything to do with partisan politics and nothing to do with public health. (In the early 1980s, cocaine is still in the "reefer madness" stage of public fear and uncertainty that marijuana was in two or three decades before. In fact, the Drug Abuse Council, in its final report, *The Facts About Drug Abuse*, concluded, "Medical experts generally agree that cocaine produces few observable adverse health consequences," and added that the biggest health problem caused by cocaine is runny noses.)

If Carter, in the safety of a second term, wanted to move the country forward on drug policy, an obvious starting point would be federal approval of the medical use of marijuana. He might also, in his quest for budget cuts, look at the hundreds of millions of dollars that are being spent in a largely futile effort to stop the importation of marijuana. On any cost-effectiveness scale, the anti-smuggling program is a joke, and much of its money would be better invested in drug-education programs. Perhaps the most useful step Carter could take would be to appoint a new presidential commission on marijuana, both to examine the scientific controversy and to propose long-term national policy on drugs.

Still, that sort of presidential leadership may or may not be forthcoming. Politicians have tended to follow, not to lead, on drug issues. The surest agent of change on the marijuana issue is likely to be simply time. If we step back a bit from the political battles of recent years—from the reform movement's successes in passing decriminalization bills, and the anti-marijuana movement's success in closing head shops—the overriding political fact is that more and more people are using marijuana. Between 1964 and 1978 the percentage of Americans who had used marijuana rose from 2 to 25 percent. Something like 50 million Americans have used it by now, perhaps half of them smoke regularly, and they spend more than $25 billion a year on the weed. The key fact is not the number of smokers—they are still a minority —but the ages involved. Government figures for 1978 said that only 7 percent of the people over age thirty-five had used marijuana, but 44 percent of those age twenty-six to thirty-four had, 62 percent of those twenty-two to twenty-five, and 58 percent of those eighteen to twenty-one. In short, the time is coming when a majority of Americans will have smoked, and there is every reason to think they will be more tolerant of marijuana than the present, nonsmoking majority. Ultimately, marijuana is a political issue. Today most politicians (and many scientists) are responding to a political majority that opposes marijuana. When a majority approves of marijuana, there is every reason to think the politicians will respond to its wishes.

Until then, we are living through a period of transition, a time of uncertainty and compromise, as the country tries to make up its mind. It may be, of course, that Rusche and DuPont are right, and the nation is at the brink of a moral renaissance, and we will begin to turn away from alcohol, tobacco, marijuana, and all drugs. Certainly one of the benefits of the marijuana controversy is that we have increasingly been forced (often by our children) to consider marijuana's ill effects in comparison to those of alcohol and tobacco. Certainly an increase in drug education in the schools, if honest and realistic, might reduce all drug use and could only benefit the nation.

But all human history teaches that people like to get high, to relax with one drug or another, and it is likely that we are entering not a period of reduced drug use so much as a period of shifting drug use. It is likely that in the years ahead, we will smoke more marijuana, drink more wine and beer, drink less hard liquor, smoke fewer cigarettes, and use less (or milder) hallucinogenic drugs. This period of change and experimentation should also be a time of learning, on both sides of the generation gap. Parents need to recognize the difference between drug use and drug abuse, to recognize that a normal teenager can smoke an occasional joint or drink an occasional beer without disaster. Parents need also to consider to what extent they have used marijuana as a scapegoat for their own failures. If a child who is unloved at three turns to drugs at thirteen, it is not NORML that deserves the blame. Young people for their part need to recognize that drug abuse really can damage their lives, and that some drugs are dangerous even on an experimental basis.

We need, in this period of transition, to examine some of the larger questions that underlie the marijuana controversy. To what extent have we become a nation of drug users—Dad with his martinis, Mom with her Valium, and Junior with his marijuana? What does it say about our schools if kids would rather be stoned all day than try to learn? To what extent have we used the marijuana laws, like the sex and obscenity laws, as tools of social control against nonconformists and especially against the rebellious young? To what extent have our pressures on the young pushed them toward drugs? (Dr. DuPont, in one of his talks, quoted an educator who said he was in the business of "creating and managing anxiety" among the young—via tests, grades, SAT scores, and the like—and DuPont went on to say it was understandable that educators would resent marijuana, because it enabled students to escape that anxiety. Perhaps so, but it is also understandable if the teenager being thus manipulated may occasionally choose to beat the game by getting stoned.) There is a great deal we need to consider before we are likely to arrive at a coherent national policy on marijuana, alcohol, or any other drug.

My own view is that we will eventually reach a national consensus that marijuana is a mild drug, like beer or wine, that should be legal and regulated. Inevitably, the issues of adult and adolescent marijuana use must be addressed separately, and the two sides in the debate will have to reach some political accommodation. The anti-marijuana forces are going to have to accept adult marijuana use and focus their energies on discouraging adolescent use. By definition, no political movement can get far that defines half the young lawyers and politicians in America as criminals. At the same time, smokers will have to support programs to discourage smoking by young people. Legalization and regulation of marijuana will not be a perfect system, but ours is not a perfect world, and it will come because it is the least-bad system.

It is truly mind-boggling to step back and look dispassionately at America's marijuana policy over the past fifty years. We have wasted billions of dollars, polarized the nation, damaged thousands of lives, and defined millions of respectable people as criminals, all over a mild intoxicant that every serious study has pronounced less harmful than beer. It is difficult to imagine how we, or indeed our worst enemies, could have developed a more wrong-headed policy. It is as if Harry Anslinger, James Eastland, Richard Nixon, and all the others had been agents of the Kremlin, hell-bent on sowing dissension among us. Our marijuana policy has become a domestic Vietnam, a national disgrace. If it weren't so tragic, it would be hilarious.

Still, there has been progress. In the 1970s, thanks to the efforts of, among others, NORML, the Marijuana Commission, and the Drug Abuse Council, America began to face up to the complexities of the marijuana issue. In just a few years we advanced from widespread arrest and jail for smokers to a national consensus that simple marijuana-smoking should not be punished by jail, and toward serious debate of marijuana's eventual legalization. NORML's role in all this was quite remarkable. There had been presidential commissions before, and Ford Foundation projects, but there had never before been a national lobby on behalf of people who were violating the law. For a few amazing years in the middle of the decade, largely because of Stroup's creativity and audacity, a well-organized pro-marijuana minority was able to seize political momentum and to pass decriminalization laws in a dozen states. Inevitably the anti- marijuana majority caught on to what was happening and a reaction set in, but the issues had been raised, progress had been made, and the debate would never be so one-sided again.

There will be more progress in the years ahead, but it will almost certainly be slow—evolutionary rather than dramatic. It may be ten or twenty years before there is a consensus for legal marijuana. Until then, we will continue to have confusion and occasional hardship, and the best we can hope for is a maximum of tolerance and a minimum of self-righteousness from those who feel so strongly on both sides of the issue.

Index

Acapulco Gold papers, 87
Agnew, Spiro T., 117
Alaska, 4, 159–61
Alcoholic beverages, 47, 181
    See also Prohibition
Aldrich, Michael R., 55–56, 67, 87–89,
    128–29, 307
Alliance for Cannibus Therapeutics,
    306
American Bar Association (ABA), 70,
    105
American Civil Liberties Union
    (ACLU), 60
American Council on Marijuana, 303
American Medical Association
    (AMA), 52
Amorphia, 14, 41, 56, 67, 80, 86–90,
    97, 99, 128
Amotivational syndrome, 131, 132
Amphetamines, 36–37, 137
Anderson, Jack, 7, 23, 65, 243, 272,
    278, 280, 283, 285

Angarola, Robert, 222, 231–35
Anslinger, Harry Jacob, 49–52
Anti-marijuana movement, 300–14,
    317–20
Apodaca, Jerry, 247
Aragon, Manny, 247
Archer, Guy, 41, 67–68, 80, 101, 118
Armstrong, Louis, 49
Arnstein, Bobbie, 44, 73, 75–79, 135,
    139–49
Ashford, Robert H.A., 89, 100–101

Baba Ram Dass (Richard Alpert), 76
Baker, Bobby, 32–33
Baker, George, 212, 213, 215
Barbiturates, 206–207
Bayh, Birch, 162–63
Beal, Dana, 18
Beatty, Warren, 77, 78
Benton, Barbi, 78, 136
BLOSSOM (Basic Liberation of
    Smokers and Sympathizers of

Marijuana), 80, 84–86
BNDD. *See* Bureau of Narcotics and Dangerous Drugs
Bonnie, Richard, 93, 163, 222
Bourne, Peter, 6–8, 191–200, 210, 216–17, 225, 227–29, 232–35, 304, 307, 318
  background of, 17
  cocaine use by, 17–24, 278–81, 283, 285–91
  medical uses of marijuana and, 242–244
  at NORML party (1977), 17–24
  paraquat spraying program in Mexico and, 17, 205–208, 250–52, 270–72, 274–75
  Quāālude prescription incident and, 275–78
Bradley, Ed, 270
Brecher, Ed, 162
Briggs, John, 155, 158
Briscoe, Dolph, 124, 125
Brooke, Edward W., 163
Brown, Edmund G. (Jerry), 152, 158
Brown, William J., 164, 167
Brown, Willie, 156
Brownell, Gordon, 8, 97–100, 128, 152–158, 224, 231, 286, 288
Bryant, Thomas, 106–108, 133, 134, 151, 153–54, 195, 233, 288, 289
Buckley, William F., Jr., 105–107, 202
Buffet, Jimmy, 291, 294
Buford, Winston, 183–85
Bureau of Narcotics and Dangerous Drugs (BNDD), 49, 70

Califano, Joseph, 250
California, 4, 88–89, 97, 99–101, 128, 150–59, 305
California Marijuana Initiative (CMI), 89–91, 97, 99–101
Cancer patients, 236, 243–48, 306
Carey, Hugh, 202
Carr, Bob, 133, 134, 233
Carter, Caron, 267–69
Carter, Chip, 7, 195, 197–99, 265–73
Carter, Jack, 192

Carter, Jimmy (Carter administration), 5–7, 12, 17, 23, 189–91, 194–99, 206, 210–11, 217, 251, 265, 266, 271, 277, 281, 284–85, 317, 318
Carter, Rosalynn, 199
Carter, Tim Lee, 64
Center for the Study of Non-Medical Drug Use, 108, 125
Chemotherapy, 245–46
Clark, Ramsey, 42–43, 59, 60, 65, 126, 129
CMI. *See* California Marijuana Initiative
Cocaine, 318
  at 1977 NORML party, 11–12, 19–24
  Bourne's use of, 278–81, 283, 285–291
Cohn, Gary, 233–35, 243, 278–79, 285
Colorado, 4, 162
Concerned Parents for Marijuana Reform, 123
Consumers' Union, 105
Controlled Substances Act of 1970, 237
Coombs, Jack, 172, 173, 294
Copetas, Craig, 18–22, 174, 177, 181, 182, 205, 219, 220, 224, 280–82, 291
Cowan, Richard, 105–106, 123
Cranston, Alan, 163

Darling, Lynn, 279, 292–93, 297–99, 308
Davis, Ed, 154, 158, 181
Davis, Roger, 126–27, 305
Dealers, 295, 307
Decriminalization, 3–6, 59, 105, 106, 150–68, 181, 195, 199–203, 211, 266, 304, 305, 308–13, 317
  in Alaska, 159–61
  in California, 151–59
  in Colorado, 162
  House hearings on (1977), 199–201
  in Maine, 161–62
  Marijuana Commission call for, 92–95

Decriminalization (*cont.*)
  in Ohio, 163–67
  in Oregon, 120–23, 134, 154
Demolli, Frank, 8, 111–17, 124–25, 295
Dennis, Walter, 63
Denver, John, 181
Dirksen, Everett, 28, 32
Dixon, Bill, 209
Dodson, Daryl, 207
Dogoloff, Lee, 304
Donahue, Phil, 253
Donovan, Hedley, 171
Drug Abuse Council, 41, 106–108,
  133–35, 154, 172, 318
Drug Enforcement Administration,
  103, 206, 208, 229, 230, 237, 240–
  242, 282
Drug Reform Act of 1970, 63
Dubois, Larry, 43, 45, 81, 82, 290
Dubois, Louise, 290
DuPont, Robert, 53, 151, 181, 200,
  307, 311–314, 317, 320
Dylan, Bob, 53–54

Earle, Ronnie, 125
Eastland, James O., 53, 129–33
Effects of marijuana, 131, 313–17
  Marijuana Commission report on,
  91–92, 94
Eisberg, Howard, 185–86, 252, 253
Eisenstat, Stu, 211
Esposito, John, 43

Falco, Mathea, 192, 206, 233, 274
Families in Action, 300, 303–305
Farnham, George, 228–30, 266, 284
Fiedler, Leslie, 56
Finlator, John, 61, 62, 122, 123, 176
Fioramonti, Frank, 41, 67–68, 105,
  118, 172, 173, 202
Fitzpatrick, Tom, 149
Food and Drug Administration, 242,
  248, 306
Forcade, Tom, 8, 13, 96, 172–79, 220,
  226, 251, 291, 294
Ford, Gerald R., 6, 150
Ford, John D., 204, 229
Ford Foundation, 106–108

Freedom of Information Act,
  128

Gaskill, Marlene, 267–68, 291
Georgia, 303
Giglotto, Herbert Joseph, 103–104
Ginsberg, Allen, 55, 56, 67
Glaucoma, 236, 238–45, 306
Goldstein, Gerald, 124, 127, 254–62,
  294, 296
Goodell, Charles, 63
Grannies for Grass, 100
Grinspoon, Lester, 61, 95, 96
Gutwillig, Bob, 43

Hallucinogens, 76, 81–83, 98
  See also specific hallucinogens
Hammond, Jay, 161
Hansell, Stafford, 121, 122, 154
Harrison Narcotic Act of 1914, 48–49
Hart, Philip, 163, 181
Hashish, 47–48, 165
Hay, John, 48
Hefner, Christie, 12, 15–18, 219, 220
Hefner, Hugh, 4, 8, 44–45, 73–79,
  135–40, 143–44, 146–49, 158, 172,
  187, 294
Hepler, Robert, 240
Herbicides, 70
  See also Paraquat
Heutlinger, Mark, 14, 22–23, 128, 222–
  224, 285–87
High Times (magazine), 13, 172, 176–
  178, 227, 301
Hines, William, 66
Hirschkop, Phil, 35
Hoover, J. Edgar, 50, 54
Horn, Vicky, 174
Horton, Pat, 121, 154, 163
Hughes, Harold, 64
Hume, Brett, 65

Indiana, 128
Initiatives. *See* Voter initiatives

Javits, Jacob, 64, 163, 181
Jocks for Joynts, 100
Johnson, Lyndon Baines, 36

Jones, Hardin, 154
Jordan, Hamilton, 195–99, 277, 318
Joseph, Burton, 44, 45, 60, 62–63

Kafoury, Steve, 120–23, 154
Kaplan, John, 43, 59, 68, 88
Kaplan, Ralph, 227
Kaye, Aaron, 13, 220–24
Kazickas, Jurate, 110, 124
Kennedy, David, 12, 20
Kilpatrick, James J., 106
Kincaid, Brain, 218
Koch, Ed, 63, 64
Kornbluth, Jesse, 207–208
Kraft, Joseph, 289
Kraft, Tim, 209, 272, 279
Kristofferson, Kris, 69–70
Kurzman, Marc, 217–18, 222–24, 231

La Guardia, Fiorello, 51
Lampe, Keith, 100
Lawyers Committee to Legalize
    Marijuana, 68
Leaflet, The (newsletter), 70–71, 125
Leary, Timothy, 130
Legalization of marijuana, 94, 95,
    310–11
Leichter, Franz, 68
LeMar (Legalize Marijuana), 55–56,
    87
Levin, Don, 227
Levitan, Stuart, 284–85
Liddy, G. Gordon, 56, 104
Linkletter, Art, 165–66
Long, Toby, 276
LSD, 83–84
Lucks, Linda, 218
Ludlow, Fitz Hugh, 47–48

McCall, Tom, 121
McCarthy, Leo, 155–57
MacDonald, Webster, Jr., 260, 262
McGovern, George, 1, 95–96
McNeally, Bob, 193, 209
Maine, 4, 161–62
Marijuana, 46–47
    decriminalization of. See
        Decriminalization

effects of. See Effects of marijuana
medical uses of, 235–48, 306, 313
National Commission on. See
    National Commission on
    Marijuana and Drug Abuse
1920s–1940s attitudes and legisla-
    tion on, 49–52
1960s spread of use of, 52–56
See also specific topics
Marijuana Commission. See National
    Commission on Marijuana and
    Drug Abuse
Marijuana Review, 56
Marijuana Tax Act of 1937, 51
Massachusetts, 123
Matthews, George, 141, 143–45
Maverick, Maury, Jr., 255
MDA, 67, 76, 81
Mead, Margaret, 60–61
Medical uses of marijuana, 235–48,
    306, 313
Meggyesy, Dave, 100
Merritt, John, 241–42
Metsky, Ellen, 7, 193, 198, 233, 275–
    278
Mexico, paraquat-spraying program
    in, 7, 17, 203–206, 211, 216–17,
    228–29, 249–52, 263, 265–67,
    269–75, 281–82
Meyers, Peter, 125–28, 218–19, 228,
    229, 249, 286
Michigan, 157
Miller, Ed, 96
Miller, Terry, 160
Minnesota, 201
Mississippi, 201–202
Mitchell, Betty, 295
Mitchell, Jerry, 182–86, 219, 252–54,
    295
Mitchell, John, 56, 71, 92
Mitchell, Roy, 295
Moore, Fred, 208–209, 269, 283–84,
    291, 292, 297
Moore, James, 162
Moore, Mary Tyler, 181
Morgan, Charles, 276, 281
Mori, Floyd, 158
Morphine, 48

Moscone, George, 152–57, 295
Mothers for Marijuana, 100
Mott, Stewart, 172

Nader, Ralph, 35, 36, 41, 58
National Commission on Mari-
    juana and Drug Abuse
    (Marijuana Commission), 2, 105,
    129–33
  1971 hearings of, 63–69
  report of, 91–95, 103, 132, 133
National Commission on Product
    Safety, 35–37, 39
National Institute for Drug Abuse
    (NIDA), 206, 208, 216, 229, 249–
    251
National Organization for the Reform
    of Marijuana Laws (NORML), 2,
    122, 124, 152, 156, 157, 167–68,
    171–74, 177–78, 321
  1971 hearings of the Marijuana
    Commission and, 63–69
  1974 conference of, 151
  1977 conference of, 216–24
  1977 party held by, 10–24
  1978 conference of, 295–97
  advisory board of directors of,
    59–62
  Drug Abuse Council and, 107–108,
    133–35, 172
  financial problems of, 171–72
  founding of, 41–43, 56–57
  The Leaflet (newsletter), 70–71, 125
  medical-reclassification project of,
    237, 239–40, 243–44
  other reform groups and, 84–90, 97,
    128
  People's Pot Conference held by
    (1972), 96
  Playboy Foundation and, 43–44, 72,
    73, 79, 172
  Stroup censured by, 290–91
  See also individual officers of
    NORML, and other specific
    topics
National Review, 105, 106
Nebraska, 203
Neier, Aryeh, 60

Nellis, Joseph, 200–201, 221–24, 231
Nelson, Gaylord, 163
Nelson, Willie, 264, 267–69, 283–85,
    289, 290
Nester, Billy, 166
Newman, Blair, 41, 56, 86–91, 99, 128,
    307
New Mexico, 237, 247, 248
Newsweek, 170–71
New York State, 68, 118, 202
New York Times, 254
New York Times Magazine, 2, 108,
    109
NIDA. See National Institute for
    Drug Abuse
Nixon, Richard M. (Nixon ad-
    ministration), 1–3, 5, 17, 42,
    56, 63–65, 71, 102–104, 117, 135,
    143, 150, 151, 155, 203, 237
  Marijuana Commission report and,
    91, 93–95
NORML. See National Organization
    for the Reform of Marijuana Laws
North Carolina, 202
Novak, Michael, 228

Office of Drug Abuse Law Enforce-
    ment (ODALE), 103–104
Ohio, 4, 150, 163–67
O'Leary, Alice, 236, 239, 306
Operation Intercept, 104
Oregon, 4, 120–23, 134, 154

Palevsky, Max, 59–60, 172
Paley, Billy, 12, 208–209, 269, 283–85,
    291, 292, 297
Paoli, Leo, 88
Paraphernalia industry, 300–304
paraquat-spraying program in
    Mexico, 7, 17, 203–206, 211,
    216–17, 228–29, 249–52, 263,
    265–67, 269–75, 281–82
Parole Commission, U.S., 127–28
People's Pot Conference (1972), 96
Percy, Charles, 205, 206
Percy Amendment, 274, 275, 282
Pertschuk, Michael, 36
Piedras Negras jail break, 127

Pierson, Lynn, 219, 236, 245–48
Pie-throwing incident (1977), 221–25, 231–32
Playboy (magazine), 4, 44, 72–74, 169, 180, 253
Playboy Foundation, 43–45, 72, 73, 79, 100–101, 172
Pollin, William, 315
Pomeroy, Wes, 231–33
Powell, Jody, 195–99, 267, 276, 284, 285
Presley, Robert, 153
Privacy, right of, 125–26, 161, 305
Prohibition, 50
Psychedelic drugs. *See* Hallucinogens

Randall, Bob, 8, 236–48, 306
Ravin, Irwin, 159, 160
Reagan, Ronald, 43, 97–99, 117–18, 152, 317
Reefer Madness (film), 51, 101
Rhodes, James, 163
Rivera, Geraldo, 180
Robinson, Richard, 158
Rockefeller, Nelson, 118–19
Roffman, Roger, 288
Rogers, Paul, 64, 200, 201
Rubin, Burt, 227
Rusche, Sue, 8, 217, 300–305, 309–11, 317
Rutherford, Tom, 247

Safire, William, 148–49
Sanders, Ed, 55, 56
Sapstein, Ira, 141–43, 145
Schang, Gabrielle, 294
Scharf, Ron, 141–46
Scheuer, James, 66, 70, 96
Schoenfeld, Eugene, 222–24
Schott, Larry, 37–39, 41, 42, 66, 72, 73, 81, 82, 95, 108–109, 125–26, 286, 288, 290, 307
Schott, Sandy, 37
Schumer, Sheldon, 256
Schur, Edwin, 62
Shafer, Raymond P., 64–66, 92
Sharp, Joe, 37–41, 102
Shepard, Martin, 218
Sieroty, Alan, 155, 156

Silverstein, Shel, 77, 78
Simon, Steve, 110
Sinclair, John, 55, 70, 96
Sirulnik, Eric, 272
Smith, Chesterfield, 105
Smith, David, 67
Smith, Griffin, 110, 210–11
Smith, Kevin, 271
Smoke-in in Lafayette Park (1977), 179
Sonnenreich, Michael, 64–65, 93
South Carolina, 128
South Dakota, 202
Spock, Benjamin, 63
Standish, Margaret, 43
State Department, 228–30, 251
Statler, Stuart, 35, 205–206, 228, 274
Stepanian, Michael, 184–85, 224, 293
Strang, Michael, 162
Stroup, Keith, 2–4, 6, 25–46, 56–91, 95–96, 99–103, 105–11, 118, 122–28, 132–35, 139–49, 152, 156, 158, 160, 162, 163, 167–93, 197–202, 205, 208–35, 237, 239–40, 243, 250–75, 282–99
   1971 Marijuana Commission hearings and, 62–69
   1977 NORML conference and, 216–224
   1977 NORML party and, 10, 14–20, 22–24
   arrested in Canada, 214–15, 227–28, 254–63
   background of, 25–39
   Bourne's cocaine use at 1977 party and, 17–24, 278–81, 283, 285–91
   drug use by, 81–84, 188–89, 297–98
   financial problems of, 186
   first experiences with marijuana, 36–38
   law firm of, 294, 295, 307–308
   personal characteristics of, 3–4, 15, 74–75
   pie-throwing incident and (1977), 221–25
   resignation from NORML, 293–96
   in Texas, 109–11, 123

Stroup, Keith (*cont.*)
  See also specific individuals and
    topics
Stroup, Kelly, 2, 37–38, 40, 43, 62, 71–
    72, 186, 289
  breakup of marriage to Keith,
    89–90, 188
  marriage to Keith, 33–34
Stroup, Larry, 25–26, 289
Stroup, Lindsey, 71, 186, 187, 270, 289
Stroup, Russell, 25–30, 34
Stroup, Vera, 25–29, 34
Sullivan, Tom, 144
Supreme Court, U.S., 104, 305

Tabankin, Margery, 62
Taylor, Bayard, 47
Teasdale, Joseph, 253–54
Television, 52–53
Texas, 77, 109–17, 123–24
THC pill, 306
Thompson, Hunter, 54, 183, 192, 219,
    224, 229, 291, 296
  at 1977 NORML party, 16, 18–21
Thompson, James, 143, 147
Time (magazine), 170, 171
Tims, Doug, 202
Topping, Robert, 302
Trachtman, Dinah, 58, 61, 108, 109
Trevino, Pete, 111
Trudeau, Pierre, 257
Tucker, Sterling, 270

Ungerleider, 218
Urry, Michelle, 73–76, 79

Vietnam war, 4–5, 34, 53, 55
Voter initiatives, 84–86, 88–89,
    99–101

Waddy, Joseph, 274
Wagstaff, Robert, 159–61
Walden, Phil, 264–66
Walker, Frank, 29
Walsh, John, 20, 267, 270
Washington, George, 47
Washington, James A., Jr., 241, 242
Washington Post, 276, 279, 283
Washington Star, 216
Washington State, 84, 86
Waters, Ron, 110, 125
Weil, Andrew, 67, 81
Weiner, David, 167
Wenner, Jann, 63
Whipple, Dorothy, 61–62, 122, 162
White, James R., III, 55
Whitten, Coy, 111
Wilcox, Steve, 84–86
Williams, Leslye, 265, 266
Wolfe, Richard M., 163–67
Wolff, Lester, 200, 221, 300
Woodward, W.C., 51

Yippies, 96, 175, 178–80, 220–23
York, Frank, 111

Zill, Ann, 18
Zinberg, Norman, 49, 52–53, 61, 66,
    132, 218, 289, 308–309